CRITICAL PERSPECTIVES ON INTERNATIONALISATION

INTERNATIONAL BUSINESS AND MANAGEMENT SERIES

Series Editor: Pervez Ghauri

Published

GEMÜNDEN, RITTER & WALTER
Relationships and Networks in International Markets

GHAURI & USUNIER
International Business Negotiations

MOROSINI
Managing Cultural Differences

NAUDÉ & TURNBULL
Network Dynamics in International Marketing

BUCKLEY & GHAURI
The Global Challenge for Multinational Enterprises

HÅKANSSON & JOHANSON
Business Network Learning

LI
Managing International Business Ventures in China

Forthcoming Titles

HENNART & THOMAS
Global Competitive Strategies

CONTRACTOR & LORANGE
Alliances and Cooperative Strategies

Other Titles of Interest

FATEMI
International Trade in the 21st Century

DUNNING
Globalization, Trade and Foreign Direct Investment

MONCARZ
International Trade and the New Economic Order

KREININ
Contemporary Issues in Commercial Policy

Related Journals
sample copies available on request

European Management Journal
International Business Review
International Journal of Research in Marketing
Long Range Planning
Scandinavian Journal of Management

CRITICAL PERSPECTIVES ON INTERNATIONALISATION

EDITED BY

VIRPI HAVILA

Uppsala University, Sweden

MATS FORSGREN

Uppsala University, Sweden

HÅKAN HÅKANSSON

Norwegian School of Management BI, Norway

SERIES EDITOR

PERVEZ N. GHAURI

2002

Pergamon
An Imprint of Elsevier Science

Amsterdam – London – New York – Oxford – Paris – Shannon – Tokyo

ELSEVIER SCIENCE Ltd
The Boulevard, Langford Lane
Kidlington, Oxford OX5 1GB, UK

First edition 2002

Library of Congress Cataloging in Publication Data
A catalog record from the Library of Congress has been applied for.

British Library Cataloguing in Publication Data
A catalogue record from the British Library has been applied for.

ISBN: 0-08-044035-5

♾ The paper used in this publication meets the requirements of ANSI/NISO Z39.48-1992 (Permanence of Paper).
Printed in The Netherlands.

To Jan Johanson

Contents

THEME ONE: CRITICAL VIEWS ON GLOBALISATION AND THE MULTINATIONAL CORPORATION

PART I: THE MULTINATIONAL CORPORATION AS A PHENOMENON AND ITS WELFARE IMPLICATIONS

PART II: WHAT KINDS OF MULTINATIONAL CORPORATIONS ARE THERE AND WHAT ARE THEIR TRUE COMPETITIVE ADVANTAGES?

Contributors

Henrik Agndal

Jönköping International Business School
Jönköping, Sweden

Poul Houman Andersen

Department of International Business
The Århus School of Business
Århus, Denmark

Ulf Andersson

Department of Business Studies
Uppsala University
Uppsala, Sweden

Björn Axelsson

Jönköping International Business School
Jönköping, Sweden

Anders Blomstermo

Department of Business Studies
Uppsala University
Uppsala, Sweden

Peter J. Buckley

Centre for International Business
University of Leeds
Leeds, United Kingdom

John Cantwell

Department of Economics
University of Reading
Reading, United Kingdom

Mark Casson

Department of Economics
University of Reading
Reading, United Kingdom

Kent Eriksson

Department of Business Studies
Uppsala University
Uppsala, Sweden

Mats Forsgren

Department of Business Studies
Uppsala University
Uppsala, Sweden

Pervez N. Ghauri

UMIST
Manchester School of Management
Manchester, United Kingdom

*Mohammed Azzim
Gulamhussen*

Department of Economics
University of Reading
Reading, United Kingdom

Amjad Hadjikhani

Department of Business Studies
Uppsala University
Uppsala, Sweden

Virpi Havila

Department of Business Studies
Uppsala University
Uppsala, Sweden

Ulf Holm

Department of Business Studies
Uppsala University
Uppsala, Sweden

Håkan Håkansson

Norwegian School of Management BI
Oslo, Norway

Hans Jansson

Center for International Business Studies
Göteborg University
Göteborg, Sweden

Jan Johanson

Department of Business Studies
Uppsala University
Uppsala, Sweden

Martin Johanson

Department of Business Studies
Uppsala University
Uppsala, Sweden

Elena Kosmopoulou   Department of Economics
University of Reading
Reading, United Kingdom

Michael Kutschker   Department of Business Administration
Catholic University of Eichstaett
Eichstaett, Germany

Peter Lorange   IMD
Lausanne, Switzerland

Anders Malmberg   Department of Social and Economic Geography
Uppsala University
Uppsala, Sweden

Asta Salmi   International Marketing
University of Vaasa
Vaasa, Finland

Andreas Schurig   Department of Business Administration
Catholic University of Eichstaett
Eichstaett, Germany

D. Deo Sharma   Department of Marketing
Copenhagen Business School
Copenhagen, Denmark

Peter Söderbaum   Department of Business Studies and Informatics
Mälardalen University
Västerås, Sweden

Örjan Sölvell   Institute of International Business
Stockholm School of Economics
Stockholm, Sweden

Jan-Erik Vahlne   Gothenburg Research Institute
Gothenburg School of Economics and
Commercial Law
Göteborg University
Göteborg, Sweden

Mohammad Yamin UMIST
Manchester School of Management
Manchester, United Kingdom

Ivo Zander Institute of International Business
Stockholm School of Economics
Stockholm, Sweden

Udo Zander Institute of International Business
Stockholm School of Economics
Stockholm, Sweden

Figures

Tables

Series Editor's Preface

For the last couple of decades there has been an increased interest in international business which is apparent from a huge amount of research on internationalisation of the firm. Most of these studies are done from a company perspective where scholars have been trying to understand why companies go international, what types of problems they face and how they formulate their strategies on how to enter new/foreign markets. The implicit objective often has been to explain and arrive at the most efficient way of going international. In other words, the researchers are trying to help companies and managers how to go international and how to manage international operations most efficiently.

This is, in a way, only one side of the coin. In order to see the complete picture, we need to study internationalisation and company strategies with a different perspective, that is the perspective of society (people) and not only that of the company. The recent developments, such as the World Trade Organization (WTO), inclusion of developing countries in G8 meetings and all the incidents in Seattle, Genoa and elsewhere, demonstrate a need for such a perspective.

This volume takes this other perspective on international activities of firms and critically analyses multinationals and the impact of globalisation. As such, it is a timely book that attempts to balance our views on internationalisation and globalisation. Most prominent scholars from all over Europe have contributed the perspective coming from many countries and companies. I am sure our readers will agree with me that it is a valuable addition to international business literature and will serve to be the base for a new stream of literature in our field, like many other contributions coming from Uppsala School.

Pervez Ghauri
Manchester School of Management
UMIST – UK

Preface

The internationalisation of business has accelerated during the postwar period and particularly in the past decade. At the same time, research on international business has grown considerably. The early efforts in the 1950s have been followed by a vast number of research projects all over the world attempting to understand and explain the processes and problems of internationalisation. The aim of this book is to continue this task by providing critical perspectives on internationalisation and on internationalisation research.

The book includes 19 contributions from a total of 32 researchers. All of the contributions have been selected from papers presented at the "Marcus Wallenberg Symposium on Critical Perspectives on Internationalisation", which took place 10–11 January, 2000. The aim of the symposium was to bring together internationally recognised scholars to discuss internationalisation from different angles. The symposium was hosted by Uppsala University, Department of Business Studies, Sweden, and was supported by the Marcus Wallenberg Foundation for International Cooperation in Science.

The book is divided into two sub-themes. Theme One, *Critical Views on Globalisation and the Multinational Corporation,* includes articles analyzing globalisation and the multinational corporation as economic and social phenomena with consequences for welfare, knowledge development and world order. Theme Two, *Critical Views on the Received Theory on Internationalisation,* includes articles that question received theories of internationalisation and the multinational corporation.

This book is dedicated to Professor Jan Johanson, who has for so long inspired so many scholars all over the world in their research within the field of international business. The large number of distinguished scholars contributing to this volume serves as strong proof of this inspiration.

May 2001

Virpi Havila　　　　*Mats Forsgren*　　　　*Håkan Håkansson*
Uppsala University　*Uppsala University*　*Norwegian School of*
　　　　　　　　　　　　　　　　　　　　　Management BI

Theme One

Critical Views on Globalisation and the Multinational Corporation

Virpi Havila, Mats Forsgren and Håkan Håkansson

In recent analyses of the post-modernistic society the concept of globalisation has received a considerable amount of attention. In some of these analyses the emphasis is on the global economy as a constant flow of capital and information, made possible by the development of information technology. It is claimed that this has led to a new world order in which states and governments have lost a considerable amount of their power to those who control the global flows (Castells, 1996). It has even been suggested that globalisation contains a paradigmatic shift to a new order, a state of "governance without government", that sweeps all actors, governments, institutions and people into the order of the whole (Hardt & Negri, 2000). In this new, all-encompassing, worldwide "empire" the multinational firms, with their global networks of resources and information, have become important parts of the upper echelons of the "empire's" hierarchy. At the bottom of the "empire's" hierarchy resides a miscellaneous and shattered group of small, underdeveloped states and non-governmental organizations, like Attac, Amnesty, International Save the Children Alliance, Greenpeace, Human Rights Watch etc, which, on behalf of different groups of people, deal with specific aspects of globalisation and its effects.

Irrespective of the type of analysis of globalisation and whether the analysis are made by economists, political scientists or sociologists, the multinational enterprise as a phenomenon seems to be at the centre. In many respects this is a renewal of the debate from the 1960s and 1970s about the welfare implications of firms' internationalisation. For instance, Stephen Hymer's discussion of the market power of multinationals and their effects on competition, geographical concentration of resources and welfare, has received renewed attention, after the relative paucity of discussions on this point during the 1980s and beginning of 1990s (Hymer, 1972a: 1972b).

However, in contemporary analyses of globalisation and the new order, the multinational firm is conceptualised somewhat differently from the way it was viewed in Hymer's and others' analyses two to three decades ago. In the latter analyses, the sheer size of multinationals and their control of resources and oligopolistic behaviour through market collusions where of major concern. The multinationals "conquered the world" through their monopolistic advantages, mainly based on resources located in the home country. In contemporary analysis, the importance of the multinationals in the globalisation process rather stems from their possibilities to build and control a network of global flows of information, capital and people. The truly new phenomenon, from a globalisation perspective, is these networks rather than the size of resources per se. The ability to create global networks and utilize geographically specialized resources, through transfer of information and knowledge between the nodes of the network, is at the core of the conceptualisation of the multinational firm. This ability is supposed to give it a superior position vis-à-vis most other groups in our post-modernistic society.

However, it is obvious that most analyses of globalisation apply relatively simplistic and "taken-for-granted" models of the multinational firm, especially among researchers outside the international business field. For instance, in the analyses mentioned above by Castells and Hardt and Negri, (Castells, 1996; Hardt & Negri, 2000), which are often considered to the most important contributions to contemporary analyses of globalisation, do not contain any analysis of the multinational firm as a concept, except for the notion that it is a "global informational network". This is surprising as their conclusions on globalisation as a "new order" and "empire" in itself rests heavily on the assumption that multinational firms are equivalent with global networks. Consequently, one is tempted to suggest that the analyses by Castells and Hardt and Negri largely contain stories about the multinational firm, without the multinational firms as an empirical phenomenon, being considered. For instance, the more or less explicit assumption that it is possible to control global, corporate networks from above by some kind of "master-mind" — for which should be read the corporate headquarters — is rarely questioned or discussed.

These deficiencies are indicative of a general need for more research addressing the multinational firm as a phenomenon, not least in conjunction with issues about globalisation and its welfare implications. The first theme of this book, *Critical Views on Globalisation and the Multinational Corporation*, is an attempt to fill this gap. The various contributions under this label differ in terms of perspectives and issues raised. Therefore, they have been placed under three different labels. The first label, *The Multinational Corporation as a Phenomenon and its Welfare Implications* contains chapters that analyse different configurations of multinational corporations, and how they affect factors of importance for host and home countries. The second label, *What Kinds of Multinational Corporations are there and what are their True Competitive Advantages?* includes three chapters that discuss the core competence of the multinational corporation more in-depth. The third label, *Impacts of Globalisation on People and Mind* contains contributions that pave the way for a broad discussion of different perspectives on globalisation and its consequences for factors like migration and environmental issues.

References

Castells, E. (1996). *The Information Age*. Oxford: Blackwell Publishers.

Hardt, M. & Negri, A. (2000). *Empire*. Cambridge, Mass.: Harvard University Press. 14.

Hymer, S. (1972a). The multinational corporation and the law of uneven development. In J. N. Bhagwati (ed.), *Economics and World Order*. London: Macmillan.

Hymer, S. (1972b). The efficiency (contradictions) of multinational corporation. In G. Paquet (ed.), *The Multinational Corporation And The Nation-state*. Don Mills: Macmillan.

Part I

The Multinational Corporation as a Phenomenon and its Welfare Implications

This topic contains three contributions. The first chapter, *Globalisation and the End of Competition: A Critical Review of Rent-Seeking Multinationals*, by Pervez N. Ghauri and Peter J. Buckley, contains an overview of the criticism against multinational firms since the 1950s. The authors argue that a new research agenda is likely to emerge concerning the external impact of the strategies of the leading MNCs, as they consolidate their hold on the global economy. An important issue of the chapter is the possibility for the MNC to attain a high degree of flexibility through decentralization of activities, vertical disintegration, networks of joint ventures etc., with increasing uncertainty for host countries and their governments. The authors conclude that the growing imbalance between powerful MNCs and less powerful states and governments, and the impact of this imbalance on factors like economic insecurity and political instability, should be a key focal point for international business researchers.

The basic message of the second contribution, *Are Multinational Firms Good or Bad?*, by Mats Forsgren, is that the socio-economic consequences of MNCs as phenomena are difficult to analyse at a general level. Although the consequences as such are often dealt with individually, for instance in terms of income distribution, economic growth, labour relations etc., models of the main actor itself, the multinational firm, has been oversimplified. By combining a classification of MNCs into Multi-domestic firms, Global Firms and Network Firms with consequences in terms of competition, bargaining power vis-à-vis governments and technology transfer across borders, the author claims that the consequences differ depending on which combination is the main focus.

However, the analysis ends up with proposition that, on the whole, the Network Firm is an ideal form, but that it might also be much less prevalent than is usually assumed.

In the third contribution, the host countries' local clusters, in which the MNC has its subsidiaries, are focused. The key topic in Anders Malmberg's and Örjan Sölvell's chapter, *Does Foreign Ownership Matter? Subsidiary Impact on Local Clusters,* is whether foreign ownership per se affects how MNC subsidiaries behave in these clusters. The authors claim that the dynamism of the cluster is the basic determining factor, rather than the ownership. The more dynamic is the cluster, of which the foreign subsidiary is a member, the more capabilities the subsidiary will built up, and the more autonomous it will be from its foreign owner. It is also argued that this situation is the most favourable one when considering the positive effects on the local economy. The authors conclude that in general foreign ownership plays a minor role, except in those situations when host and home country clusters are equally strong, the industry in question is politically sensitive or when the MNC is state-owned.

Chapter 1

Globalisation and the End of Competition: A Critical Review of Rent-seeking Multinationals

Pervez N. Ghauri and Peter J. Buckley

Introduction

This paper suggests that, for a variety of reasons, there is likely to be a renaissance of critical writing on the multinational enterprises in the first decade of the new millennium. The paper first revisits the critical literature on multinational enterprises of the 1950s to 1970s, in order to refresh our minds on the basis for that criticism. It then suggests a number of areas on which criticism is likely to focus — the strategy of multinational firms, bargaining power of multinationals versus the state, development issues, the decline of competition, and distributional issues (affecting unskilled workers in particular). These are old concerns, but the problems are emerging in new ways because of the new configuration of the globalising economy.

The paper concentrates on issues in international political economy. It does not deal with issues of globalisation that are related to the decline of local indigenous cultures, felt to be under attack from the homogenising pressure of globalisation. This is not because cultural issues are unimportant or intrinsically separable from political economy, it is simply for ease of focus of exposition.

Critical Perspectives on Internationalisation, pp. 7–28.
Copyright © 2002 by Elsevier Science Ltd.
All rights of reproduction in any form reserved.
ISBN: 0-08-044035-5

Critical Literature to the Mid-1970s

Edith Penrose (1956) wrote a classic piece, which pointed out the controversial aspects of foreign investment where, in spite of the successful
establishment of a subsidiary, the foreign capital and its possible benefits
for the local economy may be largely transmitted out of the host country.
It also explained why the returns on the initial investment could be
exceptionally high. This illustrates the 'Gambler's Earnings Hypothesis'
(Barlow & Wender, 1955), which likens the foreign investor to a compul-
sive gambler who constantly reinvests his winnings in the game, until he
makes a killing, then he withdraws a large amount (in comparison with
the initial stake). Penrose's paper discussed the implications of this form
of foreign investment for the economic policies of less-industrialised host
countries. It revealed that for the year ending 1954, GM earned a return
of 590 percent on its original dollar investment in Australia. The debate
started by this incident led to Australian economists concluding that the
country should use "some caution in giving indiscriminate encouragement to foreign investment" and that the country should concentrate less
on attracting American capital. The imputed behaviour of the multinational firm clearly has detrimental implications for the host country —
in particular, the negative impact on the balance of payments in the withdrawal period and the associated instability. This is an interesting case,
also because it is related to a typical "import replacement" investment, as
sought by most developing countries at that time.

   This study evaluated a number of options the host country could have
in such a situation, but concluded that once a foreign firm was established, it was not economically sound to limit its growth or to acquire it
wholly or partly. From the firm's perspective, the establishment of a
foreign subsidiary was no different from establishing a subsidiary in the
domestic market. Other than that, it entailed higher risk and thus led to
the fact that higher returns were expected through this growth. Moreover, even if the profitability in a particular industry declined due to
increasing competition over the years, an MNE was able to diversify
more easily and to move its capital to areas that ensured higher returns
on the capital.

   A second important study by Stephen Hymer (1991), examined 'two
basic laws of development'; namely the Law of Uneven Economic Development and the Law of Increasing Firm Size. The study strove for a
futuristic viewpoint and claimed to look towards the year 2000. Written
in 1971, it opened with the statement that until then most MNEs came

from the United States, where the firms had achieved the largest size and development. But now, (i.e., 1971), European corporations were beginning to "see the world as their Oyster". It claimed that the multinationalisation would continue through giant firms from both sides of the Atlantic. Moreover, although initially dominated by the US firms, eventually some kind of oligopolistic equilibrium will be achieved with a new structure of international industrial organisation. It also suggested that while North Atlantic MNEs will dominate, a geographical division of labour and dependence relationship, with one being superior and the others being subordinate, would emerge. This situation would lead to tensions and conflicts and to further uneven development.

The study started with the evolution of MNEs, "beasts" or "The US corporate monsters". It claimed that The Hudson Bay Company, or the British East India Company, or large mining and plantation enterprises were not the forerunners of MNEs. Instead, it was small-scale capitalist enterprises in manufacturing who were the forerunners of MNEs. The contributing factors were the industrial revolution and the railways, as suggested also by Chandler (1977), until we came to the stage where if a firm was to grow steadily, it had continuously to introduce new products. Thus product development and marketing replaced production as the factor dominating growth. A new divisionalised organisational form emerged, which also led to an increased outward FDI. In the 1950s and 1960s US FDI increased at a rate of 10 percent per annum. The rapid growth in Europe and Japan was one of the major factors stimulating this growth in FDI.

Using the Chandler-Redlich (1961) scheme, it suggested that MNEs would spread their day-to-day, i.e. manufacturing, activities all over the globe, thus diffusing industrialisation to developing countries and creating new centres of production. The other activities, i.e. coordination and communication, would stay closer to the head offices, which would be completely centralised. As a result, "the best" highly skilled and highly paid manpower would concentrate in the major cities of the US and Europe, while lower level skills and manpower would remain in other parts and cities of the world. Most new products would be developed in the "major" cities and, once accepted there, would travel to other countries. MNEs would thus be greatly interested in the markets of these less-developed countries. This system would automatically force developing countries not to develop skilled manpower above a certain level, as there would be no market for their skills. The local governments would not even be able to invest in their infrastructure, communication, education and health, to achieve growth, as it would not be able to finance these investments. They would not be able to tax MNEs to acquire finance, due to the ability of these corporations to manipulate transfer prices or to move to low-tax countries, whereas the home countries of these MNEs would be able to tax these corporations as a whole, as well as through their highly paid manpower.

The relationship between MNEs and developing countries would also be of a superior and subordinate nature. The study concluded that if MNEs could solve the following four problems for developing countries, they could survive and have continued growth. The four issues were:

1) MNEs must break foreign exchange constraints and provide local governments with imported goods for capital formation and modernisation;
2) they must help local governments in training labour and industrialisation;
3) they must solve the urban food problems created by growth;
4) they must keep the excluded two-thirds of the population under control.

Hymer's vision represents a stark picture of opposition between the interests of multinational firms and those of the populations of developing countries.

Streeten (1974) dealt with the theory of development from the perspective of the 1970s. He started with the assumption that countries were poor because they were poor and thus needed large injections of foreign capital because they could not raise their own savings. The low investment ratio was considered both the cause and effect of poverty. While discussing MNEs and developing countries, he suggested that the bulk of FDI in developing countries consisted of the re-investment of local earnings. The benefits of MNEs in terms of the training of local labour (investments in human capital), management, science and technology, and R & D depended largely upon the ability and willingness of the host government to pursue the "right" policies. The policy issues thus became of prime importance and one could see MNEs filling in the "gaps" in the policy that local governments could not achieve on their own, such as: savings, foreign exchange, tax revenues, and skills. There were some other contributions that MNEs could make, such as: appropriate technology, entrepreneurship, balance of bargaining power, and providing a network of relationships to local firms.

In a macro-economic sense, MNEs could contribute towards job creation, import substitution, and more efficient market structure. It was, however, very difficult to measure or assess the contribution of MNEs. Moreover, there were a number of contradictions in these contributions, for example, MNEs could improve foreign exchange earnings but at the same time could impose a foreign exchange burden. Another problem raised when assessing the contribution of MNEs was that many of the actions of MNEs were dependent on individuals responsible for its affairs or on host government policies. Moreover, it was suggested that a number of these activities could have been equally well or better done by other means than MNEs.

MNEs were often blamed for:

1) uneven development, dualism and inequality;
2) a fragmented consumption pattern only for a small proportion of the population;
3) local funds being wrongly allocated, not in accordance with social needs;
4) influencing government policies, often unfavourable to development;
5) creating political frictions by the suspicion that foreign capital controlled assets and jobs.

Streeten's analysis highlighted the problem of transfer pricing and the bargaining power of MNEs (often due to monopolistic or oligopolistic market structures). Because of these powers, MNEs often end up with very beneficial contracts while negotiating with host governments. Even if the specific contribution of the MNE is technical knowledge, and if this knowledge bestowed bargaining power, why had competition in the market not eroded this power? Why had there been so few inventions of low-cost, simple, appropriate products? Why did industrialised countries with a comparative advantage in manufacturing, protect, often at high cost, their agricultural and other sectors, instead of exchanging low-cost machinery and durable consumer goods for the agricultural exports of developing countries?

The analysis of Barnet and Muller (1975) was typical of the critical literature from the 1970s. It addressed the myth of development, "the struggle of human beings to realize their full potential" and an evaluation of FDI. According to them, the 1960s were considered to be the "decade of development" and the most important issue was to see whether the "free world model" or the "communist model" would survive. By the end of the 1960s, the gap between the rich and the poor world was widening. Moreover, the gap within countries was also widening, a small minority was becoming affluent but for a large majority the miseries were increasing. Yet, in absolute terms there has been growth in most countries. At the same time, global corporations proclaimed themselves to be the engines of growth. This could only be judged by understanding or defining "development". The positive impact of MNEs as regards job opportunities, could be compared with the negative impact of maintaining and increasing poverty and having conflicting interests to those of developing countries.

The primary objective of MNEs was profit maximization, thus MNEs used all their resources and power to achieve that, which had an adverse effect on the distribution of income and employment levels in developing countries. The claim that MNEs supplied capital to poor countries was a metaphor and not reality. Most of the investments came from reinvested earnings derived from the local market, while most of the profits were generated from local resources with more than 50 percent being repatriated back to developed countries. As a net result the capital or resources were moving from the developing to the developed world. It is a proven fact that where it was to their advantage, MNEs widely overvalued their imports into developing countries. By taking into consideration the over-pricing of imports and the under-pricing of exports, repatriated profits, royalties, and fees repatriated to head office, we could really evaluate the advantages or disadvantages of MNEs for developing countries. There was no doubt that the import of technology had a major impact on poor countries. In fact, the technology dependence was an obstacle to development, as when technology was controlled from abroad all funds for R & D also went abroad.

After these critical studies most of the literature of late 1970s, and of the 1980s and 1990s, has presented MNEs and FDI as positive factors and essential for economic development and the well-being of societies, rich or poor. Recent literature, as we show below, is beginning to highlight certain problems in the relationship between states and MNEs and a new dissatisfaction with the new world order is beginning to appear as the riots against the World Trade Organization (WTO) meeting in Seattle (December 1999) illustrate.

The Strategy of Multinational Firms

Buckley and Casson (1998) and Ghauri (1999) suggest that internal and external pressures on the multinational enterprise in the 1990s are producing a new strategic imperative — flexibility. The search for flexibility is a reaction to external volatility (e.g., in exchange rates) and to attempts to reduce monopolistic 'pinch-points' (e.g., single supply sources, tie-in to particular locations). The search for flexibility leads to (vertical) disintegration and foreign direct investments being seen as 'real options'. This results in a new ownership strategy with networks of joint ventures and a new location strategy based on 'hub and spoke' operations where central facilities (e.g., manufacturing) are augmented by decentralised activities (e.g., distribution). These two strategies can be combined so that wholly owned central facilities such as finance, production and R & D are combined with dispersed joint ventures in marketing, distribution and warehousing. The existence of increasingly integrated regional economic unions (EU, NAFTA) facilitates this strategy.

The ability of multinational firms to appropriate rent by adjusting their foreign market servicing strategies, partly in response to national governmental policies (Buckley, 1996), enhances their flexibility and their bargaining power. Buckley shows that the range of policies open to multinational firms makes broadbrush policies untenable, because in each policy cell (exporting, licensing, foreign direct investment), government policies will have both positive and negative effects. Targeted policies, moreover, are difficult to design, given the dynamics of the firm's evolving foreign market servicing strategies and the links between the different elements in the firm's global value chains.

The result of these strategies is to create uncertainty for the host countries. Locational policies create difficulties in that multinationals are becoming more 'footloose' and are liable to move 'offshore plants' in response to changing incentives, demand and supply conditions. The search for flexibility also means that multinationals may engineer internal competition between competing plants within the same firm with weaker plants being winnowed out by failures in internal tendering.

The arguments for policy intervention are weakening. Krugman (1994), in reviewing the arguments for interventionist policies based on externalities and strategic trade considerations, concluded that the optimal policy set is so sensitive to technological and behavioural parameters, that the results of intervention are uncertain, even in areas where externality and monopoly arguments abound. Further, the information available to government policy makers is likely to be partial, out-of-date and biased (not in the least by representations on the part of the rent-seekers). This analysis has important implications for bargaining power.

Bargaining Power

Arguments about bargaining power between multinationals and governments have moved on in the decades since the 1970s. The move from confrontation to cooperation (Dunning, 1991) or from government policies as constraint to conflict and bargaining and then to cooperation (Boddewyn, 1992) is a commonplace. However, the nature of the interaction between governments and multinational firms is much more complex than a simple two person game, be it competitive or cooperative. Stopford and Strange (1991) developed a view that multinationals and governments are colluding in order to acquire market share for 'their" firms. Strange (1997) went further and argued that "globalisation by shifting power from states to firms, has allowed international bureaucracies to undermine that accountability". This leads to dilemmas, not only economic, but also environmental (lacking countervailing power, corporations polluting the planet) and political (lack of accountability, transparency and greater insecurity for citizens because the safety net of the state is eroded). This "retreat of the state" (Strange, 1996) leads to a vacuum of governance.

Host country policies that have changed in this period include the relaxing of controls, increasing incentives to inward FDI, privatisation, provision of guarantees and arbitration. We have seen a trajectory of MNE-emerging market relations where tension increased during 1950–1975 and then reduced, whilst the host country gained bargaining strength in the first period, which relaxed as the MNE gained ascendancy (Dunning, 1992; 1994; Vernon, 1966; Wells, 1998). The reason for these shifts in bargaining power suggests three alternative scenarios for the future — 'more balanced', 'cyclical' and a continuation of present trends. Jenkins believes that it is most likely that a cyclical shift will occur taking us back to an increase in host country bargaining power and increased tension. Even those who doubt this outcome will find much interest in these projections (Jenkins, 1999). Figure 1.1 illustrates the history of the balance in bargaining between MNEs and host countries from the 1950s

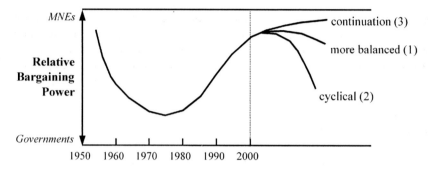

Figure 1.1: Bargaining Power of Governments versus MNEs — 1950 to
the Millennium, and Three Future Scenarios.

to the millennium with projections indicated after 2000. Recent developments suggest a continuation of current trends, the MNEs gradually
accreting bargaining power.

If we re-examine some of the issues above in the light of the Asian
crisis, we can see that the penetration of northern multinationals in the
South will increase. As asset prices fall in developing economies, more of
the firms denominated in these assets will be acquired by northern multinationals from strong currency countries. UNCTAD figures show this
happening (1998). The symmetry of the relationship will be further distorted by the decline of southern multinationals in the North, which will
be increasingly unable to fund outward FDI and which will be vulnerable
to take-over, considering the increasing size and resources of northern
MNEs due to a wave of big mergers and acquisitions. The balance of
FDI will thus swing ever more decisively to the northern firms.

All of this, of course, is not without cost to the multinationals. Prahalad and Lieberthal (1998) say "In order to participate effectively in the
big emerging markets, multinationals will increasingly have to reconfigure
their resource base, rethink their cost structure, redesign their product
development process, and challenge their assumptions about the cultural
mix of their top managers. In short, they will have to develop a new
mind-set and adopt new business models to achieve global competitiveness in the post imperialist age". Prahalad and Lieberthal thus predict the
end of corporate imperialism and a more "accommodatory" stance by
multinational firms in emerging markets. Their position approximates to
the "more balanced" scenario.

There are also grounds for believing that bargaining power will continue to move in the direction of multinational firms. They have a wider choice of investment locations as new "emerging countries" put themselves forward as export platforms — usually on a tax-free basis. Their proprietary technology is widely sought after by host countries and their branded products sell at a premium to upscale consumers globally. Flexible manufacturing and production controlled by IT systems mean that more and more of the activities of MNEs are footloose. They can use the threat of switching locations to squeeze concessions from host countries. We thus have reasons to believe that MNE-government relationship is shifting towards MNEs gaining more power, as depicted in scenario (3) in Figure 1.1.

States are, however, not without recourse to new reserves of power. Domicile in national locations still requires state guarantees of security and underwriting of property rights. Indeed, it is the inability of the states in transition economies to underwrite such rights, which is a major cause of their failure to achieve secure growth (Buckley & Ghauri, 1994; see particularly Casson's chapter, 1994). Private appropriation of the rewards of entrepreneurial activity is a key driver of growth but achieving the legitimacy of this process is not easy to accomplish in many societies — notably where it contributes to the already huge inequalities and where private wealth has heretofore been discouraged by state institutions. The role of the state in preventing the growth of corruption (in its own long-term interests) is becoming a major location factor. These issues are far more prevalent in developing than in developed countries.

Developed versus Developing Countries

In the discussion of states versus firms, a special reference is always made to governments of developing countries. The role of the government and government bodies from developing countries is relatively more crucial than the role played by these bodies in developed countries. The government bodies in developing countries regulate their economies not only to secure the best interest of their population, but also to safeguard local firms. Governments aim to plan their economies to seek goals which they believe a purely market outcome will not secure. These actions thus take the stance of developing countries versus developed countries, or governments from developing countries versus multinational enterprises (MNEs). Thus, we can expect an inharmonious conjunction of the strategies of MNEs and governments policies. However, we need to consider the fact that markets are not perfect and both firms and governments are attempting to appropriate rents in a world of imperfect markets (Buckley 1996). This opens up the possibility of collusion between governments and MNEs in dividing rents and mitigating conflicts between them. The game is not a simple one and its rules are constantly changing. It is this game which is taking place in a globalising world where markets are becoming increasingly interdependent and this is critical in allocating the benefits of improving technology, communication, productivity and output.

In terms of strategic decision-making, firms undertake FDI to achieve three main objectives:

1) "Market seeking": firms invest in countries where they see a large and/or rapidly growing market, for example, recent investments in China and India;
2) "Efficiency seeking": firms invest in countries where they can achieve efficiency in cost reduction due to lower operating costs, for example, recent investment by Philips and other consumer electronic products companies in Singapore and Malaysia;
3) "Resource seeking": firms invest in countries to get access to raw materials or other inputs, for example, investments by oil companies in the Middle East or textile companies in India and Pakistan.

Some investments may include more than one of the above elements and some of the motives are specific; for example, in banking a number of investments are made because banks follow their home country clients into the emerging markets. Firms in oligopolistic industries gain economies of scale and other advantages that enable them to be superior to local competitors in host countries (Hymer, 1976). Moreover, firms choose FDI when the transaction costs associated with other modes (such as licensing) are higher (Buckley & Casson, 1976). FDI thus enforces the internationalisation of transactions.

For years, the absence of strong local competitors in most developing markets was one of the reasons that the FDI flow was predominantly from the industrialised countries of the North to the developing countries of the South. The import substitution and protectionist strategies of most emerging markets made FDI a more viable mode than trade to gain access to these markets. Now government induced market imperfections are declining, there are some strong and competitive local firms that can beat off the entry of foreign firms. Moreover, most of the countries are moving away from protectionist politics and are opening up their markets to all types of entry by foreign firms, the nature of the resource flow has thus changed. According to a UNCTC (now UNCTAD, Division on Transnationals) (1992) study, 26 developing countries had already changed over the period 1977 to 1987 towards more hospitable and less restrictive policies towards FDI. However, in the last decade macro-economic determinants rather than the micro-economic determinants mentioned above, have become more important. Factors such as: the investments or capital flow to countries where it can achieve highest returns, the market size or potential for local sales and benefits which can be achieved through local sourcing have become more important (Brewer, 1993; Contractor, 1991; Pfefferman & Madarassy, 1992).

In addition to the above, it has been suggested that the investments flow to the markets where a certain level of FDI is already in existence. This leads to synergetic effects such as foreign firms buying from each other. Moreover, the presence of a number of foreign firms helps to develop specialised know-how and skills with regard to the availability of skilled labour, suppliers and distribution networks. This also means that firms investing abroad go to countries with a good quality infrastructure, communications, transport, energy, and a certain degree of industrialisation. Thus, it is not surprising that the stock of FDI in a given country is often a good predictor of future FDI. It has also been established that although relative cost is still important, direct labour costs in particular are not as important as previously. On the other hand, costs related to highly skilled labour and well-educated manpower have become more important (Pfefferman & Madrassy, 1992).

Privatisation (the transfer of productive assets from public to private ownership) has been part of most structural adjustment policies in LDCs since the 1980s. It has been undertaken to achieve a variety of objectives, such as enhanced economic efficiency, reduction of financial deficits and reducing the role of the state. If we summarise experiences with privatisation strategies showing that there is now a sufficient body of evidence to review its progress made and to assess what works and what does not, we end up with the cautionary point that privatisation alone is unlikely to ease significantly the burden of the state owned sector in many less developed countries.

The emergence of China as a major player in the world economy has already had an impact equal to that of Japan in earlier decades of the Post War World. An initial, almost blanket acceptance of FDI has now become more targeted in terms of priority sectors and regions. China represents a non-uniform environment for the inward investor and there are currently difficulties in the implementation and transparency of business law, contractual difficulties, regional differences and uncertainties about the direction of future economic policies. These challenges need to be addressed by careful adaptation of company strategies.

We are in a state where MNE — host country relations in middle-income countries have fully emerged onto the world stage, leaving behind a group of largely inert less developed countries which have so far been bypassed by globalisation. Increasing location 'tournaments', to attract FDI may have reduced the benefits to the host countries as have the increasing skill of the managers of MNEs in making their investments more 'footloose'. Corresponding skills on the part of host countries to make FDI sticky are not developing at the same rate. Differences within developing countries may lead to divergence between those which can develop the velocity to catch up and those which will fall behind as the world economy becomes more interdependent.

In both advanced and less developed countries, the period from the mid-1970s to the millennium has generally been one where the activist functions of the state have declined. This has been more true in equity related policies (the right hand side of Table 1.1) than in addressing market failure. Indeed, the role of the state at the turn of the millennium is much more related to market enhancing policies than heretofore. On the left hand side of Table 1.1, the state has become more active in addressing externalities, regulating monopoly and attempting to redress information imperfections than in previous decades. The prevailing fashion for "competitiveness" has led to increasing attempts to go further than this in fostering 'dynamic comparative advantage' by subsidising and otherwise encouraging clustering of industry (often in a fashion which is competitive with other states) — even within a customs unions (the EU is a prime example) and encouragement of "indigenous" research and development (Cantwell, 1989).

These market enhancing state policies, fuelled by the rhetoric of competitiveness (Porter, 1990) have encouraged competitive bidding for inward foreign direct investment and led to escalation in the effective locational subsidy for multinational firms. As the next section shows, there has been no effective international control, or even coordination, of the process.

Following the collapse of the state-dominated and centrally planned economies, the Asian crisis and firms increasingly gaining monopoly powers, there is a general feeling that the functions of state require reformulating and refocussing. The main problem in redefining the states role is that the basic conditions are constantly changing. Market failure and the concern for equality provide for economic rationale for government intervention. However, there is no guarantee that any such intervention will benefit society. As we have seen in the Asian crisis, government failure is equally possible as market failure. Thus, the challenge is to see that the political process and institutional structures get the incentives right, so that the interventions actually improve social welfare (IBRD 1997). The task of the state is first to match the state's role to its existing capability — to establish the institutional rules and norms that will enable the state to provide collective goods and services efficiently — and secondly, to reinvigorate the state's capability through rules, partnerships competitive pressures, outside and within the state. According to IBRD, the functions of the state can be represented as a continuum from activities that should not be undertaken without state intervention, to activities in which the state plays an activist role in coordinating the market or redistributing assets, as illustrated in Table 1.1.

First, countries with low state capability need to focus first on minimal basic functions, such as; provision of public goods, such as property rights, macroeconomic stability and basic infrastructure. Second, there are intermediate functions such as the management of environment, regulation of monopolies and provision of social benefits. Again, in these functions it is not a question of whether the government should or should

Table 1.1: Reinvigorating Functions of State.

State Capabilities	Handling Market Failure	Improving Equality
Minimal functions	Providing basic public goods and services	Protecting the poorest
Intermediate functions	Management of environment; Regulating monopolies; Providing social benefits	Providing social insurance
Activist functions	Coordinating markets and private activities	Redistribution of assets

Source: Based on IBRD 1997:27

not intervene, but rather how best to intervene. In this case, government can work together with market and society. Third, states with strong capabilities should play a more active role in dealing with problems related to market imperfections. Experience from the Asian crisis has strengthened the view that state should play an active role in promoting markets through industrial and financial policy. Rethinking the role of state also means that it has to explore alternative instruments and ways to enhance the effectiveness of its policies. The regulatory role of the state has become broader and more complex than before. The regulatory action needs to fit with the capabilities of state regulatory agencies and the sophistication of the market. The state's responsibility for providing basic services — education, health, etc. — has become doubtful. The state's responsibility has to be based on its capabilities and the relative strength of the market and society. To protect the weaker part of society and to improve equality it has to differentiate between insurance against the unexpected (unemployment, etc.) and providing a minimum level of living conditions for the poorest.

Decline of Competition

This scenario takes place against a world economy that exhibits strong signs that, in many markets, competition is decreasing. This exacerbates problems where little countervailing power exists. At least six factors may be adduced for the argument that globalisation is associated with the decline of competition in many markets. These are:

1) The oligopolistic structure of markets and the associated strategic behaviour of multinational enterprises;
2) The emergence of alliance capitalism and the competition reducing practices of alliances;
3) Regionalisation and its associated internal consolidation and external protection;
4) The decline of anti trust and anti-monopoly policy implementation;
5) The ability of multinational firms to become (or to be seen as) 'insiders' rather than 'outsiders' in national markets;
6) Control of information and knowledge management in multinational firms.

The culmination of these trends is to accent the political skills of lobbying and shelter seeking (insider status) over the economic value of activities. The result is that ineffective and imperfectly informed governments are unable to act to restore any kind of competitive equilibrium.

In a sense, the nature of global oligopolistic competition is 'old news'. Its effects were analysed by Knickerbocker back in 1973. The intensity of this behaviour has increased as cross border entry, particularly by merger and take-over, has become more commonplace (Flowers, 1976; Ghauri, 1999). Threats to a global oligopolistic world market share may be met by a welfare sub-optimal strategy of take-over or pre-emptive entry into a market where the oligopolist knows that profitable operation cannot take place. It is however, preferable, than allowing a rival player to have a sheltered base from which to mount a strategic attack (Lenway *et al.*, 1996).

Such strategies are reinforced by alliances designed to 'regulate markets' or 'enforce conformity to industry standards'. Competition between alliances of firms, rather than unitary firms, has become the norm in industries such as airlines. Cooperation, rather than competition, may sound a good slogan, but alliances may have deleterious effects on those shut out of them, on those coerced into membership, and on suppliers and customers who become much more price takers.

Regionalisation, the consolidation of national economies into trade and investment blocks, often implies increased concentration of industry. The EU is perhaps the best example of this.

The inability of individual nation states' laws to act against monopoly, oligopolistic practices and cartel-like behaviour in alliances, is of course exacerbated by the regional strategies of multinationals and despite the extraterritorial nature of some countries' laws (e.g., US anti-trust laws), globalisation provides shelter from such legislation.

Eden and Molot (1993) examine the ways in which foreign owned companies become insiders (in the case of the North American automobile industry). Insinuation, through lobbying and seeking government shelter, enables the companies to become insiders and raises the question 'Who is us?' (Reich, 1990).

The control of information within multinational firms and strategies to prevent its diffusion, whilst appropriating rents from proprietary knowledge, are a key focus for public policy and business strategy (Buckley & Carter, 2000). The privatisation of public knowledge provides a real challenge in the new global economy.

However, there are countervailing trends. The entry of e-commerce as a major factor in global competition is breaking some existing monopolies and providing competition at crucial points in the value chain.

This results in fragmentation of existing competitive structures and may well result in a new wave of consolidation. These effects are not confirmed to the developed world and may well have some direct effects on low cost labour locations, extending the ability of firms to control "offshore operations".

The Asian crises might, in the short term, be regarded as increasing competition by breaking down sheltered domestic monopolies but, on a global scale, it may have removed independent (nascent) multinationals. The potential destruction of "infant industry" competitors by takeovers of the newly cheap firms in emerging economies, may, in the longer run, have a detrimental effect on world competition.

Indeed, new circumstances force a reconsideration of the correct level of analysis of competition. Should it be assessed at global, regional or national levels? It is clear that large scale consolidation of activities by multinationals at regional level within, for example, the EU and NAFTA, make this an appropriate analytical domain. In matters of international financial flows, the global market may well be the crucial one. Competition issues within individual markets have to be considered against this background.

Further, competition must be assessed in the dynamic context. The role of oligopolistic structures in fostering innovation was highlighted by Schumpeter and has been a feature of economic discourse for centuries, from Smith to Marx to Marshall and Schumpeter. The "creative destruction" wrought by new combinations of factors of production is needed to push firms and industries on to new levels of attainment. The question of the reality of this picture and the extent to which there is a trade off between innovation and market power remain matters of ideological dispute and contradictory evidence.

Distributional Issues

The argument that trade and foreign direct investment in globalisation damages the interest of workers mirrors the arguments in the 1970s of the detrimental effects of outward FDI on the USA and UK (Bergsten *et al.*, 1978).

The argument now is that trade (and FDI) redistribute income away from unskilled workers, towards capital and skilled (knowledge) workers. Krugman (1994) has continually made a powerful argument that trade, based on comparative advantage, is a non-zero sum game. Partly this

Table 1.2: Inflows of Foreign Direct Investment by Region, 1996–1999 ($ billion).

	1996	1997	1998	1999
World	363	468	660	827
of which:				
Developed countries	212	276	468	609
• Western Europe	116	138	246	–
• European Union	109	128	237	269
• Other western Europe	8	9	9	–
• Japan	–	3	3	–
• United States	76	109	189	–
Developing countries	139	173	174	198
• Africa	6	8	9	10
• Latin America and the Caribbean	46	68	73	97
• Asia	85	96	90	91
West Asia	4	5	4	–
Central Asia	2	3	3	–
South, east and south-east Asia	80	88	83	84
of which China	*40*	*44*	*43.5*	*40*
• The Pacific	–	–	–	–
Central and eastern Europe	13	18	19	20

Source: World Economic Situation and Prospects 2000, United Nations, New York, and *The Economist*, April 8, 2000
Note: Due to rounding, the sum of the sub regions might not add up to the total

argument rests on the view that government policies are based on imperfect information. However, technological innovation may be the major culprit in eroding real wages for unskilled workers.

There is a further element of severe inequality in the world economy and that is the extent to which poorer nations attract inward foreign direct investment. The data in table 1.2 shows that:

1) FDI goes to a minority of less developed countries;
2) there is a very uneven distribution amongst less developed countries in the amounts they attract.

In 1999, China was the recipient of almost five percent of world FDI and more than 20 percent of FDI in developing countries.

Societies living with ineffective states have long suffered the consequences in terms of postponed growth and social development. There are great dangers of ineffective governments, such as, political and social unrest, disintegration, loss in productive capacity and human misery. Well-functioning markets are considered the most efficient means to provide social justice. But it is not always true, as markets often undersupply a range of collective goods necessary for the benefits of society. These goods can include basic infrastructure, literacy, and employment opportunities.

Provisions for basic education, health and other social services can help achieve a better match between roles and capabilities. In the long run, investment in people will cut poverty and create basic living conditions for the most vulnerable. This can be achieved through social assistance programmes to help the poorest and through unemployment and other social insurance programmes to support the poorest or lowest level of workforce.

Some developing countries have experimented with social assistance measures for meeting the basic needs of the poorest, ranging from cash assistance to subsidisation of labour intensive public or private works. In many countries, however, these programmes have failed to achieve their objective of protecting the most vulnerable (IBRD, 1997)

Conclusion

There is likely to be an upsurge of critical material on globalisation, and specifically on the role of multinational enterprises' rent-seeking behaviour which fosters globalisation. This literature will mirror the critical literature of the 1970s in some ways but will also have some new features. The revisiting of extant issues will include competitive issues, issues of bargaining and lobbying, and labour related questions such as the export of jobs. Issues likely to have a renewed focus are those relating to regional integration, insecurity of tenure (both of multinationals in individual locations and workers within multinationals), questions of monopolistic practises, and a focus on environmental damage and cultural issues.

Our analysis suggests that a new research agenda is likely to emerge in the new millennium. This agenda concerns the external impact of the strategies of the leading multinational firms as they consolidate their hold on the global economy and as they accrete the power that comes from control of scarce knowledge resources. Combined with economic abundance, the new development raises threats such as, economic insecurity, political instability and cultural decay leading to further imbalance in equality. The resulting insecurity felt by citizens is likely to be exacerbated by the declining ability of individual states to provide a safety net. Attention to the empirical reality of these issues, their extent and impact, is a key focal point for international business researchers.

References

Barnet, R. J. & Muller, R. E. (1975). *Global Reach: The Power of the Multinational Corporations*. London: Jonathan Cape.

Bergsten, C. F., Horst, T. & Moran, T. H. (1978). *American Multinationals and American Interests*. Washington, D.C.: Brookings Institution.

Boddewyn, J. J. (1992). Political behaviour research. In P. J. Buckley (ed.), *New Directions in International Business*. Cheltenham: Edward Elgar.

Brewer, T. L. (1993). Foreign direct investment in emerging market countries. In L. Oxelheim (ed.), *The Global Race for Foreign Direct Investment*. Berlin: Springer-Verlag.

Buckley, P. J. (1996). Government policy responses to strategic rent-seeking transnational corporations. *Transnational Corporations, 5(2)*, 1–17.

Buckley, P. J. & Carter, M. J. (2000). Capturing value from internationally dispersed knowledge in multinational firms. *Long Range Planning*, (forthcoming).

Buckley, P. J. & Casson, M. (1976). *The Future of the Multinational Corporation*. London: Macmillan.

Buckley, P. J. & Casson, M. (1991). Multinational enterprises in less developed countries: cultural and economic interactions. In P. J. Buckley & J. Clegg (eds), *Multinational Enterprises in Less Developed Countries*. London: Macmillan.

Buckley, P. J. & Ghauri, P. N. (1994). *The Economics of Change in East and Central Europe*. London: Academic Press.

Cantwell, J. A. (1989). *Technological Innovation and the Multinational Enterprise*. Oxford: Basil Blackwell.

Casson, M. (1994). Enterprise culture and institutional change in eastern Europe. In P. J. Buckley & P. N. Ghauri, *The Economics of Change in East and Central Europe*. London: Academic Press.

Chandler, A. D. & Redlich, F. (1961). Recent developments in American business administration and their conceptualization. *Business History Review*, Spring, 103–128.

Chandler, A. D. (1977). *The Visible Hand: The Management Revolution in American Business*. Cambridge, Mass.: Belknap Press of Harvard University Press.

Contractor, F. (1991). *Government Policies Toward Foreign Investment: An Empirical Investigation of the Link Between National Policies and FDI Flows.* Paper presented at the Annual meeting of Academy of International Business, Miami.

Dunning, J. H. (1991). Governments and multinational enterprizes: from confrontation to cooperation. *Millennium, 20,* 225–244.

Dunning, J. H. (1992). The political economy of international production. In P. J. Buckley (ed.), *New Directions in International Business.* Cheltenham: Edward Elgar.

Dunning, J. H. (1994). Re-evaluating the benefits of foreign direct investment. *Transnational Corporations, (1),* 23–51.

Eden, L. and Molot, M. A. (1993). Insiders and outsiders: defining "Who is Us" in the North American automobile industry. *Transnational Corporations, 2,* 31–64.

Flowers, E. B. (1976). Oligopolistic reaction in European and Canadian direct investment in the US. *Journal of International Business Studies, 7,* 43–55.

Ghauri, P. N. (1999). Relationship games: creating competitive advantage through cooperation. In S. Urban (ed.), *Relations of Complex Organizational Systems.* Wiesbaden: Gabler. 59–84.

Hymer, S. (1976). *The International Operations of National Firms: A Study of Direct Foreign Investment.* Cambridge MA: MIT Press.

International Bank for Reconstruction and Development (IBRD) (1997). *The State in a Changing World: World Development Report 1997.* Washington: IBRD. iii.

Jenkins, R. (1999). The changing relationship between emerging markets and multinational enterprises. In P. J. Buckley & P. N. Ghauri (eds), *Multinational Enterprises and Emerging Markets: Managing Increasing Interdependence.* Pergamon.

Knickerbocker, F. T. (1973). *Oligopolistic Reaction and Multinational Enterprise.* Boston: Harvard University.

Krugman, P. (1994). Does third world growth hurt first world prosperity? *Harvard Business Review,* July-August, 113–121.

Lenway, S., Morck, R. & Yeung, B. (1996). Rent-seeking, protectionism and innovation in the American steel industry. *Economic Journal, 106,* 401–421.

Penrose, E. T. (1956). Foreign investment and the growth of the firm. *Economic Journal, 66,* 220–235.

Pfefferman, G. P. & Madarassy, A. (1992). *Trends in Private Investments in Developing Countries.* International Finance Corporation, discussion paper No. 14. Washington DC: The World Bank.

Porter, M. A. (1990). *The Competitive Advantage of Nations.* New York: Macmillan.

Prahalad, C. D. & Lieberthal, K. (1998). The end of corporate imperialism. *Harvard Business Review 76(4),* 69–79.

Reich, R. (1990). Who is us? *Harvard Business Review, 68(1)*, 53–65.

Stopford, J. M. & Strange, S. (1991). *Rival States, Rival Firms.* Cambridge: Cambridge University Press.

Strange, S. (1996). *The Retreat of the State: The Diffusion of Power in the World Economy.* Cambridge: Cambridge University Press.

Strange, S. (1997). The erosion of the state. *Current History*, November, 365–369.

Streeten, P. (1974). The theory of development policy. In J. H. Dunning (ed.), *Economic Analysis and the Multinational Enterprise.* London: George Allen and Unwin.

UNCTC (1992). *The Determinants of Foreign Direct Investment: A Survey of Evidence.* London, New York: United Nations.

UNCTAD (1998). *World Investment Report.* Geneva: UNCTAD.

Vernon, R. (1966). International investment and international trade in the product cycle. *Quarterly Journal of Economics 80*, 190–207.

Wells, L. T. (1998). Multinational enterprises and developing countries. *Journal of International Business Studies, 29(1)*, 101–114.

Chapter 2

Are Multinational Firms Good or Bad?

Mats Forsgren

Introduction

With reference to her study of the international petroleum industry Edith
Penrose wrote "the role of the very large privately-owned companies in a
modern economy is still ill defined and controversial, and also subject to
great confusion of thought because the 'models' of the 'firm' implicit in
the prevailing theory of a private, competitive economic system, to which
both the big firms and their critics seem to cling, are inadequate, even for
analytical purposes, let alone as foundations for making judgements
about public policy" (Penrose, 1971). At the same time Stephen Hymer,
one of the founders of the mainstream theory of foreign direct investment, stated that "in a word, the multinational corporation reveals the
power of size and the danger of leaving it uncontrolled" (Hymer, 1970).
The debate about the socio-political implications of the multinational
firm reached its peak during the 1970s. Several authors claimed that the
structure and accumulation of huge resources in these firms led to extensive bargaining power in relation to governments and employees
(Negandhi, 1980; Turner, 1970). The sovereignty of the nation states was
at bay (Tugendhat, 1971; Vernon, 1971) and the labour force's usual
means by which to secure a fair share of the surplus were supposed to be
weakened by the possibility of the firm relocating its production to
another country (Hymer, 1970; Marglin, 1974).

Hymer's perspective on the multinational firm contained a concern
about reduced competition. The result of the deviation from classical
competition was at the heart of his theory. He maintained that inter-

Critical Perspectives on Internationalisation, pp. 29–58.
Copyright © 2002 by Elsevier Science Ltd.
All rights of reproduction in any form reserved.
ISBN: 0-08-044035-5

national investments, to a large degree, reflect different kinds of collusion between large firms, including mergers, acquisitions or strategic alliances across borders (Colin & Sugden, 1987; Hymer, 1968; 1970; Hymer & Rowthorn, 1970; Yamin, 1991). Through this behaviour competition between the large firms can be avoided or at least controlled in such a way that the joint profit can be optimised at the expense of consumers. Dividing up countries and markets between large actors in order to restrain competition between rivals is part of that story.

Naturally, the theory of oligopolistic behaviour, combined with the many cases of large mergers, etc., between firms in different countries and the increasing degree of concentration in many industries, sometimes on a global scale, laid the foundation for critical analyses of the political and economic implications of the multinational firm. Such analyses also became relatively common up to the middle of the 1970s, in the form of governmental investigations or investigations by trade unions. For instance several investigations were made to determine the effects on rate of employment in USA of US firms investing abroad (Bergsten *et al.,* 1978; Frank & Freeman, 1978; Hawkins, 1972; Stobaugh, 1976). Similar investigations were made in Sweden and in other countries about the consequences on employment, balance of payment and technology of outward and inward investments in Swedish industry (see, for instance, SOU, 1975; SOU, 1983).

However, for several reasons the critical analysis of the multinational firm as a phenomenon decreased considerably during the 1980s and 1990s, especially among economists within the international business field. Dunning, for instance, stated 1994 that most governments are "now acclaiming FDI as good news" after a period of hostility in the 1970s and early 1980s (Dunning, 1994; Rugman & Verbeke, 1998).

Welfare Implications According to Internalisation Theories and Resource-based Views

It is reasonable to argue that one important reason for this change is the introduction of transaction costs and internalisation as explanations for the existence of multinational firms (Buckley & Casson, 1976; Hennart, 1982; McManus, 1972). According to the internalisation approach multinational firms arise because firms tend to internalise transactions for which the transaction cost in the market is high. By carrying out these transactions within one and the same firm, rather than between independent firms, the transaction cost will be reduced. Consequently, if a firm intends to exploit a firm-specific asset in a foreign market, and this exploitation has to be done in that market due to localization factors (e.g., trade barriers, high transportation costs or other country-specific factors), the firm often tends to do so by investing abroad in own facilities, and not by selling the asset to an indigenous firm, e.g., through a license (Dunning, 1988). This tendency will be stronger the more intangible the firm-specific asset is, because intangible assets are difficult to do business with (Caves, 1982).

Although it has been claimed that Hymer was very well aware of the transaction cost problem (see e.g., Buckley, 1990; Horaguichi & Toyne, 1990), it is nevertheless true that his concern was above-normal profits and monopolistic behaviour rather than cost efficiency. Within the internalisation approach the focus is more or less the opposite. The growth of the multinational firm through foreign direct investment is basically interpreted as cost-minimizing behaviour rather than as rent-seeking monopolistic behaviour. The border of the multinational firm ends where the sum of transaction costs and administrative costs is minimized. The transaction costs are dependent on market failure, but not caused by the kind of structural imperfections Hymer was occupied with, but rather with natural imperfections because of inadequacies in market pricing due to intangible assets. While the behaviour of multinational firms, based on structural imperfections, can lead to losses for society, internalisation due to high transactions costs implies a net gain, not only for the firm itself but also for society (Hennart, 1982).

In principle the two lines of thought can be combined in one and the same model, and it is basically an empirical question which one is the most prevalent one. However, the elegance of the internalisation model and cost efficiency thinking has undoubtedly dominated the theoretical debate among economists during the last two decades. Consequently, a more critical analysis of the multinational firm based on Hymer's original reasoning has been more or less absent. The internalisation approach has in fact been efficient in disarming most attempts to question the multinationals from a socio-political point of view.

However, the internalisation "fortress" has been questioned lately with reference to models dealing with how knowledge is used as a value-creating asset in the firm. One strand of this research argues that multinational firms exist, not because of market failure, but because knowledge across borders can be transferred more efficiently inside the firm than between independent firms (Kogut & Zander, 1993). A more subtle variant of this argument is the notion that in principle transaction cost considerations imply that the firm-specific asset, notably intangible asset, in principal can be treated as a sellable asset. Very often, though, the relevant knowledge or skill cannot be detached from the firm itself and consequently cannot be treated as a public good (Yamin, 1999). Consequently, exploitation through knowledge transfer rather than through internalisation of a less efficient market transaction is claimed to be a *raison d'être* for multinationals.

It is interesting to observe that more recent thoughts on the multi-national as a phenomenon that creates capabilities and values rather than minimize costs, inspired by theories about organizational learning (Kogut & Zander, 1993; Madhook, 1996; 1998), have often been developed in opposition to internalisation theory based on transaction cost reasoning. However, these thoughts also imply that the behaviour and existence of multinationals have to do with transfer of knowledge inside the organiza-tion. The basic difference is that while internalisation theory argues that flows of knowledge between independent organizations would sometimes be an inefficient solution, learning theories propose that knowledge is basically a collective resource that must be handled inside the organiza-tion if the multinational is to reap the benefits from it (Foss, 1999; Spender, 1996). So, even if the former perspective deals with the transfer of knowledge, as an asset, the latter perspective deals with knowledge in relation to organizational learning. One could argue that both perspec-tives assume that knowledge is actually transferred within the multi-national. Consequently, in this sense the welfare implications of multinational corporations (MNCs) based on the learning approach will be rather similar to those in the internalisation approach. MNCs con-tribute to the welfare of societies because they are more efficient vehicles for knowledge transfer between countries and contexts than other forms of institutions. Whether this is owing to the minimization of transaction costs or the optimization of organizational learning is of minor impor-tance. Multinationals exist because they are efficient in handling and transferring of knowledge on a global scale. From a host country per-spective the implications are the same. A foreign investment in the country improves its possibility to get access to new technology, which will contribute to the welfare of the country.

However, scattered empirical observations concerning internationalisa-tion and the structure of multinationals casts doubt on the assumption that the multinational is dominated by learning and the transfer of know-ledge. It has been suggested that internationalisation, and consequently the present structure of many multinationals, primarily reflects a gradual exploitation of firm-specific advantages in foreign markets, which eventually lead up to a relatively dispersed, and duplicated structure (Zander and Sölvell, this volume). Acquisitions of foreign operations as the dominant mode of foreign investments contribute to this polycentric character, where the different subsidiaries tend to be relatively independent of each other. The discussion about subsidiary product mandates is also in line with this conceptualisation of the multinational as a dispersed, polycentric organization. The present localization of subsidiaries maybe more closely mirrors how competitive threats and exploitation in different markets have been handled over time than the MNCs' ambitions to combine and learn from different contexts through an appropriate localization strategy. Therefore, the logic of the multinational as a learning organization, well fitted to upgrade competence through exploring and combining capabilities residing in the different subsidiaries, is possibly misleading or greatly overemphasized. It has also been pointed out by several scholars that there are severe barriers to knowledge transfers between sub-units in organizations (Szulanski, 1996), which also imply that the metaphor of the learning MNC can be questioned.

If the perspective of the MNC as a learning organization is questioned, its role as a vehicle for knowledge transfer between countries must also be questioned. Transfer of knowledge across borders may certainly occur because of MNCs, but might not be the dominant feature of multinationality.

The analysis of the economic and political consequences of multinational firms since the 1960s is a good illustration of Edith Penrose' point cited above. The issues raised and the answers given depend heavily on the basic model adopted for the firm, and all models tend to be inadequate in the sense that they emphasize certain aspects at the expense of others.

Are MNCs Good or Bad?

The issue of the social and economic consequences of the multinational firm contains many different sub-issues. For instance, in Caves seminal book about this topic the analysis included the impact of foreign direct investment on income distribution, labour relations, international capital flows, technology, productivity, taxation and economic growth (Caves, 1982). However, these matters are related and the answers depend on certain underlying, broader factors. One such factor is the impact of the MNC on competition, because competition is considered to be of crucial importance to a country's economic growth and technological development (Hood & Young, 1979, Porter, 1990). Another factor is the bargaining power of the MNC vis-à-vis governments. Such bargaining has a profound impact on issues such as taxation, labour relations and income distribution (Dicken, 1992). A third factor is the impact of MNCs on knowledge transfer across borders. More attention is now being paid to knowledge as a factor of production, with the distribution and exchange of know-how being a crucial element of the global economic system. This has far reaching consequences for the development of technology within countries and for their economic growth (Amin & Thrift, 1994; Dunning, 1991).

The purpose of this chapter is to point out some economic and political implications of the existence of multinational firm with reference to the above-mentioned three factors. However, as has been illustrated in the introductory section, the interpretation depends on how we model the multinational firm. Up to the middle of 1980s the analysis tended to conceptualise the multinational firm as an organization exploiting its home-based, ownership advantage in foreign markets through direct investment. During the last 15 years a richer conceptualisation of the multinational firms has been developed. It is recognized that multinationals differ, both in terms of the localization of their core competence as well as in the overall configuration and degree of integration between their different units (Bartlett & Ghoshal, 1989; Ghoshal & Nohria, 1997; Porter, 1986). An attempt to use this new conceptualisation in an analysis of the impact of MNCs on competition, bargaining power and knowledge transfer will be presented in the next section, by applying a well known classification of MNCs into three archetypes. First, however, the general impact of multinationality on competition, bargaining power and knowledge transfer will be outlined below.

Competition

A usual question is whether the operation of the multinational firm violates competition and therefore benefits from monopoly rents to an extent that is detrimental to consumer welfare. Important questions here are issues involving the exercising of market power and what Hymer would have called market collusion between multinationals. The basic idea behind Hymer's view is that multinational firms tend to *create* market imperfection in order to increase the returns on their assets, which can be detrimental to welfare. The internalisation theory, on the contrary, suggest that foreign direct investments are made in order to *avoid* market imperfections, and therefore increase welfare (Buckley & Casson, 1976; Rugman, 1982; Safarian, 1993).

However, a closer look reveals that even if the two perspectives differ they are not mutually exclusive. The internalisation theory deals first of all with market imperfection as the basic reason for foreign direct investments. MNCs are created because firms internalise imperfect markets. Hymer's concern with respect to competition has more to do with MNCs behaviour, *once they have been created.* Internalisation can be a relevant explanation for foreign direct investment, but that does not exclude the possibility that the multinational firms are in a especially favourable position to reduce competition in the market through e.g., horizontal mergers, strategic alliances, bargaining with governments about subsidies etc. Consequently, an analysis of the impact of MNCs on competition must consider in which situations the MNC is able to carry out such competitive-reducing behaviour. Such analysis can be carried out independent of the received theories of foreign direct investment.

There is a classical dilemma concerning competition and competition policy in an international context. Within one country, optimal competition policy calls for competitive markets, that is markets with a sufficient number of producers to prevent any firm earning above normal profits. However, in order to maximize national income from *international transactions*, it could be argued that the nation should extract as much monopoly rent as possible from foreign markets (Caves, 1996). From a nation's point of view, therefore, the need for a competition policy differs depending on whether the competition within or between markets(countries) is considered. In the international arena, the interests firms have in achieving stronger market positions and decrease competition by different means coincides with the home nation's interest, while this is not the case for the same behaviour within the home country's own market.[1]

---

[1] The dilemma is illustrated by the discussions coming up after the EU-commission's decision not to approve Volvo's application to buy Scania. The EU commission referred to the high market shares in Sweden and the other Nordic countries resulting from the acquisition while Volvo and the Swedish government referred to the two companies needs for a stronger position in the global market. Or expressed differently, the Swedish government was prepared to sacrifice competition in the home market for a prospect of a Swedish-based company to reach a higher degree of market power abroad and (possibly) earn monopoly rents.

Bargaining Power

The relationship between the state and firms has always been an important issue (Caves, 1996; Dunning, 1993; Moran, 1993; Rugman, 1998; Safarian, 1993; Stopford & Strange, 1991; Strange, 1997; Vernon, 1971), and the relative bargaining strength of governments and multinationals has long been of major concern. Governments are supposed to maximize national incomes and social welfare within their respective countries. Multinationals investing in these countries are expected to contribute to national income and social welfare through a positive impact on growth and development. However, by demanding special treatments from governments, e.g., through tax exemption or reduction, subsidies etc., the multinational tries to optimise its return from foreign operations. Under certain conditions the result can be that the augmentation of the welfare that would otherwise result from the investments will be reduced or even eliminated. The possibility of demanding special treatments from governments depends on bargaining power, including the alternatives that are open to the MNC whilst the bargaining is being conducted. For instance, a multinational with unique assets attractive to host countries can take a tougher line, and if it lacks close international or national rivals it certainly tends to do so (Caves, 1996). The issue of multinationals' bargaining strength is most often considered with reference to host country situations, especially when considering less-developed countries (Wells 1998). However, the problem and the analysis are also applicable to the relationship between multinationals and their home country governments.[2]

The basic reason for dealing with bargaining power in relation to multinationals is the assumed operational flexibility of MNCs. It is argued that in comparison with domestic firms the multinational firm has a higher flexibility in allocating its operations between countries in response to changes in markets, governmental policies and currencies (Doz, 1986; Dunning & Rugman, 1985; Kogut, 1985). In the so called real option theory it is claimed that multinationals have a comparative advantage made available by their portfolio of investments in different countries (Buckley, 2000). These investments open up the possibility of undertaking or postponing further investments depending on the situation, and to

---

[2] A recent illustration is the discussion in Sweden about business climates and threads by some Swedish multinationals and whether to move their headquarters abroad (I huvudet på ett företag, ISAs Ekonomiska Råd, 1999).

"select an outcome only if it is favorable" (McGrath, 1997). This is done by shifting the value-chain activities across countries, which implies that the multinational firm has a higher possibility of avoiding risk than domestic firms (Reuer, 2000).

One such risk is obviously political risk. Through the choices open to it the multinational firm has a greater chance than a national firm of reducing the impact of political actions by government, and also a stronger chance of successfully influencing such actions. Or expressed otherwise, to some extent at least, the multinational firm can treat the firm-government relationship, not just as an exogenous variable through adaptation, but as an endogenous variable through lobbying and negotiation (Rugman & Verbeke, 1998).

This relationship can be analysed through a simple resource-dependence approach (Pfeffer & Salancik, 1978). The less the individual government is dependent on the multinational firm's operations, the lower the firm's negotiating power vis-à-vis the government. And the more real options the multinational firm has, in terms of alternatives to the present way of conducting operations, the higher its bargaining power.

Consequently, the bargaining power of multinationals in government relationships has very much to do with the number and type of alternatives available on both sides (Dicken, 1992). Countries base their market power mainly on the size of their market and the uniqueness of their resources, for instance natural resources or a highly developed infrastructure. The larger the market and/or the more attractive the resources of the country the more willing is the multinational firm to adapt to government policy. However, if the multinational firms is less dependent on a single country due to its large set of alternatives its bargaining power is higher and its possibility to play one country off against the other increases. Operational flexibility differs between different types of multinational firms, and consequently their bargaining power varies as well. However, we can argue that multinational firms, ceteris paribus, are more powerful negotiators in relation to governments than domestic firms, due to the simple fact that their operations cover several countries.

It has to be recognized that bargaining between governments and multinational firms is a dynamic process in which the relative strength of the parties changes over time. For instance, it has been pointed out that over time the host country's bargaining strength increases because it learns how to screen the entry of the MNC and regulate their operations. At the same time the MNC's bargaining strength tends to decrease along with its investment in the country, because of the dependence these investments create. This has sometimes been called the "obsolescing model of bargaining"(Vernon, 1971b).

However, a new dimension in the bargaining relationship between countries and multinational firms has come into play. Through bilateral and multilateral negotiations between countries different rules are decided upon that circumscribes the possibility for the individual country to take actions against multinational firms, for instance in terms of taxes on foreign ownership, performance requirements, remittance policies etc (Ramamurti, 2001). So even if there is an "obsolescing" process in the sense that relative bargaining power change in favour of the country over time, other factors work in the opposite direction.

Knowledge Transfer Across Borders

The third factor deals explicitly with the multinational as a learning organization. It concerns the explorative ability of an organization, which involves the successive upgrading of the firm's technology and knowledge base. It can be argued that the ability to learn through absorbing and combining information in new ways lies at the heart of the sustainable competitive strength of any firm. However, it can also be assumed that learning capacity at the firm level has a socio-economic impact, through the firms' own activities and through spillover effects to other parts of the business community. Within the context of the multi-national firm learning activities through the transfer of knowledge within the organization — across borders — is of special importance, since this is a process for which multinational firms are supposed to be especially suited. Consequently, the implications associated with the role of the multinational as a vehicle for knowledge transfer across borders is quite obvious.

It is assumed that MNCs have better possibilities not only to absorb new knowledge from different environments, but also particularly to use their own organization as a vehicle for knowledge transfer. The ability to transfer knowledge across borders also has important, positive welfare implications. The presence of an MNC would give a country, hosting the subsidiary of the MNC, greater opportunities to acquire knowledge about new products from abroad etc. than if it only hosted domestic firms. The discussion about technology transfer to under-developed coun-tries through foreign investments is an example of such beneficial effects (Blomström, 1991). Another example is the knowledge transfer between industrial countries arising from MNCs strategies to tap "foreign diamonds" (Sölvell *et al.*, 1991).

However, similar to the impact MNCs have on competition and bargaining power, we would expect that the welfare effects stemming from knowledge transfer differ depending on the configuration and integration of the multinational firm.

Multinational Firms — Three Archetypes

Today multinational firms differ tremendously in terms of their operational structure, internationalisation modes, technology and history. It is beyond the scope of this chapter to analyse all these categories and to examine how they are related to competition, bargaining power and the cross-border transfer of technology. However, one can argue that the strategy used by the MNC, manifested in its configuration of activities and degree of integration, also reflects its role in a socio-economic context. A first step, therefore, would be to analyse the relationship between different strategic archetypes and the socio-economic factors suggested above. In the following discussion we will use a typology advocated by several scholars (for an overview of the most common typologies, see Harzing, 2000). More precisely, we will elaborate on three well-known, but distinctive forms of multinationality: Multi-domestic firms, Global Firms and Network Firms.[3] In multinationals traits of all three archetypes can easily be found. However, quite often one is dominant.

The Multi-domestic Firm

The configuration of the Multi-domestic firm implies that the subsidiaries in the different countries operate the entire value chain, that is purchasing, production, marketing and sales activities, and sometimes even R&D. The integration between activities across subsidiaries and country borders is limited. Exporting to neighbouring countries can occur, but typically there is a high degree of concentration on the local (country)

---

[3] Similar classifications have been used by several authors; see for instance Porter 1986, Bartlett and Ghoshal 1989 and Harzing 2000. Our classification corresponds to large extent to the latter author's distinction between multi-domestic firms, global firms and transnational firms.

business (Porter, 1986). The interaction across borders between the sub-sidiaries concerns administrative and financial relationships rather than flows of products and services. The history of the multi-domestic firm is that of a firm exploiting a firm-specific advantage abroad, which for several reasons, such as differences in markets, cost of transportation, importance of a close link to specific customers etc., has to be carried out on a country-by-country basis. The firm is multinational because of the companies it owns and its presence in several countries rather than due to cross-border operations. Often foreign acquisition has been used as a dominant form of internationalisation. The strategic role of the indivi-dual subsidiary resembles the role of a local innovator according to Gupta and Govindarajan's classification (Gupta & Govindarajan, 1991).

The structure of the Multi-domestic firm is illustrated in Figure 2.1 below.

Multinational firms that over time have built up foreign subsidiaries with more or less full-fledged operations, each directed its operation first of all to the local market, resemble the multi-domestic type. For instance, before the ongoing globalisation of telecommunication Ericsson had to

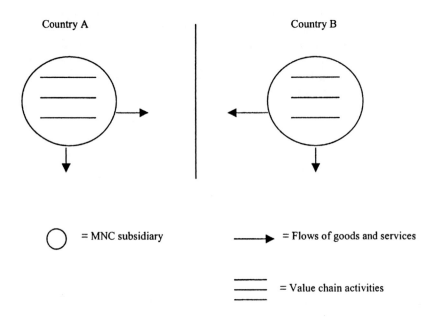

Figure 2.1: The Multi-domestic Firm.

duplicate their operations by having more or less the same type of activities in several countries.

Another example of a multi-domestic firm is AGA, the Swedish producer of gas and gas applications. Due to high transportation costs and a high degree of customer-related production and product development AGA operates subsidiaries in a large number of countries, each having more or less a complete value chain directed to the local market. Some parts of the value chain, first of all R/D, are the object of integration attempts by the headquarters. However, the multi-domestic configuration dominates and the overall integration between the subsidiaries is low.

The Multi-domestic Firm and Competition. How do multi-domestic firms affect national and international competition? As the multi-domestic firm by definition operates in each national market separately, national competition rather than international competition is of primary concern. The subsidiaries resemble their national competitors, including the possible effects of their operation on competition. The effects are limited to the competition in the host market, and the basic question is whether the presence of foreign subsidiaries stimulates or hampers rivalry between firms. The only difference would probably be a higher degree of variance in the possible outcomes arising from the possibility open to the MNC headquarters to reallocate its resources between countries and its possibility to choose between different entry modes. For instance, an acquisition of a local firm will, ceteris paribus, not change the degree of local competition, while a green-field investment might do so. The overall conclusion, though, is that the impact of the multi-domestic firm on national competition resembles those of domestic firms.

This statement needs some qualifications. If we assume that the multi-domestic firm has developed out of the exploitation of a firm-specific asset originally located at the home-base, and not only as a portfolio strategy, the presence of the subsidiary may have positive economic effects for the host country. The subsidiary may put pressure on local firms, because of the subsidiaries' access to resources, competence, etc., in the home country. If this pressure leads to an upgrading of competence and rivalry in the host country's industry positive effects will follow. However, even if exploitation of a home-based firm-specific advantage lies behind the development of the multi-domestic multinational, gradual liberation from the parent company is the typical trajectory. As long as we stick to the view that subsidiaries in such firms primarily run their operations independently, upgrading host-country competition because of the subsidiary's access of resources within the multinational system must be considered the exception rather than the rule. Consequently, contribution to increased national competition from multi-domestic multinationals is limited, but so probably are the negative effects caused by market power.

In principle, the subsidiary of the multi-domestic firm has the same access to competitive-reducing means as domestic firms, no more and no less, which implies that the national market structure rather than the multinationality per se is the crucial factor behind the subsidiary's impact on national competition. The only difference in terms of multinationality would be the larger resources available to the subsidiary through the MNC, which can be used, for instance, to acquire local rivals. However, this advantage should not be overemphasized, as the strategy of the Multi-domestic firm is the sum of the subsidiaries' individual strategies rather than a common corporate strategy.

The Multi-domestic Firm and Bargaining Power. In the Multi-domestic firm the operations of the different subsidiaries are directed to the different host-markets and their operations are run relatively independently of the parent company. In general this archetype is usually seen as a favourable situation from the host government perspective, because it is assumed that the degree of subsidiary responsiveness to the country's policy is higher if the subsidiary is not integrated in the rest of the multinational firm. The manager of the non-integrated subsidiary is also assumed to be more rooted in the national environment and therefore more positive to host government policy (Doz, 1986).

However, this conclusion must be questioned on two points. First, the assumed national responsiveness of the multi-domestic firm has most often been related to market considerations rather than political considerations. The subsidiary of the multi-domestic firm primarily adapts its products and market behaviour to the characteristics of the local market, in contrast to the standardization of products in the global firm case. The national responsiveness behaviour concerns business rather than politics, and whether the subsidiary adapts to the host country's policy or not depends on the relative bargaining power.

Second, seen from the perspective of the multi-domestic firm as a whole, each subsidiary has a limited influence on the corporation's overall business. Its dependence on an individual subsidiary, therefore, is relatively limited. The downscaling of a single subsidiary will have a limited impact on other subsidiaries. The local business will decrease, but it will not affect the other subsidiaries' business. This situation will give the multinational firm a relatively strong bargaining power in relation to the government in the country where the subsidiary is located. In a negotiating process the multi-domestic firm can always demonstrate its relative independence from local business. If the government is dependent on the subsidiary caused by its relative size or its importance for other local firms' business, there will be an asymmetry in the power with the balance in favour of the multinational firm. This asymmetry will be stronger if the firm can demonstrate its ability to move the local business to another country by extending the operations of the subsidiary elsewhere. This situation seems to be in line with the thoughts behind real option theory, where the MNC is modelled first of all as a portfolio of investments, which can be relocated in response to changes in business conditions. One such condition could be a change in government policy. The important point, though, is that this "real option" situation can be used not only to avoid or reduce the impact of government policies, such as taxes or environmental legislation, but also to demand special treatments in direct negotiations with governments.

Therefore, in contrast to the usual perspective we will argue that the bargaining power of the multi-domestic firm vis-à-vis host governments is relatively high, because of the operational independence of the subsidiary from the rest of the corporation and the duplication of resources in the MNC. The firm can compare the situations in the different countries and play off one host government against another. As long as exit is not an unrealistic option the multinational firm has a broad spectrum of possibilities in its bargaining process with host governments, including voice, accommodation or avoid (Safarian, 1993).

If we assume that the Multi-domestic firm is based on an exploitation of a firm-specific asset, the bargaining power of the host government is dependent on the relative size of the local market rather than on the country's uniqueness in terms of competitive resources. If the market is small, the host government run the risk of being more dependent on the MNC than vice versa. However, over time, some "obsolescing" can occur, especially if the subsidiary becomes more and more full-fledged in terms of value-chain activities. If a subsidiary changes from a unit that exploits locally what has been developed at the parent company to a unit with unique capabilities, for instance in product development, the MNC's dependence on the subsidiary increases. This will change the relative bargaining power in favour of the host government.

By definition, though, in the multi-domestic firm unique resources in the individual subsidiary are entirely related to its local business. If the subsidiary acquires capabilities on which other MNC units are dependent, the multi-domestic firm has turned into a situation more in line with the network firm case (see below). We can therefore conclude that in the "pure" multi-domestic firm case the relative bargaining power of the host government is weak, especially if the country market is small.

The Multi-domestic Firm and Knowledge Transfer Across Borders. By definition, exchange between different subsidiaries in the multi-domestic firm is limited. The corporate relationships are administrative and financial more than operational. Even though the individual subsidiary can have a high ability to absorb knowledge from its local market because of the character of its local business network (Andersson *et al.,* 2001), this knowledge is primarily commercialised in the subsidiary itself, rather than transferred to other subsidiaries. Some knowledge can of course be transferred between subsidiaries through the hierarchy. However, the possibility of transferring tacit knowledge is limited because of the absence of any close relationship between the subsidiaries (Lane & Lubatkin, 1998). Consequently we can conclude that the multi-domestic firm is not the best vehicle for knowledge transfer across borders.

The Global Firm

The second archetype is the global firm. This archetype is quite opposite to the multi-domestic firm. Instead of spreading its value chains to several countries the global firm strives to concentrate the activities in the value chains as much as possible to one country. The main reason behind such a strategy is economies of scale in production and other activities, the locational advantage of certain countries and the advantage of co-locating linked activities as much as possible (Porter, 1986). The integration between activities is high in the global firm, however cross-border integration is low due to the concentration of operations to one or a few countries. Contrary to the multi-domestic firm the international market is served through exports to other countries. The global firm is illustrated in Figure 2.2 below.

There are several examples of the global firm case. Commercial aircraft, for instance, consists of three main competitors, Boeing, McDonnel Douglas and Airbus, which concentrate most of their activities to USA and Europe, from which they serve worldwide markets. Another example

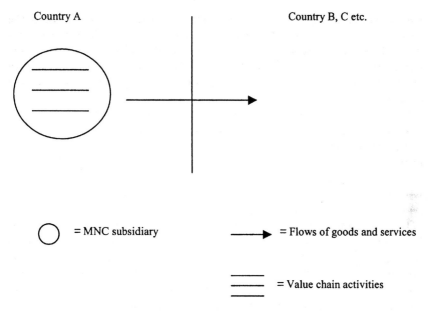

Figure 2.2: The Global Firm.

is the forest industry, in which firms typically has a concentrated configuration of its activities to the parent home country, although with some down-stream activities located in other countries. The Swedish producer of household appliances, Electrolux, has through foreign acquisitions and rationalization increased its economies of scale through geographic specialization within the white-goods sector. For instance, the development, production and marketing of top-loaded washing machines are concentrated to Italy, while France and Sweden host the same activities for washing machines and freezers/refrigerators.

The Global Firm and Competition. The strategy of the global firm is to strive for economies of scale and scope through rationalization of production, concentration of R/D and standardization of marketing activities. Common features of this strategy are mergers and acquisitions of local competitors in order to reach a scale large enough to serve the global market. The number of local competitors decreases and, as a consequence, the competition in the host country's national market will also decrease. For instance, Electrolux's development into a global firm within the white goods sector has been combined with a substantial reduction of local competitors in the Swedish market. This is the classical case of the host country giving up or reducing competition at the national level in order for the global firm to reach competitive advantage at the international arena, which hopefully also will benefit the host country in longer terms (Caves, 1982).

The impact of the global firm on international competition is more difficult to estimate. There are contradicting forces. On one hand, a restructuring of an industry into a global oligopoly, dominated by a few global firms, implies a reduction in competition in terms of numbers of rivals, actual or potential. On the other hand, the global rivals have a higher possibility of global reach, with less possibility for firms to benefit from regional or local monopoly.

However, the global firm often has a much higher market share in the host country market and in neighbouring countries than in other countries, especially in countries where its global competitors have their base. One reason for this is what Hymer used to call "removal of conflicts" and "market collusion" as strategic behaviour of global firms (Hymer, 1970). One part of these strategies is to avoid challenging other global firms in their "own" markets in exchange for a similar treatment from the competitors' side. For instance, the production of rock drills is dominated by three producers, two located in Sweden and one in South Africa. The global market share of these three producers is about 30 percent each. However, the South African producer has a much higher market share in South Africa than in Sweden, and vice versa (Forsgren & Olsson, 1992). A similar pattern is also obvious in other global oligopolies, for instance the car industry.

In principal, the reduction of competition at the host national level when the global firm is created should be perfectly balanced by competition from other global firms in the same market. However, this does not always materialize due to "market collusion". The strategies of global firms will often lead to lower competition in certain countries than would otherwise have been the case, maybe in combination with strong competition in countries where no "market collusion" is present.

The Global Firm and Bargaining Power. From a resource-dependence perspective maybe the initial conclusion is likely to be that the global firm is even more powerful than the Multi-domestic firm owing to its relatively higher market power in the local market and global dominance. However, there is a fundamental difference between the two archetypes in terms of their resource dependence that has to be considered. The main characteristics of the Global Firm are the high degree of geographic concentration and specialization of its resources. It is an "all the eggs in one basket" situation in terms of a limited duplication of resources. The country, in which the resources are concentrated, is probably highly dependent on the MNC, and a downscaling of the operations or a withdrawal would have serious consequences. However, this can also be expected to be true for the global firm. Due to its configuration it is highly dependent on the country in which it has decided to run its operations. In contrast to the Multi-domestic firm its possibility to change its geographic structure is limited, at least in the short run. This is more so, the more the localization of the global firm is based on unique qualities of the individual country, for instance in terms of infrastructure or human capital. But even if this is not the case, the mere fact that the strategy is built on economies of scale in production and other value-chain activities makes a geographic reallocation of resources difficult.

Consequently, the symmetry in bargaining power between the company and the host government will be relatively high. With reference to real options theory one could probably state that the global firm, at least in the short run, has relatively few real options. We would therefore argue that contrary to what one could expect, the global firm, ceteris paribus, may have a lower degree of bargaining power than the multi-domestic firm. Or expressed differently, bargaining with governments is more a function of reciprocity and interdependence than on unilateral power and the availability of alternatives. It is the price the global firm pays for the high degree of concentration and scale efficiency of its operational structure.

The Global Firm and Knowledge Transfer Across Borders. The configuration of the global firm indicates that knowledge transfer across borders is concentrated to downstream value activities, that is marketing, sales and services. Consequently, the global firm can function as a vehicle for the transfer of knowledge between countries through these activities. An example of such transfer, with beneficiary effects, is when an MNC based in an industrialized country establishes a sales subsidiary or an assembly unit in an underdeveloped country. Some of the knowledge developed in the former country, including technology and management practices, may be transferred and applied in the latter country, as a direct result of the MNC's operations. However, as the core strategy of the global firm is concentration and integration within one country, the contribution to knowledge transfer will be limited, although more extensive than in the Multi-domestic firm case.

The Network Firm

The network firm symbolizes the true advantages of multinationality (Harzing, 2000). As in the former archetype the firm utilizes the comparative advantage of countries. However, it does so to a much higher degree by linking the different subsidiaries in a common value-chain that cross borders. Consequently, the transfer of goods, services and knowledge between different subsidiaries is the landmark of the network firm. Every subsidiary plays a specific role in the corporate network, thus what happens in any subsidiary will affect the whole network. The network firm is illustrated in Figure 2.3.

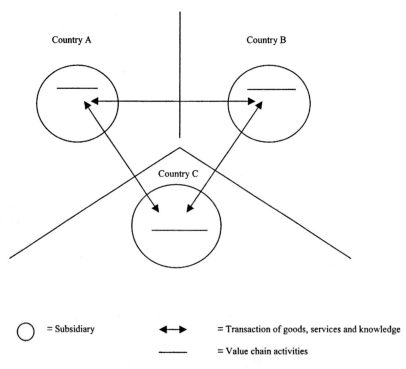

Figure 2.3: The Network Firm.

The subsidiaries of the network firm have different strategic roles depending on the type of activity they engage in. However, the roles are integrated and, to a large extent, the different subsidiaries play the role of what Gupta and Govindarajan would have called Integrated Players (Gupta & Govindarajan, 1991).

The network firm also strives for economies of scale but do so in a more sophisticated way than in the global firm. The specialization and concentration to certain countries are done at the chain activity level, rather than at the product level. The strength of the whole value chain is increased by utilizing the uniqueness of resources in every country through placing the different activities or part of the activities in the countries most suitable. For instance, SKF, the Swedish ball-bearing company, produces different qualities of ball-bearings in different countries, while marketing and sales for the whole assortment is taken care of by each subsidiary, country by country. This implies a high degree of integration between the subsidiaries in terms of exchange of products, market information and knowledge about new products and production processes.

The Network Firm and Competition

There is no reason to assume that the structure of the network firm implies reduced competition at the national level. The basic difference from the case of the global firm is the existence of operational linkages between subsidiaries across borders. The fact that each subsidiary is responsible for a certain part of a value chain, rather than the whole value chain, does not imply an increased market power in the national market per se. From the point of view of a national competition every subsidiary can be looked upon as a unit with international suppliers and customers. The fact that these suppliers and customers belong to a large extent to the same corporation does not change the market share in the national market. Whether this structure leads to a higher market share for the subsidiary depends on the efficiency of the corporate value chain compared to competitor's value chains, rather than the structure as such. Therefore, the network firm has probably a limited impact, negative or positive, on national competition.

In contrast to the multi-domestic firm and the global firm the network firm utilizes specialized resources and capabilities in different countries to optimise the efficiency of the whole value chain. This implies that there are no "home markets" or "host country markets" of the same type as in the former strategies. The only market is the global market, and the network firms compete with each other in that market. However, compared with the global firm, they do not base their competitive strength on a certain home base. Consequently, even though "market collusion" between Network Firms is a possible scenario, a mutual agreement of not entering competitors "home markets" is less likely in this case. The network firms compete first of all with the efficiency of their networks, and the markets for the final products are common to all network firms. Consequently, the possible negative impact on international competition is probably much less than in the global firm case.

The Network Firm and Bargaining Power. It has often been argued that MNCs integrating operations across borders complicate the implementation of national policies. Integration limits the ability of subsidiaries to respond to host government policy, as the MNC's requirement for success is quite different from the individual subsidiary. Therefore, the response to policy implementation is difficult to predict because the relationships between the corporate units make reactions from the MNC quite different from those of domestic firms. Another complicating factor is the conflicting interests between different host governments that occur as a consequence of the integrated MNC. It has also been pointed out that the integrated MNC has superior access to information about investment alternatives and can also avoid interventions from host governments through transfer pricing etc. (Doz, 1986).

Therefore it is often argued that the network firm has a strong bargaining position vis-à-vis governments. In fact, it has been claimed that the creation of the multinational firm as a global network is a dominating feature of the post-modern, informational society, with severe consequences for the bargaining power of the state as a democratic institution (Castells, 1996, Hardt & Negri, 2000). However, if we take into consideration the basic conditions behind the network firm this conclusion can be questioned. The special feature of this archetype is the unique role of each unit in the corporate system. Every subsidiary contributes to the integrated network in its own way, and a withdrawal of a subsidiary will have serious consequences for the whole system. The network is built on specialization and not duplication, as in the multi-domestic case, and the system benefits not only from economies of scale but also from every unit's unique competence.

This means that the MNC is more dependent on each subsidiary for the smooth functioning of the whole corporation than in the former archetypes. Each subsidiary is a "cog in the wheel" and difficult to substitute, at least in the short run. If we also assume that the structure of the network firm has evolved over a long time, with each subsidiary having a special role according to the competitive strength of its business context, the dependence on every subsidiary is extensive.

Therefore, it is reasonable to assume that the dependence of a host government on an individual subsidiary in the Network Firm is counterbalanced by the MNC being dependent on the individual country. The more the uniqueness of the subsidiary is based on context-specific factors at the local level, the higher is the latter type of dependence. Consequently, the network firm is a case of interdependence between MNCs and governments, in which neither side can use exit as a trustworthy alternative. The network is built on combinations of subsidiary-specific and localization-specific advantages and this situation reduces the possibility of both sides to execute strong bargaining power.

In a way the network firm can be seen as the antithesis to the MNC in the real option theory, because the subsidiaries cannot be seen as investment options. Instead, they are parts of a common value-chain which cross borders. Therefore, compared to the multi-domestic case, it is more difficult for the MNC headquarters to exercise unilateral power in the bargaining process with host governments. Paradoxically, one could argue that the stronger the MNC becomes in its ability to benefit from specialized resources in a global network the less its bargaining power vis-à-vis governments!

The Network Firm and Knowledge Transfer Across Borders. The knowledge flows within the network firm are lateral and vertical. Every subsidiary is involved in a complicated pattern of operational relationships with other corporate units (Bartlett & Ghoshal, 1990). If the MNC function as a network firm the communication channels between different subsidiaries will be well developed and able to cross organizational, operational and country borders at one and the same time. In the network firm, learning is a collective phenomenon, which permeates every part of the organization. Therefore, its ability to be used as a vehicle for the transfer of knowledge across borders is obviously much higher than for the other two archetypes. The only barriers that exist are related to cultural barriers, communication technology etc, not to the strategy or configuration of the MNC, as in the multi-domestic firm and global firm cases.

Concluding Remarks

The relationships between the three welfare factors: competition, bargaining power and transfer of knowledge across borders, and the three MNC archetypes are summarized in Table 2.1.

Table 2.1 illustrates that there is no straightforward relationship between multinationality and the socioeconomic implications brought about by the MNCs. The global firm tends to have a negative impact on competition between firms within a country, while high bargaining power and a "real option" situation seems to be related to the multi-domestic firms in the first instance. The global firm, though, contributes more to knowledge transfer across borders than the multi-domestic firm.

However, the table also indicates that the network firm represents the most preferable structure from a socioeconomic point of view. First, its operation in a certain country does not imply a reduction of the competition in that country or in the international arena. Second, the network structure of the firm is far from the optimal situation from the real option theory perspective. Therefore, the bargaining situation of network firms is not particularly strong in relation to that of governments. Third, and perhaps most important, the network firm is especially suited for knowledge transfer across borders. In that sense, it contributes more than the other two archetypes to economic growth due to diffusion of innovations between countries.

This conclusion can be seen in the light of the development of theories

Table 2.1: Relationships Between Different Forms of Multi-nationality and Welfare Factors.

	Multi-Domestic MNC	Global MNC	Network MNC
Negative impact on national and international competition	LOW	HIGH	LOW
Bargaining power in relation to government	HIGH	MEDIUM	MEDIUM
Vehicle for knowledge transfer across borders	LOW	MEDIUM	HIGH

about multinationals. In Hymer's reasoning the MNC was "conquering" the world by exploiting a certain product, either on a country-to-country basis through local production or through export from certain "hubs". At the time of writing this it was not foremost in his mind that the MNC would effectively provide a value-chain across borders. The multi-domestic firm or the global firm dominated his conception of multinationality. Consequently, power of the MNC, both in terms of market power and political power, was an important input to his analysis (Hymer, 1970, Hymer, 1972, Hymer & Rowthorn, 1968).

In later writings the MNC has been considered more as a vehicle for transfer of knowledge across borders. In the transaction-cost-based analyses of the MNC this "vehicle role" is treated as a question of transaction-cost efficiency. In analyses inspired by a resource-based view of multinationals' value creation through the transfer of knowledge within the organization has been emphasized. Both approaches, but especially the latter one, are more akin to looking upon the MNC as a network firm than as a multi-domestic or global firm. Consequently, in later writings the negative consequences of MNCs, arising from their perceived impact on competition and bargaining power, have been replaced by focusing on positive implications attributable to the transfer of knowledge.[4]

It must be concluded from the analysis above that the basic question of whether MNCs are good or bad from a socio-political point of view has no simple answer. First, it depends on what type of socio-economic implications we are dealing with. In this chapter we have focused on three basic implications; competition, bargaining power and ability to transfer knowledge across borders. One limitation of the analysis that these factors are not independent from each other. For instance, bargaining power can have a profound impact on how the MNC affect competition at the national level and knowledge transferability can have an impact on bargaining power.

Second, different types of MNCs have different impacts. However, we posit that in general the Network Firm is more preferable than the other two archetypes. Consequently, an important empirical question is how common the network firm is (Zander & Sölvell, 2000). To the best of our

---

[4] A corresponding change in focus can be observed in the management oriented literature about MNCs. Earlier discussions about the MNC as a globally divisionalized organization have been replaced by a conception of the MNC as a complicated network of operational and administrative relationships between subsidiaries.

knowledge there is no data that can give us a complete answer, only scattered indications. One type of indication is given by data about the integration of subsidiaries within the MNC. A high degree of integration would imply that the MNC functions more as a network than as a multidomestic firm or a global firm. For instance, in a study of 98 subsidiaries belonging to 15 Swedish MNCs, 75 percent of the subsidiaries were either not integrated at all in terms of product or production process development, or functioned as implementers of the parent company's strategy. Only 12 percent could be called integrated players in the sense that they were both receivers of knowledge from and givers of knowledge to other subsidiaries (Andersson & Forsgren, 2000). In an investigation of 255 German foreign-owned subsidiaries Kutschker and Schurig find a similar pattern (Kutschker & Schurig, this volume). Seventy-five percent of the subsidiaries were relatively isolated from the rest of the MNC, in terms of knowledge flow.

These and other figures at least indicate that it might be a mistake to argue that the MNCs Hymer had in mind 30–40 years ago have disappeared, and that the scene is dominated by the network firm. Although it has dominated our conceptualisation of the MNC lately, it might yet be found to belong to what has been called the "myths about global interdependence."[5] Whatever the truth turns out to be, it is reasonable to conclude that it can still be relevant to question the existence and behaviour of multinationals from a sociopolitical point of view.

References

Amin, A. & Thrift, N. (1994). Living in the global. In A. Amin & N. Thrift (eds), *Globalization, Institutions, and Regional Development in Europe*. New York: Oxford University Press. 1–22.

Andersson, U., Forsgren, M. (2000). *Integration in Global MNCs: The Swedish Case*. In proceedings of the University of Vaasa. Reports 58, 150–163.

Andersson, U., Forsgren, M. & Pedersen, T. (2001). Subsidiary performance in MNCs: the importance of technology embeddedness. *International Business Review, 10*, 3–23.

Bartlett, C. A. & Ghoshal, S. (1990). Managing innovations in the transnational corporation. In C. A. Bartlett, *et al.*, (eds), *Managing the Global Firm*. London: Routledge. 215–255.

[5] An expression used by John Mayor in a seminar at IIB, Stockholm School of Economics in April 2000

Bartlett, C. A. & Ghoshal, S. (1989). *Managing Across Borders: The Transnational Solution.* Cambridge, Mass.: Harvard Business School Press.

Bergsten, C. F. & Moran, T. H. (1978). *American Multinationals and American Interests.* Washington: Brookings Institution.

Blomström, M. (1991). Competitiveness of firms and countries. In J. Dunning, B. Kogut & M. Blomström (eds), *Globalization of Firms and the Competitiveness of Nations.* Lund: Institute of Economic Research, Lund University.

Buckley, P. & Casson, M. (1976). *The Future of the Multinational Corporation.* London: Macmillan.

Castells, M. (1996). *The Information Age. Volume 1: The Rise of the Network Society.* Oxford: Blackwells.

Caves, R. (1982). *Multinational Enterprise and Economic Analysis.* Cambridge: Cambridge University Press.

Caves, R. (1996). *Multinational Enterprise and Economic Analysis* (2nd ed.). Cambridge: Cambridge University Press

Cowling, K. & Sugden, R. (1987). *Transnational Monopoly Capitalism.* Brighton: Wheatsheaf.

Dicken, P. (1992). *Global Shift. The Internationalization of Economic Activity.* London: Paul Chapman.

Doz, Y. (1986). *Strategic Management in Multinational Companies.* Oxford: Pergamon Press

Dunning, J. (1988). The eclectic paradigm of international production: A restatement and some possible extensions. *Journal of International Business Studies 19,* Spring, 1–33.

Dunning, J. (1993). *The Globalization of Business.* London: Routledge.

Dunning, J. (1994). Re-evaluating the benefits of foreign direct investment. *Transnational Corporations 3(1),* 23–51.

Dunning, J. & Rugman, A. (1985). The Influence of Hymer's dissertation on the theory of foreign direct investment. *American Economic Review, 75,* 228–232.

Dunning, J. (1991). The globalization of firms and the competitiveness of countries: some implications for the theory of international production. In J. Dunning *et al.,* (eds), *Globalization of Firms and Competitiveness of Nations.* Lund: Institute of Economic Research, Lund University.

Forsgren, M. & Olsson, U. (1992). Power balancing in an international business network. In M. Forsgren & J. Johanson (eds), *Managing Networks in International Business.* Philadelphia: Gordon and Breach. 178–193.

Frank, R. H. & Freeman, T. (1978). *Distribution Consequences of Direct Foreign Investment.* New York: Academic Press.

Ghoshal, S. & Nohria, N. (1997). *The Differentiated Network. Organizing Multinational Corporations for Value Creations.* San Fransisco: Jossey-Bass Publishers.

Gupta, A. K. & Govindarajan, V. (1991). Knowledge flows and the structure of control within multinational corporations. *Academy of Management Review*, *16(4)*, 768–792.

Hardt, M. & Negri, A. (2000). *Empire*. Cambridge, Mass.: Harvard University Press.

Harzing, A.-W. (2000). An empirical analysis and extension of the Bartlett and Ghoshal typology of multinational companies. *Journal of International Business Studies, 31(1)*, 101–120.

Hawkins, R. G. (1972). *US Multinational Investment in Manufacturing and Domestic Economic Performance*. Occasional paper, No.1. Washington DC: Center for Multinational Studies.

Hennart, J.-F. (1982). *A Theory of Multinational Enterprise*. Ann Arbor: The University of Michigan Press. 77.

Hood, N. & Young, S. (1979). *The Economics of Multinational Enterprise*. New York: Longman Group.

Horaguichi, H. & Toyne, B. (1990). Setting the record straight: Hymer, internalization theory and transaction cost economics. *Journal of International Business Studies*, Third Quarter, 487–494.

Hymer, S. (1968). The large multinational "corporation". An analysis of some motives for the international integration of business. *Revue Economique*, 1–24.

Hymer, S. (1970). The efficiency (contradictions) of multinational corporations. *American Economic Review, LX(2)*, 441–448.

Hymer, S. (1976). *The International Operations of National Firms: A Study of Direct Foreign Investment*. Cambridge, Mass.: M.I.T. Press.

Hymer, S. & Rowthorn, R. (1970). Multinational corporations and international oligopoly: the non-American challenge. In Ch. Kindleberger (ed.), *The International Corporation*, Cambridge, Mass.: The M.I.T. Press. 57–91.

Kogut, B. (1985). Designing global strategies: profiting from operational flexibility. *Sloan Management Review*, Summer, 15–27.

Kogut, B & Zander, U. (1993). Knowledge of the firm and the evolutionary theory of the multinational corporation. *Journal of International Business Studies, 29(3)*, 625–645.

Lane, P. J. & Lubatkin, M. (1998). Relative absorptive capacity and inter-organizational learning. *Strategic Management Journal, 19*, 461–477.

Madhook, A. (1996). Know-how, experience and competition-related considerations in foreign market entry: An exploratory investigation. *International Business Review, 5(4)*, 339–366.

Madhook, A. (1998). The nature of multinational firm boundaries: transaction costs, firm capabilities and foreign market entry mode. *International Business Review, 7*, 259–290.

McGrath, R. G. (1997). A real options logic for initiating technology positioning investments. *Academy of Managment Review, 22*, 974–996.

McManus, J. C. (1972). The theory of the international firm. In G. Paquet (ed.), *The Multinational Firm and the Nation State*. Toronto: Collier-Macmillan.

Moran, T. H. (ed.) (1993). *Governments and Transnational Corporations.* London: Routledge

Negandhi, A. (1980). Multinational corporations: issues, context and strategies. In A. Negandhi (ed.) *Functioning of the Multinational Corporation. A Global Comparative Study.* New York: Pergamon Press.

Penrose, E. T. (1971). *The Large International Firm in Developing Countries. The International Petroleum Industry.* London: George Allen and Unwin. 266.

Pfeffer, J., & Salancik, G. R. (1978). *The External Control of Organizations. A resource Dependence Perspective.* New York: Harper & Row.

Porter, M. E. (1986). Competition in Global Industries. A Conceptual Framework. In M. E. Porter (ed.), *Competition in Global Industries.* Boston: Harvard Business School Press.

Porter, M. E. (1990). *The Competitive Advantage of Nations.* Boston: the Free Press.

Prahalad, C. K. & Doz, Y. L. (1987). *The Multinational Mission.* New York: The Free Press.

Ramamurti, R. (2001). The obsolescing 'bargaining model'? MNCs' host country relations revisited. *Journal of International Business Studies, 32(1),* forthcoming.

Reuer, J. J. (2000). *Downside Risk Implications of Multinationality and International Joint Ventures.* Unpublished paper. Stockholm: Institute of International Business.

Rugman, A. (1998). Corporate strategies and environmental regulations: an organizing framework. *Strategic Management Journal, 19(4),* 363–375.

Rugman, A. & Verbeke, A. (1998). Multinational enterprises and public policy. *Journal of International Business Studies, 29(1),* 115–136.

Safarian, A. E. (1993). *Multinational Enterprise and Public Policy. A Study of the Industrial Countries.* Bodmin: Edward Elgar Ltd.

SOU, (1975). *Internationella Koncerner i Industriländer (International Firms in Industrial Countries).* Stockholm: Liber. *50.*

SOU, (1983). *Närings Politiska Effekter av Internationella Investeringar (Economic-political Impacts of International Investments). 17.*

Spender, J.-C. (1994). Organizational knowledge, collective practise and Penrose rents. *International Business Review, 3(4),* 353–367.

Stopford, J. & Strange, S. (1991). *Rival States, Rival Firms: Competition for World Shares Market.* Cambridge: Cambridge University Press.

Strange, S. (1997). *The Retreat of the State: Diffusion of Power in the World Economy.* Cambridge: Cambridge University Press.

Szulanski, G. (1996). Exploring internal stickiness. Impediments to the transfer of best practise within the firm. *Strategic Management Journal, 17,* 27–43.

Sölvell, Ö., Zander, I. & Porter, M. E. (1991). *Advantage Sweden.* Stockholm: Norstedts.

Tugendhat, C. (1971). *The Multinationals.* London: Eyre & Spottiswoode.

Turner, L. (1970). *Invisible Empires: Multinational Companies in the Modern World.* London: Hamish Hamilton Publishers.

Wells. L.T. (1998). Multinationals and the developing countries. *Journal of International Business Studies*, First Quarter, 101–114.

Chapter 3

Does Foreign Ownership Matter?
Subsidiary Impact on Local Clusters

Anders Malmberg and Örjan Sölvell

Introduction

In recent years, a rapid increase in inward investment has stirred up sentiments in Sweden (Malmberg & Sölvell, 1998). Swedes have witnessed Saab Automobile being taken over by GM, Volvo Car by Ford, Asea merging with Brown Boveri (creating ABB), Nordbanken with Merita, Stora with Enso, Pharmacia with Upjohn, Astra with Zeneca and so forth.[1] Thus, some of the more prominent Swedish 'flagships' have become subsidiaries of large foreign multinationals. So does this change in ownership matter? Are the Swedish parts of these MNEs drained on resources or do they get a boost? What are the true implications of such a shift for the firms concerned and, perhaps more importantly, for the dynamism of the Swedish industrial clusters within which these firms are essential players? In this paper we outline a conceptual model and propose some hypotheses that we believe may be of help in the attempt to answer these questions.

Our main concern in this brief paper is to understand how inward FDI and foreign ownership affect the development of local firms and, as a

[1] Similar sentiments do tend to occur in situations when inward FDI increases in a country, such as in France and other European countries when there was an upsurge in US FDI in the 1960s, or in the US in the 1980s when Japanese investors made their entry on a broader scale.

Critical Perspectives on Internationalisation, pp. 59–78.
Copyright © 2002 by Elsevier Science Ltd.
All rights of reproduction in any form reserved.
ISBN: 0-08-044035-5

consequence, the local milieu at large. The question will be addressed in two steps. First, we review and discuss some of the positions held in the research debate since the 1970s on MNEs, foreign ownership and external control. Second, we develop a theoretical model on subsidiary impact on its surrounding cluster. This impact, we argue, is determined by the corporate strategy of the MNE on the one hand, and the characteristics of the local cluster on the other (for a similar view, see Birkinshaw and Hood 1998). The strategic aspects include the degree to which headquarters exercise control over the local unit and what formal mandate the unit is granted. The external part of the equation involves degree of dynamism in the cluster and competencies built up over time within the subsidiary unit.

Research on Foreign Ownership and External Control

There exists a voluminous research literature that, from rather different points of departure, addresses the question of effects of foreign ownership. Early on, most writers seem to have taken a fairly negative position towards foreign ownership. Typically, it was considered bad for a local (national) economy if its industry was owned and controlled from the outside. Already during the 1960s and 1970s, there was a discussion about the loss of national sovereignty in the wake of expanding FDI. Empirical studies were carried out, not least in countries with a high share of foreign ownership, such as Canada and the Netherlands. One type of studies was preoccupied with what was referred to as the geography of branch plants (Firn, 1975; Malmberg, 1990; Townroe, 1975; Watts, 1981). Here, one can find a rather pessimistic view on the impacts of external ownership. A few quotations can illustrate this:

> "The MNE tends to create a world in its own image that corresponds to the division of labour between various levels of the corporate hierarchy. It will tend to centralize high-level decision-making occupations in a few key cities in the advanced countries, thereby confining the rest of the world to lower levels of activity and income." (Hymer, 1972)

> "One aspect that has so far been relatively neglected (...) despite its obvious and important theoretical and policy implications (...) is the effects and problems associated

with a situation whereby a large amount of ownership and control of key sectors lies outside the regions concerned. When major decisions are made elsewhere (...) much of the drive, enthusiasm, and invention that lies at the heart of economic growth is removed, reduced, or at best suppressed." (Firn, 1975)

The message from this line of research was that externally owned/controlled firms for various reasons give a smaller contribution to the development of a local economy. There is, at the same time, also a literature that regards FDI and MNEs as a carrier of economic modernisation and development (see Hood & Young, 1979, for an overview). Dicken (1998) illustrates this contradiction:

"According to viewpoint, TNCs either expand national economies or exploit them; they are either a dynamic force in economic development or a distorting influence; they either create jobs or destroy them; they either spread new technology or pre-empt its wider use and so on (...) Virtually every aspect of the TNC's operations — economic, political, cultural – has been judged in diametrically opposite ways by its opponents and its proponents." (Dicken, 1998)

Some views of the effects of foreign ownership rest on interpretations of empirical data; some are based on theoretical analysis, while others are more ideologically based. It is fair to say that the criticism changed and a much more positive attitude developed during the 1980s and 1990s. However, interestingly enough, the debate at least in Sweden has recently again shifted back to a more negative stance towards inward FDI (Malmberg & Sölvell, 1998), and it is yet to see whether this will also be the case in empirically based research.

The empirical support for these arguments varies. Some of the propositions above get more or less support in different studies, but the results of such studies are far from unequivocal. In reality, we should of course expect that there could be both positive and negative effects, following, e.g., from an acquisition of a local firm by a foreign MNE. The most common arguments regarding positive and negative effects following from foreign ownership are summarised in Table 3.1 (based on Allard & Lundborg, 1998).

Table 3.1: Research Showing Positive and Negative Effects of Foreign Ownership.

Positive effects	*Negative effects*

Subsidiary Unit Level

New more efficient management techniques (Hayter, 1981)	Decreased autonomy (Steuer *et al.*, 1973)
Access to a global organisation	Erosion of top management (Ashcroft & Love, 1993)
New financial resources (Hayter, 1981)	Profit transfers (Hayter, 1981; SOU, 1989)
Production growth, increased employment	Plant closures, less qualified (paid) jobs
Increased productivity (Modén, 1998; Parry, 1980)	Rationalisation, standardisation/ routinisation (Malmberg, 1990)
New proprietary technology (Hood & Young, 1979)	Removal of technology to home centres (Britton, 1980)
Continued local R&D investment (Modén, 1998)	Lack of R&D (Hayter 1981)

Cluster / Local Milieu Level

New competition (Gorecki, 1976)	Monopolisation
Growth and new market opportunities (Hayter, 1981)	Dependence of foreign technology (Dunning, 1985)
Embeddedness & spillovers (Blomström 1990; Ivarsson 1999; Kokko, 1992; Safarian, 1966)	Weak local linkages, decreased local sourcing of inputs (e.g. HQ services)

There are, of course, huge problems related to research methods in this field of study. In order to say something certain about differences between locally owned and foreign owned firms, one would need to compare sets of twin firms: one group of locally owned and one group of foreign owned firms which are identical in terms of industry, size etc. Even if it would be possible to isolate such groups, there is still the problem of counter-factuality — what would have happened otherwise? If we are interested in the development of a certain firm unit subsequent to a foreign acquisition, we can never know for certain what would have happened had the acquisition not taken place. To this is added the long term and dynamic effects of structural change. Even if it would be possible to document cases where a firm have been acquired, only to go through tough rationalisation or even closure, we cannot know whether this, in the long term, will harm or benefit the local economy. In principle, such a restructuring may relief resources for other and possibly more productive tasks, but it may be extremely difficult to assess to what degree this potential is fulfilled. One condition, of course, is that there are well functioning markets such that resources, e.g., labour, can smoothly be transferred to other firms and industries.

Theoretical Model: Subsidiary Impact on Local Clusters

In the following, our main focus is not so much on the effects of foreign ownership on the individual subsidiary business unit, but rather on the dynamics of the local cluster. Will a local cluster be strengthened or weakened by the entry of foreign firm, either through a green-field investment or a take-over? In order to separate out when we should expect positive effects from foreign ownership and when we should expect negative effects, we will outline a theoretical model proposing four critical factors behind the long-term impact on the surrounding cluster.

Over time, a subsidiary (or a domestic unit, which is later to be acquired by a foreign firm) develops certain capabilities and builds up more or less unique resources (Birkinshaw, 1995), implying a stronger or weaker overall subsidiary competence level. This competence level determines the position of the subsidiary within the corporate network and decides to which degree the subsidiary has the power to make strategic and operational decisions. The competence of the subsidiary is in turn affected by the conditions that prevail in its local environment, notably the dynamics of the local cluster. The stronger and more dynamic the

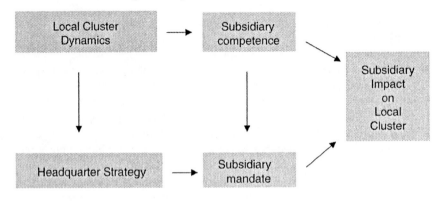

Figure 3.1: Theoretical Model.

local cluster within which the subsidiary unit is active, the more unique competencies do we expect to be controlled by that unit within the global firm.

A subsidiary is also assigned a certain mandate by corporate head-quarters, sometimes formalised in roles as centres of excellence or centres of competence. Centres of excellence often consolidate internal profit and loss statements within its product or technology mandate, and are typically the nexus for strategic and operational reporting. The given mandate in turn is driven by headquarter strategy and the degree to which headquarters exert control over the unit. A low degree of control implies a hands-off policy when it comes to operational and even strategic decisions at the subsidiary level. Such decisions include everything from investment decisions (plants, machinery, new investment and replacements), hiring decisions, product line choices (diversification and vertical integration), product features (quality levels, add-on services, pricing), and market choices (segments, exporting), and so on. The theoretical model is shown in Figure 3.1.

Local Cluster Dynamics

In the model, the starting point is taken in the dynamics of the local cluster (Porter, 1990). Despite the alleged homogenizing effects of globalisation, countries — and individual cities or regions within countries – continue to exhibit dramatic differences in terms of specialisation, competitiveness and industrial dynamics. Southern Italy has largely failed to develop a competitive industrial base despite decades of dedicated efforts. The firms in southern Italy operate within the same macro-economic and regulatory regime as those in the north. Still, there are great disparities both in the effectiveness of public institutions and in industrial growth (Putnam, 1993). Patterns of unequal regional growth are almost as evident in other European countries, where certain types of technological and industrial activity are clustered in certain cities and regions. Successful industries in a country or region often retain their leading edge over extended periods of time, despite attempts by others to imitate their success. The competitive strength is often not embedded in machinery, robots or even in patents. Anyone may get access to these. Competitiveness, or still more important, innovative capacity, has a markedly local element and is often built through a series of small steps (Maskell *et al.*, 1998).

Labour markets are still predominantly local. People rarely move between countries, even within the European Union where everyone has the formal right to live and work in another country. A clear empirical indication of this lack of mobility is seen in the fact that wage conversion is extremely slow.

Some technologies move across the globe, while other types of technology and competence are spatially "sticky" (i.e. they are kept "secret" or are retained in certain individuals) and are therefore little mobile (Malmberg & Sölvell, 1997; Markusen, 1996). Standard components and machinery may be purchased by anyone, anywhere, while the latest technology is often being fine-tuned in interaction between actors in local clusters. Network relations between buyers and suppliers within which new products and technologies are developed, and where production flows are perfected, are traditionally stronger if they are local (national) than if they are international (Gertler, 1995). In the local milieu, people speak the same language (not only do they share the same mother tongue, in addition they have often learnt to "talk the same way" through shared schooling, experience etc) and tend to trust each other. Even complex business deals can be sealed with a handshake. Furthermore, local networks often include links between firms and universities, research institutes and public authorities. Even the most modern forms of communication technology is inferior to face-to-face contacts between people when it comes to building trustful relations and to communicate non-codified types of information. In addition, personal travel is both costly and time-consuming (Malmberg & Maskell, 1997).

The more codified the knowledge involved is, the easier it can be transferred across borders. The more tacit the knowledge, the more attached it is to the local milieu. Knowledge and competencies which are embodied in people or are "in the air", e.g., in the routines of organisations (or local milieus), can often neither be articulated, nor moved from one place to another. Such tacit knowledge can sometimes only be transferred through various apprenticeship systems in the local milieu.

Porter (1990) argues that certain national circumstances determine the innovative, and thus competitive, strength of a given industry. All the four determinants in Porter's well known 'diamond model' relate to the existence of a system of interdependent firms or industries embedded in a local milieu. Specialised *factors of production* are seen as being formed historically in interaction between firms and institutions. Firms needing products with specific characteristics by and large raise *sophisticated demand*, and to meet such demand on the domestic market implies the co-existence of buyers and sellers in the same local milieu. The notions of *related and supporting industries* and *rivalry* presuppose the presence, in the milieu, of more than one firm in a particular industry.[2]

A consequence of the system of determinants is that a nation's competitive industries are not spread evenly through the economy but are connected in *clusters of industries* related by links of various kinds. One of the main empirical observations that form the point of departure for Porter's model is that a nation's successful industries are usually linked through vertical (buyer/supplier) or horizontal (common customers or technology etc.) relationships.

Clusters may differ regarding dynamism, degree of maturity, geographical extension and local embeddedness. All spatial agglomerations of similar or related industrial activity are not "Hollywoods" or "Silicon Valleys". The most decisive dimension has to do with how powerful the cluster is in terms of its long-term innovative capacity. The dynamism of the cluster is a function of the interaction between the four elements of the diamond model, and the dynamism of the cluster in turn gives rise to challenges and pressures towards the incumbent firms to be innovative and thereby upgrade their competitive advantages.

In the model proposed here, the dynamism of the local cluster is the

---

[2] Here, we will not go into the tricky discussion about at what spatial scale we should expect the cluster dynamics to unfold, and the difficulty of studying such interdependences and interactions empirically (see Malmberg, 1999 for such a discussion).

major determining force. Cluster characteristics are assumed to affect the average level of competence in all business units located in the cluster (including foreign subsidiaries) and it will affect the formal mandate given to local subsidiaries by foreign headquarters.

We expect that — ceteris paribus — the more dynamic a local cluster is, the more resources and capabilities the subsidiary will build up and a de facto stronger mandate will emerge. And the stronger the mandate a corporate unit possesses, the more autonomy it has to make its own strategic decisions. From this follows that the 'flag' of headquarters plays a less important role. The potential negative effects of foreign ownership stated in Table 3.1 above are also less likely to materialise; i.e. the risks associated with distance to corporate headquarters are less pronounced. Rather the opposite is likely to emerge, i.e., the foreign owner will add more resources (capital, complimentary skills etc) to the local units which will benefit the local cluster overall. With a weaker cluster it is more likely that the subsidiary controls less unique resources and capabilities, which makes it more vulnerable to be overrun by headquarters. The mandate is weak and the degree of autonomy low.

Dynamic local clusters are likely to attract foreign firms in search for technology, corresponding to the location-specific advantages identified in Dunning's model of firm internationalisation (Dunning & Narula, 1995). This process, when a firm enters a dynamic local cluster in order to gain valuable knowledge, is also referred to as selective tapping (Sölvell & Zander, 1995; Sölvell, *et al.*, 1991), or home base augmenting strategies (Kuemmerle, 1996). In the process of enhancing long-term local learning to be able to reap the benefits of the local cluster dynamics, the foreign firm is likely to invest more and potentially complementary resources locally, and thereby add to the local dynamism.[3] Thus, a first hypothesis is that the more dynamic a local cluster is the more positive effects we expect from foreign ownership (compare Table 3.1).

Porter's analysis of the functioning of clusters state that any business unit becomes a product of its surrounding environment, and thus we hypothesise that dynamic clusters on average lead to high levels of firm competence (Porter, 1990).

---

[3] In the case of short-term scanning strategies, we do not expect any positive spin-offs locally, since technology and skills are tapped and moved to the home base of the foreign firm.

Subsidiary Competence

The competencies of a corporate unit are created over extended periods as a firm interacts with its surrounding environment. The quality of the business conditions will therefore ultimately determine the quality of the strategies of the firm and the competencies and resources built up within the firm. In addition, internally generated acts of entrepreneurship and change will add to competence accumulation (Birkinshaw, 1995). The evolution of subsidiary competence or 'subsidiary development' has recently attracted increased interest in the research literature (for reviews see Birkinshaw & Hood, 1998; Birkinshaw & Morrison, 1996; Forsgren *et al.*, 1999). Depending on the history of a subsidiary unit — whether a greenfield unit or acquired unit — and the quality of the surrounding cluster we expect subsidiary competence to vary. Two hypotheses can be formulated. First, the more unique and valuable the competence of the subsidiary is in the corporate network, the more likely it is that the subsidiary will be assigned the mandate of centre of excellence. Second, the higher the competence of a subsidiary, the more positive spin-offs we expect on the surrounding cluster.

Headquarter Strategy

Corporate headquarters involve top management functions, including the office of the president and CEO, corporate finance, legal services, information etc, but not necessarily the legal domicile. Essentially, the long-term international strategy developed at headquarters involves two basic logics — exploitation of existing technologies and competencies or exploration to develop new competitive advantages. A third strategic approach is when headquarters decide to keep a hands-off policy, where the FDI de facto becomes a case of a portfolio investment only involving financial flows.

In the exploitation mode the MNE needs a range of local resources in order to penetrate local markets or to rationalise production on an international scale. The exploration logic on the other hand means that the MNE develops local resources to mutually learn from and add to the subsidiary unit and its surrounding cluster. In recent international business research, the aspects of global learning and the creation of new competitive advantages through international operations has come to the forefront. A diverse body of literature has been concerned with the MNE as a learning organisation, addressing the process of upgrading of competitive advantages. The need for global co-ordination in MNEs put focus on issues such as cross-border innovation processes (Ridderstråle, 1997), transfer of tacit knowledge (Kogut & Zander, 1996), and transfer of best practices (Arvidsson, 1999).

Headquarter strategy following the *exploitation logic* treats local units as sales and service organisations for the local market. This logic often involves rapid restructuring processes in order to enhance efficiency by reducing costs throughout the international network. In this scenario the foreign firm has a strong incentive to drain the local unit by not allowing further investments in products and people, and furthermore to close down plants, R&D laboratories and headquarter functions. Such a drainage can be expected in small markets like Sweden with its scale disadvantages, unless the MNE wants to utilise Sweden as a regional platform for the larger Nordic and/or Baltic Rim area. Such platforms often involve logistics functions, production and headquarter functions. Another case of the exploitation logic is related to 'pure tapping'. Pure tapping is when an MNE acquires a foreign unit or establishes a scanning unit just to 'take out' resources and competencies to be developed at home (cf. Figure 3.2 below). In this case we expect foreign ownership to lead to a weaker mandate and more likely negative consequences. In the case of an acquisition the unit is likely to be drained on resources over time.

The *exploration and learning logic*, on the other hand, typically involves the adding and combination of capabilities to facilitate mutual learning, and adding of new resources such as new capital, expatriates etc. The local unit is seen as a vehicle for building insider positions in the local cluster. The MNE can gain access to specialised and advanced factors of production, sophisticated demand, leading supplying and related industries, a unique science base (university and specialised research institutes), and proximity to the home base of leading rivals (see discussion above on cluster dynamics). Exploration and learning in this case is carried out in the local context, which is often manifested in the granting of regional/global mandates for the local subsidiary.

To facilitate exploration and mutual learning, home and host units have to be integrated to a varying degree. Headquarter strategy in terms of levels of integration tend to vary a lot, and to change over time. One can imagine a scale from zero integration with limited flows of resources and capabilities to very high levels of integration. If we first consider the case of very little integration, as we stated above the FDI becomes somewhat of a portfolio investment. Subsidiary units in such conglomerate-like MNEs typically exhibit very strong mandates and a high degree of strategic autonomy. A well-known case in Sweden has been ITT-Flygt (see SOU, 1981), which has had a unique standing within ITT ever since it was incorporated into the group in the mid-1960s.

Thus, a subsidiary mandate is determined by the 'logic' or long-term strategy imposed by corporate headquarters. Today's global firms are organised around a mix of subsidiaries with local mandates (e.g., local sales and service support, and manufacturing for the local market) and subsidiaries with regional or global mandates, often referred to as strategic centres of excellence (Holm & Pedersen, 2000) or multiple home bases (Sölvell & Zander, 1995). Three hypotheses are put forward in the model. First, with a headquarter strategy following the exploitation logic, the subsidiary unit will gain a weak mandate including local sales or, possibly, standardised production for the local market. Second, with an exploration strategy we expect stronger subsidiary mandates to emerge. The corporate rationale for tapping into a foreign cluster is to learn, and such learning presupposes that the local subsidiary unit becomes an insider in the cluster. The success of such a strategy can be expected to rest upon the assignment of strong and fairly autonomous mandates to the local unit and one can expect new resources to be added to the unit. Third, we expect headquarter strategies following a portfolio logic to lead to a strong mandate of a subsidiary unit (both in the case of acquired or green-field establishments).

Subsidiary Mandates

The classical greenfield subsidiary (sales and/or manufacturing unit) has a weak mandate, where strategic choices related to product range and market coverage is severely limited. For example, a typical sales subsidiary cannot export its products if home demand weakens since other markets belong to other sales subsidiaries within the MNE (SOU, 1981). Similarly, a typical sales subsidiary cannot get involved in other product areas or areas of technology than decided by headquarters. In tightly organised MNEs, local sales units do not even have the autonomy of setting prices or hiring key personnel. A domestic firm, on the other hand, can always look for new products, new technologies and skills, and new markets to secure survival and future growth.

For corporate units with a long history (including newly acquired units with a prior 'domestic' history) the 'subsidiary' role sometimes changes over time due to local entrepreneurial effort and the long-term build-up of local resources. Depending on the size and uniqueness of these resources, subsidiary units can play more strategic roles (Hedlund, 1980). Especially, subsidiaries in large and sophisticated markets and within leading clusters tend to develop their own unique capabilities and fields of technological expertise (Behrman & Fischer, 1980; Chiesa, 1995; Dunning, 1958; Gerybadze *et al.*, 1997; Patel & Pavitt, 1998; Pearce, 1994; Pearce & Singh, 1992; Ronstadt, 1978; Zander, 1997). These unique capabilities seem to play an important role in the formation of multi-centre structures with clear assigned mandates within the MNE, particularly when foreign acquisitions add new product areas and technologies to the acquiring firm (Dunning, 1981; 1988; Forsgren, 1989; Ghauri, 1990; Stopford & Dunning, 1983). In some cases, the result is a weakening of traditional centre-periphery relationships in the MNE and the establishment of divisional headquarters outside the country of origin (Forsgren, *et al.*, 1991; Holm, 1994; Sölvell, *et al.*,1991).

Overall, the mandates of foreign units have tended to become more diverse, reflecting an increasing number of units capable of contributing overall to the development of the MNE. Several attempts to classify subsidiaries have been presented in the literature. One of the more prominent taxonomies makes a distinction between 'strategic leaders' who are granted formal responsibility to develop, manufacture and market specific products on a global corporate-wide basis, and 'contributors' whose distinct capabilities could be employed as inputs into projects of corporate importance (Bartlett & Ghoshal, 1986). Most researchers working on similar frameworks would ascribe to the natural progression towards more sophisticated and independent foreign operations (Birkinshaw & Hood, 1998; Gupta & Govindarajan, 1991; Taggart, 1996; 1997; White & Poynter, 1984).

Impact on the Local Cluster

As we discussed in the introduction to this section, we can expect both positive and negative effects from foreign ownership. In our model we have outlined two major forces or mechanisms: one is related to the strength of the cluster and evolving subsidiary competencies, the other to headquarter strategy and formal mandates. In both cases, the overall impact may be to the benefit or to the detriment of the future development

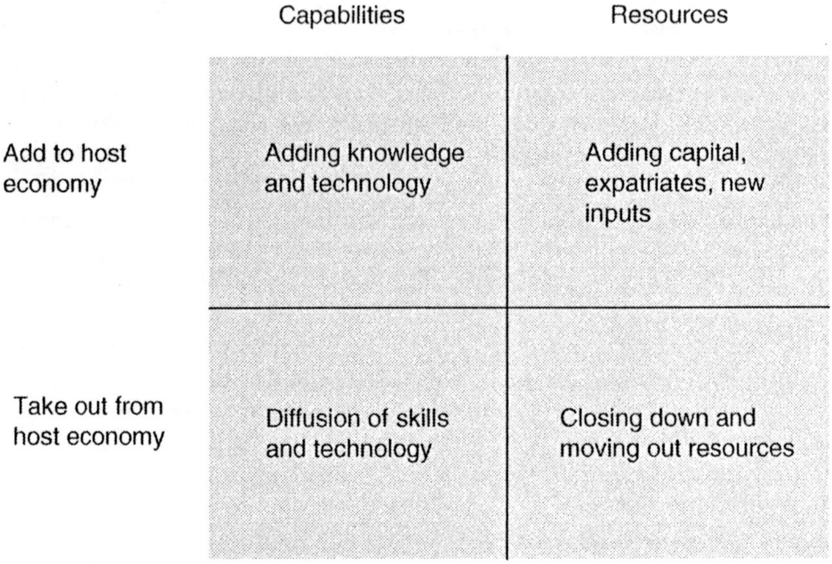

	Capabilities	Resources
Add to host economy	Adding knowledge and technology	Adding capital, expatriates, new inputs
Take out from host economy	Diffusion of skills and technology	Closing down and moving out resources

Figure 3.2: Dynamic Effects From Inward FDI.

of the local cluster. Thus, foreign firms may add to the local cluster by bringing in valuable capabilities and resources, such as new knowledge and technology, capital, expatriates and other inputs (see Figure 3.2). However, the entry of foreign firms may also erode the basis of future cluster dynamics by "taking out" resources and competencies from the cluster. This may be done either actively by transferring resources form one subsidiary/cluster to another, or more indirectly by not making continuous investment in the build-up of the competencies and resources of the local unit. The latter outcome, we argue, is more likely to materialise in cases where headquarter strategies are geared towards an exploitation logic and, as a consequence, the local subsidiary has a weak mandate.[4]

---

[4] It should be noted, in relation to Figure 3.2, that it is fully possible, even likely, that the processes of "adding" and "taking out" occur simultaneously. Corporate headquarters following the exploration logic have the intention to develop strong integration between home and host units. Often, as in the case of acquisitions, the acquiring firm has the intention to move and combine a set of resources and capabilities. In search for corporate-wide synergies, such integration processes can involve one or more of the four boxes in Figure 3.2. Think of Ford's recent acquisition of Volvo Cars. A number of integration processes have started, involving "taking out" competencies related to automotive safety as well as

The basic assumption in this paper, of course, is that the effects of foreign ownership on a local cluster are more positive, the more foreign firms add to the local economy. The hypotheses put forward in the model are that 1) the stronger the competence of a subsidiary unit the more positive effects we expect in the local cluster, and 2) the stronger the formal mandate of a subsidiary unit the more positive effects we expect in the local cluster.

Concluding Remarks

In this paper, we have proposed a model and some mechanisms that we believe could be helpful in analysing the impact on foreign ownership on local business units and, more importantly, the long-term dynamics of local cluster. In doing so, we have been arguing in favour of a type of analysis where such impacts are seen in relation to the characteristics of local clusters on the one hand, and the strategies of corporate head-quarters, on the other. In essence we have argued that foreign sub-sidiaries will tend to have a positive impact on the local cluster if they have developed valuable competencies and resources "on their own", or if they are assigned strong corporate mandates by corporate head-quarters. Furthermore, we have argued that it is more likely to find sub-sidiary competence and strong mandates if the subsidiary units are located in dynamic clusters.

The arguments put forward in this paper are based on the assumption that all actors involved are economically rational.[5] If a cluster is both

---

footnote 4 continued
"adding" manufacturing skills to Volvo's unit in Gothenburg. Thus, resources including certain R&D units or manufacturing units can be closed down and even transferred abroad, parallel to a process where Ford moves new resources into Sweden in the form of capital and people.

[5] One could of course ask how the argument would be affected if we introduce an element of irrationality in the form of some "local patriotism" in this process. Is it possible, if we think of a Swedish cluster as an example, that Swedish actors will evaluate the local milieu differently than actors which lack the "sense of place" that follows from being born and raised inside Sweden? It is well known that what is sometimes referred to as psychic, or mental, distance may lead to a favouring of spatially proximate business units, even if technical or business data would speak in favour of making an investment somewhere else. Local or national patriotism, whether draped in the Swedish yellow and blue flag or any other, will be heightened because politicians, public authorities and firms are embedded in complex interdependencies such that for example a decision to close down a business unit

dynamic and locally embedded it is of course rational – for local firms which have their roots in the milieu as well as for existing or potential newcomers – to retain their presence in this cluster, and thereby to contribute to its further dynamism. If, on the other hand, the cluster has lost its dynamism, it would be rational — again for locals as well as for foreign firms – to try to shift their resources to other, more dynamic clusters. In clear cases like those above, the conclusion seems pretty straightforward: ownership location is of subordinate importance. A strong and dynamic cluster will do well while a weak cluster is in a more vulnerable position, regardless of the degree of foreign ownership. One could perhaps argue that increased capital mobility, with fewer barriers of entry and exit in a local cluster, in general serves to speed up restructuring processes. With an inflow of foreign FDI, a strong cluster can expand and strengthen its dynamism more rapidly. In a weak cluster, the inevitable process of restructuring and adjustment will accelerate, but one cannot say whether this is good or bad for the local economy in the long term.

The model and hypotheses presented in this paper should be seen as a first attempt to develop an analysis of the impact on foreign ownership on subsidiary business units and local cluster. We are convinced that such analyses will gain from dropping the assumption that foreign ownership in inherently "good" or inherently "bad". In contrast to such points of departure, we believe that a more fruitful starting-point is to analyse the impacts of foreign ownership as it materialises in the intersection of the two forces of local cluster dynamics and corporate headquarter strategies. Of course, the real value of this model can only been assessed by trying to employ it in empirical analysis. That exercise will, however, have to be carried out in another context.

---

footnote 5 continued
will be connected with all kinds of political costs and where technical and economic rationality will be sacrificed. It is not self-evident whether such "patriotism" is good or bad for a local economy. It introduces an element of inertia that may guarantee some temporary stability. Against this, one may argue that if a process of adjustment is inevitable, its consequences may be more severe if adjustment is delayed. The "protection" of the local milieu that may result from "patriotism" may thus give negative effects in the long run. One should not rule out local biases, but overall we expect these to work on the margin and not be the key driving force in investment decisions across nations. Three critical cases when national biases could be expected are 1) when home and host clusters are equally strong and clearly competing, 2) when the MNE is active in a strategically sensitive industry (e.g., defence and infrastructure), and 3) when the MNE is a state-owned firm. This is discussion is not developed in this paper, however.

References

Allard, P. & Lundborg, L. (1998). *Foreign Acquisitions of Swedish Companies — A Study of Internal and External Effects.* Stockholm: ISA Report 1998/5.

Arvidsson, N. (1999). *The Ignorant MNE — The Role of Perception Gaps in Knowledge Management.* Doctoral dissertation, Institute of International Business, Stockholm School of Economics, Stockholm.

Ashcroft, B. & Love, J. H. (1993). *Takeovers, Mergers, and the Regional Economy.* Scottish Industrial Policy Series 5, Edinburgh University Press.

Bartlett, C. A. & Ghoshal, S. (1986). Tap your subsidiaries for global reach. *Harvard Business Review,* Nov.–Dec., 87–94.

Behrman, J. N. & Fisher, W. A. (1980). *Overseas R&D Activities of Transnational Companies.* Cambridge, Mass.: Oelgeschlager, Gunn & Hain.

Birkinshaw, J. (1995). *The Entrepreneurial Process in Multinational Subsidiaries.* Unpublished doctoral dissertation, University of Western Ontario, London, Ontario.

Birkinshaw, J. (1998). *Foreign Investment and Industry Cluster Development.* ISA studies on foreign direct investment, *1998/3.* Stockholm: Invest in Sweden Agency.

Birkinshaw, J. & Hood, N. (1998). *Multinational Corporate Evolution and Subsidiary Development.* London: Macmillan.

Birkinshaw, J. M. & Morrison, A. J. (1995). Configurations of strategy and structure in subsidiaries of multinational corporations. *Journal of International Business Studies, 26,* 729–754.

Blomström, M. (1990). *Host Country Benefits of Foreign Investment.* Research Paper 6433, EFI, Stockholm School of Economics.

Britton, J. N. H. (1980). Industrial dependence and technological underdevelopment: Canadian consequences of foreign direct investment. *Regional Studies 14,* 181–199.

Chiesa, V. (1995). Globalizing R&D around centres of excellence. *Long Range Planning, 28,* 19–28.

Dicken, P. (1998). *Global shift. Transforming the World Economy,* (3rd ed.). London: Paul Chapman.

Dunning, J. (1958). *American Investment in British Manufacturing Industry.* London: Allen and Unwin.

Dunning, J. H. (1981). *International Production and the Multinational Enterprise.* London: Allen & Unwin.

Dunning, J. (1985). *Multinational Enterprises, Economic Structure and International Competitiveness.* Geneva: IRM Series.

Dunning, J. H. (1988). The eclectic paradigm of international production: A restatement and some possible extensions. *Journal of International Business Studies, 19,* 1–31.

Dunning, J. H. & Narula, R. (eds) (1996). *Foreign Direct Investment and Governments: Catalysts for Economic Restructuring.* London: Routledge.

Firn, J. R. (1975). External control and regional development: the case of Scotland. *Environment and Planning A, 7,* 383–414.

Forsgren, M. (1989). *Managing the Internationalisation Process. The Swedish Case.* London: Routledge.

Forsgren, M., Holm, U. & Johanson, J. (1991). Internationalisering av andra graden. In R. Andersson, *et al.,* (eds), *Internationalisering, Företagen Och det Lokala Samhället.* Stockholm: SNS Förlag.

Forsgren, M., *et al.,* 1999). *The Subsidiary Role for MNC Competence Development — Information Bridgehead or Competence Distributor.* Paper presented at the European International Business Association (EIBA) in Manchester, December.

Gertler, M. S. (1995). "Being there": Proximity, organization, and culture in the development and adoption of advanced manufacturing technologies. *Economic Geography, 71,* 1–26.

Gerybadze, A., Meyer-Krahmer, F. & Reger, G. (1997). *Globales Management von Forschung und Innovation.* Stuttgart: Schäffer-Poeschel.

Ghauri, P. N. (1990). Emergence of new structures in Swedish multinationals. In S. B. Prasad (ed.), *Advances in International Comparative Management.* Greenwich, CT: JAI Press.

Gorecki, P. K. (1976). The determinants of entry by domestic and foreign enterprises in Canadian manufacturing industries: some comments and empirical results. *Rev. Econ. Statis. 58,* November, 485–88.

Gupta, A. K. & Govindarajan, V. (1991). Knowledge flows and the structure of control within multinational corporations. *Academy of Management Review, 16,* 768–92.

Hayter, R. (1981). Patterns of entry and the role of foreign-controlled investments in the forest product sector: an assessment of foreign ownership and control. *Tijdschrift voor Economische en Sociale Geografie, 72,* 99–111.

Hedlund, G. (1980). The role of foreign subsidiaries in strategic decision-making in Swedish multinational corporations. *Strategic Management Journal, 1,* 23–26.

Holm, U. (1994). *Internationalization of the Second Degree.* Doctoral dissertation No. 53. Department of Business Studies, Uppsala University.

Holm, U. & Pedersen, T. (eds), (2000). *The Emergence and Impact of MNC Centres of Excellence — A Subsidiary Perspective.* London: Macmillan Press, New York: St Martin's Press.

Hood, N. & Young, S. (1979). *The Economics of the Multinational Enterprise.* London: Longman.

Hymer, S. (1972). The multinational corporation and the law of uneven development. In J. N. Bhagwait (ed.), *Economics and World Order.* London: Macmillan.

Ivarsson, I. (1999). Competitive industry clusters and inward TNC investments: The case of Sweden. *Regional Studies, 33*, 37–49.

Kogut, B. & Zander, U. (1996). What firms do? Coordination, identity, and learning. *Organization Science, 7(5)*, (September-October), 502–518.

Kokko, A. (1992). *Foreign Direct Investment, Host Country Characteristics, and Spillovers*. Published doctoral dissertation. Stockholm: Economic Research Institute.

Kuemmerle, W. (1996). *Home Base and Foreign Direct Investment in Research and Development — An Investigation into the International Allocation of Research Activity by Multinational Enterprises*. Doctoral dissertation, Graduate School of Business Administration, Harvard University, Boston.

Malmberg, A. & Maskell, P. (1997). Towards an explanation of regional specialization and industry agglomeration. *European Planning Studies, 5*, 25–41.

Malmberg, A. & Sölvell, Ö. (1997). Localized innovation processes and sustainable competitive advantage of firms: a conceptual model. In M. Taylor & S. Conti (eds), *Interdependent and Uneven Development: Global-local Perspectives*. Aldershot: Avebury.

Malmberg, A. & Sölvell, Ö. (1998). *Spelar det någon roll? Om ökat utländskt ägande i svenskt näringsliv*. Rapport från ISA's Ekonomiska Råd 1998. Stockholm: Invest in Sweden Agency.

Malmberg, B. (1990). *The Effects of External Ownership — a Study of Linkages and Branch Plant Location*. Geografiska Regionstudier No. 24. Uppsala: Department of Social and Economic Geography, Uppsala University.

Markusen, A. (1996). Sticky places in slippery space: a typology of industrial districts. *Economic Geography, 72*, 293–313.

Maskell, P., et al., (1998). *Competitiveness, Localised Learning and Regional Development. Specialisation and Prosperity in Small Open Economies*. London: Routledge.

Modén, K.-M. (1998). *Foreign Acquisitions of Swedish Companies — Effects on R&D and Productivity*. Stockholm: Invest in Sweden Agency.

Parry, T. (1980). *The Multinational Enterprise:International Investment and Host Country Effects*. Contemporary studies in Economic and financial analysis, Vol. 20, Connecticut: JAI Press Inc.

Patel, P. & Pavitt, K. (1998). The wide (and increasing) spread of technological competencies in the world's largest firms: a challenge to conventional wisdom. In A.D. Chandler, Jr., P. Hagström & Ö. Sölvell (eds), *The Dynamic Firm*. Oxford: Oxford University Press.

Pearce, R. D. (1994). The Internationalization of research and development by multinational enterprises and the transfer sciences, *Empirica 21*, 297–311.

Pearce, R. D. & Singh, S. (1992). Internationalization of research and development among the world's leading enterprises: survey analysis of organization and motivation. In O. Granstrand, et al., (eds), *Technology Management and*

International Business — Internationalization of R & D and Technology. Chichester: John Wiley & Sons.

Porter, M. E. (1990). *The Competitive Advantage of Nations*. London and Basingstoke: Macmillan.

Putnam, R. D. (with Leonardi, R. and Nanetti, R. Y.) (1993). *Making Democracy Work. Civic Traditions in Modern Italy*. Princeton: Princeton University Press.

Ridderstråle, J. (1997). *Global innovation —Managing International Innovation Projects in ABB and Electrolux*. Published doctoral dissertation, Institute of International Business, Stockholm School of Economics, Stockholm.

Ronstadt, R. C. (1978). International R&D: The establishment and evolution of research and development abroad by seven US multinationals. *Journal of International Business Studies, 9*, 7–24.

Safarian, A. E. (1966). *Foreign Ownership of Canadian Industry*. McGraw-Hill of Canada.

SOU (1981). 33 *Effekter av Investeringar Utomlands: en Studie av Sex Industrier. Delbetänkande av Direktinvesteringskommittén*. Stockholm: Liber Förlag/Allmänna förlaget.

SOU (1981). 43 *De Internationella Iinvesteringarnas Effekter: Några fallstudier. Delbetänkande av Direktinvesteringskommittén*. Stockholm: Liber Förlag/Allmänna förlaget.

SOU (1989). *Utländska Forvärv av Ssvenska företag — En studie av Utvecklingen. Betänkande av Företagsförvärvsutredningen*. Stockholm: Liber Förlag/Allmänna förlaget.

Steuer, M. D. *et al.*, (1973). *The Impact of Foreign Direct Investment on the United Kingdom*. London: Her Majesty's Stationery Office.

Stopford, J. M & Dunning, J. H. (1983). *Multinationals: Company Performance and Global Trends*. London: Macmillan.

Sölvell, Ö. & Zander, I. (1995). The dynamic multinational firm. *International Studies of Management & Organization, 25*, 1–2.

Sölvell, Ö., Zander, I. & Porter, M. E. (1991). *Advantage Sweden*. Stockholm: Norstedts Juridik.

Taggart, J. H. (1996). Multinational manufacturing subsidiaries in Scotland: Strategic role and economic impact. *International Business Review, 5*, 447–68.

Taggart, J. H. (1997). Autonomy and procedural justice: A framework for evaluating subsidiary strategy. *Journal of International Business Studies, 28*, 51–76.

Townroe, P. M. (1975). Branch plants and regional development. *Town Planning Review 46*, 47–62.

Watts, H. D. (1981). *The Branch Plant Economy — a Study of External Control*. London: Longman.

White, R. E. & Poynter, T. A. (1984). Strategies for foreign-owned subsidiaries in Canada, *Business Quarterly*, 59–69.

Zander, I. (1997). Technological diversification in the multinational corporation — historical trends and future prospects. *Research Policy, 26*, 209–227.

Part II

What Kinds of Multinational Corporations are there and What are their True Competitive Advantages?

Under this label there are contributions that deal with basic conceptualisations of Multinational Corporations from a critical perspective. In the first chapter by Ivo Zander and Örjan Sölvell, *The Phantom Multinational*, the authors question the usual assumption that the "typical" MNC is an organization that exploit and explore opportunities on a global basis. On the basis of observations how multinationals have built up their geography and resources over time, the authors claim that MNC can equally well be considered to be organizations with rather dispersed and duplicated structures. These structures are some way from the global system of knowledge flows between sister units, about which most of the international business literature seems to talk. The authors also point out that, with reference to the welfare implications of MNCs, a distinction should be made between exploitation and exploration activities of these firms. They conclude that currently there is little empirical evidence to support extreme positions with regard to positive welfare implications from exploration and knowledge exchange in global networks.

The question of the configuration of the MNC and the extent to which it contains a network of knowledge flows is also taken up in the next chapter, *Embeddedness of Subsidiaries in Internal and External Networks: A Prerequisite for Technological Change*, by Michael Kutschker and Andreas Schurig. To a certain degree the chapter tries to determine the existence of the "Phantom Multinational", brought up by Zander and Sölvell in the previous chapter. This chapter contains an empirical investigation of the role of the subsidiary as a "change agent", in terms of channelling knowledge from its business environment to the rest of the corporation, or vice versa. Among the 255 investigated foreign-owned subsidiaries in Germany, about half of them were "stand alones", in terms of relationships with their corporate and external network. The authors conclude that it takes time to integrate subsidiaries in both corporate and external networks, which indicates that the role of the individual subsidiary in providing knowledge between the external and corporate environment is more difficult to establish than is usually assumed in the literature.

In *Subsidiary Entrepreneurship and the Advantage of Multinationality*, Mo Yamin turns this lack of integration of the subsidiaries into what he perceives to be an advantage for the MNC. In a thought provoking discussion he argues that in fact the diversity within the MNC and the relative isolation of subsidiaries, especially, inadvertently and paradoxically, creates a competitive advantage. The reason given for this is that such a structure would leave room for enough exploration and entrepreneurship at the subsidiary level, without too much interference from the corporate headquarters. This statement is based on the assumption that organizations in general suffer from a tendency that "exploitation drives out exploration". Consequently, the advantage of multinationality, in comparison with domestic firms, therefore is that they can even out the odds between exploitation and exploration. Yamin's analysis offer a radically different view on the welfare implications of MNCs compared to analyses that emphasize the importance of MNCs as global networks.

Chapter 4

The Phantom Multinational

Ivo Zander and Örjan Sölvell

Introduction

Over the past decade, there has been a significant shift in understanding the *raison-d'être* of the multinational enterprise. Increasingly, the MNE is seen as a superior creator of new advantages through global exploration rather than a simple exploiter of firm-specific advantages in international markets. This shift partially reflects changing organizational structures and the perceived need to develop more coordinated networks of foreign subsidiaries in large multinationals, but also growing academic interest in the issues of knowledge creation, learning and upgrading of competitive advantage in the business firm.

To some extent, interest in the exploration activities of the MNE can be traced back to the general discussion of advantages of multi-nationality. Vernon (1979) introduced the idea that global firms could leverage their international experience by exchanging information across dispersed units, whereas Dunning (1981) suggested that the multinational could gain competitive advantages by structuring its foreign direct invest-ments according to particular host-country strengths. These competitive advantages were associated with access to pools of low-cost and skilled labour, or close relationships with advanced research institutions. In a discussion of the well-established and dispersed MNE, Hedlund (1986; 1993) and Hedlund and Rolander (1990) suggested that it may exploit unevenly distributed skills and resources in the international business environment within a system of globally coordinated units.

Eventually, a new and more radical line of thinking evolved in which

Critical Perspectives on Internationalisation, pp. 81–106.
ISBN: 0-08-044035-5

the multinational was expected to systematically leverage its experience and international network to create new competitive advantage. Specifically, it was claimed that the use of global or cross-border innovation projects would constitute a unique advantage from multinationality, significantly adding to the firm's upgrading and renewal capabilities (Ghoshal & Bartlett, 1988; Hedlund & Ridderstråle, 1995; Ridderstråle, 1997). Both cross-fertilization and the identification of new combinations of knowledge would produce innovations of extraordinary quality and impact. In what developed into a received view of the modern MNE, it was widely assumed that multinationals by means of changing structures and coordination mechanisms constitute the ultimate vehicle for exploration and creation of competitive advantage on a global scale.

Currently, the geographical dispersion of business activities and in particular the emergence of advanced capabilities in foreign units are often viewed as indications that the multinational is actively seeking out new skills on a global basis and implements strategies for integrating knowledge within the multinational network. In this paper, we argue that this received view essentially represents a phantom picture of the MNE.[1] By revisiting and interpreting the internationalisation process as an outcome of exploitation rather exploration motives, we suggest caution in accepting global creation of competitive advantage as a reality in today's multinational. Specifically, we present and discuss some significant problems that relate to the exploitation logic of the internationalisation process and address some unexplored organizational challenges in establishing innovation that cuts across geographically dispersed units.

A few comments about the contents of the paper are in order. In our interpretation of internationalisation processes and the evolution of the MNE, the separation of the development of multinationals into distinct phases such as the interwar and post-war period is to a certain extent arbitrary. Transitions between phases and the formation of new trends are gradual and affected by occasional setbacks, especially as individual firms are concerned. Second, any condensed account of historical processes contains elements of over-simplification, and the current paper is no exception to this. It focuses on selected aspects of international business operations, and is biased towards what has been going on among European multinationals with small home markets. With some exceptions, the paper does not comment upon variations in the foreign invol-

---

[1] Phantom as in Webster's Collegiate Dictionary: "something apparent to sense but with no substantial existence".

vement of multinationals from different home countries (or multi-nationals of recent origin), or how the proposed patterns of development need qualifications to account for a wide range of industry- and firm-specific characteristics and circumstances.[2]

The Growth of the Traditional Multinational

For most firms, the internationalisation process has been and still is a question of exploiting a perceived set of firm-specific advantages in foreign markets. For most of today's leading industrial firms, exploitation historically proceeded through technology or knowledge transfer and gradually enhanced resource commitments to foreign markets (Aharoni, 1966; Johanson & Vahlne, 1977; Johanson & Wiedersheim-Paul, 1975; Luostarinen, 1979; Mudambi, 1998).[3] Initially, foreign activities would involve sales and service, local assembly and packing, and occasionally the adaptation or modification of products according to specific needs of the local market. When demand was sufficient to promise potential economies of scale, foreign manufacturing as a means of overcoming transportation costs (and uncertainties associated with international shipments), tariffs, and customer preferences for local producers became an economically interesting option. Thus, the largest and most protected markets were often endowed with manufacturing responsibilities, the output primarily being geared towards the local or regional market.

While many multinationals developed extensive international structures already before the turn of the century, exploitation of firm-specific advantages in the increasingly divided world economy of the interwar period amplified the geographical dispersion of manufacturing resources. Political pressures, trade barriers, and currency controls required the formation of self-sustained and highly autonomous units lest sales in local markets were sacrificed. Sometimes, the maintaining of foreign market shares required extensive transfers of firm-specific knowledge, blueprints and production

---

[2] For example, the paper focuses on what have been termed market- or efficiency-seeking multinationals, as well as firms in the asset-seeking category (Dunning, 1993). In all probability, the proposed logic of internalisation and evolutionary dynamics is quite different among firms which have internationalised primarily to secure access to raw materials.

[3] The step-wise or gradual evolution of foreign activities has been confirmed in a number of country and firm settings (Johanson & Vahlne, 1990), although there are exceptions which speak for occasionally faster and non-linear internationalisation processes in specific firm contexts (Hedlund & Kverneland, 1984; Jones & Tagg, 1999; Lindqvist, 1991).

manuals. As a result, a significant number of multinationals would develop polycentric or decentralized networks of foreign operations (Bartlett, 1986; Perlmutter, 1969), in which foreign units could be characterized as minia-ture of truncated replicas of the parent organization. As trade across country borders was difficult there would be comparatively little cross-flows of products and components within the international network — overall, structures were dispersed but little coordinated.

The closing of markets and self-sustained operations supported a general tendency among foreign units to become embedded in their local markets (Andersson, 1997; Andersson & Forsgren, 1996; Andersson *et al.*, 1999; Forsgren, 1996; Forsgren & Johanson, 1992; Holm *et al.*, 1995). Although technology transfer from the home country in most cases remained the main vehicle for upgrading local firm-specific advantages,[4] the pursuit of local business opportunities and ties to local clusters of industrial activity would grow in importance. As local managers made use of transferred technology and deepened local business contacts, fre-quently unbeknownst to corporate staff, some foreign units gradually took on rather prominent roles in the international network. Their self-perceived role was transformed from one of selling and modifying pro-ducts originally developed by the parent organization to identifying and exploiting business opportunities that may even be of commercial interest outside the local market.

Overall, the mandates of foreign units thus tended to become more diverse, reflecting an increasing number of accomplished units capable of significantly contributing to the development of the multinational group. For example, one foreign subsidiary taxonomy made a distinction between 'strategic leaders' who could be granted formal responsibility to develop, manufacture and market specific products on a corporate-wide basis, or 'contributors' whose distinct capabilities could be employed as inputs into projects of corporate importance (Bartlett & Ghoshal, 1986). Most researchers working on similar frameworks would ascribe to the natural progression towards more sophisticated and independent foreign opera-tions (Birkinshaw & Hood, 1998; Gupta & Govindarajan, 1991; Taggart, 1996; 1997; White & Poynter, 1984), although some found that subsidiaries with extensive local responsibilities sometimes lost some of their functions to become more integrated within the multinational network (Jarillo & Martinez, 1990).

---

[4] As pointed out by Cantwell (1995), some firms deviated from the overall pattern and experienced rapidly diminishing dependence on technology developed in the home country.

Exogenous Changes and Reaction Patters in the Postwar Period

In the immediate postwar period, traditionally profitable and thus power-ful foreign units would continue to lead a life of their own in the interna-tional organization. They would sell products based on technology that had been transferred from the home organization and in parallel take own initiatives to exploit locally emerging business opportunities. Inde-pendence based on locally accumulated resources, powerful managers who may be described as "country kings", and only gradually alleviated tariffs and trade restrictions made attempts to coordinate and rationalize across national subsidiaries a difficult endeavor (Hedlund & Åman, 1983). Indeed, incentives for rationalization and coordination were weak in the two decades after the war, and there would also be mounting poli-tical pressure to circumscribe the operations of local subsidiaries, espe-cially in the developing countries. Yet all of this did not matter, because as long as profits were generated and competitors did not undertake major changes to their international organization, dispersed and uncoor-dinated structures remained a workable solution to securing customers worldwide.

Rationalization and Specialization, Phase 1

The periods that followed saw a number of developments which even-tually would have a significant impact on the organization of the MNE. In particular, these changes related to the integration of the world economy and the emergence of international or global competition. The most significant elements in the integration of the world economy were reduced tariffs, creation of economic unions, homogenisation of stan-dards, lowered transportation costs, and enhanced speed of communica-tion (Dicken, 1998). In parallel, technological advancements produced increasingly flexible manufacturing systems and information systems that could be used for improved international communication or advanced inventory control and coordination of logistics. As a result, formerly separated 'islands' in the archipelago of competition were increasingly connected through bridges built by multinational enterprises entering and further penetrating each others' home markets (Sölvell, 1987).

The organizational imperatives introduced by these changes eventually had to clash with the dispersed networks of manufacturing capabilities that many multinationals had developed in the interwar period. While previously it was necessary to maintain a set of miniature or truncated replicas of the parent organization, the rationale for maintaining smaller foreign units was in many cases lost. Now, firms could increasingly centralize activities such as manufacturing and research and development to one or a few locations, benefit from economies of scale, and ship products and components across geographically dispersed units (Doz, 1986; Vahlne & Sölvell, 1981). Some firms recognized the potential gains from specialization on a regional or worldwide basis, thus launching a series of international acquisitions under the credo to restructure their industries on an international scale.

In many instances, international rationalization and specialization proceeded hand in hand with the implementation of increasingly sophisticated systems for inventory and logistics control (Hagström, 1991). If local manufacturing of certain items was to be abandoned, the supply of these products from other units had to be guaranteed. However, change was slow because of historical heritage or resistance among established units in the international network, and it appears that cross-border product and process specialization and international industry restructuring were phenomena of relatively late occurrence. For example, most US multinationals maintained truncated and independent replicas of the parent corporation at least until the 1960s (Dunning, 1993). Studies of Swedish multinationals showed that cross-border product and process specialization and associated organizational changes were still only emerging in the early 1980s (Hedlund, 1981; Hedlund & Åman, 1983; Vahlne & Sölvell, 1981).

Rationalization and specialization efforts, however tentative at first, highlighted some unintended consequences of the polycentric structure which concerned the upgrading of products and their related services. Specifically, a growing number of established foreign units, especially those in the large and sophisticated markets, had upgraded transferred technology and eventually branched out into their own unique fields of technological expertise (Behrman & Fischer, 1980; Chiesa, 1995; Dunning, 1958; Gerybadze et al., 1997; Patel & Pavitt, 1998; Pearce, 1994; Pearce & Singh, 1992; Ronstadt, 1978; Zander, 1997; 1999a).[5]

---

[5] Several contributions have emphasized that the internationalisation of advanced technological capabilities is dependent on industry or country of origin (Cantwell, 1989; 1991; Cantwell & Kosmopoulou, 1999; Pavitt, 1988; Pearce, 1989). Moreover, some research however suggests a significant amount of management discretion with regard to the amount and

These unique fields of technological expertise seem to have played an important role when formal production and research and development mandates were awarded in the restructuring of the multinational network (Dunning, 1981; 1988; Forsgren, 1989a; 1990; Ghauri, 1990; Stopford & Dunning, 1983). Generally, acknowledgement of foreign capabilities resulted in a weakening of traditional centre-periphery relationships in the MNE and sometimes in the establishment of divisional headquarters outside the country of origin (Forsgren *et al.*, 1995; Holm, 1994).

For most firms, increasingly advanced technological capabilities in foreign units represented a distinct and largely unforeseen phenomenon that had to be dealt with for two reasons. First, as independent foreign units tried to solve their immediate market problems on their own, often because of insufficient inter-unit communication and sometimes because of faltering supply of new technology from home, costly overlap in dispersed innovation had followed. This was particularly troublesome in the face of escalating development costs and shortened product life cycles that became part of the post-war period. Secondly, unique and diverse technological capabilities in foreign units brought about questions concerning technological thrust and strategic direction of the multinational group.

Whereas practical and conceptual work on multinational strategy traditionally had concerned structures for the exploitation of firm-specific advantages,[6] the secondary and in some respects unintended effects of internationalisation thus forced a focus on exploration issues. How was

footnote 5 continued
nature of technological capabilities in foreign units (Patel & Pavitt, 1997; Zander, 1999b), and varying degrees of operational and technological freedom granted to foreign affiliates (Fischer & Behrman, 1979). As a result, the international dispersion of technological capabilities may involve significant variation even across firms engaged in similar lines of business.

[6] Some early contributions to the strategy literature suggested the importance of exploiting economies of scale in research and development and manufacturing (Hout *et al.*, 1982), or the need to develop an ability to attack and defend positions in international competition (Hamel & Prahalad, 1985). Subsequent work emphasized the need for balancing efficiency and local responsiveness in the multinational network (Bartlett, 1986; Bartlett & Ghoshal, 1989; Prahalad & Doz, 1987). These latter frameworks probably reflected difficulties in reconciling redundant duplication of resources and resistance to change among traditionally self-sustained units, but they may also be seen as a comment on the allegedly ethnocentric organizations of multinationals originating in the United States and Japan. If these firms were to become truly international players and compete on the back yard of entrenched competitors, they surely would have to learn to respect and actively exploit the particular needs of local markets (Vernon, 1980).

the multinational to structure the development of new technology and thus secure upgrading of firm-specific advantages?[7] Perhaps reflecting the view that foreign units were primarily responsible for securing customers and profits, much of the practical and academic work fundamentally regarded uncoordinated, duplicated and diverse structures as a problem. Research on the management of geographically dispersed research and development acknowledged the need for loosening the reins on technological activity in foreign units (Håkanson & Zander, 1986), but overall the organizational solution spelled increased headquarter involvement or direction and optimisation through division of labour in the international network (Behrman & Fischer, 1980; Cheng & Bolon, 1993; De Meyer & Mizushima, 1989; Gassman & Von Zedtwitz, 1999; Kuemmerle, 1997). The literature also dealt with how communication could be improved within the geographically dispersed organization, but communication was first and foremost seen as a means of control and providing sales support to foreign units.

Rationalization and Specialization, Phase 2

If the integration of the world economy provided incentives to rationalize and specialize international networks of manufacturing units, the competitive situation in many cases pulled firms in another direction, at least from the short-term perspective. Specifically, any ambitions to reap global economies of scale, continue foreign expansion and enter new markets ultimately meant confronting established competitors in their home markets.[8] This in turn was associated with significant problems in terms of building distribution, brand names and local market share. In most cases, sustained internationalisation therefore required the use of acquisitions and in some cases involved large-scale mergers

---

[7] Although the paper is mainly concerned with firm-specific advantages such as proprietary technology or the ability to organize human skills and resources, other advantages became part and parcel of the geographical dispersion of activities and resources. To capture the differences between initial advantages built up in the home country from advantages of multinationality, Sandén and Vahlne (1976) introduced the concept of the advantage-cycle. Kogut (1983; 1989; 1990) later refined this idea in his discussion of the sequential advantages of MNEs with a long-term involvement in international markets.

[8] As noted by Cantwell and Kosmopoulou (Theme 2, this volume), the location of foreign technological activity suggests that internationalising firms have typically avoided making substantial investments in the home markets of major competitors.

(Andersson *et al.,* 1997; Forsgren, 1989b). Some firms used explicit foreign acquisition strategies to realize long-term goals of rationalizing the internal network and using efficiency gains to outperform local rivals. As many acquisition targets were full-fledged international competitors, the short-term effect was enhanced overlap and diversity of activities while the preferred structures were and in many cases still are to be realized.

Overall, competitive imperatives seem to have gained the upper hand in the 1980s and 1990s. The proliferation of international acquisitions and mergers, to a certain extent driven by the internationalisation of financial markets, caused increased dispersion, overlap and diversity of activities in the international organization. A growing number of the world's largest multinationals thus came to operate very dispersed networks of subsidiaries of both overlapping and distinct resources. Most importantly, the amount of overlap in the most important fields of technology as well as the number of distinct technological capabilities was significantly enhanced.[9] Perhaps as a repeat of history, sales and competitive considerations thus had side effects on the capabilities available for upgrading firm-specific advantages. However, this time the question of how to structure and organize the development of new technology would be even more paramount than before.

Consider a white goods manufacturer such as Electrolux, which began to consolidate the Swedish white goods industry in the 1960s and eventually turned its attention to the international arena.[10] Initial foreign acquisitions included Norwegian Electra (1967), Danish Scan-Atlas (1967), French Arthur Martin (1979), and American Tappan (1979). Many of the acquired plants were closed down and production was rationalized so that each plant would specialize in a certain line of appliances. During the 1980s, Electrolux acquired some 200 additional firms and increased its turnover from SEK 15 to 85 billion. The more significant acquisitions included Italian Zanussi (1986), American WCI (1986), and the white goods division of British Thorn-EMI (1987). In the late 1980s,

---

[9] Zander (1999b) shows an overall increase in technological diversification and duplication among Swedish multinationals, but also finds considerable differences across firm groupings.
[10] Electrolux was originally founded as Lux AB in 1901. The company started out in the production of gas-operated light bulbs, merged with Elektromekaniska in 1919, and shifted focus towards the manufacturing and sales of vacuum cleaners. Refrigerators and refrigeration equipment were added to the product portfolio through own and acquired inventions in the 1920s.

the Electrolux group operated some 500 subsidiaries in 50 countries and employed around 150,000 people.[11]

After almost three decades of international acquisitions, the location of Electrolux' upgrading capabilities had undergone dramatic changes. What started out as a home-centred structure in terms of advanced technological capabilities was eventually transformed into a dispersed, duplicated and diverse assortment of technological capabilities (Figure 4.1). Very similar pictures would be displayed by other firms engaged in substantial foreign acquisition activity, and notably by merger cases such as ABB (electrotechnical equipment), PharmaciaUpjohn (pharmaceuticals), Akzo Nobel (health products and chemicals), Daimler-Chrysler (automobiles), Stora-Enso (pulp and paper) or Linde-AGA (industrial gases).

Although many multinationals thus developed increasingly dispersed, duplicated and diverse technological capabilities in the multinational network, cases like Electrolux suggest caution in the interpretation of how these changes affected the nature of the multinational in general and its upgrading capability in particular. It is clear that the selection of locations was generally the outcome of ambitions to sell or exploit existing firm-specific advantages in foreign markets, and eventually competitive interaction in an increasingly integrated world economy.[12] The pursuit of markets may have coincided with the establishment of research capabilities in locations which fit the technological needs of the internationalising firm, but on the whole these capabilities came out of evolutionary dynamics in foreign subsidiaries rather than decisions based on knowledge considerations (Ronstadt, 1978). In a somewhat different formulation, multinationals did not actively hunt the international environment for knowledge or new technology, nor did they *choose* the type and location of foreign technological activity primarily on knowledge

---

[11] As the international restructuring of the industry continued, so did the company's acquisition activity. Electrolux acquired Hungarian Lehel (1991), the household division of German AEG (the first steps towards ownership were taken in 1992), Romanian Samus (1997) and Brazilian Refripar (majority ownership in 1997).

[12] For example, a large number of studies confirmed access to new markets or the need to follow major customers abroad as the main drivers of internationalisation, whereas access to locations which in one respect or another were particularly conducive to innovation would play a very insignificant role. Dunning's (1993) review of the literature suggests the predominance of motives such as size and growth of the market, the competitive moves of rival firms, the lack of opportunities for expansion in the home market, or the extent to which local product adaptation and customization is required.

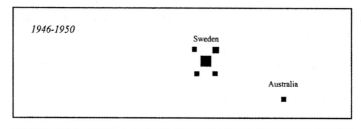

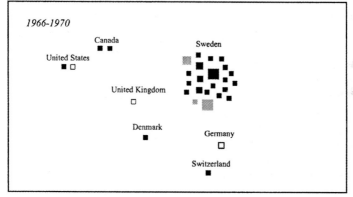

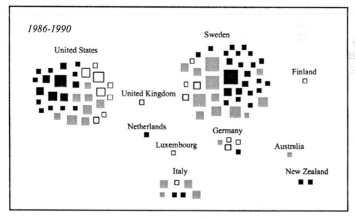

■ Location represents 100 per cent of technological capabilities
▓ Location represents a leading share of technological capabilities
□ Location represents a minority share of technological capabilities

Figure 4.1: Electrolux, Three Networks of Technological Capabilities
Based on U.S. patenting data, Zander, 1999b

grounds (Kuemmerle, 1999). The question is, could the established multi-national nevertheless become more actively involved in utilizing and perhaps combining technological capabilities on a worldwide basis?

New Currents — The Modern Multinational

As a number of researchers observed increasingly dispersed, duplicated and diverse capabilities in the multinational network, frameworks dealing with international organization and management picked up on the idea of knowledge exchange and learning through interaction within the international network (Bartlett & Ghoshal, 1989; 1990; De Meyer, 1993; Hedlund, 1986; 1994; 1996; Hedlund & Rolander, 1990; Nohria & Ghoshal, 1997; Prahalad & Doz, 1987). In these conceptions of the modern multinational, internationally dispersed capabilities were commonly seen as an asset rather than a problem, and the primary concern became how to foster the development and integration of these assets on a worldwide basis. Somewhat simplified, duplicated capabilities would allow for international cross-fertilization whereas specialized capabilities would lend themselves for recombination or technology fusion within the multinational network. In this context, international strategy became a simple and in many ways appealing exercise — exploit *and* explore through increasingly interconnected units in the international network.

It was implicitly or explicitly assumed that the modern multinational would gain superior long-term advantage by implementing systems for the integration of an increasingly heterogeneous innovation structure. As opposed to firms with their upgrading capabilities concentrated in one single location, the multinational could thereby uncover new solutions to existing problems and use its access to a large and diverse set of technologies to respond to the imperatives of technology fusion in complex products and systems. Specifically, it could make use of unplanned variation due to differences in development paths across individual organizational units as well as idiosyncrasies of the local environments in which these units were embedded.[13]

---

[13] The latter observation gained support from a number of studies that illustrated the local dependency of innovation and upgrading activity (Almeida, 1996; De Vet & Scott, 1992; Dorfman, 1983; Feldman, 1993; Frost, 1998; Jaffe *et al.*, 1993; Marshall, 1890/1916; Porter, 1990; Russo, 1985; Saxenian, 1991).

One central assertion was increasing reciprocity in inter-unit relationships, in particular with respect to headquarter-subsidiary relationships but also in terms of interaction across subsidiaries of the multinational network. Concerning the managerial requirements for creating and effectively operating the integrated multinational, Hedlund and Ridderstråle (1995) affirmed that the managerial challenge was one of moving from controlling a set of bilateral relationships between a clear strategic centre and a set of implementing subsidiaries to utilizing the creative abilities of an integrated global network. Exactly how MNEs would go about learning and creating new practices on a global scale was theoretically derived, and case-based research revealed current practices rather than evolutionary trends (Ridderstråle, 1997). Only recently have a number of empirical projects tried to penetrate the issues of cross-border learning and transfer of skills on a broader basis.

The Phantom Multinational

By adhering to the principle of knowledge-maximization, the multinational actively seeks out dispersed sources of technological knowledge, encourages diversity and experimentation in the international organization, and uses its integrated international network to rapidly transform accumulating knowledge into new products and services. It implements an explicit, coordinated strategy for long-term upgrading of competitive advantage, using management practices that maximize cross-border learning through lateral and reciprocal knowledge flows. This has become the increasingly adopted view of the modern multinational, which in our opinion has created a phantom picture of the multinational enterprise.

It is clear that the multinational has undergone significant change over the past century, and it may be appropriate to summarize the more recent development as follows. As a result of structural reconfigurations to support the exploitation of firm-specific advantages in a changing world economy, lately through international mergers and acquisitions, the multinational's international network now contains an unprecedented set of dispersed, duplicated and diverse technological capabilities. In terms of the exploitation of firm-specific advantages, emerging structures over the past two decades appear to involve an increasing amount of coordination of intra-firm flows of components and products. The question is whether similar changes should be expected with regard to knowledge flows and upgrading or innovation activities.

In terms of organizational structures, established multinationals seem to have several plausible choices to deal with duplicated and diverse capabilities in the international network. With regard to duplication, continued merger and acquisition activity will undoubtedly build further overlap in core strategic areas, but the long-term ambition is likely to be concentration or differentiation of skills at a narrow level (e.g., according to equipment type or customer segment). Duplication goes against the overall logic of exploiting economies of scale in an integrated world economy, particularly in the face of escalating development costs in many industries and product areas. Firms may of course opt to sustain duplication and seek benefits from reciprocal knowledge flows and cross-fertilization (or intra-firm competition), but overall economic arguments and the long-term objectives of international acquisition strategies generally speak against this development.

Most probably, diversity through dispersed centres of excellence will be sustained to a relatively large extent, both because international acquisitions will remain an important response to the integration of world markets and because unique skills in foreign subsidiaries can contribute to the overall upgrading and growth of the multinational. However, it is important to emphasize that making use of these foreign centres of excellence does not necessarily differ from traditional and established modes of operation. Innovation and upgrading may remain a predominantly local process while results are exploited by means of one-way transfer of technology throughout the international network of sales and manufacturing units.

In terms of the upgrading processes of the MNE, we suggest caution in assigning reality to the phantom picture of the multinational. We do not argue against the fact that global or cross-border innovation efforts are sometimes a necessity or that they may offer qualitative benefits in terms of learning and upgrading. Our major concern is with the order of magnitude and also the impediments to changing traditional patterns of localized exploration for international exploitation. Specifically, we perceive limitations associated with the exploitation logic of the internationalisation process and some traditionally unexplored organizational challenges in establishing collaboration and interaction across geographically dispersed units. Prudence is also advised in light of the lack of broad-based empirical studies of evolving innovation processes in the modern multinational.

The Exploitation Logic of the Internationalisation Process

As suggested, it is difficult to argue that access to advanced technological capabilities in foreign locations has been a first-order driver of the internationalisation process. Although multinationals are known to have gained improved access to the technological activity in certain geographical locations (Cantwell & Iammarino, 2000; Cantwell & Piscitello, 2000; Dunning & Narula, 1995; Florida, 1997), most have probably discovered internationalisation of technological capabilities as a side-effect of overall internationalisation[14] — in some cases resisted, in some cases accepted, and arguably in a more limited number of cases actively supported as an important generator of new ideas and corporate renewal. There is limited systematic evidence to suggest that the motives for foreign expansion have recently shifted towards a more active search for new knowledge and technological capabilities residing in foreign markets.

In the context of technological fusion, internationalisation may have promoted unforeseen encounters with new technology that can be used creatively within the multinational network. However, it is important to emphasize that structures, systems and procedures are mainly designed and re-designed to optimise sales and profits, not to further learning and knowledge flows within the multinational network. Internationalisation decisions predominantly rest with managers under pressure from financial markets and competitors' activities, not with technical staff and engineers involved in the creation of new products and production processes. For example, major international mergers and acquisitions are the result of efficiency and market share considerations, and it is likely that employment levels, manufacturing capacity and sales channels rather than knowledge exchange processes will receive primary attention in the immediate re-organization process.

Unexplored Organizational Challenges in Global Innovation

When internationalisation results in access to new technological capabilities, a distinction must be made between tapping into foreign tech-

---

[14] In a study of foreign-owned companies in the United States, Dalton and Serapio (1999) conclude that "a large part of the globalization of patents and R&D results from mergers and the requirements of companies to meet customer demands and adapt products to local market."

nology for growth or marketing reasons and ambitions to actively combine and re-combine several knowledge bases within the multi-national network. Indeed, it has been argued that isolation rather than integration can be a valuable factor in promoting entrepreneurship and innovation in a geographically dispersed organization (Yamin, Theme II).

In our opinion, a number of traditionally under-emphasized factors must be considered in the assessment of the degree to which global exploration may become a major force in the modern multinational. First, the broad-based introduction of internationally integrated innovation requires implementation of systems that reward occupation in projects that are temporary and fall in-between organizational entities. These systems seem hard to come by spontaneously, and most managers would testify that involvement in temporary projects without an organizational "home" is not conducive to individual careers.[15] Second, recent findings suggest that information processing in the established multinational is not necessarily based on objective data (Arvidsson, 1999). The difficulties involved in correctly evaluating the capabilities of dispersed subsidiaries seem to suggest important limitations to implementing a systematic and optimized approach to knowledge exchange in the international network. Third, theoretical and empirical evidence points to the existence of an insider-outsider paradox in the expansion of activities in foreign locations (Forsgren et al., 2000; Forsgren & Pedersen, 2000; Sölvell & Zander, 1998). In essence, accumulating resources and increasing embeddedness in host country environments — all essential in getting access to local knowledge — appear to evolve together with processes that build independence and distance resourceful units from others in the multinational network.

Finally, globally integrated innovation efforts must be seen in the light of recent organizational changes that have come with international mergers and acquisitions. The international context adds complexity in that dispersed units tend to have their own identity and understanding of what constitutes an effective development process. Unless projects that cut across different units are carried out with regular frequency, these differences will continue to have a negative effect on inter-unit collaboration and the effectiveness of knowledge exchange (Kogut & Zander, 1992; 1996). Issues of organizational survival are also involved, which become

---

[15] Findings by Lagerström (2001) suggest that members of transnational projects in the great majority of cases remain subject to the conflicting demands of both line and project responsibilities.

particularly accentuated in the long-term reorganization and specialization of the international network. Individual units may be reluctant to share information because this would reduce bargaining power and eventually undermine their existence as full-fledged units in the international network.

Admittedly, all of these things may change over time, thus pushing the frontier of integrated innovation further into the international domain. Also, depending on their starting point firms may be better or worse equipped to deal with the challenges of innovating across geographically dispersed units (Zander, 2000). However, the threshold or collective hurdle that must be cleared suggests limitations in terms of how *fast* and how *far* multinationals can generally move in the direction of globally integrated innovation activity.

Limited Empirical Evidence

At present, there is growing awareness and empirical interest in how internationalisation has changed the upgrading processes of large multinationals, but empirical evidence is still both scarce and scattered (Zander & Sölvell, 2000). While the international network on several occasions has been found useful for transferring and reviving individual research projects, empirical studies on knowledge exchange in joint international innovation efforts are based on a small number of case studies. In spite of projecting the need to develop increasingly sophisticated processes for inter-unit collaboration, the more extensive studies seem to confirm the organizational complexities as well as the additional costs associated with international innovation projects. Gassman's (1997) suggestion that cross-border innovation is "used to the required amount" but "as little as ever possible" is perhaps a representative summary of current conditions in larger multinationals.

Recently, projects on managing international networks (MIN) and centres of excellence (COE) at Uppsala University have supplied a broad empirical foundation for testing what is going on in terms of creation of new capabilities in today's MNEs (Holm & Pedersen, 2000). Results are mixed and underline the many and rather complex roles played by resourceful units in the multinational network. Some findings suggest that capabilities are not developed through a process of tapping into and integrating the specific skills and capabilities of different subsidiaries. However, subsidiaries may play an important role in bridging or linking headquarter units with industrial and innovation clusters around the world. These findings are in line with observations by Sölvell & Bresman, (1997), who found that subsidiary networks are complements to direct linkages between headquarter units and external actors in various host countries, phrased as 'duplicated bridges'.

Concluding Comments

Undoubtedly, internationalisation in the long run enhances the potential to leverage diverse sources of innovation in the multinational network. Most evidence suggests that multinationals over time have developed increasingly dispersed and complex structures of technological capabilities, and that the pre-conditions for various forms of international integration of these capabilities are at hand. In this paper, we have nevertheless expressed caution regarding the formation of globally integrated upgrading efforts, specifically because of the exploitation logic that underlies the internationalisation process and some traditionally underemphasized factors influencing knowledge exchange in the multinational network. The integration and sharing of technological knowledge is certainly practiced in the multinational, most likely to a larger extent than before, but we maintain that the magnitude of change in most cases has been limited or at least remains an empirical question.

The predominant exploitation logic of the internationalisation process has some obvious implications for host country economies, some of which are elaborated upon in other chapters of this volume (see Malmberg and Sölvell). If exploitation rather than exploration is the fundamental logic of the internationalising MNE, its impact in terms of international dissemination and integration of knowledge may typically be overstated. Indeed, if firms devote most of their attention to restructuring and improving the overall cost-effectiveness of operations, individual host countries may experience substantial setbacks in terms of local employment and research activity in the wake of international mergers and acquisitions. However, the picture becomes more complex in a perspective which emphasizes limited amounts of information, control and coordination in the dispersed multinational. Indeed, resourceful foreign units may well be allowed to continue operating as relatively independent entities and thereby draw upon and substantially contribute to their respective local environments.

To conclude, we find it very important not to confuse changing structures with changing processes in the multinational enterprise, especially with regard to the integration of technological capabilities and the upgrading of knowledge within the modern multinational. Unfortunately, the distinction is too often missed or ignored with the result that the modern multinational is increasingly projected as a globally exploiting as well as globally exploring organization. Apart from some of the doubts that have been expressed in this paper, there is currently little empirical evidence to support extreme positions with regard to exploration and integrated innovation efforts within the international network. Further research will undoubtedly produce a clearer and more refined picture of global exploration in the years to come, but we project that innovation that cuts across geographically dispersed units will remain a significant challenge to the established multinational enterprise.

Acknowledgments

The authors would like to thank the Swedish Council for Research in the Humanities and Social Sciences (HSFR) for financial support, and participants at the Uppsala workshop for stimulating discussions. Helpful comments and suggestions from the editors of this volume are gratefully acknowledged.

References

Aharoni, Y. (1966). *The Foreign Investment Decision Process*. Boston, MA: Division of Research, Graduate School of Business Administration, Harvard University.

Almeida, P. (1996). Knowledge sourcing by foreign multinationals: Patent citation analysis in the U.S. semiconductor industry. *Strategic Management Journal 17* (winter special issue), 155–165.

Andersson, U. (1997). *Subsidiary Network Embeddedness — Integration, Control and Influence in the Multinational Corporation*. Doctoral dissertation no. 66, Department of Business Studies, Uppsala University.

Andersson, U. & Forsgren, M. (1996). Subsidiary embeddedness and control in the multinational corporation. *International Business Review, 5(5)*, 487–508.

Andersson, U., Forsgren, M. & Holm, U. (1999). *Subsidiary Embeddedness, Expected Performance and MNC Competence Development*. Paper presented at the EIBA 25th Annual Conference, Manchester, December 12–14.

Andersson, U., Johanson, J. & Vahlne, J.-E. (1997). Organic acquisitions in the internationalization process of the business firm. *Management International Review, 37*, 67–84.

Arvidsson, N. (1999). *The Ignorant MNE — The Role of Perception Gaps in Knowledge Management.* Doctoral dissertation, Institute of International Business, Stockholm.

Bartlett, C. A. (1986). Building and managing the transnational: The new organizational challenge. In M. E. Porter (ed.), *Competition in Global Industries.* Boston, MA: Harvard Business School Press.

Bartlett, C. A. & Ghoshal, S. (1986). Tap your subsidiaries for global reach. *Harvard Business Review*, November–December, 87–94.

Bartlett, C. A. & Ghoshal, S. (1989). *Managing Across Borders: The Transnational Solution.* Boston, MA: Harvard Business School Press.

Bartlett, C. A. & Ghoshal, S. (1990). Managing innovation in the transnational corporation. In C. A. Bartlett et al., (eds), *Managing the Global Firm.* London & New York: Routledge.

Behrman, J. N. & Fischer, W. A. (1980). *Overseas R&D of Transnational Companies.* Cambridge, MA: Oelgeschlager, Gunn & Hain Publishers Inc.

Birkinshaw, J. & Hood, N. (eds) (1998). *Multinational Corporate Evolution and Subsidiary Development.* Macmillan Press.

Cantwell, J. (1989). *Technological Innovation and Multinational Corporations.* Oxford: Basil Blackwell.

Cantwell, J. (1991). The international agglomeration of R&D. In M. Casson (ed.), *Global Research Strategy and International Competitiveness.* Oxford: Basil Blackwell.

Cantwell, J. (1995). The globalization of technology: What remains of the product cycle model? *Cambridge Journal of Economics, 19*, 155–174.

Cantwell, J. & Iammarino, S. (2000). Multinational corporations and the location of technological innovation in the UK regions. *Regional Studies, 34(4)*, 317–332.

Cantwell, J. & Kosmopoulou, E. (1999). *Patterns of Technological Internationalisation and Corporate Technological Diversification.* Paper presented at the EIBA 25th Annual Conference, Manchester, December 12–14.

Cantwell, J. & Piscitello, L. (2000). Accumulating technological competence: Its changing impact on corporate diversification and internationalization. *Industrial and Corporate Change, 9(1)*, 21–51.

Cheng, J. L. C. & Bolon, D. S. (1993). The management of multinational R&D: A neglected topic in international business research. *Journal of International Business Studies, 24(1)*, 1–18.

Chiesa, V. (1995). Globalizing R&D around centres of excellence. *Long Range Planning, 28(6)*, 19–28.

Dalton, D. H. & Serapio, M. G. (1999). *Globalizing Industrial Research and Development.* Washington: U.S. Department of Commerce, Office of Technology Policy.

De Meyer, A. (1993). Management of an international network of industrial R&D laboratories. *R&D Management. 23(2)*, 109–120.

De Meyer, A. & Mizushima, A. (1989). Global R&D management. *R&D Management, 19(2)*, 135–146.

De Vet, J. M. & Scott, A. J. (1992). The Southern Californian medical device industry: Innovation, new firm formation, and location. *Research Policy, 21*, 145–161.

Dicken, P. (1998). *Global Shift: Transforming the World Economy*. London: Paul Chapman Publishing.

Dorfman, N. S. (1983). Route 128: The development of a regional high technology economy. *Research Policy 12*, 299–316.

Doz, Y. (1986). *Strategic Management in Multinational Companies*. Pergamon Press.

Dunning, J. H. (1958). *American Investment in British Manufacturing Industry*. London: George Allen & Unwin.

Dunning, J. H. (1981). *International Production and the Multinational Enterprise*. London: George Allen & Unwin.

Dunning, J. H. (1988). *Explaining International Production*. London: Unwin Hyman.

Dunning, J. H. (1993). *Multinational Enterprises and the Global Economy*. Addison-Wesley Publishing.

Dunning, J. H. & Narula, R. (1995). The R&D activities of foreign firms in the United States. *International Studies of Management & Organization, 25(1–2)*, 39–73.

Feldman, M. P. (1993). An examination of the geography of innovation. *Journal of Industrial and Corporate Change, 2(3)*, 451–470.

Fischer, W. A. & Behrman, J. N. (1979). The coordination of foreign R&D activities by transnational corporations. *Journal of International Business Studies, 10(3)*, 28–35.

Florida, R. (1997). The globalization of R&D: Results of a survey of foreign-affiliated R&D laboratories in the USA. *Research Policy, 26*, 85–103.

Forsgren, M. (1989a). *Managing the Internationalization Process — The Swedish Case*. London and New York: Routledge.

Forsgren, M. (1989b). Foreign acquisitions. In L. Hallén & J. Johanson (eds), *Advances in International Marketing*. Greenwich, CT: JAI Press.

Forsgren, M. (1990). Managing the international multi-centre firm: Case studies from Sweden. *European Management Journal, 8*, 261–267.

Forsgren, M. (1996). The advantage paradox of the multinational corporation. In I. Björkman & M. Forsgren (eds), *The Nature of the International Firm — Nordic Contributions to International Business Research*. Copenhagen Business School Press.

Forsgren, M. & Johanson, J. (eds) (1992). *Managing Networks In international Business*. Philadelphia: Gordon and Breach.

Forsgren, M., Johanson, J. & Sharma, D. (2000). Development of MNC centres of excellence. In U. Holm & T. Pedersen (eds), *The Emergence and Impact of MNC Centres of Excellence — A Subsidiary Perspective*. Macmillan Press Ltd.

Forsgren, M., Holm, U. & Johanson, J. (1995). Division headquarters go abroad — a step in the internationalization of the multinational corporation. *Journal of Management Studies, 32(4)*, 475–491.

Forsgren, M. & Pedersen, T. (2000). Subsidiary influence and corporate learning — centres of excellence in Danish foreign-owned firms. In U. Holm & T. Pedersen (eds), *The Emergence and Impact of MNC Centres of Excellence — A Subsidiary Perspective*. Macmillan Press Ltd.

Frost, A.S. (1998). *The Geographic Sources of Innovation in the Multinational Enterprise: U.S. Subsidiaries and Host-country Spillovers, 1980–1990*. Doctoral dissertation. Cambridge, MA: MIT, Sloan School of Management.

Gassman, O. (1997). F&E-projektmanagement und Prozesse länderübergreifender Produktenentwicklung. In A. Gerybadze *et al.*, (eds), *Globales Management von Forschung und Innovation*. Stuttgart: Schäffer-Poeschel Verlag.

Gassman, O. & Von Zedtwitz, M. (1999). New concepts in international R&D organization. *Research Policy, 28*, 231–250.

Gerybadze, A., Meyer-Krahmer, F. & Reger, G. (1997). *Globales Management von Forschung und Innovation*. Stuttgart: Schäffer-Poeschel Verlag.

Ghauri, P. N. (1990). Emergence of new structures in Swedish multinationals. In S. B. Prasad (ed.), *Advances in International Comparative Management*. Greenwich, CT: JAI Press Inc.

Ghoshal, S. & Bartlett, C. A. (1988). Innovation processes in multinational corporations. In M. L. Tushman & W. L. Moore (eds), *Readings in the Management of Innovation*. Ballinger Publishing Company.

Gupta, A. K. & Govindarajan, V. (1991). Knowledge flows and the structure of control within multinational corporations. *Academy of Management Review, 16(4)*, 768–792.

Hagström, P. (1991). *The 'Wired' MNC — The Role of Information Systems for Structural Change in Complex Organizations*. Doctoral dissertation, Institute of International Business, Stockholm.

Hamel, G. & Prahalad, C. K. (1985). Do you really have a global strategy? *Harvard Business Review*, July–August, 139–148.

Hedlund, G. (1981). Autonomy of subsidiaries and formalization of headquarters-subsidiary relationships in Swedish MNCs. In L. Otterbeck (ed.), *The Management of Headquarters-subsidiary Relationships in Multinational Corporations*. Gower.

Hedlund, G. (1986). The hypermodern MNC — A heterarchy? *Human Resource Management, 25(1)*, 9–35.

Hedlund, G. (1993). Assumptions of hierarchy and heterarchy, with applications to the management of the multinational corporation. In S. Ghoshal &

E. Westney (eds), *Organization Theory and the Multinational Corporation*. London: Routledge.

Hedlund, G. (1994). A model of knowledge management and the N-form corporation. *Strategic Management Journal, 15*, 73 –90.

Hedlund, G. (1996). The intensity and extensity of knowledge: Implications for possible futures of the global firm. *CEMS Business Review, 1*, 111–126.

Hedlund, G. and Kverneland, Å. (1984). *Investing in Japan — The Experience of Swedish Firms*. Stockholm: Minab/Gotab.

Hedlund, G. & Ridderstråle, J. (1995). International development projects — key to competitiveness, impossible, or mismanaged? *International Studies of Management & Organization, 25(1–2)*, 158–184.

Hedlund, G. & Rolander, D. (1990). Action in heterarchies: New approaches to managing the MNC. In C. A. Bartlett, Y. Doz & G. Hedlund (eds), *Managing the Global Firm*. Routledge.

Hedlund, G. & Åman, P. (1983). *Managing Relationships with Foreign Subsidiaries — Organization and Control in Swedish MNCs*. Stockholm: Sveriges Mekanförbund.

Holm, U. (1994). *Internationalization of the Second Degree*. Doctoral dissertation, Department of Business Studies, Uppsala University.

Holm, U. & Pedersen, T. (eds) (2000). *The Emergence and Impact of MNC Centres of Excellence — A Subsidiary Perspective*. Macmillan Press Ltd.

Holm, U., Johanson, J. & Thilenius, P. (1995). HQ knowledge of subsidiary network contexts in the MNC. *International Studies of Management & Organization, 25(1–2)*, 97–119.

Hout, T., Porter, M. E. & Rudden, E. (1982). How global companies win out. *Harvard Business Review*, September–October, 98–108.

Håkanson, L. & Zander, U. (1986). *Managing International Research & Development*. Stockholm: Mekan.

Jaffe, A. B., Trajtenberg, M. & Henderson, R. (1993). Geographic localization of knowledge spillovers as evidenced by patent citations. *Quarterly Journal of Economics, 108(3)*, 577–598.

Jarillo, J. C. & Martinez, J. I. (1990). Different roles for subsidiaries: The case of multinational corporations in Spain. *Strategic Management Journal, 11*, 501–512.

Johanson, J. & Vahlne, J.-E. (1977). The internationalization process of the firm — A model of knowledge development and increasing foreign market commitments. *Journal of International Business Studies, 8(1)*, 23–32.

Johanson, J. & Vahlne, J.-E. (1990). The mechanisms of internationalization. *International Marketing Review, 7(4)*, 11–24.

Johanson, J. & Wiedersheim-Paul, F. (1975). The internationalization of the firm — four Swedish cases. *Journal of Management Studies*, October, 305–322.

Jones, M. V. & Tagg, S. K. (1999). *International Growth and Development of Small Firms: Patterns of Start-up and Internationalization*. Paper presented at the EIBA 25th Annual Conference, Manchester, December 12–14.

Kogut, B. (1983). Foreign direct investment as a sequential process. In C. P. Kindleberger & D. Audretsch (eds), *The Multinational Corporation in the 1980s.* Cambridge, MA: MIT Press.

Kogut, B. (1989). A note on global strategies. *Strategic Management Journal, 10,* 383–389.

Kogut, B. (1990). International sequential advantages and network flexibility. In C. A. Bartlett *et al.,* (eds), *Managing the Global Firm.* Routledge.

Kogut, B. & Zander, U. (1992). Knowledge of the firm, combinative capabilities, and the replication of technology. *Organization Science, 3(3),* 383–397.

Kogut, B. & Zander, U. (1996). What firms do? Coordination, identity, and learning. *Organization Science, 7(5),* 502–518.

Kuemmerle, W. (1997). Building effective R&D capabilities abroad. *Harvard Business Review,* March–April, 61–70.

Kuemmerle, W. (1999). The drivers of foreign direct investment into research and development: An empirical investigation. *Journal of International Business Studies, 30(1),* 1–24.

Lagerström, K. (2001). *Transnational Projects Within Multinational Corporations.* Doctoral dissertation, no. 84, Department of Business Studies, Uppsala University.

Lindqvist, M. (1991). *Infant Multinationals — The Internationalization of Young, Technology-based Swedish Firms.* Doctoral dissertation, Institute of International Business, Stockholm.

Luostarinen, R. (1979). *Internationalization of the Firm — An Empirical Study of the Internationalization of Firms with Small and Open Domestic Markets with Special Emphasis on Lateral Rigidity as a Behavioral Characteristic in Strategic Decision-making.* Helsinki: Acta Academiae Oeconomicae Helsingiensis, Series A:30.

Marshall, A. (1890/1916). *Principles of Economics — An introductory Volume* (7th ed.). London: Macmillan.

Mudambi, R. (1998). The role of duration in multinational investment strategies. *Journal of International Business Studies, 29(2),* 239–262.

Nohria, N. & Ghoshal, S. (1997). *The Differentiated Network — Organizing Multinational Corporations for Value Creation.* San Francisco: Jossey-Bass Publishers.

Patel, P. and Pavitt, K. (1997). The technological competencies of the world's largest firms: Complex and path-dependent, but not much variety. *Research Policy 26,* 141–156.

Patel, P. & Pavitt, K. (1998). The wide (and increasing) spread of technological competencies in the world's largest firms: A challenge to conventional wisdom. In A. D. Chandler *et al.,* (eds), *The Dynamic Multinational Firm.* Oxford University Press.

Pavitt, K. (1988). International patterns of technological accumulation. In N. Hood & J.-E. Vahlne (eds), *Strategies in Global Competition.* London: Croom Helm.

Pearce, R. D. (1989). *The Internationalization of Research and Development by Multinational Enterprises.* Macmillan.

Pearce, R. D. (1994). The internationalization of research and development by multinational enterprises and the transfer sciences. *Empirica, 21,* 297–311.

Pearce, R. D. & Singh, S. (1992). Internationalization of research and development among the world's leading enterprises: Survey analysis of organization and motivation. In O. Granstrand *et al.,* (eds), *Technology Management and International Business — Internationalization of R&D and Technology.* Chichester: John Wiley & Sons.

Perlmutter, H. V. (1969). The tortuous evolution of the multinational corporation. *Columbia Journal of World Business,* January–February, 9–18.

Porter, M. E. (1990). *The Competitive Advantage of Nations.* The Free Press.

Prahalad, C. K. & Doz, Y. (1987). *The Multinational Mission — Balancing Local Demands and Global Vision.* The Free Press.

Ridderstråle, J. (1997). *Global Innovation — Managing International Innovation Projects at ABB and Electrolux.* Doctoral dissertation. Stockholm: Institute of International Business.

Ronstadt, R. C. (1978). International R&D: The establishment and evolution of research and development abroad by seven U.S. multinationals. *Journal of International Business Studies, 9(1),* 7–24.

Russo, M. (1985). Technical change and the industrial district: The role of interfirm relations in the growth and transformation of ceramic tile production in Italy. *Research Policy, 14,* 329–343.

Sandén, P. & Vahlne, J.-E. (1976). *Impact of Multinationality on Performance.* Working paper, Centre for International Business Studies, University of Uppsala.

Saxenian, A. (1991). The origin and dynamics of production networks in Silicon Valley. *Research Policy, 20,* 423–437.

Stopford, J. M. & Dunning, J. H. (1983). *Multinationals — Company Performance and Global Trends.* London: Macmillan Publishers.

Sölvell, Ö. (1987). *Entry Barriers and Foreign Penetration — Emerging Patterns of International Competition in Two Electrical Engineering Industries.* Doctoral dissertation, Institute of International Business, Stockholm.

Sölvell, Ö. & Bresman, H. (1997). Local and global forces in the innovation process of the multinational enterprise — An hour-glass model. In H. Eskelinen (ed.), *Regional Specialisation and Local Environment — Learning and Competitiveness.* Stockholm: NordREFO.

Sölvell, Ö. & Zander, I. (1998). International diffusion of knowledge: isolating mechanisms and the role of the MNE. In A. D. Chandler *et al.* (eds), *The Dynamic Firm — The Role of Technology, Strategy, Organization, and Regions.* Oxford University Press.

Taggart, J. H. (1996). Multinational manufacturing subsidiaries in Scotland: strategic role and economic impact. *International Business Review, 5(5),* 447–468.

Taggart, J. H. (1997). Autonomy and procedural justice: A framework for evaluating subsidiary strategy. *Journal of International Business Studies, 28(1),* 51–76.

Vahlne, J.-E. & Sölvell, Ö. (1981). *Effekter av Investeringar Utomlands — En Studie av Sex Industrier.* SOU, 33.

Vernon, R. (1979). The product cycle hypothesis in a new international environment. *Oxford Bulletin of Economics and Statistics, 41,* 255–267.

Vernon, R. (1980). Gone are the cash cows of yesteryear. *Harvard Business Review,* November–December, 150–155.

White, R. E. & Poynter, T. A. (1984). Strategies for foreign-owned subsidiaries in Canada. *Business Quarterly,* Summer, 59–69.

Zander, I. (1997). Technological diversification in the multinational corporation — historical trends and future prospects. *Research Policy, 26,* 209–227.

Zander, I. (1999a). Where to the multinational? The evolution of technological capabilities in the multinational network. *International Business Review, 8(3),* 261–291.

Zander, I. (1999b). How do you mean 'global'? An empirical investigation of innovation networks in the multinational corporation. *Research Policy, 28,* 195–213.

Zander, I. (2000). *The Formation of International Innovation Networks in the Multinational Corporation — An Evolutionary Perspective.* Paper presented at the AIB Annual Meeting, November 17–20, Phoenix, Arizona.

Zander, I. & Sölvell, Ö. (2000). Cross-border innovation in the multinational corporation — a research agenda. *Journal of International Studies of Management & Organization, 30(2),* 44–67.

Chapter 5

Embeddedness of Subsidiaries in Internal and External Networks: A Prerequisite for Technological Change

Michael Kutschker and Andreas Schurig

Introduction

When skimming through modern concepts of multinational corporations a lot is said about the advantages of exploiting activities on a global scale and simultaneously realising local responsiveness. "Think global, act local" has become a well-known slogan. Emphasis is especially put on the ability of learning by tapping into local centres of innovation, transferring these innovations to other corporate units by interlinking the centres, and then exploiting these innovations on a worldwide basis. Taking a look at the global economy today, one can see that large multinationals are continuously shifting their activities abroad. The number of foreign affiliates has risen from 206,000 in 1993 to 508,239 in 1998. The value of the total FDI outward stock has reached 4.1 trillion USD in 1998. Companies such as General Electric and The Ford Motor Company have allocated up to 30 percent of their assets abroad. Companies from smaller countries such as Nestlé or Unilever have even accumulated up to 85 percent of their assets in foreign countries (UNCTAD, 1999). It seems as if the multinational corporations were trying to build up these "heterarchical/transnational" structures in order to realise the advantages associated with these organizational modes as mentioned above. At a first glance these evidences might be striking but there still is

Critical Perspectives on Internationalisation, pp. 107–132.
ISBN: 0-08-044035-5

little empirical proof that multinational corporations are actually realising these theoretically pronounced advantages. Especially the role foreign units play in the learning and transfer process between the multinational corporation and the local environment has rarely been analysed in depth.

Recently the transfer of knowledge in the MNC has become a focal point of interest in the literature on international management (for an overview see Bendt, 2000). Some scholars have even emphasised the role of the subsidiary in the transfer process. Most of these studies though have either concentrated on the knowledge transfer between different units within the MNC (Gupta & Govindarajan, 1991; 1994; Randoy & Li, 1998) or the exchange of knowledge between a focal foreign subsidiary and its local environment (Andersson & Forsgren, 1994). To the best of our knowledge only few studies have analysed the role of a foreign subsidiary as a "knowledge broker" or "pipeline" enabling a through flow of knowledge between the MNC and the local environment of the subsidiary (Forsgren *et al.*, 1999; Forsgren *et al.*, 1997; Hakanson & Nobel, 1998). This is an astonishing observation taking into consideration that this function is seen as one of the competitive advantages of multinational firms vis-à-vis firms with a more concentrated asset structure (Birkinshaw & Hood, 1995: 340; DeMeyer, 1992: 169; Pearce & Singh, 1992: 138). We want to contribute to this string of research by analysing the role of foreign subsidiaries in Germany. We are especially interested in the question whether these subsidiaries can act as "technological change agents" — influencing the technological development of their corporation and/or their local environment — by exercising the role of a knowledge pipeline.

Based on this background we want to answer three questions in this paper:

1) Which roles do subsidiaries exercise in the knowledge development process in their corporation and their local environment?
2) Can subsidiaries act as technological change agents?
3) How can differences in role behaviour be explained?

In five steps we shall try to find an answer to the questions pointed out. First, we shall give a detailed insight into the theoretical background of our argumentation. Then we shall analyse the different knowledge relationships the subsidiaries can engage in within the MNC. Further, reflecting the network literature of industrial marketing, we shall describe the knowledge relationships subsidiaries can undertake in their external environment. In a third step, we combine the internal and the external knowledge relationships giving an overview of all possible knowledge flows a subsidiary can engage in. In the fourth step, we shall concentrate on those subsidiaries acting as change agents offering a pipeline for the knowledge transfer and try to explain the differences of these subsidiaries and their surrounding network configuration. In the last chapter we shall summarise our findings and draw some conclusions.

Theoretical Background

In the field of international management it has long been accepted that knowledge is a basic source of advantage in international competition. Dunning is even seeing the global economy entering into a new form — a knowledge-based form — of capitalism (Dunning, 1999). It has been realised though that this source of competitive advantage — the world's stock of knowledge — is unevenly distributed domestically and internationally (Hedlund, 1999; Teece, 1981). It therefore can be argued that since economic growth requires the utilization of this differentially distributed stock of available knowledge, mutually advantageous transfer opportunities must exist. Or in other words, the ability to create new knowledge, and to replicate it through knowledge transfer, lies at the heart of the process of economic growth (Kogut & Zander, 1993; Mansfield *et al.*, 1983).

One of the first and still very dominant lines of reasoning in the literature on international management, which has touched upon the aspect of knowledge transfer, is the internalisation theory (Buckley & Casson, 1976; Caves, 1971). It is argued that the MNC develops — that is to say extends its activities abroad by foreign direct investments — in response to imperfections in the market for intermediate products especially for knowledge. Rising transaction costs prohibit the transfer of knowledge through market mechanisms. It is assumed that these imperfections are caused by the fact that the transfer process of knowledge is accompanied by a high degree of spill-over or externality (Johnson, 1970) and that market partners are characterised by bounded rationality and a tendency to opportunism (Hennart, 1982). The MNC can overcome these imperfections and reduce the transaction costs either by creating an internal market of its own (Rugman, 1980) or by replacing the price system with a mode of organization — the extension of managerial control — where a central party directs the exchange (Conner & Prahalad, 1996; Hennart,

1991). The MNC can therefore be seen as a vehicle by which knowledge can be transferred more efficiently and cheaply than by independent market partners.

It has to be stated though that the focus of the internalisation theory has mainly been on knowledge flowing outward from the centre, the parent company, to the periphery, the subsidiaries. Other directions of knowledge flows such as between the subsidiary and its local environment or other subsidiaries were often neglected. (Chesnais, 1988; Ghoshal, 1987). This disregard can partially be explained by the dominant paradigm in international management which saw the headquarter as the focal point of analysis. Internationalisation was basically seen as the exploitation of a firm-specific advantage through foreign direct investments. The firm-specific advantage has normally been generated at the centre (Ghoshal, 1987). Recently there has been a change in the perspective of the MNC shifting the view from a hierarchical to a multi-centre perspective (Schmid et al., 1998). On the one hand this alternative perspective has taken into consideration that geographically dispersed subsidiaries can be seen as a major source of knowledge and therefore a source of competitive advantages for the MNC. Foreign subsidiaries may control resources relevant for the further development of the MNC — a stage often described as "internationalisation of the second degree" (Andersson, 1997; Forsgren, 1997). On the other hand it is argued that the MNC can no longer be seen as an hierarchical entity, but has to be looked at as a network of multiple units. (Bartlett & Ghoshal, 1989; Doz et al., 1997; Ghoshal & Bartlett, 1998; Hedlund, 1986). Each unit is further part of a network between entities outside the MNC within its local environment. Large MNCs are therefore best viewed as organizations in which different units are embedded in a number of intersecting networks both internal and external to the organization. (DeMeyer, 1992; Ghoshal & Bartlett, 1990 ; Yamin, 1997). Internal networks consist of actors or counterparts such as the headquarter or other corporate subsidiaries. External networks include actors such as customers, suppliers, government agencies etc. The relationships between the subsidiary and these actors, both corporate and non-corporate are often interpreted as exchange relationships. These relationships cannot only be differentiated by their content but also through their extent and direction (Gupta & Govindarajan, 1994). As mentioned above knowledge can be seen as one important element being exchanged within these relationships. The subsidiary therefore can either function as a receiver of knowledge flows or as a provider of knowledge flows to other actors in the internal and external network. By combining these aspects — concentration on the single subsidiary, network theory, knowledge flows — it becomes clear that the single subsidiary can be seen as a focal actor engaged in four different vectors of knowledge flows:

1) inflowing knowledge from other corporate units;
2) outflowing knowledge to other corporate units;
3) inflowing knowledge from non-corporate units;
4) outflowing knowledge to non-corporate units.

Subsidiaries' Knowledge Flow Within the MNC's Internal Network

Inflowing Knowledge from Other Corporate Units

This vector has long been part of the research in international management especially when it comes to analysing the motivation for fdi. Hymer (1976), Kindleberger (1969) and Caves (1982), for example, explained foreign direct investments as the outcome of firm-specific monopolistic advantages. These advantages (e.g., technology) were transferred from the headquarter internally across international borders, thus allowing the local subsidiary to compete with host country firms (Fayerweather, 1969). From an empirical study Mansfield concluded that if firms could not utilize their foreign subsidiaries as a channel for transfer they would reduce their R&D expenditures by 12 to 15 percent. The authors also concluded that large companies draw about 30 percent of the returns from their R&D projects from overseas markets. The total annual output of countries outside the home country would have been at least one percent less if technology transfer of this sort had not occurred (Mansfield *et al.*, 1983). In modern literature though these resource flows are no longer viewed only as a bundle of headquarter-subsidiary relationships but as a complicated system of reciprocal inter-dependencies between corporate units in different countries (Hedlund, 1986). Since innovative capabilities are dispersed and subsidiaries are often in control of strategic assets the headquarter is no longer seen as the only provider of knowledge for other corporate units. The underlying theoretical approach lies in the possibility of linking together a set of actors with the purpose to exploit exchange opportunities in the single local markets through economies of scale and scope and learning (Kogut, 1989).

Outflowing Knowledge to Other Corporate Units

Recent research in international management looks upon subsidiaries not just as exploiters of home country knowledge but also as units that share their knowledge with other parts of the organization (Hedlund, 1986). In fact, the ability to learn and use knowledge elsewhere in the firm is one of the primary advantages of multinationality (Kogut, 1989). The transfer of knowledge from the overseas subsidiaries to the parent company and other corporate units has long been neglected. Increasingly though scholars have recognized that foreign units are also used as a means to access and develop new technologies (Cantwell, 1991; Cantwell & Janne, 1997; Cantwell & Piscitello, 1997; Pearce & Singh, 1992; Yamin, 1997). Internationally dispersed units facilitate the technological development of the firm, since they can tap into alternative streams of innovation in different "hot spots". Empirical studies have indicated that the effect of knowledge transferred from subsidiaries to the parent corporation has generated technologies that contributed about four percent of the total profits of manufacturing firms (Mansfield & Romeo, 1984).

Subsidiaries' Knowledge Flow Within the MNC's External Network

In the previous section we discussed the different roles a subsidiary can exercise in the corporation's internal network. We now change the perspective and ask which role the subsidiary can play vis-à-vis customers, suppliers and governmental institutions within its external networks. In the literature on international management the subsidiary is often seen as a focal unit maintaining relationships and handling the day-to-day work with external counterparts such as customers and suppliers (Andersson *et al.*, 1999; Andersson, Furu & Holmstroem, 1999; Forsgren *et al.*, 1999; Hakansson & Johanson, 1993). On the one hand the relationships are a necessity for the subsidiary to survive in the local market, resulting in adjustments and equipment that are customised to the requirements of local partners (Forsgren *et al.*, 1997; Powell *et al.*, 1996). On the other hand the local or external environment seems to play an important role especially in the context of technological knowledge creation (Andersson, 1997). Forsgren for example argued that the intensity of the interaction with external counterparts influences the innovative capacity of the corporation (Forsgren, 1997). The MNC cannot only be influenced by its local counterparts but it can itself bring about change in its environment. It has long been accepted that through dealing with suppliers, distributors, creditors etc. the MNC will serve as a medium of exchange of marketing and technical know-how and of lifestyles. Directly or indirectly, the MNC will also be a transmitter of organizational know-how and a transformer of attitudes in general and of business in particular (Thorelli, 1966). Therefore the increasing presence of foreign firms raises the question of knowledge acquiring and sharing patterns of these multinationals through the relationships of their subsidiaries with non-corporate units.

Inflowing Knowledge from Non-corporate Units

A recent flood of fdi into high-technology regions suggests that multinationals are using fdi to gain access to local information channels and thus source location-specific knowledge (Mariotti & Piscitello, 1995; Tsurumi, 1976). It has also been suggested that overseas R&D is undertaken to gain access to knowledge in foreign centres of excellence and to benefit from localized R&D spillovers (Fors, 1996; Rugman & Verbeke, 2001). A possible explanation to these phenomena lies in the assumption that the socio-cultural milieu in which the subsidiary is embedded has a major influence on how the subsidiary evolves and behaves (Porter, 1990). This argument can also be found in modern network theory. It is often argued that relationships with external counterparts are critical as a means of developing competence, new products and processes as well as for the modification of old existing ones. It can be expected that some of the business relationships provide knowledge, which is critical for long-term survival in the market, and some business relationships might provide knowledge relevant for the development of the entire corporation (Easton, 1992; Hakansson & Johanson, 1993; Hedlund, 1999). Even though the important role of a subsidiary as a change agent between the external context and the rest of the corporation is being analysed (Forsgren *et al.*, 1999), Almeida has found that some of the newly gained knowledge remains localized (Almeida, 1996). This circumstance is often explained by the fact that these working business relationships contain a strong element of mutual knowledge of which some is tacit and cannot be transferred to others (Kogut & Zander, 1992).

Outflowing Knowledge to Non-corporate Units

A question of equal importance is whether MNCs contribute to the host countries technological development. As shown above the subsidiary located in a region becomes part of the regional knowledge network (Cohen & Levinthal, 1989). This network facilitates not only the absorption of external knowledge but also allows the leakage of firm knowledge to others in that particular region. Some studies seem to prove this phenomenon, arguing that the productivity gains of the host country could have resulted from the diffusion of knowledge and expertise from the subsidiary to host firms or from the effects of greater competition and better resource allocation (Almeida, 1996; Dunning, 1994; Young *et al.*, 1988). These gains in the host country can result in the undeliberate diffusion of knowledge by the subsidiary. The subsidiary though might deliberately transfer knowledge to local partners in order to improve the local "infrastructure" for its own competencies. In an empirical study it was indicated that local partners had realized savings resulting from training programmes and from the transfer of know-how offered by the foreign subsidiary to suppliers. About two-thirds of the firms felt that their technological capabilities were raised by technology transfers of this sort (Mansfield & Romeo, 1980).

Pipelines as a Prerequisite for Technological Change

As pointed out above most studies have concentrated on just one vector of knowledge flow. Even though many studies have contributed to a better understanding of the MNC they were limited to a special content, extent or direction of knowledge flows. In what follows we want to combine several vectors of knowledge flow by especially analysing the role of the subsidiary as a technological change agent. We will provide some insight on the knowledge transfer between the MNC and its environment. The subsidiary thereby functions as a knowledge broker between the external environment and the other units of the corporation offering a "pipeline" for the knowledge flow. We thereby differentiate between a micro economic perspective (contribution to the technological progress of the parent company) and a macroeconomic perspective (contribution to the technological progress of the host country). In the former the internal and external networks of a subsidiary serve as a transmission line of knowledge on the level of the firm. Externally acquired knowledge is passed into the corporation by the subsidiary. In the latter the subsidiary functions in analogy to the role of a change agent in the corporation as a change agent within the host country offering a pipeline for the knowledge transfer from the MNC to the local network partners. The local network partners thereby use the social, technological, and managerial knowledge base of the MNC for their own technological development. In conclusion it can be stated that from both the micro and the macro-economic perspective, it is necessary that knowledge can flow freely from the MNC to the external environment or from the external environment to the MNC. That is to say the link between the internal and external networks must be locked.

The role of a subsidiary is hereby comparable to the role of a boundary spanner as pointed out in the literature on organizational ecology where the firm is seen as an open system interacting with its environment. Boundary roles link organizational structures to environmental elements either by buffering, moderating, or influencing the environment. These roles are vital to the transfer of technology and information across boundaries. Substantial research indicates that boundary spanners are an important mechanism for linking their organization or subunit to external sources of information. Several studies concluded that boundary spanners are an efficient way to gather information from and transfer information to external areas. (Aldrich & Herker, 1977; Keller & Holland, 1975; Tushman & Scanlan, 1981a). Social ties are thereby often used as channels for information and resource flows (Tsai & Ghoshal, 1998). The effectiveness and outcome of the transfer process though is not only determined by the nature of the individual bilateral interaction but also by the overall structure and characteristics of the larger network of relations in which the unit is embedded (Granovetter, 1985).

Furthermore it is argued that only those units, which are well connected internally and externally, accomplish informational boundary spanning. This is due to the fact that only those units can span boundaries effectively and search for relevant information on one side and disseminate it on the other which understand the coding schemes and are attuned to the contextual information on both sides of the boundary. Internal and external linkages are necessary to translate across communication boundaries and to be aware of contextual information on both sides of the boundary (Tushman & Scanlan, 1981b).

This supports the suggestion that effective knowledge diffusion — either from the corporation to the environment or vice versa from the environment to the MNC — actually requires dual embeddedness on part of the subsidiary, i.e., embeddedness in both external and internal networks (Hakanson & Nobel, 1998). In the following we want to pick up this argument assuming that embeddedness — intensive contact and interaction with network partners — on the one hand enhances the ability of subunits to assimilate and generate new technical knowledge and on the other hand ensures the awareness about such technology and its potential use by other units. This line of reasoning runs parallel to the debate about the new heterarchical/transnational MNC and the question how and if foreign subsidiaries can remain integrated with the rest of the corporation while simultaneously maintaining strong local linkages to customers, suppliers and governmental agencies.

Method

Sample

The data used in this analysis were collected through the mailing of a standardized questionnaire sent to the heads of the biggest 1,500 foreign subsidiaries in Germany. The Scandinavian scholars participating in the international research project directed by Jan Johanson and Ulf Holm designed the questionnaire. In order to obtain comparability between the different country samples all participating research institutions used this questionnaire. In the German sample the total number of employees measured the size of the subsidiary. In overall terms the participation was fairly good with a response rate of 20 percent. All in all 255 subsidiaries were included in the sample. The size of the subsidiaries varied considerably from 15 to 44,000 employees with an average of 1,740 employees. The average turnover of the subsidiaries amounted to 527 million USD, varying between 0.2 and 16,140 million USD. The headquarters of the subsidiaries were located in North America (34.4%), Europe (60.3%) and Asia (5.4%). The subsidiaries are operating in all three sectors whereby subsidiaries from the secondary sector clearly dominate the sample (85.2%). Within the secondary sector the chemical industry accounts for 24.1 percent and the industry of manufacturing fabricated metal products, machinery and equipment for 40.7 percent of the subsidiaries.

Measures

Since knowledge flows cannot be traced as easily as product or capital flows we will concentrate our analysis on the prerequisites or outcomes of knowledge flows. That is the embeddedness of the subsidiary in internal and external networks as pointed out above. Since there is no homogeneous definition of embeddedness we will focus on the influence structure of the subsidiary and its surrounding network. We thereby follow the literature on the organizational ecology, the resource dependence theory, and literature dealing with intra-organizational power. In this literature it is argued that the integration of knowledge is not just a reactive process but also a forming or moulding process in which attitudes, perceptions and values of the receiving unit are changed (Leifer & Delbecq, 1978). Bringing about a change in the status quo though requires the use of power and influence to persuade others of the desirability of the change (Tushman & Scanlan, 1981a). Sources of power can be seen in specific technological knowledge, control over communication channels, boundary spanning position between the organization and its environment, and hierarchical legacy (Crozier & Friedberg, 1979). Empirical studies indicate that expert power followed by legitimate power seems to be the most frequently mentioned basis of influence within corporations (Spekman, 1979). It is further argued that boundary spanners are in an excellent structural position to convert their access and control over information into actual power (Aldrich & Herker, 1977). Enlarging this line of reasoning to the subsidiary's internal and external network configuration one can say that the focal subsidiary can on the one hand be influential on other network partners due to the possession of critical knowledge. On the other hand the subsidiary can also be dependent on the knowledge of other network partners and therefore be liable to the influence of these units. We therefore conclude that the possibility to exercise influence on the behaviour of other units is related to the possession of resources e.g. knowledge in the relevant area of influence. A high degree of influence on the behaviour of others is therefore comparable to a high degree of embeddedness. In the following we therefore identify pipelines as subsidiaries that on the one hand are being influenced by partners from "one side" of the network (internal or external) and on the other hand influence partners on the "other side" of the network (external or internal).

Several questions in the questionnaire were used as indicators in order to analyse the extent and the direction of technological knowledge and influence from corporate and external counterparts on the subsidiary and from the subsidiary on corporate and external counterparts. The identified questions were combined to four vectors indicating:

1) the degree of influence on other corporate units;
2) the degree of influence from other corporate units;
3) the degree of influence on non-corporate units;

4) the degree of influence from non-corporate units (for further detail see appendix).

For each of the items, the respondents were asked to answer on a likert-type seven-point scale (ranging from "not at all" to "a very great deal"). Finally, median splits along these composites measures were used to determine a threshold differentiating the extent of influence described by each vector. By combining the different vectors to several two-dimensional spaces it was possible to identify different types of subsidiaries according to the extent and direction of influence.

Results

Influence Structure Within the Internal Network

As can be seen from Figure 5.1 the degree of embeddedness of the subsidiaries within the corporation varies considerably.

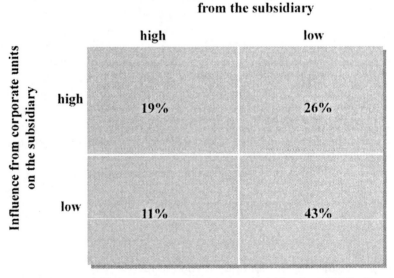

Figure 5.1: Subsidiaries' Influence Structure Within the MNC's Internal Network.

Over 40 percent of all subsidiaries show a low degree of embeddedness in the internal network of their corporation. They neither exercise a high degree of influence on other corporate units nor are other corporate counterparts influencing them. The "mirror inverted" position, accounts for 19 percent of the German sample. Only few subsidiaries are highly influential and influenced at the same time. Twenty-six percent of the subsidiaries in the German sample are being influenced by other corporate units but exercise no or a low degree of influence themselves. These subsidiaries could act as technological change agents in their host country (Germany) if and only if they had an influence on their local stakeholders. Eleven percent of the subsidiaries exercise influence on other corporate units but are not influenced by other units. These subsidiaries might act as change agents transferring externally gained knowledge into the MNC if they are additionally being influenced by the external environment. However, 43 percent of the sample is not enabling the knowledge flow from the MNC to the local environment and vice versa at all. Whether the remaining 57 percent actually offer a pipeline for knowledge transfer efficiently, is a matter of the embeddedness in the external networks.

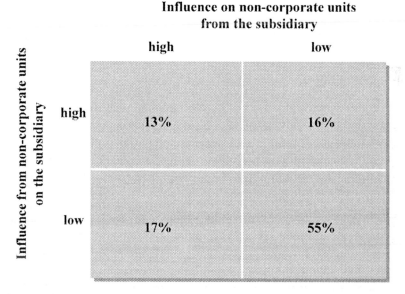

Figure 5.2: Subsidiaries' Influence Structure Within the MNC's External Network.

Influence Structure Within the External Network

The analysis of the external network configuration shows a similar picture. An overwhelming part (55%) of the subsidiaries in the German sample neither have a high degree of influence on their external business network nor are they being influenced by the external partners. Only 13 percent are highly integrated in their local network, that is to say being influenced by and being influential on their external network at the same time. Sixteen per cent of the subsidiaries are influenced by their external network but show little signs of influencing activities themselves. The remaining 17 percent exert influence on their external network but show no tendency of influence by non-corporate units. These two groups could act as change agents, if and only if these subsidiaries are engaged in relationships in their internal network, opening a pipeline for knowledge flows from the MNC to the local environment and enabling that externally gained knowledge can pass through to the corporation.

Subsidiaries Influence Structure Within the MNC's External and Internal Network

So far the subsidiaries have been looked at from two different angles — the corporate side and the external side. The combined analysis of both the subsidiaries' corporate and non-corporate networks though is important when investigating the subsidiaries' function as a pipeline offering the possibility of knowledge transfer from the MNC to the local environment and vice versa from the local environment to the MNC as argued above. In order to fulfil this task we combined the analysis of the subsidiary's influence structure with internal and external network partners. The result can be seen in Figure 5.3. The matrix shows all 16 different positions of influence relationships a subsidiary can take on.

Only 7.1 percent of the subsidiaries in the German sample resemble the role of a fully integrated player, influencing their internal and external environment as well as being influenced by their internal and external counterparts (square 1). These 18 subsidiaries act as pipelines allowing the subsidiary to exert influence in both directions. These subsidiaries are labelled "**All flows**". Further subsidiaries can also be identified as pipelines. The squares 2,3,5,6,9,11 account for another 16.4 percent of subsidiaries possibly functioning as pipelines. All in all 23.5 percent of all subsidiaries included in the sample can be labelled as "**Pipelines**".

External influence structure

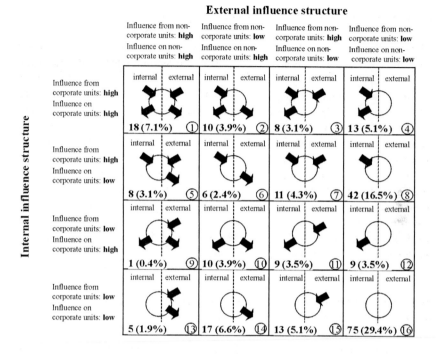

Figure 5.3: The Subsidiaries' Influence Structure Within the MNC's Internal and External Network.

A larger share (29.4%) of the sample though does not show any intense relationships neither with internal nor with external counterparts. These subsidiaries were labelled "**No flows**". The remaining 46.9 percent are being influenced either from internal and/or external network members or influencing internal and/or external actors. These subsidiaries labelled as "**Weak flows**" cannot be considered as Pipelines since their through flow of knowledge seems to be "interrupted".

Concerning the first research question, we can state that the subsidiaries included in the German sample do exercise different roles in their internal and external network — Weak flows, No flows and Pipelines. More than 75 percent of the sample does not fulfil the prerequisite for functioning as a Pipeline for knowledge transfer crossing the internal and the external network. And almost 30 percent of the subsidiaries in Germany are just slightly engaged in influence structure with internal or external counterparts. Both results are remarkable since the German market can be considered important as well as attractive to foreign MNCs. And since we have addressed the 1,500 largest foreign corporations in Germany one would expect an even higher degree of influential relationships.

The second research question — whether the subsidiary acts a Pipeline — has partially been answered. It was found that 23.5 percent of the subsidiaries in the German sample have been identified as Pipelines. The subsidiaries fulfilling the function of a Pipeline though can be further differentiated according to the direction of knowledge flows passing through the Pipeline. As stated above 7.1 percent of the subsidiaries were identified as "**All flows**" offering a Pipeline for knowledge flow in both directions — from the internal network to the external one and vice versa. The remaining Pipelines (16.4%) can be differentiated into "**In flows**" (squares 3,9,11) allowing a knowledge transfer from the external network into the MNC (7.1%) and "**Out flows**" (squares 2,5,6) enabling the subsidiary to act as a change agent in the local environment by supporting knowledge flows from the MNC to the external network (9.4%).

Recapitulating the results it can be stated that the subsidiaries exercise different roles according to their knowledge and influence relationships with internal and external network partners. In the next section we want to analyse to what extent these differences in the subsidiary roles can be explained by systematic determinants.

Determinants of Differences in Network Clusters

The development of networks as well as the role exercised by a single actor within the network takes time: "... a business network develops over a long time and a subsidiary's role in such a network is formed from long-lasting interactions..." (Hakansson & Johanson, 1993). This assumption is further supported by the Uppsala model of internationalisation (Johanson & Vahlne, 1977; 1990) viewing the development of the multinational corporation as an incremental process. Therefore it can be suggested that the degree of integration into the corporate network as well as into the external network is dependent on the age of the subsidiary, its market position in the local market as well as its degree of internationalisation. An additional positive effect on the network integration of the subsidiary can be exerted by the degree of internationalisation of the parent company.

Further we argue that the possibility to build network relationships and manage Pipelines is correlated with the size of the focal actor. Larger subsidiaries can mobilize more "boundary personal" enabling them to exert a higher degree of influence on the local environment than smaller subsidiaries. A greater amount of boundary personal also enables the subsidiary to receive more signals from the external counterparts and to transfer them to other corporate units. Similarly it can be argued that larger parent companies can fall back upon a greater surface and network structures with its own controlling overlayers in which the subsidiary can be embedded more easily. It therefore can be expected that subsidiaries of large MNCs show a greater possibility of offering a Pipeline for knowledge transfer than subsidiaries of small MNCs. Size is indicated through the turnover and the number of employees as often suggested in organizational theory. Another determinant indicating the size of the parent company as well as its degree of internationalisation is represented by the total number of subsidiaries maintained in the local environment. Similarly the size and the degree of internationalisation of the subsidiary can be indicated by the units reporting directly to the focal subsidiary.

As argued above we differentiated the sample primarily into three different sub-samples: No flows, Weak flows and Pipelines as shown in Table 5.1. By conducting an ANOVA analysis we have tried to give an answer to the question whether the differences in the identified roles of the subsidiaries can be explained by the determinants listed above. Even though only few determinants show significant differences according to the three sub-samples, they do indicate a clear order from No flows over Weak flows to Pipelines. Pipelines are older, are more successful, show a higher degree of internationalisation both according to the parent company as well as to the subsidiary itself. Further the parent company shows a greater surface according to the total amount of subsidiaries in Germany than the No flows and the Weak flows. According to most of the determinants the Weak flows are ranked in-between the Pipelines and the No flows. It therefore can be stated that the degree of integration into the internal and the external network, or put differently that the possibility to act as a Pipeline for knowledge transfer is dependent on age, size, market position, degree of internationalisation of the local subsidiary as well as on the size and degree of internationalisation of the parent company.

In a second step we have differentiated those subsidiaries acting as Pipelines into three sub-samples: All flows, In flows and Out flows (Table 5.2). Due to the low quantity of subsidiaries in these sub-samples we could not calculate an ANOVA analysis trying to explain differences in

Table 5.1: Determinants of Differences in Network Clusters I.

	No flows	Weak flows	Pipelines (all)	Average over all subsidiaries
Count	75	120	60	**255**
Age	1980	1975,67	1974,67	**1976,72**
Internationalisation degree parent company	54,64	58,57	65,58	**59,44**
Turnover parent company (USD)	8470,51	11624,44	14582,35	**11448,42**
Employees parent company	31972,9	43366,93	69230,61	**46420,44**
Further units in Germany reporting to the parent company	5,36	6,19	8,53	**6,52**
Further units reporting to the subsidiary	2,69	18,42	7,53	**11,02**
Employees subsidiary	661,68	1769,88	3027,85	**1739,93**
Turnover subsidiary	168,46	614,02	807,38	**527,68**
Internationalisation degree subsidiary	12,8	19,44	19,29	**17,42**
Rank	7,71	4,96	2,86	**5,17**
significant at .05				

the Pipelines caused by the determinants listed above. According to tendency though it can be stated that subsidiaries labelled as In flows seem to be smaller in terms of size measured by the amount of generated turnover, the number of employees as well as the amount of units directly reporting to the subsidiary than Out- and All flows. Additionally the parent companies of subsidiaries acting as In flows seem to be smaller in size too. On the other hand In flows seem to be older and more successful than other subsidiaries acting as pipelines. By extending these analyses with samples from other research-teams participating in this research-project we hope to confirm our conjectures.

Conclusion

In this article we intended to give some insight into the question whether MNCs are building heterachical/transnational structures. We focussed on

Table 5.2: Determinants of Differences in Network Clusters II.

	No flows	Weak flows	Pipelines (all)	Average over all subsidiaries
Count	18	18	24	**255**
Age	1973	1971,61	1978,79	**1976,72**
Internationalisation degree parent company	66,6	67,47	63,31	**59,44**
Turnover parent company (USD)	14943,5	7682,39	19486,46	**11448,42**
Employees parent company	70402,53	39600,5	90623,08	**46420,44**
Further units in Germany reporting to the parent company	8,35	4,5	11,83	**6,52**
Further units reporting to the subsidiary	9	3,56	9,48	**11,02**
Employees subsidiary	4404,44	1245,72	3332	**1739,93**
Turnover subsidiary	809,61	464,26	1059,2	**527,68**
Internationalisation degree subsidiary	23,5	22,69	12,98	**17,42**
Rank	3,59	2,18	2,83	**5,17**

the question whether foreign subsidiaries can act as technological change agents either by passing knowledge from the MNC to the local in their local environment or visa versa from their local environment to other units within their corporate network. This function is seen as one of the competitive advantages of multinational firms. The knowledge flows were traced through the influence structure between the subsidiary and network partners both in the corporation and the external network. We stated that a distinct influence structure is comparable to a high degree of embeddedness — a prerequisite to engage in this role. This prerequisite has been labelled pipeline-effect.

The empirical results have shown that only 23.5 percent of 255 investigated subsidiaries fulfil this prerequisite. 16.5 percent of the subsidiaries can thereby be viewed as technological change agents in their local environment transferring knowledge from the MNC to their external counterparts. 14.2 percent of subsidiaries fulfilling the prerequisite act as a technological change agent in the corporation transferring externally gained knowledge into the MNC. The remaining 75 percent of the subsidiaries do not seem to be embedded in their internal and external networks at the same time and seem to make little use of their possibility to function as a pipeline. This seems somewhat astonishing since over 35 percent of the respondents indicated that their subsidiary acts as a "Centre of Excellence" within the corporation and the German market can be considered important as well as attractive to foreign MNCs.

By revealing that many subsidiaries seem to act as "stand alones" in their corporate network (43%) and their external network (54%) — 30 percent are neither exerting influence on their external or internal network, nor are they being influenced by their internal or external counterparts in technological matters — we can partly explain the frail use of internal and external network relationships in the German sample. It seems as if the subsidiaries do not fully exploit all positive effects of international knowledge transfer due to their low degree of corporate embeddedness. One can say that the ideal structure as pointed out by modern concepts of the MNC is far from being implemented by international corporations today. For once the theoretical concepts seem to be ahead of the economy.

By taking a look at several structural determinants of the network configuration that enables the subsidiary to function as a pipeline we concluded that it takes time to fully integrate or embed the subsidiary both in the internal and external networks. Furthermore older, larger and internationally more experienced corporations seem to have come closer to the ideal concept of the MNC. For smaller and younger corporations this indicates that they deliberately have to navigate and control the embeddedness of their subsidiaries to realise the advantages of heterachical/transnational structures and fall behind the "established" corporations.

Appendix

A) Influence on the corporate network:
   In order to determine this vector three aspects were taken into consideration. First the respondents were asked to indicate to what extent the German subsidiary's distinctive competencies in research and development activities are of use for other units in the foreign corporation. Secondly the respondents had to estimate the impact of the German subsidiary on the development of research and development

competencies in other units within the foreign corporation. Finally the managers were asked to state to what extent the German subsidiary had influenced the corporate investments in R&D and the corporate introduction of new products.

B) *Influence from the corporate network:*
In order to trace this vector the respondents were asked to indicate which relationships with the following counterparts had an impact on the development of the German subsidiary's distinctive competencies.
   1) The foreign corporate headquarter
   2) Specific internal corporate customers
   3) Specific internal corporate suppliers
   4) Specific corporate R&D units

C) *Influence on the external business network:*
This vector was determined by asking the managers to estimate the extent of contributing influence exerted by the German subsidiary on its local business environment when it comes to the creation of new technology, the diffusion of technology or the development of start-up companies.

D) *Influence from the external network:*
In order to trace this vector the respondents were asked to indicate which relationships with the following counterparts had an impact on the development of the German subsidiary's distinctive competencies.
   1) Specific external market customers
   2) Specific external market suppliers
   3) Specific distributors
   4) Specific competitors
   5) Specific external R&D units
   6) Governmental institution

References

Aldrich, H. & Herker, D. (1977). Boundary spanning roles and organization structure. *Academy of Management Review*, April, 217–230.
Almeida, P. (1996). Knowledge sourcing by foreign multinationals: patent citation analysis in the U.S. semiconductor industry. *Strategic Management Journal 17*, Winter Special Issue, 155–165.

Andersson, U. (1997). *Subsidiary Network Embeddedness. Integration, Control and Influence in the Multinational Corporation.* Unpublished doctoral dissertation, Department of Business Studies, Uppsala University, Sweden.

Andersson, U. & Forsgren, M. (1994). *Degree of Integration in Some Swedish MNCs.* Working paper 1994/4, Department of Business Studies, Uppsala University, Sweden.

Andersson, U., Forsgren, M. & Holm, U. (1999). Subsidiary embeddedness, expected performance and MNC competence development. *Proceedings of the 25th Annual EIBA conference.* Manchester: European International Business Academy.

Andersson, M., Furu, P. & Holmstroem, C. (1999). *Development, Recognition, and Integration of Competence of Subsidiaries in the Multinational Corporation.* Proceedings of the 25th Annual EIBA conference. Manchester: European International Business Academy.

Bartlett, C. & Ghoshal, S. (1989). *Managing Across Borders. The Transnational Solution.* Boston Mass.: Harvard Business School Press.

Bendt, A. (2000). *Wissenstransfer in der Multinationalen Unternehmung.* Wiesbaden: Gabler.

Birkinshaw, J. & Hood, N. (1995). An empirical study of development processes in foreign owned subsidiaries in Canada and Scotland. In R. Schiattarella (ed.), *New Challenges for European and International Business.* Proceedings of the 21st Annual EIBA Conference. Urbino: European International Business Academy.

Buckley, P. & Casson, M. (1976). *The Future of the Multinational Enterprise.* Houndmills: The Macmillan Press.

Cantwell, J. (1991). A survey of theories of international production. In S. Pitelis & R. Sugden (eds), *The Nature of the Transnational Firm.* London: Routledge. 16–63.

Cantwell, J. & Janne, O. (1997). Technological globalisation and innovative centres. In K. Macharzina *et al.*, (eds), *Global Business in the Information Age.* Proceedings of the 23rd Annual EIBA Conference Stuttgart: University of Hohenheim. 103–127.

Cantwell, J. & Piscitello, L. (1997). The emergence of corporate international networks for the accumulation of dispersed technological competences. In K. Macharzina *et al.*, (eds), *Global Business in the Information Age.* Proceedings of the 23rd Annual EIBA Conference Stuttgart: University of Hohenheim. 165–191.

Caves, R. (1971). Industrial economics and foreign investment. *Journal of World Trade Law, 5,* 303–314.

Caves, R. (1982). *Multinational Enterprise and Economic Analysis.* Cambridge: Cambridge University Press.

Chesnais, F. (1988). Multinational enterprise and the international diffusion of technology. In G. Dosi *et al.* (eds), *Technical Change and Economic Theory.* London: Pinter Publishers. 496–527.

Cohen, W. & Levinthal, D. (1989). Innovation and learning: the two faces of R&D. *Economic Journal, 141,* 569–596.

Conner, K. & Prahalad, C. (1996). A Resource-based theory of the firm. Kowledge versus opportunism. *Organization Science, 7,* 477–501.

Crozier, M. and Friedberg, E. (1979). *Macht und Organization: Die Zwaenge Kollektiven Handelns.* Koenigstein: Athenaeum.

Doz, Y., Asakawa, K., Santos, J. & Williamson, P. (1997). *The Metanational Corporation.* Working paper 97/60/SM. Fontainebleau: INSEAD.

Dunning, J. (1994). Re-evaluating the benefits of foreign direct investment. *Transnational Corporations, 3,* 23–51.

Dunning, J. (1999). The changing nature of firms and governments in a knowledge-based globalizing economy. In J. Engelhard & W. Oechsler. (eds), *Internationales Management.* Wiesbaden: Gabler. 3–20.

Easton, G. (1992): Industrial networks: a review. In: B. Axelsson & G. Easton (eds), *Industrial Networks. A New View of Reality.* London: Routledge. 3–17.

Fayerweather, J. (1969): *International Business Management — A Conceptual Framework.* New York: McGraw Hill.

Fors, G. (1996). *R&D and Technology Transfer by Multinational Enterprises.* Unpublished doctoral dissertation. Stockholm: Stockholm School of Economics.

Forsgren, M. (1997). The advantage paradox of the multinational corporation. In I. Bjoerkman & M. Forsgren (eds), *The Nature of the International Firm.* Copenhagen: Munksgaard International. 69–85.

Forsgren, U., Holm, U., Pedersen, T. & Sharma, D. (1999). *The Subsidiary Role for MNC Competence Development — Information Bridgehead or Competence Distributor?* Proceedings of the 25th Annual EIBA conference. Manchester: European International Business Academy.

Forsgren, M., Holm, U. & Thilenius, P. (1997). Network infusion in the multinational corporation. In I. Bjoerkman & M. Forsgren (eds), *The Nature of the International Firm.* Copenhagen: Munksgaard International. 475–494.

Ghoshal, S. (1987). Global strategy: an organizing framework. *Strategic Management Journal, 8,* 425–440.

Ghoshal, S. & Bartlett, C. (1990): The multinational corporation as an interorganizational network. *Academy of Management Review, 15,* 603–625.

Ghoshal, S. & Bartlett, C. (1998). *The Individualized Corporation. A Fundamentally New Approach to Management.* London: Heinemann.

Granovetter, M. (1985). Economic action and social structure: the problem of embeddedness. *American Journal of Sociology, 91,* 481–510.

Gupta, A. & Govindarajan, V. (1991). Knowledge flows and the structure of control within the multinational corporation. *Academy of Management Review, 16,* 768–792.

Gupta, A, & Govindarajan, V. (1994). Organizing for knowledge flows within MNCs. *International Business Review, 3,* 443–457.

Hakanson, L. & Nobel, R. (1998). Organizational characteristics and reverse technology transfer. In Jaffe *et al.*, (eds), *International Business Strategies and Middle East Regional Cooperation*. Proceedings of the 24th Annual EIBA conference. Jerusalem: European International Business Academy.

Hakansson, H. & Johanson, J. (1993). Networks as a governance structure. In E. Grabher (ed.), *The Embedded Firm: On the Socioeconomics of Industrial Networks*. London: Routledge.

Hedlund, G. (1986). The hypermodern MNC — a heterarchy? *Human Resource Management, 25,* 9–35.

Hedlund, G. (1999). The intensity and extensity of knowledge and the multinational corporation as a nearly recomposable system (NRS). *Management International Review, 39,* Special Issue, 5–44.

Hennart, J. (1991). The transaction cost theory of the multinational enterprise. In C. Pitelis & R. Sugden (eds), *The Nature of the Transnational Firm*. London: Routledge. 81–116.

Hymer, S. (1976). *The International Operations of National Firms: A Study of Direct Foreign Investment*. Cambridge Mas.: MIT Press.

Johanson, J. & Vahlne, J.-E. (1977). The internationalization process of the firm. *Journal of International Business Studies, 8,* 23–32.

Johanson, J. & Vahlne, J-E. (1990). The mechanism of internationalization. *International Market Review, 7,* 11–24.

Johnson, H. (1970). The efficiency and welfare implications of the international corporation. In C. Kindleberger (ed.), *The International Corporation*. London: MIT Press. 35–56.

Keller, R. & Holland, W. (1975). Boundary-spanning roles in a research and development organization. *Academy of Management Journal, 18,* 388–393.

Kindleberger, C. (1969). *American Business Abroad: Six Lectures on Direct Investments*. New Haven Conn.: Yale University Press.

Kogut, B. (1989). A note on global strategies. *Strategic Management Journal, 10,* 383–389.

Kogut, B. & Zander, U. (1993). Knowledge of the firm and the evolution theory of the multinational corporation. *Journal of International Business Studies, 24,* 625–645.

Kogut, B. & Zander, U. (1992). Knowledge of the firm, combinative capabilities and the replication technology. *Organization Studies, 3,* 383–397.

Leifer, R. & Delbecq, A. (1978). Organizational/environmental interchange. *Academy of Management Review,* January, 40–50.

Mansfield, E. & Romeo, A. (1980). Technology transfer to overseas subsidiaries by US-based firms. *Quarterly Journal of Economics,* December, 737–750.

Mansfield, E. & Romeo, A. (1984). "Reverse" transfer of technology from overseas subsidiaries to American firms. *IEEE Transaction on Engineering Management, EM-31,* 122–127.

Mansfield, E., Romeo, A. & Schwartz, M. (1983). New findings in technology transfer, productivity and economic policy. *Research Management, 26,* 11–21.

Mariotti, S. & Piscitello, L. (1995). Information cost and location of FDIs within the host country: Empirical evidence from Italy. *Journal of International Business Studies, 26,* 815–842.

DeMeyer, A. (1992). Management of international R&D operations. In O. Granstrand *et al.,* (eds), *Technology Management and International Business.* Chichester: John Wiley & Sons. 163–179.

Pearce, R. & Singh, S. (1992). Internationalisation of research and development among the world's leading enterprizes: survey analysis of organization and motivation. In O. Granstrand *et al.,* (eds), *Technology Management and International Business.* Chichester: John Wiley & Sons. 137–162.

Porter, M. (1990). *The Competitive Advantage of Nations.* New York: The Free Press.

Powell, W., Kogut, B. & Smith-Doerr, C. (1996). Internationalisation, collaboration and the locus of innovation: networks of learning in biotechnology. *Administrative Science Quarterly, 41,* 116–137.

Randoy, T. & Li, J. (1998). Global resource flows and MNE network integration. In J. Birkinshaw & N. Hood (eds), *Multinational Corporate Evolution and Subsidiary Development.* London: Macmillan Press. 76–101.

Rugman, A. (1980). Internalization as a general theory of foreign direct investment. *Weltwirtschaftliches Archiv, 116,* 365–379.

Rugman, A. & Verbeke, A. (2001). Subsidiary-specific advantages in multinational enterprises. *Strategic Management Journal, 22,* 237–250.

Schmid, S., Baeurle, I. & Kutschker, M. (1998). *Tochtergesellschaften in International Taetigen Unternehmen.* DiskussionsBeitraege der Wirtschaftswissenschaftlichen Fakultaet, Nr. 104, Katholische Universitaet Eichstaett.

Spekman, R. (1979). Influence and information: an exploratory investigation of the boundary role person's basis of power. *Academy of Management Journal, 22,* 104–117.

Teece, D. (1981). The multinational enterprise: market failure and market power considerations. *Sloan Management Review,* Spring, 3–17.

Thorelli, H. (1966). The multinational corporation as a change agent. *Southern Journal of Business, 1,* 1–9.

Tsai, W. & Ghoshal, S. (1998). Social capital and value creation. *Academy of Management Journal, 41,* 464–476.

Tsurumi, Y. (1979). Two models of corporation and international transfer of technology. *Columbia Journal of World Business,* Summer, 43–50.

Tushman, M. & Scanlan, T. (1981a). Characteristics and external orientations of boundary spanning individuals. *Academy of Management Journal, 24,* 83–98.

Tushman, M. & Scanlan, T. (1981b). Boundary spanning individuals: their role in information transfer and their antecedents. *Academy of Management Journal, 24,* 289–305.

UNCTAD (1999). *World Investment Report 1999 — Foreign Direct Investment and the Challenge of Development*. New York: United Nations.

Yamin, M. (1997). An evolutionary analysis of subsidiary innovation and reverse transfer in multinational companies. In K. Macharzina *et al.*, (eds), *Global Business in the Information Age*. Proceedings of the 23rd Annual EIBA Conference. Stuttgart: University of Hohenheim.

Young, S., Hood, N. & Hamill, J. (1988). *Foreign Multinationals and the British Economy*. London: Croom Helm.

Chapter 6

Subsidiary Entrepreneurship and the Advantage of Multinationality

Mohammad Yamin

Introduction

This paper proposes a view of the advantage of multinationality based on the premise that in a complex, multiunit organisation, autonomous action at 'subsidiary' levels has strategic consequences beneficial to the organisation as a whole. From this perspective, the advantage of multi-nationality is that it is an organisational structure in which the possibi-lities for autonomous action in subsidiaries are enhanced. More specifically, we argue that, compared to sub-units of a national firm, foreign subsidiaries in an MNE are 'organisationally isolated' from the centre. Organisational isolation is likely to be greater in multinational compared to multi-unit national firms because two key mechanisms that help to provide cross-unit organisational integration, namely, replication of routines and (formal and informal) control instruments work less effectively *across national boundaries than within the same country*. We argue that organisational isolation is beneficial to the MNE as a whole. Thus, because organisational isolation enhances the potential for entre-preneurial action by subsidiaries, it increases the likelihood of a *differ-entiated* set of competencies within the MNE the existence of which can counteract strategic inertia at the HQ and improve adaptive capabilities in the MNE.

In developing the argument of the paper we assume that MNE sub-sidiaries are established through Greenfield entry. MNE expansion

Critical Perspectives on Internationalisation, pp. 133–150.
ISBN: 0-08-044035-5

through mergers and acquisition does not totally invalidate the advantage of multinationality as envisaged in this paper though it may weaken it. This is clearly a limitation of the argument proposed in the paper. We return to this issue in the concluding section of the paper. A more crucial assumption is that MNE subsidiaries and sub-units of national firms have equal support in terms of the provision of key assets by the organisation of which they are a part. It is also important to stress that the comparison is specifically with multi-unit or multi-business national firms rather than with national firms in general. This comparative context is appropriate as we wish to stress the role of multinationality in counteracting the strategic inertia that may characterise large and multi-unit organisations

The remainder of the paper is organised as follows. Section II explains the conceptual basis of the argument presented in this paper. This relates to the organisational consequences of autonomous action within complex (by which we mean large, multi-unit and multi-layered) organisations. Section III provides an explanation of the basic proposition advanced in this paper, namely that, ceteris paribus, MNEs are subject to a greater degree of organisational isolation compared to multi-unit national firms. Sections IV and V draw out the implications of organisational isolation for subsidiaries and for the MNE as a whole. Section VI concludes the paper by pointing out the limitations and some implications of the argument advanced in the paper.

Conceptual Background: Organisational Consequences of Autonomous Action

A number of management scholars have highlighted the relevance of exploration in the strategic activities of firms (e.g., Hedlund & Rolander, 1990; March, 1991; Levinthal & March, 1993). Thus whereas exploitation is the utilization, refinement and extension of existing capabilities, exploration is the search for alternative capabilities that may underpin future exploitative potential. The value of exploratory activities is therefore that they help to create *adaptive* capabilities for the organisation. Of course, it is true that organisations cannot focus exclusively on either exploitation or exploration and that maintaining an appropriate balance between exploration and exploitation 'is a primary factor in system survival and prosperity' (March, 1991). However it is generally agreed that 'exploitation drives out exploration' (Birkinshaw & Ridderstrale, 1999;

Levinthal & March, 1993; March, 1991). Whilst in most organisations exploratory/adaptive capabilities could be beneficially enhanced, the question of interest to this paper is what factors may determine the exploratory potential of companies.

We suggest that the ability of 'subsidiary' units within an organisation to undertake initiatives independently of the centre is an indication of that organisation's exploratory capabilities. In this sense, exploratory capability is at least partly a consequence of the 'weakness' of the centre to control the behaviour of sub-units. In tightly controlled multi-unit organisations, the ability of sub-units to detect new ideas, develop initiatives around these ideas and hence generate new 'local' competencies is severely curtailed. In such corporations exploratory capability is likely to be low.

Linking an organisation's exploratory potential with its sub-units' ability to undertake initiative reflects the premise that exploratory initiatives are unlikely to stem from the centre. The reason for this is that top decision-makers are likely to have a strong commitment to the firm's current concept of strategy and thus a preference for activities that are 'consistent' with it. Typically, top executives display a high degree of attachment to the *status quo* (Hambrick *et al.,* 1993). And, as Burgelman (1983) suggests, because top managers have an inflexible stance in relation to current strategy, their 'capacity to deal with substantial issues pertaining to new technological and market developments can be expected to be low'. Thus even in apparently dynamic and progressively managed companies, there is a remarkable degree of inertia in official corporate strategy. Top level commitment to current strategy remains strong even when environmental changes have eroded the value of the competencies that underlined the strategy (Burgelman, 1994).

By comparison, operational and middle-level managers are naturally sensitised or exposed to exploratory stimuli because, to a large extent, the operational locus *is* where the opportunities and pressures for change are most keenly felt (Brown & Duguid, 1991; Dutton *et al.,* 1997). Top managers are deprived from this important source of exploratory stimuli, because by the very nature of their position in the organisation, they are too distant or removed both spatially and cognitively, from the operational locus.

Furthermore, top management's inflexible adherence to the current concept of corporate strategy inevitably implies that it overlooks or even suppresses non-canonical knowledge at the 'periphery' or at the operational domain. In Burgelman's words, top managers rely 'on the structural context to bring autonomous behaviour under control' (1983). As Birkinshaw and Ridderstrale (1999) convincingly argue, corporations develop a strong 'immune system' the function of which is to repel or resist initiatives even though they may promise an improvement in performance.

Consequently, exploratory activities are often manifested as 'autonomous behaviour' — that is, strategic activities by operational and middle-level managers that are not authorised or even encouraged by top level decision-makers in the firm (Birkinshaw & Hood, 1998; Burgelman, 1983). And, given the multi-layered structure of large organisations, some leeway or opportunity is likely to exist for these managers to undertake autonomous activities unnoticed by top decision-makers. Thus some autonomous behaviour is inevitable in complex organisations. The importance of autonomous behaviour is that new strategic directions are often charted through initiatives by the operational and middle level mangers. In fact, as Burgelman (1991; 1994) suggests, in companies where autonomous activities are strong, strategy making should not be considered purely as a prerogative of the top decision-makers. Rather, strategy making should be viewed in terms of an 'intra-organisational ecology' or internal selection environment in which autonomous initiatives *offer strategic choices to top management.* An immediate advantage of this is that considering simultaneous alternatives may reduce excessive commitment to any one strategic option. The danger that core competencies become core rigidities may be somewhat reduced (Dutton *et al.,* 1997; Leonard-Barton, 1992). Furthermore, given that environmental changes will inevitably undermine the value of competencies that underpin any current strategy, the existence of alternative capabilities within the firm enhances adaptive capabilities.

The Advantage of Multinationality: The Relevance of Organisational Isolation

A stream of recent literature has focused on the development of MNE subsidiary capabilities for strategic actions. Different authors have focussed on different manifestations of this such as competence for product development (e.g., Andersson & Forsgren, 1996; Andersson & Pahlberg, 1997; Forsgren *et al.,* 1999a; Fratocchi & Holm, 1998); subsidiary mandate development (Birkinshaw, 1996; Birkinshaw & Hood, 1998); subsidiary initiatives and entrepreneurship (Birkinshaw, 1997; Birkinshaw

& Ridderstrale, 1999) and subsidiary contribution to the development of firm-specific assets in MNEs (Birkinshaw *et al.*, 1998). The question of interest to this paper is whether the propensity for initiative and autonomous competence development is greater for MNE subsidiaries compared to sub-units of national firms? We believe that the answer to this question is affirmative.

The reason for this is rooted in the fact that subsidiaries are a part of an organisation that is dispersed internationally. Note that, by assumption, the advantage envisaged does not derive from *access* to the resources (such as R&D output from the centre or other units) of the MNE organisation. On the contrary, the emphasis is on the fact that, compared to a sub-unit of a national firm, the subsidiary operates in an organisational context characterised by international dispersal and, consequently, by a greater degree of organisational separation between different units. Units of the MNE are not only separated by geographical distance (which may be equally the case for national firms) but also by the fact they operate within distinct legal, political, cultural and economic domains. Any organisation whose sub-units operate in fragmented environments may be characterised by some degree of organisational 'isolation'. We define organisational 'isolation' as a condition, in which *the constraints* forcing sub-unit fidelity to organisational norms and strategies are weak. Note that the emphasis is on weak constraints. The sub-unit may choose to conform to organisational norms or strategies but the constraints are relatively ineffective. Our basic proposition is that MNEs are subject to a greater degree of 'organisational isolation' than multi-unit national firms are. The logic underlying this proposition is that, compared to national firms, MNEs are characterised to a greater extent by the following interdependent phenomena:

1) Incomplete control and coordination from the centre;
2) Imperfect organisational replication.

Incomplete Control and Coordination from the Centre

There is a large literature addressing control and co-ordination issues in MNEs (e.g., Birkinshaw & Morrison, 1995; Ghoshal *et al.*, 1994; Ghoshal & Nohira, 1989; Hennart, 1993; Nohira & Ghoshal, 1994; Roth & O'Donnell, 1996). The starting point of this literature is the recognition that in MNEs 'the control problem is particularly acute' (Hennart, 1993). However, no study explicitly compares MNEs and national firms from the control perspective. Nevertheless, it is self-evident that the control environment facing MNEs is significantly more demanding. As will be pointed out more fully in the next sub-section, each subsidiary will operate in an environment that is increasingly 'enacted' by itself in terms of more extensive and intensive linkages in the host market. Holm *et al.* (1995) have suggested that a subsidiary's 'network context' is not necessarily transparent and hence the headquarters' ability to effectively control the subsidiary is progressively compromised.

Furthermore, the MNE's control environment is significantly more variegated than that faced by national firms. Each subsidiary presents the MNE with a somewhat differentiated control task depending on the characteristics of the environment in which it is operating and the organisational capabilities that the subsidiary possesses (Ghoshal & Nohira, 1989; Nohira & Ghoshal, 1994). Sub-units within a national firm, by comparison, operate in a relatively more homogenous environment. For MNEs greater differentiation at the subsidiary level, clearly translates to significant control-task complexity at the headquarter level.

The complexity is intensified as control is often multi-dimensional, involving not only elements of centralisation and formalisation but also 'more subtle' informal methods including normative integration (Martinez & Jarillio, 1989). Recent empirical analysis by Birkinshaw and Morrison (1995) indicates a high reliance on normative integration for all categories of subsidiaries. This is an interesting finding. Traditional control mechanisms — centralisation and formalisation — may be relatively ineffective and Birkinshaw and Morrison's finding may indicate the gradual recognition of this by the MNEs. As Sundram and Black (1992) note, an MNE is affected by multiple sources of external (legal and political) authority while all sub-units of a national firm reside within a single external authority domain. Consequently, the parent in a multi-unit national firm would be less constrained in imposing conformity to organisational goals by sub-units, as long as the rules of external authority allows such imposition. On the other hand, the ability of the MNE parent to demand or impose conformity to organisational goals is constrained by the fact that the sub-units reside in different legal and political domains. This has an important implication for control mechanisms in MNEs. In particular, it may be *impossible* for the parent to force all subsidiaries to implement centrally made decisions that run counter to pressures in the host country. Thus, within an MNE, the prevalence of socialisation as a coordination mechanism 'may substitute for the void in the superstructure to mediate conflicts' (Sundram & Black, 1992).

Broadly speaking, the control literature has been concerned with determining the 'right' or 'optimal' degree of control and the appropriate mix of instruments to achieve it. The relevant point, from the perspective of this paper, is that the MNE will inevitably experience a residual degree of control 'gap'. Whilst in any complex system the 'optimal' degree of control falls short of complete control (reflecting rising marginal control cots), it is likely that this residual is *greater in an MNE* than in a comparable (in terms of size, number of sub-units, business activity etc) national firm. Furthermore, it is reasonable to suggest that a subsidiary of an MNE has more opportunity for utilising a given level of 'control gap' than a sub-unit of a national company. The MNE subsidiary can, more easily than a sub-unit of a national firm, engage in an 'unauthorised' initiative that is oriented towards the local market and external networks. The process of developing such initiatives is more likely to remain 'hidden' from the centre until it is a fait accompli (Birkinshaw, 1996; Birkinshaw & Ridderstrale, 1999).

Imperfect Organisational Replication and the Development of Subsidiary Capabilities

Kogut and Zander (1993) note that the 'cornerstone' of their evolutionary approach to the theory of the MNE is the 'treatment of the firm as a social community whose productive knowledge defines a comparative advantage'. However, precisely because a firm is a social community, its extension across *national boundaries* must be particularly problematic as national boundaries demarcate different societal arrangements. In fact this is the reasoning behind the Uppsala model of internationalisation in which 'psychic distance' between countries is the main obstacle to the rapid expansion of foreign operations. More recent analyses articulate a similar logic. For example Kogut (1991) and Kostova (1999) argue that 'organisational principles' and 'strategic organisational practices' are deeply embedded both locationally and organisationally and hence are relatively immobile compared to well packaged or embodied technologies (see also Badaracco, 1991; Sölvell & Zander, 1998).

More generally, as Nelson and Winter (1982) have pointed out, the feasibility of close (let alone perfect) organisational replication is quite problematic. Replication is practically always partial. Organisational routines, it may be said, do not 'travel' well. Knowledge, and more generally routines that are transferred to the subsidiary by the parent lose some of their value and effectiveness simply because they are largely context dependent (Madhok, 1997). Significantly, Nelson and Winter (1982) note that routines 'have their clearest relevance at the establishment level' and that 'the memory of an organisation that comprises many *widely separated establishments* exists mainly in the establishments' (emphasis added). If 'widely separated establishments' are located in different countries, then it is only reasonable to assume that the original, replicated routines only provide a rather weak 'glue' for coupling or binding the different establishments (see also Kilduff, 1992; 1993). The work of Szulanski (1996) is also useful in this context. His empirical investigation indicated that internal transfers of best practices are mainly impeded by three factors: 'causal ambiguity' (of knowledge to be transferred), lack of 'absorptive capacity' by the recipient and 'arduous' relationship between the source and the recipient. The last factor may be particularly relevant in the present context; internal transfers, of routines (e.g. best practices) across national boundaries (within MNEs) may, other things being equal, encounter a more 'arduous context' than internal transfers within a national firm. Furthermore, it is important to consider the possibility that subsidiaries cannot be merely *passive* recipients of routines. In fact, precisely because initial organisational replication from the parent to the subsidiary is imperfect and incomplete, a process may be triggered that propels the long-term development of the subsidiary. Because subsidiaries inevitably inherit an incomplete 'template', they are *forced* to engage in a process of searching for market and other knowledge about the local environment. Such knowledge, due to its often tacit, localized and experiential nature, will not be transparent to the parent and could not thus have been given to the subsidiary 'at birth'. Incomplete replication makes it imperative that the subsidiary establishes external (to the MNE) avenues for attracting additional resources, particularly from its host environment and consequently it may well develop linkages with various information, finance, technology and production oriented networks in the host country. Thus 'embeddedness' in external networks may be viewed as a deliberate compensation strategy by the subsidiary to 'anchor' itself onto a significant resource base.

Implications of Organisational Isolation for Subsidiaries

The discussion in the previous section suggests that, compared to subunits of a national company, MNE subsidiaries are more likely to develop an 'entrepreneurial' orientation. One consequence of weak orga-nisational ties is that sub-units have greater search opportunities and tend to be more adaptive than sub-units in tightly coupled organisations (Hansen, 1999). More specifically, Birkinshaw, (1997) identifies three aspects of an entrepreneurial orientation: 'a predisposition to proactive or risk- taking behaviour', 'use of resources beyond the individual's direct control' and 'departure from existing practices'.

We argue that the subsidiary's isolation from the rest of the MNE forces it to behave in ways similar to the above descriptions. For example, seeking linkages with local networks is essentially proactive or risk-taking behaviour for a foreign subsidiary, and it is in part motivated by gaining access to or benefiting from resources at present outside its control. In this sense, embeddedness of a foreign subsidiary is qualita-tively different when compared to that of 'native' companies. For a foreign subsidiary embeddedness is an *induced and proactive* process rather than a passive or 'natural' one. It signals a highly active stance with respect to the local environment in which the subsidiary finds itself. Finally, 'departure from existing practices' is, at least initially, what a subsidiary has to do to survive. This is simply the logical implication or consequence of imperfect organisational replication. It is also relevant that compared to sub-units of a national firm, a foreign subsidiary has (or, more accurately, gradually gains) greater independence to do what it has to.

Moreover, compared to its national competitors, a subsidiary's development is inevitably shaped by dual influences from the host environment and the MNE organisation (Rosenweig & Singh, 1991; Westney, 1993). A degree of diversity is 'built-in' in the perspective of the subsidiary. It is therefore less at risk of becoming too 'accultu-rated' or socialised into the host environment or to the MNE system and hence losing the entrepreneurial edge (Levinthal & March, 1993; March, 1991).

In summary, compared with a sub-unit of a national firm, an MNE subsidiary:

1) has a higher degree of organisational freedom to undertake initiatives;
2) by virtue of its *foreignness,* it faces greater pressure to develop cap-abilities appropriate to its local market and the various networks in which it needs to operate effectively;
3) by virtue of its membership of an *internationally dispersed organisation* it has a more diverse perspective (in terms of markets, technologies

and networks) that may enhance its ability to define and develop initiatives.

Thus, tentatively we can put forward the following hypothesis:

Hypothesis 1: Compared with sub-units of a national firm, MNE subsidiaries will display a greater degree of entrepreneurial orientation.

Will a foreign subsidiary also have an innovative advantage over its national competitors? To a certain degree, of course, entrepreneurial and innovative processes do overlap. To the extent that entrepreneurship is a precursor of innovation, the foreign subsidiary will perceive greater opportunities for innovation in a given environment compared to subunits of national firms. Furthermore the subsidiary's linkages with exchange partners in production and technology networks tend to boost its innovative capabilities. (Andersson & Forsgren, 1996; Andersson & Pahlberg, 1997; Forsgren *et al.*, 1999a). Clearly, membership in local networks also gives the subsidiary a degree of independence from the rest of the corporate system (Andersson & Pahlberg, 1997) and such independence also reinforces the subsidiary's ability to devote resources to its innovative projects. There are clearly a number of other factors that will effect innovative success. For example, the importance attached to customer or user needs, and the effective coordination of R&D activities with marketing and production are widely recognised as important to innovative success. However there is no analytical reason to expect that multinationality as such will affect these factors very strongly one way or another. Thus, given the aforementioned advantages that may be enjoyed by foreign subsidiaries, we put forward the following hypothesis:

Hypothesis 2: Compared with sub-units of a national firm, MNE subsidiaries will have a greater ability to undertake innovation successfully.

Implications of Organisational Isolation for the Development of the MNE as a Whole

The concept of organisation isolation suggests that the MNE is likely to develop into differentiated system, and that the degree of differentiation and sub-unit diversity within MNEs is, ceteris paribus, greater than in national firms. Initially, of course, subsidiary capabilities are limited and rely totally on technological and other skills transferred from the parent. In a 'young' MNE therefore, there may be little differentiation. However, the evolution of each subsidiary reflects a unique combination of market, technological and institutional influences that may give the subsidiary distinctive market and technological capabilities. By comparison, sub-units of a national firm will have capabilities more closely *tied* to that of the parent unit and thus the national firm will display a lower degree of differentiation in terms of competencies. Recent work by Zander (1998; 1999) provides interesting evidence on the pattern of technological differentiation within MNEs. He identifies four patterns for Swedish MNEs reflecting different combinations of technological duplication and diversification. Duplicated capabilities refer to subsidiary capabilities in the same broad field as the parent. It is important to note that 'duplication' of technological capabilities does not imply the absence of differentiation within the MNE. As Zander (1998; 1999) notes, subsidiaries with duplicated capabilities have evolved unique competencies in adapting, developing and upgrading it. Furthermore, Zander (1999) suggests that most MNEs included in his study have been evolving towards increasing technological diversification and dispersal whereby subsidiaries have developed technological competencies in different direction from those of the parent unit.

The existence of differentiated competencies within the MNE suggests that it should be viewed as a *federation* rather than as a unitary system (Ghoshal & Bartlett, 1993) in which the possibilities for inter-unit transfers are relatively limited. Limited intra-MNE transferability results from exactly the same considerations that make subsidiary competencies differentiated in the first place. Thus even though the subsidiary's capabilities may be based on technological and market skills inherited from the parent, subsequent development will be increasingly shaped by the subsidiary's attempt to meet the market and competitive challenges in the host country or in its regional/global mandate areas. From the point of view of the subsidiary, it becomes more important to nurture local/regional relationships by tailoring innovation to customer needs than to produce less customised, or more 'standardised' products that may also be of interest to other units within the MNE as a whole.

Low network transferability could be interpreted as implying that subsidiary competencies have only a limited value for the MNE as a whole (Forsgren, 1997). This is a valid inference in the context of the MNE's *current or dominant* strategy and in relation to the set of competencies that underpin this strategy. From this perspective, subsidiary competencies will tend to be highly valued by the centre only if they can be utilised to support company-wide products and technologies. Subsidiary competencies that do not easily fit into the MNE's current strategy may impose extra control and co-ordination costs on the MNE.

However, from the point of view of the MNE's adaptive capabilities — its ability to replace current competencies — low transferability may be an advantage. For the MNE as a whole, low transferability does imply that, (some) subsidiary competencies are currently partially 'redundant' as they are utilised only locally, with limited intra-MNE transfers. However, such redundancy can be a dynamic advantage in a rapidly changing environment. The deliberate creation of spare capacity has long been recognised as an important competitive instrument in oligopolistic markets (e.g., Spence, 1977; Steindl, 1976). In an MNE, 'spare capacity', in form of differentiated but under-utilised competencies within subsidiaries is an unintended consequence of organisational isolation. Low network transferability is a necessary condition for the maintenance of differentiation and diversity within the MNE. If it were the case that knowledge transfers across national boundaries were totally smooth and 'un-sticky', the organisational differentiation that is characteristics of MNEs would itself be gradually eroded. In this sense, organisational isolation helps both to generate and maintain differentiation within the MNE. In terms of Burgelman's (1991) analysis, this means that the MNE possesses a richer internal selection environment. The existence of differentiated competencies potentially provides the MNE with a wide range of strategic choices. If major technological or market changes undermine the value of the MNE's currently dominant technology, then alternative proven competencies, which can become the basis of a new strategic direction for the MNE, may well exist within the network. In particular, subsidiaries that have successfully gained global mandates through their own initiatives will have broadly-based competencies that can underpin a new strategic direction for the MNE as a whole (Birkinshaw *et al.*, 1998). Such transformation is by no means an easy process, a fact confirmed by recent case studies (Burgelman, 1994; Macnamara & Baden Fuller, 1999). But the prior existence of a wider range of alternative competencies within an MNE compared to a national firm gives the former a potential advantage. A major obstacle facing organisational renewal is the risk associated with abandoning current competencies when new competencies are not fully operational (Kogut & Zander, 1992; Macnamara & Baden Fuller, 1999). This risk is clearly attenuated in an MNC to the extent that it may avoid the need to generate wholly new competencies. In this sense, it can be said that organisational isolation may enhance the survival prospects of an MNE.

Concluding Remarks

This paper has argued that a key advantage of multinationality is that its dispersed structure *inadvertently* creates conditions conducive to entrepreneurial and innovative activities by the subsidiaries. This is a valued characteristic of the MNE as a generic organisational form if one accepts a) the view that, the hierarchical structure of large firms tends to frustrate entrepreneurial and innovative activities at the 'periphery' and b) that this is an undesirable outcome. The notion that in most organisations, 'exploitation drives out exploration' holds that both these statements are true. From this perspective, the advantage of multinationality can be captured in the following statement: *multinationality evens out the odds between exploitative and exploratory aspects of firm activities.*

It is important to stress that the conclusion of this paper is based on a particular organisational attribute of MNEs. Thus we envisage 'isolation' as a structural attribute of a multi-unit organisation the impact of which, ceteris paribus, is to weaken the constraints on sub units. A limitation of the analysis is that we have not considered managerial processes or policies. Clearly managerial authority can in principle be used to counter (or, of course, reinforce) the impact of isolation. It is always possible for the centre to create monitoring structures and control devices to enforce a high degree of conformity by sub-units. This can extend to limiting the degree and scope of subsidiary initiatives. However whilst it is clearly feasible for the centre to impose a tight control regime, the logic of organisation isolation suggest that this can only be achieved at great costs in terms of the amount of time and effort that headquarter managers would need to devote to the control function.

Another limitation of our analysis is the assumption that all subsidiaries are greenfield. This is clearly unrealistic as perhaps a majority of subsidiaries are formed through acquisition of local firms. Furthermore it is less clear analytically whether acquired subsidiaries would be more entrepreneurial than national sub-units. On the one hand, acquired subsidiaries can be at least as autonomous as Greenfield subsidiaries. Furthermore, the fact that acquired subsidiaries operate in an internationally dispersed organisation may widen subsidiary management outlook and thus sharpen their entrepreneurial edge. On the other hand, the pressure to acquire new local skills and relationships — a key driver for subsidiary entrepreneurship — would be lacking in the case of acquired subsidiaries. Overall it would seem that for MNE systems that have expanded through acquisition, the advantage we have envisaged is certainly weakened. This suggests that the proposition of this paper should be modified to state that organisational isolation creates an advantage for organically expanded MNEs.

One implication of the analysis deserves mention. Traditionally the multinational is viewed as an institution for the international transfer of knowledge from the centre. Subsidiaries embody advantages generated by the parent and this more than compensate the disadvantage of foreignness. More recently the multinational is viewed as an institution not only for the international transfer of knowledge but also for international generation of knowledge. The analysis of this paper suggests an additional function of multinationality — to encourage sub-units to innovate locally. To the extent that such innovations reflect the host economy's resource structure and institutions, multinationality may be viewed as helping to stimulate the local economy's innovative potential. A related implication is that multinationality actually accentuates technological and innovative diversities across nations rather than generating homogeneity.

Acknowledgements

I am grateful to an anonymous reviewer and to Mats Forsgren for a number of useful comments and suggestions. I am also grateful to Torben Pedersen for a number of stimulating discussions around the topic of this paper. An earlier version of this paper was presented at seminars in Copenhagen Business School, IIB Stockholm School of Economics and at the Department of Business Studies, Uppsala University. I am grateful to participants in all these seminars for a number of valuable comments and suggestions. I would also like to thank Fred Burton for his comments on the first version of this paper. The usual caveat applies.

References

Andersson, U. & Forsgren, M. (1996). Subsidiary embeddedness and control in the multinational corporation. *International Business Review*, 5, 425–446

Andersson, U. & Pahlberg, C. (1997). Subsidiary influence and strategic behaviour in MNCs: an empirical study. *International Business Review*, 3, 319–334.

Badaracco, J. (1991). *The Knowledge Link: How Firms Compete Through Strategic Alliances.* Boston: Harvard Business School Press.

Bartlett, C. & Ghoshal, S. (1990). Managing innovations in the transnational corporation. In C. Bartlett *et al.*, (eds), *Managing the Global Firm.* London: Routledge.

Birkinshaw, J. (1996). How multinational subsidiary mandates are gained and lost. *Journal of International Business Studies, 3,* 467–496.

Birkinshaw, J. (1997). Entrepreneurship in multinational corporations: the characteristics of subsidiary initiatives. *Strategic Management Journal, 3,* 207–230.

Birkinshaw, J. & Hood, N. (1998). Multinational subsidiary evolution: capability and charter change in foreign-owned subsidiaries. *Academy of Management Review, 4,* 773–796.

Birkinshaw, J., Hood, N. & Johnsson, S. (1998), Building firm specific advantages in multinational corporations: the role of subsidiary initiative. *Strategic Management Journal, 3,* 221–241.

Birkinshaw, J. & Morrison, A. (1995). Configurations of strategy and structure in subsidiaries of multinational corporation. *Journal of International Business Studies, 4,* 729–754.

Birkinshaw, J. & Ridderstrale, J. (1999). Fighting the corporate immune system: a process study of subsidiary initiatives in multinational corporations. *International Business Review, 2,*149–180.

Brown J. & Duguid, P. (1991). Organisational learning and communities of practice: towards a unified view of working, learning and innovation. *Organisation Science, 1,* 41–57.

Burgelman, R. (1983). A model of the interaction of strategic behaviour, corporate context, and the concept of strategy. *Academy of Management Review, 1,* 61–70.

Burgelman, R. (1991). Intraorganisational ecology of strategy making and organisational adaptation: theory and field research. *Organisation Science, 3,* 239–262.

Burgelman, R. (1994). Fading memories: a process theory of strategic business exit in dynamic environments. *Administrative Science Quarterly, 1,* 24–55.

Cohen, W. & Levinthal, D. (1990). Absorptive capacity: a new perspective on learning and innovation. *Administrative Science Quarterly, 1,*128–152.

Dutton, J. *et al.*, (1997). Reading the wind: how middle managers assess the context for selling issues to top managers. *Strategic Management Journal, 5,* 407–425.

Forsgren, M. (1997). The advantage paradox of the multinational corporation. In I. Bjorkman & M. Forsgren (eds), *The Nature of the International Firm: Nordic Contributions to International Business Research.* Copenhagen: Copenhagen Business School Press.

Forsgren, M., Pedersen, T. & Foss, N. (1999a). Accounting for the strength of MNC subsidiaries: the case of foreign-owned firms in Denmark. *International Business Review, 2,* 181–196.

148 Mohammad Yamin

Forsgren. M., Holm, U., Pedersen, T. & Sharma, D. (1999b). The subsidiary role for MNC competence development: information bridgehead or competence distributor. In F. Burton *et al.,* (eds), *International Business and the Global Services Economy*. Proceedings of 25th Annual Conference of EIBA, Manchester

Fratocchi, L. & Holm, U. (1998). Centres of excellence in the international firm. In J. Birkinshaw & N. Hood (eds) *Multinational corporate Evolution and Subsidiary Development*. London: Macmillan.

Ghoshal, S. & Bartlett, C. (1993). The multinational corporation as an inter-organisational network. In S. Ghoshal & E. Westney (eds), *Organisational Theory and the Multinational Corporation*. New York: St Martin's Press.

Ghoshal, S., Korine, H. & Szulanski, G. (1994). Interunit communication in multinational corporations. *Management Science, 1*, 401–418.

Ghoshal, S. & Nohira, N. (1989). Internal differentiation within multinational companies. *Strategic Management Journal, 4*, 96–102.

Hambrick, D., Geletkanycz, M. & Fredrickson, J. (1993). Top executive commitment to the *status quo:* some tests of its determinants. *Strategic Management Journal, 6*, 401–418.

Hansen, M. (1999). The search-transfer problem: the role of weak ties in sharing knowledge across organisational subunits. *Administrative Science Quarterly, 44*, 82–111.

Hedlund, G. and Rolander, J. (1990). Action in heterarchies – new approaches to managing the MNC. In C. Bartlett *et al.* (eds), *Managing the Global Firm*. London: Routledge.

Hennart, J. (1993). Control in multinational firms: the role of price and hierarchy. In S. Ghoshal & E. Westney (eds), *Organisation Theory and the Multinational Corporation*. New York: St Martin's Press.

Holm, U., Johanson, J. & Thilenius, P. (1995). Headquarters knowledge of subsidiary network contexts in the multinational corporations. *International Studies of Management and Organisation, 1(2)*, 97–120.

Jarillio, J. & Martinez, J. (1990), Different roles for subsidiaries: the case of multinational Corporations in Spain. *Strategic Management Journal, 7*, 501–513.

Kilduff, M. (1992). Performance and interaction routines in multinational corporations. *Journal of International Business Studies, 1*, 133–146.

Kilduff, M. (1993). The reproduction of inertia in multinational corporations. In S. Ghoshal & E. Westney (eds), *Organisation Theory and the Multinational Corporation*. New York: St Martin's Press.

Kogut, B. (1991). Country capabilities and the permeability of borders. *Strategic Management Journal*, Special Issue, 33–48.

Kogut, B. & Zander, U. (1992). Knowledge of the firm: combinative capabilities and the replication of technology. *Organisation Science, 3*, 3.

Kogut, B. & Zander, U. (1993). Knowledge of the firm and the evolutionary theory of the multinational corporation. *Journal of International Business Studies, 4*, 625–646.

Kostova, T. (1999). Transnational transfer of strategic organisational practices: a contextual perspective. *Academy of Management Review, 2*, 308–322.

Leonard-Barton, D. (1992). Core capabilities and core rigidities: a paradox in managing new product development. *Strategic Management Journal,* 111–125.

Levinthal, D. & March, J. (1993). The myopia of learning. *Strategic Management Journal,* special issue, 95–113.

MacNamara, P. & Baden-Fuller, C. (1999). Lessons from the Celltech case: balancing knowledge exploration and exploitation in organisational renewal. *British Journal of Management, 4*, 291–315.

Madhok A. (1997). Costs, value and foreign market entry mode: the transaction and the firm. *Strategic Management Journal, 1*, 39–61.

March, J. (1991). Exploration and exploitation in organisational learning. *Organisation Science, 1, 15–28.*

Martinez, J. & Jarillio, J. (1989). The evolution of research on coordination mechanism in multinational corporations. *Journal of International Business Studies, 3*, 489–514.

Nelson, R. & Winter, S. (1982). *An Evolutionary Theory of Economic Change.* Boston: Harvard University Press.

Nohira, N. & Ghoshal, S. (1994). Differentiated fit and shared values: alternatives for managing headquarter subsidiary relations. *Strategic Management Journal, 6*, 491–503.

Pearce, R. (1999). The evolution of technology in multinational enterprises: the role of creative subsidiaries. *International Business Review, 2*, 125–148.

Rosenzweig, P. & Singh, J. (1991). Organisational environments and the multinational enterprise. *Academy of Management Review, 2*, 340–361.

Roth, K. & O'Donnell, S. (1996). Foreign subsidiary compensation strategy. *Academy of Management Review, 3*, 678–701.

Spence, N. (1977). Entry, capacity, investment and oligopolistic pricing. *Bell Journal of Economics, 3*, 535–544.

Steindl, J. (1976). *Maturity and Stagnation in American Capitalism.* New York: Monthly Review Press.

Sundram, A. & Black, J. (1992). The environment and internal organisation of multinational enterprises. *Academy of Management Review, 4*, 729–757.

Szulanski, G. (1996). Exploring internal stickiness: impediments to the transfer of best practice within the firm. *Strategic Management Journal,* Winter Special Issue, 27–33.

Sölvell, Ö. & Zander, I. (1998). International diffusion of knowledge: isolating mechanisms and the of the MNE. In A. Chandler *et al.*, (eds), *The Dynamic Firm: the Role of Technology, Strategy, Organisation and Regions.* Oxford: Oxford University Press.

Westney, E. (1993). Institutional theory and the multinational corporation. In S. Ghoshal & E. Westney (eds), *Organisational Theory and the Multinational Corporation.* New York: St Martin's Press.

Zander, I. (1998). The evolution of technological capabilities in the multinational corporation —dispersion, duplication and the potential advantages from multinationality. *Research Policy, 1*, 17–35.

Zander, I. (1999). How do you mean "global"? An empirical investigation of innovation networks in the multinational corporation. *Research Policy, 2(3)*, 195–213.

Part III
Impacts of Globalization on People and Mind

This section includes contributions that discuss the implications of globalization in general rather than with reference to the multinational firm in particular.

In *When Muhammed goes to the Mountain: Globalization, Cathedrals of Modernity and a New World in Order*, Udo Zander challenges the idea that globalization provides homogeneity on a global scale. Instead Zander argues that globalization actually leads to a more polarized world. The reason behind this is that the improved interconnection between different countries stimulates a self-sorting migration based on ideas of what constitutes "a better life". Instead of staying in their home-countries and fight for what they think is a better life, people leave for other countries known to possess ideas about life that they would like to share. This migration creates what Zander calls "cathedrals of modernity", strong magnets to which people, with possibilities to do so, move. Zander exemplifies with USA being such a cathedral. The polarization between these "cathedrals" and the rest of the world, in terms of resources, people and technology, belongs to the basic features of globalization.

In *Business Corporations, Markets and the Globalization of Environmental Problems* Peter Söderbaum focuses on the relationships between globalization and environmental issues. Starting from the recent discussions of the roles of WTO, IMF and the World Bank he argues that the criticism against globalization must be seen against the background of these organizations' usual perspectives, rooted in neoclassical economics. Söderbaum argues that, with reference to global environmental problems, globalization requires a change in ideology, in which economic man of neoclassical economics is replaced by the political economic man, more in accordance with institutional economics. At the firm level this implies that the behaviour of firm, in terms of environmental problems, must be guided by values other than shareholder wealth. At the individual level every person must take social and environmental responsibility for his/ her own action and for the actions taken by the firm(s) in which they are stakeholders. The vast environmental problems the world is faced with today make it impossible for firms and individuals from hiding behind the neoclassical economic paradigm.

Chapter 7

When Muhammed Goes to the Mountain: Globalization, Cathedrals of Modernity and a New World in Order[1]

Udo Zander

The Globalization Discourse in the Late 2nd Millennium

Preoccupation with the 'global' has become one of the emblematic features of the late 2nd millennium. The term is repeated as a mantra by politicians, business leaders, academics, and others who try to stay with it, i.e., try to be 'modern'.

The rhetoric is familiar (and almost inevitably our eyes glaze over at the following list):

- we need to be open and compete in *global markets;*
- we are helpless subjects to fluctuation of *global industries, global demand and global business;*
- we need to adapt rapidly to the fast-changing *global economy;*
- transnational corporations, through their geographically extensive operations, and states, through their liberal trade, foreign investment and industrial policies (both as single actors and in such regional groupings as the EU or NAFTA) have shaped and reshaped the *global economic map;*

[1] Short version published in Academy of Management *Best Paper Proceedings,* 2000.

Critical Perspectives on Internationalisation, pp. 153–177.
ISBN: 0-08-044053-5

- revolutionary changes in the technologies of transport and communication and in production processes have facilitated *the globalization of manufactured goods and service production.*

The scenario is often one of unstoppable global forces leading to an ultimately homogenized world in which local differences will be virtually eradicated.[2] Globalization becomes the new economic, as well as political and cultural, order. Nation states are no longer seen as significant actors or meaningful economic units; consumer tastes and cultures become homogenized and satisfied through the production of standardized global products created by global corporations with allegiance to neither place nor community. Both the 'death of the nation state' (Ohmae 1995a) and 'the end of geography' (Castells, 1996), as well as 'the end of history' (Fukuyama, 1992) have been proclaimed recently by quite enthusiastic scholars. This paper questions the idea of an efficient history and an end-state of a world of rational actions (implicitly displaying properties of optimality).

Emergence of the Global System

The basis of the system seen today as penetrating the world is capitalist and originated and developed in quite specific geographical locations (Braudel, 1984). The beginnings of a world economy were first evident in the expansion of trade during the 'long sixteenth century' (1450–1640).[3] This 'world' was dominated by a small number of expansive, trading, European nations. By the middle of the 17th century economic leadership was centered on northwest Europe. This is also where industrialization started. The relative fortune of the industrialized countries waxed and waned, with the USA and Germany gradually overtake the previously undisputed leader, Britain, around the turn of the 20th century. Transnational corporations, once labelled 'chartered trading companies' also developed in Europe from the 15th century onwards. Succeeding the vast trading empires, like the East India Company and the Hudson Bay Company, the first firms to engage in production outside their home country emerged during the second half of the 19th

---

[2] Major proponents of the globalization position include Levitt (1983), Reich (1991), Barnet and Cavanagh (1994), Ohmae (1985; 1990; 1995a,b). The underlying concept may be traced back to McLuhan's (1960) notion of the 'global village'.

[3] Wallerstein (1979).

century. Only on the eve of World War I was there substantial overseas manufacturing by US, British, and continental European companies.

Immediately prior to World War II, the US and northwest Europe dominated production; 71 percent of world manufacturing was concentrated in just four countries and almost 90 percent in only eleven countries (League of Nations, 1945). Alone of all the major industrial nations, the US emerged from the war strengthened rather than weakened. It had the economic and technological capacity and the political will to lead the way. The institutional basis for a new order was created at Bretton Woods as early as 1944. It resulted in the creation of two international financial institutions: the IMF and the IBRD (later renamed the World Bank). The financial 'lubricant' for a reconstructed world economy was created, and free trade uninhibited by tariff barriers was promoted by establishing GATT, heir to the defunct International Trade Organization. Subsequent events produced the Marshall Plan and the European Coal and Steel Community. Finally, the Organization for Economic Cooperation and Development was launched to consolidate the system. The postwar 'economic architecture' was an order containing many traces of what had earlier occurred (de la Torre, 1992; Dicken, 1998).

It is clear from this brief account that a very small group of societies, sharing the same peculiarities, is responsible for a remarkable gradual build-up of wealth, protection from unexpected and uncontrollable evil, and technological development over the last 400–500 years. Human beings' way of going about their ordinary lives in these parts of the world has changed dramatically during this time. To capture the essence of the parts of the globe seen as the leading drivers of the global system, they will henceforward be labelled 'Cathedrals of Modernity'.[4]

Philosophy and Ordinary Life in Cathedrals of Modernity

Modernity is the historical phase that begins with Galileo's and Descartes' commitment to new, rational methods of inquiry in astronomy and mechanics as well as logic and epistemology (Toulmin, 1990). The

---

[4] Given the historical background of capitalist ideas, possibly 'Churches of Rationality' would be a better label, but the attractive glamor and mystique surrounding a Catholic mass made me choose 'Cathedrals'. 'Modernity' is chosen since it is more encompassing (and enchanting) than 'rationality'.

ideal of '*rationality*' formulated by Descartes in logic and natural philosophy in the early 17th century is central. Thirty years later, the commitment to rationality was extended into the practical realm, when the political and diplomatic system of the European states was recognized on the basis of *nations*. The modern project aims at uncertainty reduction by focusing on formal logic, common principles, abstract axioms, and permanent structures. European thinkers developed an appetite for the written, the universal, the general, and the timeless. In modernity there is long-term faith that science is the proven road to human health and welfare.[5] This dream still carries conviction for many people today: what underlies their continued trust in science and industry is their commitment to the conception of 'rationality' that promises intellectual certainty and harmony. Scientific blessings are seen as happy outcomes of scientific inquiries that have made continuous progress over the last four hundred years.

Toulmin (1990) describes the assumptions of philosophers and people in all walks of life underlying the 'modern' way of thinking of the world:

> "In a dozen areas, the modes of life and thought in modern Europe from 1700 on (modern science and medicine, engineering and institutions) were assumed to be more rational than those typical of medieval Europe, or those found in less developed societies and cultures today. Further, it was assumed that uniquely rational procedures exist for handling the intellectual and practical problems of any field of study, procedures which are available to anyone who sets superstition and mythology aside, and attacks those problems in ways free of local prejudice and transient fashion."

The dream of a modern, rational society has spawned numerous projects featuring social engineering, where emotions and sentimentality for good and for bad were stopped from interfering.[6] Based on the Cartesian

---

[5] Eriksson (1991) points to the importance of science and its development for European-Western culture, as well as to the Faustian damnation that comes with it.

[6] Neocleous (1997) urges us to see fascism as the destructive potential of modernity. The train became a living symbol for fascist Italy — an electrified, technologically advanced and tightly interconnected industrial nation founded on the values of efficiency, speed, and technical innovation (Schnapp, 1992).

division between body and mind, nature is seen as an object to observe, conquer, and use.

Weber (1958) connected modernity and capitalism when he emphasized that 'rational conduct on the basis of the idea of the calling' is a fundamental element of all modern culture, and of the spirit of modern capitalism. He sees modern man as being forced to work in a calling, since asceticism dominates world morality and helps building the modern economic order. In Puritanism, emotions play an unimportant role and the all-important aspiration is void of 'white magic'. This disenchantment of the world ('Entzauberung der Welt') is, according to Weber, the kernel of rationalism. The modern order is also bound to the technical and economic conditions of machine production. Weber sees the modern obsession with external goods as an 'iron cage':[7]

> "...material goods have gained an increasing and finally an inexorable power over the lives of men as at no previous period in history. ... In the field of its highest development, in the United States, the pursuit of wealth, stripped of its religious and ethical meaning, tends to become associated with purely mundane passions, which often actually give it the character of sport." (Weber, 1958)

In a study of 'ordinary life' in Silicon Valley, by many seen as spearheading modernity, anthropologists Darrah, English-Lueck, and Freeman find that the borders between work and family life are disappearing, more and more things are 'managed' (including family members), and technological solutions are sought for almost everything.[8] Possibly related to the work-home inter-penetration, 'outsourcing' of anything from shopping to scheduling in-law visits takes place. Long working hours (10 to 12 hours not uncommon), career pressure at a young age, extreme levels of mobility and communication, and an obsession with scheduling are other hallmarks of life in the hypermodern fast-lane.

---

[7] Reactions to disenchantment brought about by ever-present rationality are abundant. The interest in new age, astrology, earth radiation, UFOs, homeopathy, numerology, crystals, tarot cards, aura healing, and spiritual cleansing are just a few examples of what is also going on, in parallel to a rational approach, inside the Cathedrals of Modernity.

[8] See the Silicon Valley Cultures Project (http://www.sjsu.edu/depts/anthropology/svcp/SVCPoverv.htm).

The Process of Globalization

The Cathedrals of Modernity play a double role in the process of globalization. First, they are the source of much of the modern culture of rationality and of expectations regarding consumption and lifestyles diffused worldwide. Second, the same process of global diffusion has taught an increasing number of people about economic opportunities in the modern world that are absent in their own countries.

We are all familiar with the view that especially through the mechanisms of the market, a version of the contemporary modern way of life will eventually spread to every corner of the planet. Dallas, MacDonalds and Coca-Cola are the main symbols of this process, to the extent that 'Cocacolonization' has become an alternative label for the process as a whole among, e.g., anthropologists. The global homogenization scenario emphasizes a centre-periphery pattern where flows of ideas and lifestyles are closely aligned with those of political and economic power. The centre is the Cathedrals of Modernity (North America and western Europe) and the rest of the world to varying degrees is peripheral — or at least semi-peripheral (Hannerz, 1992).

A second story — often told by economists — emphasizing efficiency and the power of design instead of implying raw, profit-seeking imperialism, starts with Winston Churchill and Theodore Roosevelt sailing aboard a US destroyer in the North Atlantic in the winter of 1941. Prodded by the decision of these leaders to prevent the world from falling into protectionism and competitive devaluations, many of the best economic minds led by Keynes figured out an institutional framework that should guarantee an open and progressive world economy in the aftermath of war (de la Torre, 1992). The result was global integration: steady growth in the trade of goods and services, accelerating financial market integration, rapid expansion of foreign direct investment, and faster technology diffusion. From a standard neoclassical economic standpoint, economic integration (under a "modern system") increases competition, equalizes the capital-labour mix, and leads to increased productivity and income.

A third way of explaining globalization is offered by organizational sociologists. Institutional theorists examine cultural, normative and cognitive processes producing homogeneity of forms within organizational fields — diverse organizations interacting within a broad societal domain (DiMaggio & Powell, 1983; Meyer & Rowan, 1977; Powell & DiMaggio, 1991). They call attention to the role of ideational forces, knowledge systems, beliefs, and rules as key components in the structure and operation of organizations. Institutions consist of cognitive, normative, and regulative structures and activities that give stability and meaning to social behaviour (Scott, 1995). The argument in Meyer & Rowan, (1977) is that modern societies contain many complexes of institutionalized rules and patterns — products of professional groups, the state, and public opinion. These socially constructed realities provide frameworks for the creation and elaboration of formal institutions. These institutions of modernity are likely to take the form of 'rationalized myths'. Organizations around the world receive support and legitimacy to the extent that they can conform to modern norms concerning the 'appropriate way' to organize. They are not insulated from culture, and the modern conception of rationality is in itself a social and cultural conception (Berger, *et al.*, 1973; Berger & Luckman, 1967). Modern people have a collective, socially realized and enforced agreement emphasizing the value of identifying specific ends and developing explicit, formalized means of pursuing them. According to Dobbin (1994),

> "... rationalized organizational practices are essentially cultural, and are very much the core of modern culture precisely because modern culture is organized around instrumental rationality."

Scott (1993) echoes the idea that this rational culture is spreading over the globe:

> "Of course, the proliferation of specialized, purposeful organizations can be viewed as one of the major creatures and carriers of the modernization project".

Whoever wants to demonstrate seriousness about achieving a goal or protecting some value must, in the eyes of people from the Cathedrals of Modernity, create an organization to symbolize commitment. Legitimate organizations embody the primary values that distinguish modern cultural beliefs from more romantic or traditional forms (Scott, 1998).[9]

---

[9] The process of institutional environments 'enacting' organizations, the multiple ways in which institutional processes socially construct organizational forms and activities, is more important than Weickian (1979) organizations 'enacting' their environment through selective attention and cognitive framing processes (Scott, 1995).

As for the actual diffusion of consumption patterns, institutional frameworks, and rationalized myths, anthropologists like Hannerz (1992) see globalization as driven by the increased mobility of people, as labour immigrants, refugees, businessmen, or tourists, which carry some of their ideas and values along. Also, material goods and media are seen as playing an important role in the homogenization process.

Explicitly or implicitly, *'globalization' is thus used to describe the further expansion of the economic and symbolic architecture of modernity.* The language chosen is one of 'national borders becoming less important', and 'economies and cultures becoming increasingly interwoven'. The logic is, however, clearly one of *adaptation* — the rest of the world slowly but surely adapts to the modern system, life-style, and world view. This is not seen as surprising since the last viable alternatives failed with the collapse of so-called communism and the Soviet Union.[10] Over time a modern, homogenous world displaying efficiency and prosperity is built.

But there are signs that modern ideas and ways of life do not always spread easily despite increased global interconnectedness and fierce attempts to modernize by many elites. The experience is that rapid, top-down modernization is not an easy process: fierce resistance to rapid adaptation to modern values and lifestyles in countries like Iran, Egypt, Pakistan, Sudan, and Algeria are a fact. Strong forces advocating the re-establishment of traditional ways of living surfaced in these cases and put a halt to the modernization process and even in some cases reverted society to extreme traditionalist ways of life.[11] The fact that potential gains from modernization were not distributed evenly by the often isolated elite most likely contributed to these 'backlashes'.

A fundamental question is raised by post-modern theory, when challenging the assumption that 'rationality' in the service of unity and efficiency requires the suppression of the diversity of voices, components and interests, within organizations.[12] Thus, the scenario of global homogenization is not so widely held in this group. Postmodernist fashions in

---

[10] In many ways the Soviet experiment however bore the clear signs of a modernization project, just like Peter the Great's efforts to build St Petersburg in the swamps.

[11] Recently, renewed attempts to change traditional Iranian society were made by students in Tehran, calling for 'death or freedom'. Iran's supreme leader said students were acting as proxies for Iran's foreign enemies (in other words the U.S. and Israel) and Islamist Ansar-e Hizbullah helped by police attacked demonstrators (*Economist*, 1999a).

[12] See e.g., Cooper and Burell (1988), Clegg (1990), Smircich and Calas (1987), who build on the work of social theorists like Derrida (1976), Foucault (1977), and Lyotard (1984).

intellectual life emphasize, despite an acknowledgement of global inter-connectedness, fragmentation, diversity and the local games of language and living. The global homogenization scenario is seen as one of those overarching 'master narratives' of history toward which postmodernism is generally sceptical. To a certain degree in line with this thinking, I will in the following propose *human migration* as a main outcome of increased interconnectedness of the world.[13] Modernity-supporting people in non-modern societies, self-select and congregate in Cathedrals of Modernity out of discontentment over the slow changes in this direction, if any, in their home countries. The outcome of this type of process, happening more rapidly than the migration of ideas and ways of life, is not increased homogeneity on the worldwide level. Applying the exit, voice, loyalty framework of Hirschman (1970) on people's decisions on where to live, a process of self-sorting is proposed in the following.

The Individual's Choices and Councillors

The individual's decision regarding in what context to go about daily life is the critical and most often ignored factor in the globalization debate. But decisions are not made in vacuum, and the contemporary individual is exposed to many carefully planned ways of educating him about how (and thereby where) he/she should lead his/her life.

The state desires loyal citizens, and works on constructing them through its apparatus of schools, media, museums, national holidays, monuments, etc. (Hobsbawm & Ranger, 1983). The nation state draws a large part of its legitimacy from its claim to be the guardian of a way of going about everyday life which is voluntarily shared and historically rooted. Consequently, diversity within national borders, or linkages cutting across borders are problematic for the state. Borders are some-times closed and censorship applied, officially of course never to avoid unrest or the exit of unhappy citizens, but to 'stop evil forces from enter-ing the sanctuary'. Often it is in the interest of the state that the con-ceptual difference between state and nation is blurred. This is obvious in states having to live with arbitrary borders that are remnants of colonial-ism (Hannerz, 1992).

---

[13] Interconnectedness might by some be seen as an alternative to migration, but in order to change the way of going about daily life, 'being in touch on-line with something better' will not do the trick.

In addition to influences from the state, the individual is also increasingly exposed to products and messages from outside the area taxed by the nation state. Three well-known and fundamental enablers for this exposure are the improvements in media, communication equipment and transport: Electronic media, for example, are the instant windows on 'global' events, i.e., events occurring locally which are projected globally. It is important to realize that the amount of messages available for interested ordinary people far away from senders in, for example, Cathedrals of Modernity is increasing. We, however, cannot be sure how these messages are interpreted. The naive assumption is often that modern 'propaganda' is received well, understood in the way it is intended, and lures people to aspire to being part of the Modern Project. A more realistic view includes both admirers of modernity and recipients frowning at the immoralities, violence, vulgarities, and lack of sophistication characterizing messages from the Modern Cathedrals.

The bias towards catastrophic events constituting 'news', in combination with an expanded geographical scope of media coverage, may also ironically lead to increasing many recipients' xenophobia. Given that most news is negative in character and that the international proportion increases, foreign lands will over time in some people's eyes inevitably end up on the list of dangerous countries to be avoided.

The globalizing effect of improved communication equipment allowing us to be 'at two locations simultaneously' assumes that many people are indeed communicating across national borders. Also, the development of aluminium tubes with wings and wheels has made travel much easier than just half a millennium ago when we navigated toward inland British cities with the help of lighthouses on moonless nights. Individuals can more easily see for themselves what life in different parts of the world is like. Through some combination of this improved possibility of reliable communication and rapid and secure transport, a considerable variety of social networks can today be maintained across national borders, oceans and continents. Dispersed families, ethnic Diaspora, multinational corporations (MNCs), and professional communities can be maintained.

It is important to realize that although the improvement of transportation, communication, and media technologies increases the potential exposure to other lifestyles, *individuals are by no means isolated from the lifestyle they are exposed to going about their ordinary lives.* Neither do the changes in technology, in themselves, overnight make individuals like or dislike lifestyles that differ fundamentally from their own. Increased international coverage of the human condition and increased potential mobility, however, makes it easier (but not always easy) for individuals to form an opinion on how their society is doing in relation to other countries.

According to Ohmae (1995a), these changes have contributed to large numbers of people from all over the globe having aggressively come forward to participate in history after the end of the Cold War:

> "They have left behind centuries, even millennia, of obscurity in forest and desert and rural isolation to request from the world community — and from the global economy that links it together — a descent life for themselves and a better life for their children. A generation ago, even a decade ago, most of them were as voiceless and invisible as they had always been. This is true no longer: they have entered history with a vengeance, and they have demands — economic demands — to make." (Ohmae, 1995a)

As a contrast, back in the 19th century, countries like the US were growing and becoming industrialized countries that needed labour, but had to resort to deliberate recruitment.[14] US life standards were not a global model and its economic opportunities not well known. American migration agents were sent to Mexico, Ireland, Southern Italy, and the Austro-Hungarian empire to market "better meals and higher wages" for work in canal companies, railroads, and later on in industry (Lebergott, 1964).

If a decline in relative performance of a society can indeed be more easily observed today — and matters to individuals — Albert Hirschman's (1970) framework of exit, voice and loyalty may be applicable in order to understand the mechanisms underlying human reactions. Let us just remember that although the above examples as well as Hirschman's original reasoning deal with economic demands and material well-being, the notion of 'an under-performing society' is multidimensional.

If Hirschman's individual decides to *exit* his/her society because it under-performs, he/she is seen as pressuring and disciplining the community he/she leaves to improve. Alternatively, rather than just leaving for something better, the individual can 'kick up a fuss', i.e., attempt to change practices and policies. Attempting to change, rather than escaping

---

[14] Let us here just remind ourselves about a palpable kind of "recruitment" across borders carried out by Europeans under the label "slave trade".

from, an objectionable state of affairs through individual or collective appeal to high authorities is labelled '*voice*' by Hirschman. Either exit or voice will have the role of dominant reaction mode. The third alternative is acquiescence or indifference. We know for example that people unhappy with societal performance are not always alert, active, and vocal when given their chance to voice opinions in a democracy (Dahl, 1966).

Voice is the only way in which dissatisfied individuals can demonstrate their dissatisfaction whenever the exit option is unavailable. Hirschman claims that this is very nearly the situation in such basic social organizations as the family, the state, or the church. As we have argued, the perceived possibilities to exit states for something better have increased recently. He also states that voice is a much more commanding position in less developed countries, while dissatisfaction in advanced countries more likely takes the form of silent exit. The decision to exit will often be taken in the light of the prospects for the effective use of voice. To Hirschman, once an individual has exited, he/she has lost the ability to use voice, but not vice versa; exit will be an action of last resort after voice has failed. In Hirschman's world, the decision to 'stick' with the society is based on an evaluation of the chances of getting society 'on track' and a judgement that it is worthwhile to trade the certainty of a better system which is available here and now against these chances. It is, as we have discussed, clear that the cost of obtaining information about societies to which one intends to switch has become lower in many cases.

Hirschman's Nigerian railway example, which gave him the idea to develop his framework, is very illuminating for our purposes; when the railway under-performed, exit did not have its usual attention-focusing effect since the loss of revenue was not of utmost gravity for management. Voice wouldn't work since the most aroused and therefore potentially most vocal customers were the first to abandon the railway for trucks. People having an alternative that functioned well stopped things from improving, unless loyalty moderated the process. As we have discussed, globalization and technological development increases the awareness of both well-functioning alternatives and the possibilities for exit.

Migration Mechanisms

Who will then use the exit-option in an increasingly interconnected world? Why should people embark on costly journeys, sometimes surreptitiously, battle immigration (and sometimes emigration) authorities, learn new languages and culture, and sacrifice work, friends, and family back home? Given the sometimes huge differences in income levels between even neighbouring countries, we might alternatively ask why only a minuscule proportion of people leave their home countries with difficult economic and political conditions. For example, fewer than seven percent of Mexicans have crossed the porous border to the US, where per capita income is three times that of Mexico (adjusted for differences in purchasing power).

The groups of people that migrate are almost always self-selected from the people of the source countries. What then is the self-selection mechanism? There has been no lack of interesting suggestions: The lack of intelligence was proclaimed a driver by Benjamin Franklin who in 1753 wrote that German immigrants were "the most stupid of their own nation" (Abbott, 1969). General Patton emphasized the love of freedom as a driver when firing up his troop against possible distant relatives when liberating Sicily in 1943 (Kennedy, 1996). It is also often argued that desperate poverty, squalor, and unemployment are the main factors motivating emigration (Briggs, 1975; Lamm & Imhoff, 1985; Teitelbaum, 1980). A large number of scholars suggest the size of economic gains as the single driver. Often the explanations of how this type of mechanism works become rather complex. Borjas (1999), for example, starts by letting workers compare economic conditions in their home country and the US. Workers from countries where the payoff to human capital is low (for example, Sweden) will migrate if they have high skill levels, while workers from countries where the payoff to human capital is high (for example, Mexico and the Philippines) will migrate if they are among the least skilled.

A more plausible driver might be the individuals' *perceived gap between life aspiration and expectations, and the means to fulfil them in the home country within reasonable time.*[15] Different groups feel this gap with varying intensity, and the form the gap takes of course varies. In addition to fundamental economic conditions, freedom, security, or the possibility of 'widening the horizon' may be valued. For skilled workers and small farmers, migration may be a means of stabilizing family livelihoods and increasing consumption, while urban professionals may want to reach lifestyles commensurate with prior achievements and to progress in their careers. It is important to realize that relative and not absolute

---

[15] Borrowing from Festinger's (1957) terminology, migrants could possibly be seen as looking for increased cognitive consonance.

deprivation lies at the core of the adventurous behaviour leading to emigration. In our view, a main driver would be one of sympathy with the ideas and (perceived) way of conducting ordinary life in the country of destination. Not for a second denying the importance of material well-being, it feels important to emphasize the power of ideas over human beings, and assert that the vision of an everyday life in accordance with basic philosophical values is important for individual exit decisions.

Building on Hirschman's thinking, we would expect *impatient, non-influential minorities* to migrate. Hirschmanian thinking would also lead to large-enough groups not exiting but collectively using voice and in some cases creating their own separate homogenous units. The characteristics of people using exit as an option are of course varied depending on the composition of a country's population: poor or rich, educated or non-educated, modernists or traditionalists. *The point is that in exiting to find a 'better life', the migrants will look for societies that to the best of their knowledge promise a way of life that they have been dreaming of.* [16] Let us now investigate the characteristics of exit to one important type of society, the US Cathedral of Modernity.

Congregating in a Modern Cathedral

After a lapse of half a century, when the US Cathedral of Modernity was effectively closed to large parts of the world,[17] American society has again become a country of immigration. In 1990, the foreign-born population reached 7.9 percent of the total; eighty years earlier the percentage was 14.7. Comparing the 'new' with the 'old' inflow at the turn of the century, we find that similarities include the predominantly urban

---

[16] The aftermath of successful immigration often includes some form of circulation of family members between systems and capital flows — possibly including reinvestment in the 'old home' society.

[17] The first Great Migration was halted by restrictive policies in 1924, and the restrictions stood until 1965. A national origins quota system was established for the Eastern Hemisphere. 150,000 annual visas were allocated to nationals of a country depending on the representation of that ethnic group in the US population as of 1920. As a result, Germany and the UK received almost two thirds of the available visas. Immigration from Asia was effectively banned. Until the early 1960s, for instance, India and the Philippines were each allotted one hundred visas annually (Borjas, 1999).

destinations of most newcomers,[18] their concentration in a few port cities, and their willingness to accept the lowest paid jobs. Differences are that the 'old' immigration was overwhelmingly European and white, while the present inflow is, to a large extent, nonwhite and comes from Third World countries (Borjas, 1999). Because the sending countries are generally poor, it is often believed that the immigrants themselves are uniformly poor and uneducated.

> "Their move is commonly portrayed as a one-way escape from hunger, want, and persecution and their arrival on US shores as not too different from that of the 'huddled masses' that Emma Lazarus immortalized at the base of the Statue of Liberty. ... The reality is very different." (Portes & Rumbaut, 1996)

Never before has the US received immigrants from so many countries, from such different social and economic backgrounds, and for so many reasons.

Considering legal immigration, the proportion of professionals and managers among occupationally active immigrants in the US consistently exceeds the average among US workers. For 1990, US census data show that immigrants show a higher percentage completing four or more years of college than US natives (US Bureau of the Census 1993). The number in professional specialty occupations is the same in both groups.

As for illegal immigrants to the US, studies show that the very poor and unemployed seldom migrate, and that unauthorized immigrants tend to have above-average levels of education and occupational skills in comparison with their homeland populations. It seems that it is not the lack of jobs, but the lack of *well-paid* jobs, which fuels migration to the US. Up to 48 percent of the unauthorized Mexican immigrants[19] to the US have been found to originate in cities of twenty thousand or more, in comparison with 35 percent of all Mexicans (Portes & Rumbaut, 1996). Findings from research in the Dominican Republic conclude that Dominicans who migrate internationally are more likely to come from the cities,

---

[18] Los Angeles' Mexican population is next in size to those of Mexico City, Monterrey, and Guadalajara. Havana is not much larger than Cuban Miami, and Santo Domingo hold a precarious advantage over Dominican New York (Portes & Rumbaut, 1996).
[19] Mexico is the source of over 95 percent of unauthorized aliens apprehended in the US during the last two decades.

have much higher levels of literacy, are relatively more skilled, and have lower levels of unemployment than the Dominican population as a whole. These migration data are compatible with the view that fundamental ideas regarding the way of life drive migration.

A group of people that is especially interesting to study, if we are interested in the magnetism of ideas, are migrants who are relatively well off in their home countries. In 1993, almost 110,000 persons classified as professionals and managers arrived as permanent residents of the US. The main contributors included mainland China, the Philippines, India, Great Britain, and Taiwan. Since 1992, the number of these visas is triple the level that had been the annual norm for the previous twenty-five years. Since the 1970s, many immigrants coming to the US have also arrived with a Ph.D. in their pocket. The Cathedral has incorporated this influx of talent so well that the top ranks of the scientific establishment are now replete with foreign-born workers (Levin & Stephan, 1999). When analysing membership rolls of the National Academy of Sciences, the National Academy of Engineering, citation indices, patent citations, and boards of American biotechnology firms, foreign-born scientists are found to be over-represented. In California's high-tech industries, Asians already hold over 50,000 jobs and produce US$17 billion worth of revenue (*Economist,* 1999b). A fertile ground for this type of migration is countries in which university students are trained in advanced Western-style professional practices, but find the prospects and means to implement their training blocked because of poor employment opportunities or lack of equipment (Glaser & Habers, 1974; Portes & Ross, 1976). When these immigrants have to turn to other pursuits, they stay in the US and commonly go into small business or even the unregulated practice of their profession while awaiting better times (Stevens *et al.,* 1978). This is a good example of how the diffusion of modern ideas, being more rapid than modernization of societies itself, leads to self-selection and migration for other reasons than purely economical.[20]

Refugees are another interesting group to study, since they leave a way of life that has often for some reason seemed unbearable for another

---

[20] The phenomenon of talent seeking challenging environments is of course not new, but the extent to — and distances over — which people migrate have increased. In the 1820s, the unparalleled commercial and scientific opportunities related to the building of the Erie Canal attracted migrant inventors, but in those days mainly from the equally highly modernized southern New England (Khan & Sokoloff, 1993).

more appealing existence. The official label of 'refugee' conceals differences not only between national groups but within each of them as well.
Portes and Rumbaut (1996) point to two categories generally found in
most refugee flows. First, there is an elite of former notables who left
early because of ideological or political opposition to their countries'
regimes. Second, there is a mass of individuals and families of modest
background who left later because of the economic expectations and
hardships imposed by the same regimes. Depending on the relationship
between their home country and the US, they can be classified as bona
fide refugees or as illegal aliens. If entry is denied, it may take a few
iterations to end up where one feels 'at home', but once the original home
is left, it seems relatively easy to move on in search of greener pastures.
The existence of the two types of refugees seems to suggest that ideas
matter more for elites (minorities losing their influence), or alternatively
for people making early exit decisions.

It is not surprising that most of today's immigrants to the US, even the
undocumented ones, are from the groups most thoroughly exposed to
influences from the Cathedrals of Modernity. They are also the groups
for whom the gap between aspirations and local realities is most poignant
and among whom one finds the individuals most determined to overcome
the situation. Contemporary immigration into the US is thus a direct
consequence of the spread of modern ideas from the Cathedrals of Modernity to every corner of the globe:

> "The bewildering number and variety of today's immi-
> grants reflect this worldwide reach and the vision of
> modern life and individual fulfillment that goes with it."
> (Portes & Rumbaut, 1996)

It is apparently seen as more appealing for millions of people to exit
for an instant flash of modernity than to struggle to change societies
where most people are not interested in modernity and modern lifestyles.

The result of migration is the slow sorting of world population according to affinity for ideas that determine ways of going about ordinary life.
In the case of Cathedrals of Modernity, for example, we will see a continued concentration of people believing in 'rationality,' while the relative
concentration of non-modernists increases in the countries of exit. The
combined result of these processes is *a 'New World in Order'* where very
different internally homogenous societies co-exist, not a homogenous
global society.

Discussion and Conclusions

We have proposed that improved interconnection between different parts of the world, often labelled globalization, lead not to global homogenisation but to more homogenous societies, and thereby *increased polarization at the global level*. The mechanism we propose is one of self-sorting according to ideas about what constitutes 'a better life' for oneself and the next generation. The notion of 'a better life' not only includes financial considerations, but also compatibility of ideas and philosophies that permeate ways about ordinary life. People that have been exposed to foreign ways of life, and feel they are unable to influence their disappointing home environment in the short run,[21] exit to countries known for ideas of ways of life they would like to share. This mechanism was exemplified by discussing properties of so-called Cathedrals of Modernity, and immigration to important such Cathedral, the USA.

The argument is general and does not necessarily hinge on the importance of Cathedrals of Modernity in more than that these Cathedrals are at this point in history acting as strong "magnets" and are responsible for developing technologies that enable globalization.[22] The internationalized media, communication, and scope for travel lead to a dissemination of ideas, lifestyles, and products that is more rapid than fundamental changes in the local reality of people. The most dissatisfied and impatient believers in the foreign messages often choose to exit instead of trying to change society by 'voice'. The country of destination has to fulfil dreams of a better life, where basic values, like a belief in the virtues of modernity and rationality, play an important role.

Interestingly, *the very belief in the virtues of modernity may lead to increased levels of adventurism (and thereby exit)* through a belief in the merits of "Gesellschaft". Adventurism, according to Hamilton (1978) refers to the act of taking great risks whose outcomes are not calculable in advance, to achieve sizable social, economic, or political gains that may occur. The adventurer "departs from the routine expectations of everyday life, appeals to chance to guide the way in the face of uncertainty, and engages in concerted though often sporadic activity."

---

[21] 'Short run' is here used to mirror the concern of many people for the lives of themselves and their children.

[22] People from the Cathedrals also exit to find more appealing ways to go about their ordinary lives. This is an important part of the self-sorting story, as is the migration between different societies where modernity does not have a foothold, which has not been discussed in this paper.

According to Asplund (1992), life in "Gesellschaft" is composed of incidents and coincidences, which leads us to think that a belief in modernity would imply an acceptance of the fact that life is intermittent and accidental rather than permanent and substantial (as in "Gemeinschaft"). In conclusion, the individuals that are most drawn to the Cathedrals of Modernity might also be the ones most apt to leave for them.

As for the people remaining in their countries of birth, they might feel that conditions improve by 'adventurous, strange people' exiting and society increasingly embracing their ideas of what principles should govern human life. Local homogenization through self-sorting reduces intra-country friction.

Some scholars argue that the world was more open and integrated in the half century before World War One labelled 'the age of cosmopolitan capitalism' (Glimstedt & Lange, 1998). If this is the case, did we see processes of intra-country homogenization after 1870? There was, as an example, indeed proof of the magnetism of Cathedrals of Modernity around the turn of the century. Nearly 26 million immigrants entered the US between 1880 and 1924. The "new" immigrants then came from Poland, Russia, and Italy following the earlier wave of immigrants from Great Britain, Germany and Sweden (Borjas, 1999). A smaller but important stream of supporters of communist ideas was also finding its way to the Soviet Union after the Russian revolution. Self-sorting was obviously going on, but seemingly within a smaller geographical context than today.[23]

The central question remains, however: why do we see signs of a proliferation of system properties especially from the Cathedrals of Modernity to other societies if self-sorting is going on? Market economy is indeed under construction in many parts of the world, and modern ideas and products *can* be found in remote corners of the world. To the extent that new ideas, knowledge, competence, and expertise can be imported without interfering with basic values and lifestyles, the process is fairly uncomplicated. It is also entirely possible to, metaphorically speaking, "go to Mass every Sunday without necessarily being religiously devoted". Window-dressing to please the representatives of alien systems, for instance the IMF, is nothing new. The people associated with imports however always have to tread carefully so as not to offend the silent

---

[23] Of course, intra-country regional self-sorting has always gone on, possibly destabilizing certain states, but we have decided to focus on the process at the international level in this paper.

majority of the population. The process of creolization, suggested by Hannerz (1992), might well also be at work when alien ideas are imported. We must not forget or underestimate the common strong counter-reactions, often on part of people under 'missionary' pressures, which result in a deliberate, often rather romantic fostering of the local tradition.

As for the proliferation of products and services from the Cathedrals, we are not denying that these are attractive to consumers around the world.[24] It is however unclear whether the purchase of different types of vehicles and consumer goods profoundly changes people's way of going about their everyday lives. This type of superficial globalization is not seen as fundamental to the reasoning in this paper.

The activities of MNCs are often described as flag-waving crusades of modernity into heathen territory — 'conquering a market' is not an uncommon expression. We see MNCs much more as channelling the ongoing self-sorting of individuals by providing accessible alternatives to the local environment through their subsidiaries. The number of expatriates sent to foreign subsidiaries is often small and not a process of self-sorting, since managers rarely have a choice of destination. This leads these kinds of 'migrants' to return to their home countries, unless they by chance find 'perfect life' during one of their postings. Also in education and high-technology industries, there is the perception that phenomena like the American-style business school INSEAD in France and the 'new Silicon Valley' in Bangalore, India are evidence of world homogenization. We feel that these types of foreign satellites like the MNCs do affect the local landscape, but to a much higher degree operate as suppliers, assembly points, and gateways for the societies that launched them. As an example, the Swedish telecom manufacturer Ericsson regards arranging visas for Indian experts to stay in Silicon Valley as one of the main strategic issues in their US joint ventures and acquisitions.[25]

It could also be argued that most emigrants sooner or later return to their home countries, now often in influential positions, and that this tendency would go against the ideas of the development of a multi-polar world proposed in this paper. However, a number of psychological

---

[24] In an amusing account, Ohmae (1995a) discusses 'the ladder of development'. At the equivalent of US$ 3,000 per capita income, there is usually a strong but steady increase in the desire to buy basic consumer goods. Before that, at US$ 1,500–3,000 per capita the emphasis is on motorbikes, and below 1,500 on bicycles. At 5,000 we all want cars and to host the Olympics...

[25] Interview with Lars Stålberg, Vice President, Ericsson, in the spring 1999.

factors such as pride of enduring self-inflicted hardship without complaining, the drive to project success, and the perceived decay of the 'old country' (i.e., observations of the effects of exit through self-sorting) moderate the urge to go back to home countries. Multi-dimensionality and ambiguity as to the degree of dream fulfilment add to the number of immigrants that stay in their new country. Return to one's home at old age is probably not uncommon, but these returnees rarely have a wish or the energy to impact the development of a society.

Let us finally think about the implications of self-selection of migrants going on for an extended period of time. Is the produced local homogeneity good, bad, both, or neither? A decrease in variety is always worrying from an exploration point of view, and the question is if renewal through innovation in this case will increasingly take place at the international level. Theoretically, the creation of new ways of life could in this case take place through a combination of ideas from two countries, synthesized in one of them. These locally created syntheses could in turn be re-imported to the society where the thesis originated, as sometimes seen in so-called creolization of literature and popular music. It should be remembered that the kind of self-selection on ideological grounds, described in this paper, provides not only homogeneity in dreams about the future, but also heterogeneity along a number of different dimensions in the Cathedrals of Modernity. This may make fears of decreased requisite variance for innovation exaggerated when it comes to the "magnets".

The multi-polar global structure could however at the same time create tensions at the international level. A worrying thought in this context is that World War I followed a period of Cosmopolitan Capitalism and the first Great Wave of Migration. The dynamics when ways of life can increasingly be taken to an extreme without bothering local opposition may also turn out to be less than desirable. Boredom and lack of tolerance for deviant ideas and behaviour along certain dimensions are possible outcomes. If these tendencies are combined with extensive "missionary" activities directed at converting the "heathens" who differ in their view of where the world should be moving, *major conflict is indeed a possibility.* In a locally homogenous world produced by self-selection of individuals, dreams of inclusive and universal nature (which have been reinforced by success) are potential detonators of a most unappealing explosive charge. Modernity has until now been such a dream.

To complicate matters, the concerns about and possible negative sides of the ordering of the world according to ideas, have to be compared to the less appealing but historically not uncommon option of forcing people to stay where they were born. A thought-provoking statement in this context is Pareto's (1901/1991) claim that a dominant group survives only if it provides opportunities for the best persons of other origins to join freely in its privileges and rewards.

Acknowledgements

I would like to thank the late Gunnar Hedlund for inspiring us to read and write things for pure pleasure, and now and then give important but unwieldy issues a shot.

Thanks also to Eleanor Westney, Mats Forsgren, Timo Hämäläinen, Jerker Denrell, the participants at the IIB Seminar, the SCANCOR workshop "The Roots and Branches of Organizational Economics" at Stanford University, and the Marcus Wallenberg Symposium on Critical Perspectives on Internationalization in Uppsala.

References

Abbott, E. (ed.) (1969). *Historical Aspects of the Immigration Problem*. New York: Arno Press and NYT.

Asplund, J. (1992). *Storstäderna och det Forteanska livet*. Göteborg: Bokförlaget Korpen.

Barnet, R. J. & Cavanagh, J. (1994). *Global Dreams: Imperial Corporations and the New World Order*. New York: Simon & Schuster.

Berger, P. L., Berger, B. & Kellner, H. (1973). *The Homeless Mind: Modernization and Consciousness*. New York: Random House.

Berger, P. L. & Luckman, T. (1967). *The Social Construction of Reality*. New York: Doubleday.

Borjas, G. J. (1999). *Heavens Door: Immigration Policy and the American Economy*. Princeton, NJ: Princeton University Press.

Braudel, F. (1984). *Civilization and Capitalism, 15th–18th Centuries*. London: Collins.

Briggs, V. M. (1975). The need for a more restrictive border policy. *Social Science Quarterly, 56*, 477–484.

Castells, M. (1996). *The Rise of Network Society*. Volume 1. Oxford: Blackwell.

Clegg, S. (1990). *Modern Organizations: Organization Studies in the Postmodern World*. London: Sage.

Cooper, R. & Burrell, G. (1988). Modernism, postmodernism and organizational analysis: an introduction. *Organization Studies, 9*, 91–112.

Dahl, R. (1966). *Modern Political Analysis.* Englewood Cliffs, NJ: Prentice-Hall.
de la Torre, J. (1992). *The Advent of the Global Economy: A Highly Personal and Rambling View of Where We Have Been, and Where We May be Heading.* Mimeo: Anderson Graduate School of Management, University of California of Los Angeles.
Derrida, J. (1976). *Speech and Phenomenon.* Evanston, IL: Northwestern University Press.
Dicken, P. (1998). *Global Shift: Transforming the World Economy.* (3rd ed.). London: Paul Chapman.
DiMaggio, P. J. & Powell, W. W. (1983). The iron cage revisited: institutional isomorphism and collective rationality in organizational fields. *American Sociological Review, 48,* 147–160.
Dobbin, F. R. (1994). Cultural models of organization: the social construction of rational organizing principles. In: D. Crane (ed.), *The Sociology of Culture: Emerging Theoretical Perspectives.* Cambridge, MA: Blackwell.
Economist (1999a). Protesting in Tehran, July 17–23, 45.
Economist (1999b). Imported brains: alien scientists take over USA!, August 21–27, 40.
Eriksson, G. (1991). *Den Faustiska Människan: Vetenskap som Europeiskt arv.* Stockholm: Natur och Kultur.
Festinger, L. (1957). *A Theory of Cognitive Dissonance.* Evanston, Ill: Row Peterson.
Foucault, M. (1977). *Discipline and Punish.* New York: Pantheon.
Fukuyama, F. (1992). *The End of History and the Last Man.* New York: Free Press.
Glaser, W. A. & Habers, C. (1974). The migration and return of professionals. *International Migration Review, 8,* 227–244.
Glimstedt, H. & Lange, E. (eds) (1998). *Globalisering: Drivkrefter og konsekvenser.* Årbok, Handelshoyskolen BI, Oslo: Fagbokforlaget.
Hamilton, G. G. (1978). The structural sources of adventurism: the case of the California gold rush. *American Journal of Sociology, 83,* 1466–1490.
Hannerz, U. (1992). Center-periphery relations and creolization in contemporary culture. In: A. Sjögren & L. Janson, (eds). *Culture and Management in the Field of Ethnology and Business Administration* Stockholm: The Swedish Immigration Institute and Museum and the Institute of International Business. 30–41.
Hirschman, A. O. (1970). *Exit, Voice, and Loyalty: Responses to Decline in Firms, Organizations, and States.* Cambridge, MA: Harvard University Press.
Hobsbawm, E. & Ranger, T. (eds) (1983). *The Invention of Tradition.* Cambridge: Cambridge University Press.
Kennedy, D. M. (1996). Can we still afford to be a nation of immigrants? *Atlantic Monthly,* November, 54.
Khan, B. Z. & Sokoloff, K. L. (1993). Entrepreneurship and technological change in historical perspective: a study of 'great inventors' during early American

industrialization. In G. D. Libecap (ed.), *Advances of Entrepreneurship, Innovation, and Economic Growth — New Learning on Entrepreneurship*. Vol.6. Greenwich, CT: JAI press.

Lamm , R. D. & Imhoff, G. (1985). *The Immigration Time Bomb: The Fragmenting of America*. New York: Dutton.

League of Nations (1945). *Industrialization and Foreign Trade*. New York: League of Nations.

Lebergott, S. (1964). *Manpower in Economic Growth: The American Record Since 1800*. New York: McGraw-Hill.

Levin, S. & Stephan, P. (1999). *Innovation and Productivity in U.S. Industry: The Role of Foreign Scientists and Engineers*. Mimeo: University of Missouri-St. Louis and Georgia State University.

Levitt, T. (1983). The globalization of markets. *Harvard Business Review*, May-June, 92–102.

Lyotard, J.-F. (1984). *The Postmodern Condition: A Report on Knowledge*. Minneapolis: University of Minnesota Press.

McLuhan, M. (1960). *Understanding Media*. London: Routledge and Kegan Paul.

Meyer, J. W. & Rowan, B. (1977). Institutionalized organizations: formal structure as myth and ceremony. *American Journal of Sociology, 83*, 340–363.

Neocleous, M. (1997). *Concepts in Social Thought: Fascism*. Minneapolis: Minnesota University Press.

Ohmae, K. (1985). *Triad Power: The Coming Shape of Global Competition*. New York: Free Press.

Ohmae, K. (1990). *The Borderless World: Power and Strategy in the Interlinked Economy*. New York: Free Press.

Ohmae, K. (1995a). *The End of the Nation State: The Rise of Regional Economies*. New York: Free Press.

Ohmae, K. (ed.) (1995b). *The Evolving Global Economy: Making Sense of the New World Order*. Boston, MA: Harvard Business School Press.

Pareto, V. (1901/1991). *The Rise and Fall of Elites — an Application of Social Theory*. New Brunswick, NJ: Transaction Publishers.

Portes, A. & Ross, A. R. (1976). Modernization for emigration: the medical brain drain from Argentina. *Journal of Inter-American Studies and World Affairs, 13*, 395–422.

Portes, A. and Rumbaut, R. G. (1996). *Immigrant America: A Portrait*. (2nd ed.) Berkeley, CA: University of California Press.

Powell, W. W. & DiMaggio, P. J. (eds.) (1991). *The New Institutionalism in Organizational Analysis*. Chicago: University of Chicago Press.

Reich, R. B. (1991). *The Work of Nations*. New York: Alfred A Knopf.

Schnapp, J. T. (1992). Epic demonstrations: fascist modernity and the 1932 exhibition of the fascist revolution. In R. J. Goslin (ed.), *Fascism, Aesthetics, and Culture* Hanover, NH: University Press of New England. 16.

Scott, W. R. (1993). Recent developments in organizational sociology. *Acta Sociologica 36*, 63–68.

Scott, W. R. (1995). *Governance in Organizational Fields: Decentralization and Evaluation in Context*. Mimeo: Stanford University.

Scott, W. R. (1998). *Organizations: Rational, Natural, and Open Systems*. (4th ed.). London: Prentice Hall International.

Smircich, L. & Calas, M. B. (1987). Organization culture: a critical assessment. In F. M. Jablin, *et al.*, (eds), *Handbook of Organizational Communication*. Newbury Park, CA: Sage. 228–263.

Stevens, R., Goodman, L. W & Mick, S. (1978). *The Alien Doctors: Foreign Medical Graduates in American Hospitals*. New York: Wiley.

Teitelbaum, M. S. (1980). Right versus right: immigration and refugee policy in the United States. *Foreign Affairs, 59*, 21–59.

Toulmin, S. (1990). *Cosmopolis: The Hidden Agenda of Modernity*. Chicago: University of Chicago Press.

U.S. Bureau of the Census. (1993). *The Foreign-Born Population in the United States*.

1990 Census of Population, CP-3-1. Washington, DC: U.S. Department of Commerce.

Wallerstein, I. (1979). *The Capitalist World Economy*. Cambridge: Cambridge University Press.

Weber, M. (1958). *The Protestant Ethic and the Spirit of Capitalism*. Charles Scribner's Sons.

Weick, K. E. (1979) *The Social Psychology of Organizing*. (2nd ed.). Reading, MA: Addison-Wesley.

Chapter 8

Business Corporations, Markets and the Globalisation of Environmental Problems

Peter Söderbaum

Interpretations of Globalisation

The dominant idea of development in our part of the world is increased welfare through maximum economic growth in GDP-terms. Competitiveness of nations and business corporations in international markets are among the main considerations. Transnational corporations are now penetrating almost all parts of the globe and 'globalisation' has become a key word to describe what is happening. Representatives of national governments and transnational corporations lobby for institutional arrangements that will further facilitate moves in the direction of free trade and free movements of financial capital.

The idea that economic growth and international trade in goods and services will increase welfare is largely built on neoclassical economics and legitimised by this theory. As part of this, business corporations are interpreted in a specific way as profit maximising organisations. Markets are similarly interpreted as an interaction of the impersonal forces of supply and demand. Neoclassical theory suggests specific interpretations of Man, of economics, efficiency, rationality and so on.

The interpretations of phenomena such as business corporations and markets suggested by neoclassical economists are certainly of interest. The argument here is rather that there are other interpretations of business companies, markets etc. that also deserve attention. It is furthermore

Critical Perspectives on Internationalisation, pp. 179–200.
ISBN: 0-08-044053-5

argued that the definitions, models or interpretations put forward for consideration are not only a matter of science but also of politics.

Recent events connected with the meeting of the World Trade Organisation (WTO) in Seattle and in April 2000 with the meeting by the International Monetary Fund (IMF) in Washington D.C. can be interpreted in this light. A number of Civil Society Organisations and other groups went together to express their protests about the current state of affairs concerning the WTO, the IMF and the World Bank.

The easy way of dealing with such protests is to argue that there are people who do not understand what is good for them and good for society as a whole. Another way of viewing the same pattern of events is to try to listen to the messages expressed by the various groups. As I see it, it is this latter project that is the most promising. Three themes seem to have been important when questioning dominant ideas about progress and macroeconomic development of the WTO, IMF and the World Bank. One is about the social and cultural aspects of the policies chosen and implemented by the three organisations. A second is about environmental impacts and a third about the implications of current policy for democracy at various levels.

According to the first theme, there are doubts about the beneficial social and cultural impacts of current policies. Following the rhetoric, equality should be enhanced and poverty reduced, if not eliminated altogether, through trickle down effects. But this very seldom happens in practice. Globalisation does not seem to be a good idea for poor people. International trade furthermore does not respect the cultural diversity of the world but rather leads to cultural homogeneity. A transnational company will market the same or very similar products in different parts of the world and these products often compete with local varieties with the probable result of reducing diversity.

Our second theme is about the environmental impacts of the current development trend largely supported by the three organisations. In addition to globalisation of the national economies into something that more and more becomes a global economy, we have a trend towards globalisation of environmental problems and the two may not be totally unrelated. As an example, the European Union in its environmental policy lists a number of serious environmental problems and the reader is invited to contemplate their relation to current trends in international trade and the market economy. The areas identified are: greenhouse gases and climate change, ozone depletion substances, dispersion of hazardous substances, transboundary air pollution, water stress, soil degradation, waste generation and management, natural and technological hazards, the release of genetically modified organisms (GMOs) to the environment, human health issues, biodiversity/ecosystems (European Environmental Agency 1999). To the extent that international trade and globalisation leads to increased transportation globally, this is probably adding to the problem with greenhouse gases, at least within the scope of current technology. Losses of biodiversity occur in more ways than one and this is sometimes the result of the operations of transnational companies. It appears clear that things can go seriously wrong in more ways than one, not only at the local but also the global level. This would degrade 'welfare' for many people according to any reasonable definition of the term. At issue is how much those who work for transnational corporations or the WTO know of or bother about these environmental aspects.

The third theme has to do with tendencies not to respect normal ideas about democracy. Transnational corporations for example only operate according to market laws in some limited sense and try to lobby to increase their power and 'freedom' through the WTO in all countries. This obviously does not lead to improved control by local or national governments. Another example is the position taken by Joseph Stiglitz, professor of economics at Stanford University. In an article, he argues that when IMF is said to 'negotiate' with individual countries, this is in reality no negotiation at all. IMF rather dictates what should be done by national governments and representatives of the organisation do not respect the knowledge often available in individual countries about the local situation (Stiglitz, 2000).

The main point here, however, is not to exclusively blame the three global organisations mentioned. If I were to walk in the streets to protest against major failures among experts and other establishment actors, I would rather turn to universities and in particular departments of economics to argue for pluralism as an alternative to the present neoclassical monism. This would probably not lead to any immediate action and would be too complex a message for many. As will be explained below, one has to live with some degree of complexity. Expressed in a different manner, the task ahead for us as economists and students of business is to add to the conceptual options available for all citizens, establishment actors included. As part of a pluralistic strategy, alternative ways of interpreting the world can be articulated. Such an effort may even, as we will see, lead us to an economics that differs significantly from the neoclassical version.

In the first part of the chapter the role of interpretation in institutional change processes is discussed. Individuals as professionals and in other roles are then identified as the main actors and it is suggested that the way an actor interprets specific phenomena such as 'business company' or 'market' plays a crucial role. Such interpretations are related to ideology as well as paradigms in economics and business management. In the final section, it is argued that by supporting and accepting certain interpretations in favour of others it is possible for us as individuals to influence globalisation processes in what we see as an attractive direction.

The Need for a Pluralist Political Economics

At the time of the classical economists, such as Adam Smith, David Ricardo and Thomas Malthus, economics was seen as a political project. Reference was made to 'political economics' and value issues were addressed rather than avoided. From 1870 until recently a positivistic tradition has been influential with the scholar standing outside watching what goes on in an alleged objective and value neutral manner. A 'pure' economics, free from values and politics, was what the neoclassical economists hoped to accomplish.

Already in the 1930s, Gunnar Myrdal, among economists, started to question such claims. According to him, "values are always with us" in social science research (Myrdal, 1978). The scholar is making a choice of problem and of conceptual frame of reference among several possibilities. He or she is choosing one method rather than another and presenting results in specific ways. To argue that all these options can be handled in a purely scientific and objective manner becomes increasingly strained. More recent developments in the social sciences emphasise the importance of the subjective aspects of scholarly work. Hermeneutics, social constructivism, action research, narrative analysis — all point in this direction. Scientists have become interested in listening to and interpreting the stories told by various actors in society and to contemplate how their own preconceptions and values influence the outcome of research.

I will here stress this interpretative aspect of scholarly work. It will furthermore be argued that values, ideology and politics are normally present in social science research. The 'pure economics project' of the nineteenth century is regarded as a failure and neoclassical economics should be seen as one political economics among several possibilities. Science, at least in the case of the social sciences, cannot be separated from politics. Similarly, all other actors in society, such as owners or professionals representing a business corporation, will be interpreted not only in scientific but also in political terms. Just as it is our assumption that science cannot be separated from politics, the same working hypothesis is used for actors in business and in the market place. As in all politics, democracy becomes a hallmark and the choice of one interpretation and conceptual framework rather than another is a politically sensitive matter. Expressed in a different manner, in a democracy, nobody has the right to dictate how people should interpret the world or how we should understand specific phenomena. Competition among schemes of interpretation and pluralism is a preferable state of affairs.

Interpretation and Institutional Theory

Not all economists were enthusiastic about the neoclassical project of a pure economics where laws or regularities are identified and 'proven' to be 'true' in a way comparable to the laws of physics and chemistry. Thorstein Veblen and John R. Commons were among the early sceptics and they developed an alternative paradigm that came to be referred to as institutional economics. Veblen and Commons saw economics as an evolutionary science with important relationships to biology, and among social disciplines, to sociology. Today institutional economists are organized in the US-based Association for Evolutionary Economics (AFEE) and the European Association for Evolutionary Political Economy (EAEPE).

The popularity of institutional theory in the social sciences, for instance sociology (Scott, 1995), business management (Powell & DiMaggio, 1991) and economic history (Magnusson 1994; Magnusson & Ottosson, 1997) suggests that this group of theories plays an important role. Institutional theory may even be dominant in the social sciences as a whole. While the neoclassical paradigm is relatively coherent in logical terms, the work by institutionalists seems to be characterised by a degree of heterogeneity. As an example, those interested in the study of 'institutions' often make a distinction between 'old' institutionalists (that is those working in the tradition of Veblen and Commons) and 'new' institutionalists, the latter being closer to neoclassical theory (Rutherford, 1996).

Even the term 'institution' has been defined in more ways than one. In the mentioned study Malcolm Rutherford refers to an institution as "a regularity of behaviour or a rule that is generally accepted by members of a social group, that specifies behaviour in specific situations, and that is either self-policed or policed by external authority" (Rutherford, 1996). My previous emphasis on schemes of interpretation suggests that 'institution' can be defined as 'a phenomenon that has a similar meaning for a larger or smaller number of individuals'. 'Institution' here refers to both the cognitive aspect of 'shared meaning' and the related symbolic, behavioural or organisational manifestations of this shared meaning. (The regularities and rules emphasised by Rutherford and others then belong to the 'manifestation'-aspect of institutions.) A handshake and a national symbol, such as a flag, exemplify the symbolic and manifest aspect of institutions. In relation to environmental issues, standardised 'environmental management systems' (ISO 14001, for instance) as well as 'eco-labelling' exemplify institutions.

The word 'meaning' in the above definition points to the importance of 'schemes of interpretation'. Where do such schemes of interpretation come from and how do they change? Is there a competition going on between groups that advocate different schemes of interpretation or models of specific phenomena? Could one speak of a dynamics where the meaning of words are changing gradually and new words emerge to replace, compete with, or complement other words?

I see it as very relevant to refer to such a dynamics if we want to understand what is going on in society. In part this is a matter of rather unconscious processes where language is formulated and reformulated as a result of the interaction between people in daily affairs. In some other part it appears relevant to speak of a political power game between actors and actor categories. And science and scientists have played and are playing a crucial role in this power game.

The concepts of 'institutionalisation' and 'legitimation' are at the heart of institutional theory. A specific phenomenon, such as Environmental Management Systems or even specific 'paradigms' such as the theory and language of neoclassical economics, may be strengthened over time as part of institutionalisation processes. The opposite may also occur, i.e., 'deinstitutionalisation' implying a reduced role for neoclassical economics in society. The processes of institutionalisation and legitimation normally follow each other. 'Deinstitutionalisation' is similarly connected with delegitimation. 'Reinstitutionalisation' is a further possibility, i.e., an institution that first appears and is strengthened, then for some time looses support in relation to competing institutions and later reappears on the scene.

Reasoning in terms of competition between various ways of interpreting the world can thus be applied to paradigms in economics. Scientific organisations and journals with the purpose of developing 'institutional economics' or 'ecological economics', exemplify manifestations of institutions and efforts to influence the relative importance of various interpretations of society and the economy.

Scientists have traditionally argued in favour of one clear specification and definition of each phenomenon. This is of course helpful but it is here suggested that also some ambiguity can be a good thing and that we sometimes should reinterpret phenomena and redefine concepts. It may even be a good thing to live with complementary or competitive interpretations. Many are those who see business corporations exclusively as profit maximising entities operating in markets. But there are other ideas of the business corporation. The increased popularity of Environmental Management Systems in business was previously mentioned. As part of this process, an increasing number of interested parties or stakeholders in relation to business companies extend their interpretations of co pany performance beyond monetary profits to include environmental performance. In this case, the institution of ISO 14001 (a standardised Environmental Management System) changes the meaning of another institution (business company). A competition is going on between a more narrow (only monetary profits) and a broader interpretation of business (also environmental performance).

A way of summarising the above is to refer to 'institutional change' that stands for a relationship between a phenomenon and specific individuals. This change can be described in terms of:

- change in the interpretation of phenomena by individuals;
- change in terminology and change in the meaning of specific terms from the point of view of the individual;
- change in the manifestation of a phenomenon (as official or voluntary rules, as organisations, cultural symbols or artifacts etc);
- change in emotional support for a phenomenon (i.e. affective aspect or credibility);
- change of the behaviour of the individual(s) in relation to the phenomenon;
- change in strategies and the organised support of the phenomenon with its manifestations, by individuals and interested groups.

According to this view, many partly overlapping aspects and processes are involved in institutional change. To further exemplify the competition that goes on between schemes of interpretation, I will first focus on alternatives to the neoclassical view of human beings, then turn to business corporations and finally to market relationships. While institutional change in the above sense is going on all the time in some respects, it is equally true that our world-views and conceptual frames of reference are characterised by considerable inertia and path dependence.

Individuals and Organisations as the Main Actors

In my interpretation the criticism of present policies of the WTO, IMF and the World Bank and the representatives of national governments acting through these organisations has to do with the dominance in the work of these organisations of a theoretical perspective largely connected with neoclassical economics. It might therefore be meaningful to search for other schemes of interpretation that will make the individual more visible in all her or his different roles, that will look at efficiency and rationality in multidimensional and ideologically open ways and that will take democracy seriously. In a democracy individuals (in their different roles) and organisations are the main actors and any attempt to move in the direction of social, ecological and financial sustainability has to involve these two categories of actors.

Our political economics approach suggests that individuals should be regarded as political beings and responsible actors. A Political Economic Person is therefore suggested (Söderbaum, 1999; 2000) as an alternative to the present reliance on neoclassical Economic Man assumptions. According to the PEP-view, the individual is a political being with many roles, many relationships and engaged in many kinds of activities. At a more integrated level, the individual has an identity, is part of various networks and can be described with respect to a pattern of activities or a lifestyle. When adapting to her context, our individual has some power and resources at her disposal. The motives and interests of the individual furthermore relate to each other as part of a 'ideological orientation', i.e., a worldview consisting of schemes of interpretation and connected language. The term ideological orientation is used to suggest that the ideas about means and ends of an individual are often fragmentary, tentative and uncertain and that values, ethics and ideology are involved. In Table 8.1 an attempt is made to more systematically compare the neoclassical with the suggested institutional view of individuals.

Table 8.1: The Individual; a Comparison Between Two Schemes of Interpretation.

	Economic Man	**Political Economic Person**
History	Not considered relevant	The individual is a product of her history
Context	Markets for products and factors of production	Political, socio-cultural, institutional, physical man-made, ecological
Roles	Consumer	Citizen, parent, professional, market related roles etc.
Relationships	Market relationships between selfish market actors	Market and non-market relationships of a cooperative and non-cooperative kind
Values	Maximum utility of commodities within budget constraint	Ideological orientation as guiding principle
Behaviour	Optimising	Habitual, 'rule following' Also learning and conscious choice (decisions)

The tendency in neoclassical economics is to emphasise static analysis. The future is considered while history is regarded as irrelevant since it cannot be changed. According to the Political Economic Person view (PEP-model), history is important, 'path dependence', inertia and irreversibility being key concepts. In neoclassical economics, the human being is regarded as a consumer and the relevant context is one of markets for commodities and factors of production. The consumer can sell her or his services in the labour market, for instance. The political economics model builds on a more complex idea of the individual's context. A political, social, cultural, institutional, physical man-made and ecological context is potentially relevant. And this context is not stable over time implying that the individual has to develop strategies to adapt to changes in various parts of the environment.

The PEP-model similarly considers many roles where the one of being consumer becomes a specific case. The role as citizen is of primary importance as part of any political model. As citizens and professionals many of us can influence social and environmental issues more than in our roles as consumers. The relationships considered by neoclassical economists are market relationships. Seller and buyer have each their motives and self-interest is assumed (as in the arguments about the beneficial role of the 'invisible hand'). The PEP-view recognises egoistic as well as 'other-related' motives. Amitai Etzioni, the sociologist, has suggested an 'I & We Paradigm' (Etzioni, 1988) according to which each person, in addition to a hopefully strong ego, has a feeling for others connected with the fact that the person perceives herself as being part of many 'we-categories'. Any tendency to speak of egoism and altruism in either-or terms is rejected in favour of a theoretical perspective where consideration of interests related to the 'ego' do not necessarily contradict a concern for the well-being of others. This suggests that relationships can be cooperative or non-cooperative, or a mixture of both. Relationships may furthermore be market relationships, non-market relationships or, again, a mixture of both (Table 8.1).

While neoclassicists refer to optimising behaviour and a consumer maximising utility, the institutional approach emphasises habitual behaviour and rule following. Among students of business, James March argues that decision makers may "pursue a logic of appropriateness, fulfilling identities and roles by recognising situations and following rules that match appropriate behaviour to situations they encounter" (March, 1994). Figure 8.1 suggests a similar approach. It is based on Political Economic Person assumptions with an individual's ideological orientation as the basis for valuing various alternatives or other phenomena. 'Matching' and 'pattern recognition' are key concepts in understanding this second idea of rationality and decision-making. Herbert Simon is one of those who have discussed limits and potentials of human cognition and who argues that the ability to recognise patterns is one of the strengths of humans (1983). It may be added that also some higher animals and other life forms probably have a developed ability to recognise patterns such as images of various kinds.

Thus rationality is regarded as a matter of the compatibility of an individual's ideological orientation with the expected impact profiles of specific alternatives considered. A more holistic idea of economics and resource allocation follows where visual, multidimensional and qualitative elements have a place as part of an essentially multidimensional idea of ideological orientation and of expected impacts. I believe this is a

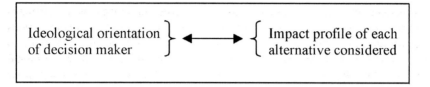

Figure 8.1: A Holistic Idea of Rationality and the Decision Act. The Ideological Profile of Each Decision Maker is Matched against the Expected Impact Profile of Each Alternative. *Source*: Söderbaum, 1999

fruitful scheme of interpretation for the case that one wishes to deal constructively with environmental and other development problems. A disaggregated approach to the comparison of alternatives (investment projects, for instance) means that monetary and non-monetary impacts are systematically kept separate throughout the analysis. This should of course not be interpreted as an assertion that monetary impacts are unimportant. It means, however, that estimates of monetary impacts only tell part of the story. A monetary calculation represents a partial analysis. The disaggregated view also opens the door for an idea that non-monetary impacts may be of importance by themselves (and not only through some imagined monetary equivalent). According to this view, the relative importance of various monetary and non-monetary impacts has to do with the knowledge position and ideological orientation of the observer.

Business Corporations and Other Organisations: Two Schemes of Interpretation

Another interest of ours is the organisation, whether business corporation or other. 'Business environmental organisations' such as the World Business Council for Sustainable Development (WBCSD) with its office in Geneva has made a number of studies which suggest an increasing awareness of the seriousness of environmental problems and the need to reconsider some parts of conventional business ideology. The WBCSD is a co-operative organisation for 120 transnational corporations. According to one interpretation, WBCSD exists to influence the agenda and policies concerning business corporations at the national and global levels and does not differ much from other pro-industry organisations. Another interpretation is that some actors in business understand that with increasing size (in terms of turnover, for instance) and power follows an increased social responsibility. The limited liability idea connected with the joint-stock company was perhaps useful and reasonable for some time but should today be replaced by principles of an 'extended responsibility'. Also broader issues about the continued growth of transnational corporations (the current 'merger mania' being one aspect) as wealth-creating machines (in a specific sense) in the global arena have to be raised (Korten 1995; 1999).

Something similar may hold for universities. Logical positivism as a theory of science with its ideas about objectivity and value-neutrality can be regarded as a limited responsibility doctrine for universities, departments and individual scholars. Actors within universities can be accused of sleeping behind curtains of objectivity and value-neutrality, while social and environmental problems are accumulating in the societies they are supposed to serve. A new doctrine is perhaps needed where the ideological and political character of research and education is recognised, where scientific rigour takes on a new meaning and where — as in the case of business — extended (rather than limited) responsibility becomes a key consideration.

There are many possible interpretations of organisations (e.g., Morgan, 1986) and even for business, one can point to models, other than that of the profit maximising firm. As an example, a stakeholder model has gained some popularity in the business management literature. The shareholders of a company are among the stakeholders, i.e., those who have something at stake in relation to the policies and activities of the company. But a number of other stakeholders or interested parties can be identified such as financial partners, other than shareholders, those employed by the company, customers, suppliers, the local municipality or the national society. Those living in the neighbourhood of a factory may suffer from pollution and so on. As part of the stakeholder model, the Chief Executive Officer (supported by the board) often get a role similar to that of a broker in relation to the various groups and interests.

The stakeholder model is not as simplistic as the idea of a centralised, profit maximising organisation. It represents a recognition that potential and real conflicts exist between the different stakeholder categories. One may add that there may be serious conflict also within one stakeholder category and even among shareholders. Some of us shareholders do not like the assumption often made that we are exclusively interested in 'shareholder value', i.e., dividends and the market price of shares. Rather

Table 8.2: Organisations; a Comparison Between the Neoclassical and an Institutional View.

	Profit maximising firm	**Political Economic Organisation**
History	Not considered relevant	The organisation is a product of its history, path-dependence
Context	Markets for products and factors of production	Political, socio-cultural, institutional, physical man-made, ecological
Purposes served	Profits for shareholders	Business concept, mission statement, 'Core Values', political ideology, 'social responsibility'
View of individual	Largely invisible	PEP, guided by an ideological orientation. Polycentric organisation
Relationships	Internally: largely invisble. Externally: market relationships	Interaction (cooperative and non-cooperative) between individuals as actors. Internally: administrative Externally: administrative and market
Interests related to corporation	Consensus idea based on assumed shareholder values	A complex of common and conflicting interests between stakeholder categories and individuals as actors
Decision act	Optimisation: maximum profits	Also 'rule-following', multi-dimensional impact studies. Matching ideology with expected impacts

than speaking of stakeholder groups as if they were homogenous, a model of Man that allows for differences as well as similarities between individuals is needed.

The Political Economic Organisation model (Table 8.2) builds on the indicated PEP-model in the sense that there is an (political) ambition to make individuals visible as responsible actors also in their professional roles. The 'Greening' of an organisation does not take place simultaneously for all employees, or for all members of other stakeholder categories. Normally, some will be reluctant to new ideas while others may act as 'environmental entrepreneurs'. Making individuals visible in an organisation is a way of recognising their importance for the company and in the economy and also a way of putting some pressure on them to behave in a responsible manner.

Another idea behind the PEO-model is that it should be useful and relevant not only for business companies but for all kinds of organisations, universities and civil society organisations included. Representatives of organisations of these kinds nowadays often speak about their environmental policies, e.g., as part of environmental management systems. In addition they may have personnel (or human resource) policies, financial policies, public relations policies etc. Reference to a Political Economic Organisation therefore appears reasonable, while assumptions that these organisations somehow operate outside the sphere of policies and politics become increasingly strained.

Market Relations: Two Schemes of Interpretation

Each actor connected with an organisation is related to a number of other actors. Relationships can be of many kinds such as administrative relationships between actors within the organisation, market relationships or more private relationships. Although non-market relationships are of importance also for business, our interest in the policies of international organisations will make us focus on market relationships.

The neoclassical view of markets in terms of supply and demand is rather mechanistic. Market actors have objectives that are fixed (in monetary or utility terms) and respond as robots to changes in market forces. The model is admittedly useful for some purposes, i.e. in discussing markets where commodities are in fact highly homogenous. Currency markets and the stock market can be given as examples.

In the case of agricultural products like wheat, an increasing number of consumers make distinctions between wheat that is produced in the conventional way with chemical pesticides and the like and wheat that is the product of 'ecological agriculture'. This suggests that, in analysis, one should distinguish between (at least) two commodities that each can be relatively homogenous. In the case of industrial markets, e.g. the relationship between Volvo (or ABB) and its suppliers (see Ford, 1990; Forsgren & Johanson, 1989; Håkansson & Snehota, 1995), the idea of focusing on prices of homogenous products becomes even less relevant. The quality of commodities purchased by Volvo change gradually as a result of new designs of cars or other vehicles produced. Actors employed by Volvo may furthermore engage in technological co-operation with actors in a supplier company, implying that the borders between the two become less clear. The social relationship between actors could be one of trust and friendship. A firm may furthermore own shares in a supplier company and vice versa. Transaction costs are involved in abandoning one relationship in favour of another.

In the case of Volvo above, and more generally for all market actors, there are potential ethical issues involved in all selling and purchasing decisions. Etzioni's 'I & We paradigm' is relevant here. The buyer may bother about the impacts on the seller and vice versa. Each of the buyer and seller can perceive herself and the other as involved in a 'we-category' as opposed to ideas of two actors who each selfishly is seeking maximum gain. John R. Commons, one of the early American institutional economists, argued that the issue is one of prices that are judged to be 'reasonable' or 'fair' by both parties, rather than prices that are the result of mechanistic forces. Earlier religious thinkers like Thomas ab Aquino argued in favour of 'just' prices as early as in the 13th century. In more recent times John Kenneth Galbraith has pointed to 'administered' prices and prices as the outcome of social dialogue and negotiation processes. Among present institutionalists, especially Yngve Ramstad points to the continued importance of Commons' ideas about fair or reasonable prices and wages (Ramstad, 1987).

The important thing, once more, is not to question the neoclassical view of markets, but to argue for a pluralistic economics. There are more interpretations than one, even of the market for one specific commodity, like coffee, with specific market actors involved. In Table 8.3, an attempt is made to compare the neoclassical idea of a market with my institutional view. And again, the choice of one model or interpretation in favour of another is in some part a choice based on ideological orientation.

Table 8.3: The 'Market' as a Phenomenon; Two Schemes of Interpretation.

	Neoclassical	**Institutional**
View of Man	Economic Man	Political Economic Person
View of organisation	Profit-maximising firm	Political Economic Organisation
Interaction between buyer and seller	Supply and demand	Multifaceted relationship between responsible actors
Goods and services	Homogeneous	Heterogeneous
Motives for purchasing decisions	Utility related to quantity and monetary price (optimisation)	Ideological considerations; 'monetary price and beyond' (matching)
Relation to other actors	Emphasis on personal gain (Belief in 'invisible hand')	Inclusive ('I & We Paradigm', 'Person in Community')
Features of relationship	Independence. Contract between parties with conflicting interests	Also cooperation. Considerations of trust and fairness

Table 8.3 can throw some light on the current debate about business companies and markets. With neoliberalism has followed a tendency to expand the sphere of economic reasoning. Ideas of 'economic rationality' and 'market efficiency' connected with neoclassical economics have been used in public debate for almost every sphere of human life or social relationships. This so-called 'economism' is often criticised and it is argued that the role of such arguments should be reduced rather than expanded. I agree, but like to emphasise that also for spheres of social life where it is generally accepted that the market has a role, there is an issue about the kind of market interpretation to be used.

In Sweden and various European countries 'eco-labelling' is more or less institutionalised. Another recent trend is to offer certain products with a 'fair trade' label. Sometimes the two are combined as in the case of coffee sold in Sweden with 'Four Seasons' as its trademark. Actors indoctrinated in neoclassical economics will probably have even more difficulties with the fair trade idea than they already have with eco-labelling. Producers and traders are expected to limit attention to their own interests and the same is true of the consumer. If some market actors start to bother about other market actors, it becomes difficult or impossible to forecast their behaviour on the basis of traditional models. One get the impression that market actors should behave in a way that minimises problems for the neoclassical model builders.

In the case of coffee, the idea of 'fair trade' means that some consumers in Sweden are no longer exclusively interested in a price as low as possible for a given quality of coffee. They also take an interest in the way that the coffee is produced, for instance with respect to environmental impacts, health impacts and social impacts. Will the smallholders producing coffee in Uganda and Tanzania receive a 'fair' price for their product or not? As suggested by the right hand side of Table 8.3, rather than the neoclassical commodity approach, a multidimensional systems view, is applied. Lifecycle Analysis with its 'from cradle to grave' approach can be used in the sense that the product is followed from its cultivation (with connected inputs), transportation, treatment, consumption and disposal. Price and quality still matter, but so do a number of other parameters.

Against this background we can return to our concerns about the World Trade Organisation and the Seattle events. An increasing number of representatives of civil society organisations, labour unions etc. formulated their arguments in terms that rather are compatible with the right hand side in Table 8.3. Susan George as an example referred to 'multi-functionality' in her effort to explain the view of some of the critics (George, 1999). Representatives of transnational corporations and some governments appear to have difficulties in understanding this broader view, or they resist it for ideological reasons and considerations of their own power positions in society. In the WTO dialogue as an example, representatives of the USA only regard neoclassical theory as a legitimate conceptual framework. The commodity and its price are relevant while arguments connected with the social and ecological context of its production are 'forbidden' or considered irrelevant. I see this as a good example of the role of neoclassical theory to legitimise a neoliberal ideology. It seems to me that the monopoly of neoclassical theory at many American, European and other universities plays an important and questionable political role.

While neoliberalism and much neoclassical theory come close to market fundamentalism, our alternative scheme of interpretation can be understood as a 'conditional view of markets'. The market is neither inherently good, nor bad. It all depends on the ideological orientation of the observer and the market actors involved with their respective ideological orientation, the impacts on market actors themselves and on third parties and the rules of interaction in the market under study, which in turn may be given by law, or be of a voluntary kind. Instead of dogmatically arguing that market transactions are always beneficial, this view suggests that impacts have to be identified in a multidimensional manner and that it is a matter of the kind of ideology and ethics applied, whether a specific market or market relationship turns out as a good or bad one.

Role and Responsibility of Business Leaders and University Scholars

Considering the serious environmental and social threats facing mankind, actors in business companies and universities alike have to reorient many of their activities to become part of a solution rather than aggravate the problems. Scientists are political economic persons like other actors in society. Criteria to distinguish between good science and bad science will still be there, but criteria that seriously consider ethical, ideological and political aspects, will differ a bit from traditional ones.

For the two fields of business management and economics, possible ways of relating to environmental issues can be divided into three categories, namely 1) no adaptation to environmental concerns and demands, 2) adaptation within the scope of traditional conceptual framework, theory and method, and 3) adaptation by reconsidering conceptual framework, theory and method as part of a pluralistic attitude.

A large part of textbooks in economics and business management still fall into the 'no adaptation' category. It is still possible, if not normal, to achieve a degree in economics and/or business management without taking any course or reading any textbook addressing environmental issues. And when the environment and natural resources are brought into the picture, the usual approach is to extend the dominating paradigm (category 2) above). Neoclassical economists point to negative 'externalities' or third-party impacts and the possibility to 'internalise' such externalities through environmental charges. Cost-benefit analysis can similarly be broadened to include the monetary value of 'environmental commodities'. Similarly, students of business and other organisations can try to estimate the monetary value of investments in preventive measures or otherwise look for environmental strategies that maximise monetary profits.

Economists in the third category, i.e., those who look for alternatives to neoclassical theory and method are increasing in number (cf. category 3)). In addition to early contributions in *Journal of Economic Issues*, one can point to the popularity in the 1990s of the International Society for Ecological Economics with a number of regional chapters. Some institutional economists like myself, regard neoclassical economics as an important part of the environmental problems faced. Getting closer to a socially, ecologically and financially sustainable society is not only a matter of science, but also one of ideology, and neoclassical economics tends to legitimise an ideology and development pattern that appears increasingly problematic.

When students of business management similarly extend or reconsider their frameworks (cf., category 3)), they are — when compared to neoclassical economists — in a favourable position to do so. They are less restricted to traditional ideas of science connected with logical positivism and are more open to the subjective aspects of scholarly work. Students of business furthermore seek relevant knowledge for practical purposes and often consider models developed in other disciplines or at an interdisciplinary level. Organisation theory is such a field where sociology and social psychology is of importance. In addition to simplistic ideas of a profit maximising firm, stakeholder theories and other models of organisations are considered. Phenomena such as environmental management schemes (ISO 14001, for example) are not readily understood as part of traditional ideas of profit maximisation, but can be interpreted as part of organisation theory.

Many business actors will similarly move in a direction of extended responsibility. Environmental management systems will continue to play a role in this, but will hardly be enough. At a more fundamental level, simplistic business ideologies in terms of profits and shareholder value will have to be reformulated. Competing or complementary views of individuals, economics, and markets as discussed in this paper, will play a role in this transformation process. There is also a need for a broader discussion about the kind of market economy that is compatible with dominating ideas about democracy. David Korten's books mentioned above are relevant here.

Ideologies of Globalisation: Neoliberalism and its Alternatives

In many ways we are living in a world that can be described as global. New developments in information technology are an example of this. At issue is what kind of social and institutional change processes we will see in the future — locally, regionally and at the global level.

Since the beginning of the 1980s, neoliberalism has been the dominant ideology among leading actors in the West. Margaret Thatcher came to power and guided to a large extent the neoliberal revolution in Britain. It was argued that there is no alternative to neoliberalism and the desirability of competition at all levels (between nations, regions, firms and individuals) became a leading doctrine (George, 2000). The egoism and even greediness of individuals was encouraged as a way of increasing economic growth and welfare. It was believed that organisations and infrastructure owned by the state could not be efficient and that privatisation was a necessity even in cases of 'natural monopolies'. This ideology was largely made legitimate through the work and messages of influential economists such as Friedrich von Hayek and Milton Friedman.

The protests in Seattle and at other places suggest that the political propaganda of neoliberal propaganda centres has not been as successful as intended. Many are those who look for a different future where cooperation is as important as competition and where the rights and responsibilities of various actors in society are discussed openly. The transfer of power from citizens and the state to transnational corporations is not compatible with normal Western imperatives of democracy and has to be reversed. In this chapter I have argued that scholars at the universities have a role in the debate about conceptual framework, language and even ideology.

Also representatives of industry and other actors who have supported neoliberalism and tended to avoid debate in the past have to participate in this dialogue. Their responsibility for the sad state in social and environmental terms of our planet should not be underestimated. New forms of cooperation between business and NGOs and between business and universities will hopefully emerge (Bendell, 2000). Why should business actors not listen to other arguments than the most simple ones i.e. those connected with neoliberalism? A return to the mixed economy is one option for those who now regard neoliberalism as an illusion (Passset, 2000).

The road ahead can be looked upon in many ways. In the present chapter, I have argued that 'protectionism' in the sense of monopoly for neoclassical economics is a threat to all of us and that this monopoly for one paradigm does not go well with democracy. In the same sense business actors have been protectionists concerning business ideology and ideology for society as a whole. Pluralism — and even 'competition' between advocates of different theoretical perspectives and ideologies is a better idea. Individuals and business corporations can be understood in more ways than one and the same is true of markets. Fortunately we are still 'free to choose' how we want to approach and understand the world.

References

Bendell, J. (Contributing ed.) (2000). *Terms for Endearment. Business, NGOs and Sustainable Development*. Sheffield: Greenleaf Pub.

Etzioni, A. (1988). *The Moral Dimension. Toward a New Economics*. New York: Free Press.

European Environmental Agency *http://themes.eea.eu.int*

Ford, D. (ed.) (1990). *Understanding Business Markets. Interaction, Relationships, Networks*. London: Academic Press.

Forsgren, M. & Johansson, J. (eds) (1989). *Managing Networks in International Business*. Uppsala University, Department of Business Studies.

George, S. (1999). Seattle prepares for battle. Trade before freedom. *Le Monde Diplomatique*. http://www. Monde-diplomatique.fr/en/1999/11

George, S. (2000). A short history of neoliberalism. Twenty years of élite economics and emerging opportunities for structural change. In B. Walden, N. Bullard & K. Malhotra (eds), *Global Finance. New Thinking on Regulating Speculative Capital Markets*. London: Zed Books.

Håkansson, H. & Snehota, I. (eds) (1995). *Developing Relationships in Business Networks*. London: Routledge.

Kapp, K. W. 1971 (1950) *The Social Costs of Private Enterprise*. New York: Shocken Books.

Korten, D. C. (1995). *When Corporations Rule the World*. West Hartford CT: Kumarian Press.

Korten, D. C. (1999). *The Post-Corporate World. Life After Capitalism*. West Hartford CT: Kumarian Press.

Magnusson, L. (ed.) (1994). *Evolutionary and Neo-Schumpeterian Approaches to Economics*. Dortrecht: Kluwer.

Magnusson, L. & Ottosson, J. (eds) (1997). *Evolutionary Economics and Path Dependence*. Cheltenham: Edward Elgar.

March, J. G. (1994). *A Primer for Decision Making*. New York: Free Press.

Morgan, G. (1986). *Images of Organization*. London: SAGE.

Myrdal, G. (1978). Institutional economics. *Journal of Economic Issues 12*, December, 771–783.

Passet, R. (2000). *L'illusion néo-liberale*. Paris: Fayard.

Powell, W. W. & DiMaggio, P. J. (1991). *The New Institutionalism in Organizational Analysis*. Chicago: Chicago University Press.

Ramstad, Y. (1987). Free trade versus fair trade: import barriers as a problem of reasonable value. *Journal of Economic Issues, 21(1)*, 5–32.

Rutherford, M. 1996 (1994). *Institutions in Economics. The Old and the New Institutionalism*. Cambridge: Cambridge University Press.

Scott, R. W. (1995). *Institutions and Organizations*. London: SAGE.

Simon, H. A. (1983). *Reason in Human Affairs*. London: Basil Blackwell.

Stiglitz, J. (2000). IMF underminerar demokratin (IMF is undermining democracy). *Dagens Nyheter*, Kultur B2, April 19.

Söderbaum, P. (1999). Values, ideology and politics in ecological economics. *Ecological Economics 28*, 161–170.

Söderbaum, P. (2000). *Ecological Economics. A Political Economics Approach to Environment and Development*. London: Earthscan.

World Business Council for Sustainable Development (WBCSD) (1997). *Signals of Change. Business Progress Towards Sustainable Development*.

Theme Two

Critical Views on the Received Theory of Internationalisation

Virpi Havila, Mats Forsgren and Håkan Håkansson

Internationalisation is a topic that has received a great deal of attention over the years. As the word indicates, internationalisation refers to a process of change, in which companies that had previously done little (or no) business internationally begin to do more. The main argument is that companies, at least in the Western world, have generally become more international, and the questions are, why, how and what are the consequences?

When trying to identify the causes of increased internationalisation, economic researchers face a huge problem. It is impossible to use a static economic model to explain a change. Instead, there are two other options for seeking an explanation. The first is to keep the static model and to explain the change by finding a change in an exogenous variable/condition that can explain the development. For example, there might be a political change, such as the creation of the EU, that creates a new situation (new set of factor costs) to which the companies will adapt. The second option is to develop a dynamic model. Within this option there are different alternatives. For example, internationalisation can be seen as a unique process that must be investigated and conceptualised separately. Another alternative is to see internationalisation as one type of effect of a more basic dynamic process; that is, it may be seen as one among several results of a certain process, such as an increased general specialisation, for example. If we look at the contributions in this volume we can see that they all belong to the dynamic group. There is also a clear focus on the view of internationalisation as a unique process that must be conceptualised and investigated in itself.

Focusing on internationalisation, a researcher can choose either to look for explanations within the units that are becoming more interna-

tional — in this case, the companies — or they can look at the environment. In the first alternative, the researcher assumes that *the companies
becoming more international have developed some special features*, which in
turn influence the internationalisation process. It can be changes in the
total amount of controlled resources or in the way companies are structured, or the development of some special objectives (goals) or some specific experience that can cause the change. Size and the existence of
suitable internal capabilities (e.g., language abilities) are two such examples. The Uppsala internationalisation model, for example, uses explanations of this type. In that model, internationalisation is seen as a process
in which increased knowledge is combined with successive economic
commitments in foreign markets. Thus, the model focuses mainly on
internal factors to find explanations for the development.

In the second alternative, *factors influencing the internationalisation
process can be found in the environment*. It can be factors in the task
environment — the environment within which the company directly
works (including customers and suppliers), or it can be in the wider
environment, such as the level of development in the country in which the
company originates or to which it is heading. The explanations might be
related to the existence of specific counterparts, or they may be linked to
more basic factors such as the growth of the market. The classical
Vernon model based on the product life cycle model is a good example.
In that model, the development is assumed to be driven by a general
factor such as sophisticated demand and the age of the technology/
product, and the companies are adapting to how the age is influencing
economic opportunities.

The internal and external factors can also be combined *(it is the third
alternative, see the text)*. In this case some internal feature in relation to a
specific environmental factor or sector is used to explain changes. This is
also, at least in an indirect way, the case for the models referred to above.
For example, the Uppsala model uses market commitment to relate internal and external factors to each other. The experience curve type of argument in the model is another. In these situations the development of the
internal capabilities are related to a specific aspect of the environment.

The internal and external factors can also be related to each other
more systematically and actively *(it is the fourth alternative, see the
text)*. The focus in this case is on the interaction between the unit and
the environment, i.e., the environment in terms of specific counterparts.
Starting with interaction leads to an interest in some kind of joint development taking place where the unit influences and at the same time is

influenced by the environment. In this case we have to study how different factors and features in the unit influence, and are influenced by, specific factors in these other units. Internationalisation is, in this case, a process that is closely related to the overall development of the interface between the company and its environment, in terms of the network of which it is part.

This interface can be viewed in terms of interdependency. All models that focus on internationalisation assume that there exists a certain level of interdependency between the unit and the environment. In most cases the interdependencies are formulated in general terms, that is, relating a certain feature in the unit to a certain factor in the environment. An alternative is to assume that there is a set of interdependencies between the company and individual counterparts and that the interaction between the companies results in the development of these interdependencies: thus, the interdependencies that exist within and between business relationships develop over time. The interface between the unit and the environment in such cases is seen as a dynamic set of relationships within a dynamic larger network of relationships.

Below, we have brought together the contributions discussing models of the internationalisation process under two headings based on the above characterisation. In the first section, entitled *Internationalisation from a Company Perspective,* we have placed the contributions that focus on internal factors and in which the environment is seen mainly as creating certain opportunities. In the second section, entitled *Internationalisation from a Network Perspective,* contributions viewing internationalisation as a result of interaction between the company and the surrounding actors are presented.

Part IV

Internationalisation from a Company Perspective

Many of the contributions in this section take the Uppsala internationalisation model as their starting point (Johanson & Vahlne, 1977). This model suggests that internationalisation is accomplished in a stepwise manner, in which companies, in a successive and incremental way, expand their foreign operations geographically as well as within each foreign country in which they operate. The basic mechanisms behind this process are learning and risk handling.

We start this section with a contribution by two of the researchers behind the Uppsala model, Jan-Erik Vahlne and Jan Johanson. In their contribution, *New Technology, New Companies, New Business Environments and New Internationalisation Processes?*, they discuss how changes in the environment in terms of the "new economy" are affecting the way companies approach international markets. In other words, they discuss the validity of the internationalisation process model for the new millennium (Johanson & Vahlne, 1977; 1990). The authors compare how modern companies internationalise with how Swedish companies did 100 years ago. The conclusion is that there are some important differences due to recent developments, but that the model is still relevant and useful for predicting and understanding internationalisation processes of individual companies.

In the second contribution, *Internationalisation — Real Options, Knowledge Management and the Uppsala Approach*, Peter J. Buckley, Mark Casson and Mohammed Azzim Gulamhussen connect to the Uppsala model and try to develop a bridge to a more rational model with the use of real options. Internationalisation is looked at from an investment point of view, and one important assumption is that it is costly to invest in several directions at the same time. Internationalisation involves investments in foreign facilities and organisational units, as well as investments in information regarding the international conditions.

In the third and fourth contributions, two dimensions in the Uppsala internationalisation model are examined, namely, time and expectation. In the contribution, *Knowledge and Time: A Forgotten Factor in the Internationalisation Process of Firms*, Anders Blomstermo, Kent Eriksson and D. Deo Sharma elaborate on the effect of time on knowledge and learning. The authors base the discussion on a review of how time, seen as duration of international operations, has been treated in international business literature. The review shows that time is often treated implicitly, and therefore the authors call for more research on how time affects learning in the internationalisation process. In the fourth contribution, *The Fifth Dimension — Expectations in the Internationalisation Process Model*, Amjad Hadjikhani and Martin Johanson discuss the need to include expectation as a separate dimension, besides market knowledge, market commitment, current activities and commitment decisions. In this way the authors want to meet the criticism that there exists an imbalance in the model regarding experiental knowledge and market commitment.

The connection between internationalisation and technology is taken up by John Cantwell and Elena Kosmopoulou in the fifth contribution, *What Determines the Internationalisation of Corporate Technology?*. They start out with a critical analysis of two classical propositions stating that large firms from small countries tend to internationalise technology more quickly than large companies from large markets, and that less research-intensive industries tend to be more international in their technological acting compared with industries that are highly research-intensive. The authors claim that in order to understand the international location of innovative activity in large firms, there are reasons to include two more variables. One is to make a distinction between inward and outward investments, and the other is to make a distinction between industry and technology. The new, more comprehensive, model is then tested on a data material based on patents.

In the last contribution in this section, *Developing an Internally Driven Growth Strategy in Network Organizations: An Organizational Learning Approach*, Peter Lorange discusses the possibilities for firms to take their own initiatives in changing the environment. It is a question of renewing the company, either through finding new partners or through developing new solutions for the existing ones (or by combining the two). The issue is formulated from a strategic point of view, and it indicates the possibilities for the individual company to influence its own position. However, the development cannot be done in isolation from the environment but rather must be done in close interaction with it. The environment is not given — it can be influenced. Furthermore, the resources within the company are not given, but can also be developed. Thus, the theme in this contribution is a natural link to the final group of contributions.

References

Johanson, J. & Vahlne, J.-E. (1977). The internationalization process of the firm — a model of knowledge development and increasing foreign market commitments. *Journal of International Business Studies, 8*, 23–32.

Johanson, J. & Vahlne, J.-E. (1990). The mechanism of internationalization. *International Marketing Review, 7*, 11–24.

Chapter 9

New Technology, New Companies, New Business Environments and New Internationalisation Processes?

Jan-Erik Vahlne and Jan Johanson

Sociologist Manuel Castells' concept of "the new economy", which implies that the economy, thanks to information technology, can enjoy rapid growth with few disadvantages, is almost daily an object of public debate. Is the economy really functioning in a novel way, or is it just a matter of a temporary phenomenon, and will we soon be back to normal in terms of, for example, inflationary pressure? But proponents and non-believers seem to be united in the opinion that the information era has indeed changed the business environment. This change has triggered the idea that it would be useful to somewhat update our knowledge on inter-nationalisation behaviour. For this purpose, we study the inter-nationalisation of a number of IT firms — e-commerce and Internet consultants — and a set of more "traditional businesses" that have recently gone abroad. In this study we use the Johanson and Vahlne (1977, 1990) internationalisation process model as a framework for ana-lysis. This model has been criticized on several grounds, among them, that changing environmental conditions would make the model invalid. Thus, as a secondary result of the study, we get some feeling of the present empirical validity of the model.

   The chapter is organized as follows: first, we present and comment on some aspects of the new business environment which can be expected to have a bearing on the pattern and pace of the internationalisation of firms. Second, based on a short presentation of the internationalisation

Critical Perspectives on Internationalisation, pp. 209–227.
Copyright © 2002 by Elsevier Science Ltd.
All rights of reproduction in any form reserved.
ISBN: 0-08-044053-5

process model, we outline how we use a number of case studies for the analysis of internationalisation behaviour. Third, we present the case studies and discuss some of the results. In this discussion we also compare the cases currently under study with a set of firms that went abroad a fairly long time ago. Finally, we draw some conclusions.

The New Business Environment

Many authors like to paint pictures of the changing business environment in very dramatic colours. For us, it started with Igor Ansoff stating that the environment is becoming turbulent. The latest, but presumably not the last, is Nordström and Ridderstråhle (1999) arguing that there is a revolution going on (p. 24). "Change and then change again. We are facing a world of chaos and genuine uncertainty" (p. 36). They, like many others, believe that the development of information technology, especially the Internet, is the main cause of this alleged dramatically accelerated change process.

"Think of the Internet not as a network of connected computers but as the testbed for a new market economy, one that is global, continuously operating, and increasingly automating the process of buying, selling, producing and distributing" (Downes & Mui, 1998). It creates a business environment where time, distance, location and communication are no longer hurdles for doing business (Mougayar, 1998, as referred to by Ekström & Persson, 1999). It is true, of course, that information and knowledge have been made much more accessible, suggesting that experiential learning is no longer as important as it used to be. But that knowledge is mainly of an objective nature in Penrose's (1966) terms. It is available to all firms, and information on suppliers, customers, products and prices, for example, will make competition more intense without really changing uncertainty. Value chains are reorganized and, in principle, a supplier can deal directly with end-users without relying upon intermediaries. It is also possible to develop one-to-one customer relationships via the Internet (Ekström & Persson, 1999).

The volume of Internet users seems to be growing rapidly. At the end of 1997 the percentage of the population in Western Europe having access to the Internet was 5.8; in 1998 it was 10.6, and in 1999 the percentage was 16.5. By the end of the year 2002 this percentage is expected to have grown to 35 (Winram & Steib, 1999). The three Nordic countries Finland, Norway and Sweden had a penetration rate of around 30 percent in 1998, while the US, according to the same source, (Ekström & Persson, 1999) in that year had a penetration rate of 32 percent, the highest in the world. Electronic commerce, the buying and selling of products and services over the Internet, has grown surprisingly slowly, according to some observers. So far it seems as if the business-to-business segment has been developing more rapidly than the business-to-consumer segment of the total electronics market. However, expectations are enormously high, manifested in the skyrocketing prices of so called IT-stocks on some exchanges. The most extreme cases in Sweden happen to be included in the sample for this paper. Information Highway, an Internet consulting company, increased its stock price by 2200 percent during 1999, while the two competitors, Icon Medialab and Framfab, stayed with 600–900 percent. Of these, only Framfab has shown "black figures" so far. Icon Medialab has been rated as by far the most overvalued company on the Swedish stock exchange (*Dagens Industri* Jan. 7, 2000).

Globalisation is often mentioned as a key aspect of environmental change. The essence of this idea is given in the metaphor of "the global village", that is, everything is within reach, and location is of little relevance from a general business point of view. International trade, international production, international mergers and acquisitions as well as international alliances have increased rapidly, which may be seen as indications that globalisation is indeed a real phenomenon. The tendency towards globalisation has run parallel to "localization", an effort to go local, especially in relation to development activities, where face-to-face communication is judged to be critical.

A step towards globalisation is regionalisation, the formation of regional economic unions and free-trade areas. When Sweden joined the European Union in the early 1990s it considerably facilitated the process of internationalisation, at least for smaller companies.

It is frequently said that cultural differences, due to phenomena such as the above-mentioned, are decreasing (Levitt, 1983) and that our ability to deal with remaining differences has increased. Nordström (1991), relying upon researchers such as Levitt and Porter, argues that homogenisation may be one reason why internationalisation processes seem to be more rapid, both in terms of increasing geographical scope and "leapfrogging" modes, compared with what has been found in earlier studies (Hörnell, Vahlne & Wiedersheim-Paul, 1973). However, a close look at the empirical results of Nordström's study shows that the pattern and pace of firm internationalisation in his sample is surprisingly like those in the older sample (Nordström, 1991).

At this point it can really be questioned whether the initially cited statement by Nordström and Ridderstråle, that we are living in a time of "genuine uncertainty", is more correct now than it would have been earlier. The general competitive climate and rapid technological change may merit such characterization, but if we consider the environment for conducting international business in a narrower sense, it may be the other way around: there may well be less uncertainty than previously.

The Model

The model we use in describing and discussing the internationalisation processes of modern companies was developed to explain an observed incremental internationalisation behaviour with its two dimensions: the geographical scope and degree of commitment to each market (Hörnell *et al.*, 1973). Its critical assumptions are that internationalisation is characterized by uncertainty and that actors are managing risk in seeking long-term profitability of companies. The most important means to achieve this is assumed to be growth.

Basic to our view is that the model as such concerns how uncertainty is coped with. In the face of uncertainty the firm commits resources to foreign markets and operations incrementally as it learns from experience. Since the critical knowledge is of an experiential nature, performing regular business activities is seen as the means for learning. In the 1990 version we explicitly incorporated the network view in the model. It assumes that critical business activity concerns exchange, which is a matter involving at least two parties, and consequently the processes of learning and building commitment occur in both the internationalising company and its counterparts.

So, this is the model. It is a black box, which we did not look into empirically. The observed pattern of gradual geographical extension and deepened commitment to each market is seen as a manifestation of the internationalisation process and, consequently, as an indication of the validity of the model. But exactly what modes, or order of modes and national markets are applied depend on various contextual aspects and are consequently not to be seen as a part of the model. Parenthetically, as the most important change aspect of the model is learning, and the specific modes of dealing with a foreign market are of no importance, we always resisted its being labelled a "stages" model.

The Empirical Base

Currently supervizing students performing their thesis work allowed one of us to initiate case studies on internationalisation. Armed with what has been written on internationalisation processes, the students interviewed people at HQs of Swedish companies to describe and explain the internationalisation processes of the firms to which they had access. Four such teams have kindly shared their raw data with us. The subjects of the case studies, respectively, were: fifteen mostly young industrial and trading companies in "traditional businesses" having rather recently started to internationalise; the four best-known Swedish e-commerce companies, and the four best-known Internet consulting companies.

Finally, four case studies from one of the empirical inputs into the internationalisation process model are revisited (Johanson & Wiedersheim-Paul, 1975).

The Case Studies

Below, we briefly summarize the various case studies in relevant dimensions. The summary is structured according to business mission: the non-IT companies ("traditional businesses"), the electronic commerce companies and the Internet consulting companies. Then the four Swedish cases are revisited.

The Non-IT Companies

Fifteen "traditional businesses" were studied by Dahlén and Åkerblom (2000) and Kjellman, Landqvist and Olson (2000), about one-half them in producer goods and services and the other half in consumer goods. A few are high-tech, most are low-tech. There is, for example, clothing, garden furniture and chemical substances, but also equipment for testing of certain specialized electronic devices and market research services. The companies are small, with at the most a hundred employees, but one had fewer than ten employees. A large majority is family owned.

In several cases it was realized at the outset that the Swedish market would be too small and, consequently, internationalisation started at the founding of the company. In other cases it started later, typically somewhat incidentally, when, for example, visiting or actively participating in an exhibition in Sweden, contacts leading to business in foreign markets were initiated. In a couple of cases searching or being approached via the Internet opened up new relationships on both the input and output sides. In a few cases internationalisation started at the input side or was at least parallel with starting to market in foreign markets.

In terms of geographical scope, these companies typically followed the traditional sequence of starting close to home and then gradually entering more distant, in terms of cultural differences, markets. Most seemed interested in securing the "home market", which was considered to be the four Nordic countries, and then proceeding to other North European markets. There were, of course, exceptions to this general pattern. A few companies explicitly recognized that potential demand was more promising in markets more distant than their European neighbours, notably the US. Two examples are a company marketing clothes for outdoor leisure activities and a company marketing testing equipment for electronic devices. In the first example, the existence of the Internet, the Internet penetration and the fact that potential customers could be expected to use the Internet, were important determinants.

Possibly (but this rests on somewhat arbitrary judgement) the speed has increased: some companies go international immediately, and many proceed quickly once they start. According to statements given by interviewees in the companies studied (Dahlén & Åkerblom, 2000), some companies go for markets where the Internet penetration is high. This, on the other hand, seems to correlate well with indices of psychic distance (Ekström & Persson, 1999), as Northern European countries score high in this regard. The exception is the US, being the country with the highest Internet penetration, but being only the eighth or ninth country in order of psychic distance from Sweden, according to by now relatively old rankings produced by Nordström (1991) and Hörnell et al. (1973).

In terms of the second dimension of the internationalisation process, the incrementally increased degree of commitment to each market, there are some interesting observations. However, in many cases companies have been active in most markets a short time only, and hence it is somewhat early to conclude. The observations made so far in the companies studied indicate that, typically, companies proceed from ad hoc types of exporting activities into a stage of more regular, routinized business. Typically, contracts have been closed with importers or agents. But only in a small minority of the cases has the process proceeded into the formation of the company's own sales subsidiaries. And the expressed opinion is often that the combination of previous relationships and the

Internet will suffice. Such statements will have to be taken cautiously, of course, but they happen to be consistent with observations that some companies with their own offices or subsidiaries in foreign markets in fact consider withdrawing these (Dahlén & Åkerblom, 2000). It is believed that tasks currently performed by local subsidiary employees can instead be done via the Internet by staff at head office. In this way information will not be "filtered".

Dahlén and Åkerblom (2000) explicitly investigated companies' use of the Internet. All companies had home pages and communicated extensively via e-mail. A majority of the companies performed search activities on the Net, and several new relationships on both the input and the output sides had been established as a result of this. Few companies actually conduct e-commerce business. Those who do, see it as a supplement to the traditional way of doing business. But all of these actually foresee that e-business may be the more dominant mode in future. The larger companies among those studied, which also happen to be the oldest and those with the highest average age of employees, were the most reluctant to engage in Internet-related activities. It was suggested that one reason for this was resistance from established partners such as importers and, sometimes, customers.

The companies engaging in e-commerce were managed by someone who strongly believed in the advantages of using the Internet taking a proactive view while the others were reacting, doing what was considered necessary "to keep up with what is going on".

In all cases, the various functions of the Internet were made use of one after the other, in an incremental fashion.

The E-commerce Companies

There were four such companies studied by Ekström and Persson (1999). They are Bokus, Boxman, Dressmart and LetsBuyIt. The first two were started in 1997, and the two others in 1998, all by private, young entrepreneurs. Bokus is now owned by KF (top organization of the consumer co-operative movement); Boxman is majority owned by investors; Dressmart is majority owned by outside investors such as the sixth AP-fund (a publicly controlled pension fund); and Emerging Technologies (controlled by venture capitalist Kjell Spångberg) and LetsBuyIt is majority controlled by foreign investors. Bokus is in books; Boxman started with CDs but has recently expanded into "home entertainment products", including videos and computer games; Dressmart is in men's clothes, shoes and accessories; and, finally, LetsBuyIt "is providing co-shopping (community shopping), meaning that the Internet is used for gathering customers who are interested in the same product and thereby get a lower price from the supplier" (Ekström & Persson, 1999). They all rely upon established manufacturers whose products they market. The logistics function is out-sourced. The four companies are operating at a loss.

All four companies started to internationalise about one year after foundation. They all entered the three neighbouring Nordic markets rapidly, within a year at the most. LetsBuyIt in August 1999, nine months after its foundation, in three consecutive days established sub-sidiaries in the three countries. Bokus, so far, stopped with that, while the others continued to set up offices or subsidiaries in the UK, and/or Germany and the Netherlands. Bokus has declared as its objective to be one of the leading European on-line booksellers. The other three have stated that they are going to be the number one in Europe within their respective businesses.

All four companies entered greenfield, without previous relationships, and hired people locally to take care of marketing and adaptation of the product range to local tastes. Considerable resources are spent on marketing. Dressmart, as an example, is said to spend an amount corre-sponding to 50 percent of sales on on-line and off-line marketing. Boxman has become known for its PR approach, whereby well-known artists, IT-specialists and investors help provide publicity in the media. This has been repeated in each market entered. Boxman strongly stresses the need to adjust to local circumstances in each market (*Svenska Dag-bladet*, 1999). All the companies prefer to be considered as local in the eyes of the general public. After acquisition of a UK competitor, Boxman has moved its head office to London. LetsBuyIt is headquartered in Amsterdam.

Ekström and Persson (1999) point out that the three most aggressive companies are all majority owned by venture capitalists, and they claim that these not only provide the financial resources but also express demands for rapid growth. Bokus, the slowest growing of these com-panies so far, is owned by a large corporation and is facing a loss of SEK 40 to 50 million on a turnover of SEK 110 to 120 million. The operations set up in foreign countries resemble each other; it is a sort of replication. Because of this, one of the founders of Boxman has started a consulting agency selling advice on how to internationalise e-commerce businesses.

The Internet Consultants

Four Internet consulting companies were studied by Andersson *et al.*, (2000). The business of these consulting agencies is to assist companies preparing to exploit the Internet for commercial purposes. The list of Swedish and foreign customers contains many well-known corporations and supports the notion that the Net is indeed going to be widely used. The spokesmen for this industry are well known by the public in Sweden, and they maintain that Sweden has an advantage in IT applications, as we were early out adopting the new technology. These consulting companies combine knowledge areas such as management, design, systems-building and e-commerce in helping the clients to develop "interactive strategies". The four case companies are: Icon Medialab, Cell Networks, Information Highway and Framfab. Started by young, private entrepreneurs (although Cell is the result of a merger) in the mid-1990s, they are now all listed.

Internationalisation has been a way of growing right from the start. Icon, as an example, was started in March 1996, and in August that same year the first foreign office was started. The stated objective is, as soon as possible and before the US competitors enter, to build a strong position in the European market. All four companies have Europe as the prime objective, but they are already looking towards other continents for further expansion. Icon is so far the only company already realizing this to some extent.

The neighbouring Nordic markets have been the first target for three of the companies, with Icon as the exception. But Germany, France and the UK have also been popular markets. The preferred mode for entry has been acquisitions. To some extent, multinational and other customer demand influence which markets are entered. But apart from that, efforts are spent on screening markets to find out about market potential and acquisition candidates. Such activities are going on in several markets in parallel, and to some extent the exact order in which things happen is a matter of chance. Initiatives are also taken by outside parties, companies interested in being acquired, interested IT-specialists with ideas about potential business in the respective markets. Framfab, as an example, acquired four companies in 2000 and has plans for more.

Icon Medialab's internationalisation process took a different shape. It started with five greenfield investments in the following order: Spain, the US, the UK, Malaysia and Denmark. Spain was on the list of interesting markets, and then there were relatives to one of the founders living in

Spain, who had excellent contacts and knowledge about the market. As to the US, Icon had excellent relations with a number of Swedes living in Silicon Valley, who were going to set up something anyway. They decided to do it for Icon, seeing it as advantageous to be present in the largest and most competitive market. In the UK and Denmark, again, personal relationships with competent people and promising market prospects triggered the investments. In Malaysia, a large customer order initiated the move. Most of the later coming investments in foreign markets, all in Europe, were made as acquisitions. Icon did not have any previous contacts with any of the acquired companies.

Once established in a foreign market, the companies typically proceed in an organic manner, even if, after a greenfield entry, an acquisition has been made. Financial resources are made available for the foreign subsidiaries to expand and recruit competent individuals, as effective staffing is regarded as essential for further growth.

Four Swedish Cases Revisited

To make a more specific comparison with firms that went abroad earlier and were not involved in Internet dealings, we revisited four Swedish cases (Johanson & Wiedersheim-Paul, 1975). Those cases were used as one of the empirical inputs into the formulation of the internationalisation process model. The firms were, in order of going abroad: Sandvik, Atlas Copco, Facit, and Volvo.

Sandvik is the oldest of the firms and also started internationalisation before the others. Steel production in Sandviken started in 1862 to exploit the Bessemer process. The founder of Sandvik, G.F. Göransson, had brought the process to Sweden from the UK through contacts he had made when he was a general manager of a Swedish trading firm that had extensive international contacts. The first firm soon went bankrupt, but in 1868 the company now known as Sandvik was formed. In the same year, relationships with representatives in Denmark, Norway and the UK were established, and, one year later, in Germany. In 1870 a representative in France was linked to Sandvik. A representative in Switzerland was taken over at the start. A number of representative relations were established in the following decades. The first sales subsidiaries were established in the UK (1914), Germany (1918), the U.S.A. (1920), France (1923) and Canada (1925) during the years around World War I. At the start of World War II Sandvik had a number of sales subsidiaries, but it had manufacturing subsidiaries in only two countries: France and Italy. The representative relations were formed in the order suggested by psychic distance, while sales subsidiaries were established in those countries with large markets.

Atlas Copco started in 1873. Exports were substantial already in 1880, but it seems that the first relations with representatives abroad were not formed until 20 to 30 years later. The first sales subsidiaries were started in the 1930s, and a great number in the 1940s. The order of establishment is similar to that of Sandvik, although less pronounced.

Facit was formed after a reconstruction in 1922, when it took over the production of calculating machines from a bankrupt firm. Until 1933, foreign sales were constant around 2,5 MSEK. At that time the firm embarked on a rapid internationalisation, with a great number of representative relations formed within a four-year period. There was no clear tendency to start in neighbouring countries. Sales subsidiaries were established in the years after World War II, and those establishments were correlated with psychic distance, but not with market size.

Volvo was launched in 1927. Its founder, Assar Gabrielsson, was general manager of the French subsidiary of SKF. Export sales formed a part of the first plans, and it began establishing representatives abroad shortly after the start, in 1928 and 1929, in the Nordic countries, and the year after in the Netherlands, Spain, Portugal and Brazil. Sales subsidiaries were established almost at the start in Finland and Norway. Subsidiaries in other countries were not formed until the 1950s. Although the first establishments were made in the Nordic countries, agency establishments were not correlated with psychic distance. They were instead strongly, and negatively, correlated with market size, meaning that Volvo avoided the big markets.

Summarizing the Case Studies

The order of foreign markets entered is similar to what has been observed before: starting by entering markets with a small psychic distance from Sweden and then proceeding to gradually more distant markets. There are exceptions, of a sort well known from before: a high-tech product line or psychic-distance-eliminating circumstances affecting the order of markets entered. With the US as the exception, the degree of Internet penetration correlates with psychic distance. Presumably there is also a causal relationship between the two variables.

In comparing the geographical extension in the current study with that in previous studies (as exemplified by the four cases) it seems that the speed is now greater than in the past. The process seems to start earlier after the establishment of the company and then proceeds faster, perhaps supporting Nordström's interpretations of his data (1991). The difference can, however, be discussed. Sandvik and Volvo obviously had plans for rapid internationalisation right from the beginning, and they also realized those plans, much in the same way as today's firms have done. Atlas Copco was a slower starter, while Facit, after having been a domestic firm for many decades, suddenly and rapidly started internationalisation in the 1930s.

In the second dimension of the internationalisation process, the entry mode and subsequent increases of commitment, there is variation among the three groups of companies studied, although they all gradually increased commitment. The non-IT companies typically entered via non-regular export and later made that export a regular activity, often relying on a middleman such as an importer or an agent. But only in a few of the cases were sales subsidiaries established, and statements indicated that these might in fact be closed down. The e-commerce companies entered greenfield and "leapfrogged" the potential and less committing alternative of working up the market from home. The foreign entities were then given resources to make possible local marketing and other measures to create a strong customer base. The Internet consulting agencies typically entered by making acquisitions and then providing the subsidiaries with resources to enable them to grow organically. Some of these acquisitions were preceded by customer demand for services. There were also some greenfield entries, building on previous relationships with competent individuals. As compared with the four Swedish cases, the new firms seem to have increased their commitments in each market more rapidly. They have increased their investments in foreign markets at a very different tempo.

Analysis

Judging from the small number of cases examined, it appears that the changed environment has had an impact on internationalisation behaviour. The manifestations of the internationalisation process model, the gradually extended geographical extension and the gradually deepened commitment to the respective markets entered, do not appear to be the same as was found a couple of decades ago (Johanson & Wiedersheim-Paul, 1975), although the differences seem to be a matter of degree rather than of kind.

It appears as if psychic distance, measured by indices produced some years back, still has an impact on the order in which national markets are entered. However, this probably gives a somewhat incorrect impression as the psychic distance correlates nicely with the degree of Internet penetration, with the US as the exception. And the Internet penetration, to many of the companies studied, serves as an indicator of market size. Also, the psychic distances have probably decreased and our ability to cope with such distance has increased, bringing North European countries closer to (in our case) Sweden and making it possible to think about a large North European home market (cf., Nordström, 1991). An indication that this may be so is that the e-commerce companies and the Internet agencies prepared entry into several markets in parallel, making the order in which the markets were entered a matter of chance (Andersson *et al.*, 2000; Ekström & Persson, 1999). Once again, this happened in some of the older cases as well. Our conclusion is that psychic distance does matter, but because of small differences, it has little explanatory value regarding the order in which Swedish companies enter North European markets. It should also be remembered that the role of psychic distance is not as unambiguous in the specific older cases as is frequently assumed.

In this context, it is worth mentioning that we have seen no sign that firms in the new economy demonstrate a different behaviour with regard to the domestic market as compared with foreign markets. They started in Sweden and, to the extent that they went to the other Nordic countries, they treated those country markets as separate markets. The local markets are the same local markets as they were in the old economy.

One more word on Internet penetration. One may suspect that the rapidity of introduction of PCs and the Internet, and hence the current degree of penetration, is not independent of culture. And one may also suspect the reverse: that the use of the Internet probably has a homogenising impact on the various national cultures.

How, then, can we understand the enormous speed with which the e-commerce and Internet consulting agencies entered new markets? Probably several factors contribute to this. One is ownership. Venture capitalists, spreading their risks, are willing to accept a very high risk connected with an individual project. These companies are valued according to the position, in terms of brand recognition, size of customer base, etc., that they manage to establish in the market, as it is hoped that once demand takes off, the well-positioned companies will earn huge profits. "The winner takes it all". A first-mover advantage, real or imagined, is exploited to gain the position sought. There seems to be a combination of risk-willing venture capitalists and imitative behaviour.

There was a difference between the two groups: the e-commerce companies entered greenfield, while the Internet consultants typically entered via an acquisition. Probably, the difference lies in the perceived need of size. The e-commerce companies can get by with a small number of people in each national market, while the Internet consulting agencies were eager to reach a "critical mass" of about 100 persons quickly. Recruiting such a large number was perceived to take too long (Andersson et al., 2000).

Also, the non-IT companies seem to expand faster than was found in previous studies, even if the speed is not nearly as dramatic as for the other two groups. The conclusion drawn by Dahlén and Åkerblom (2000) is that the Internet can explain this. The Internet, equally available to small and large companies, was used to identify potential new customers and suppliers, and it has made other objective knowledge easier to find than before. Also, the world "appears to be smaller", and it is suddenly easy to communicate with someone "who is no longer so far away".

Moreover, the other dimension of the manifestation of the internationalisation process, the deepening of the commitment to each market, seems to have been affected by the changes in the business environment.

The combined effect of the harmonization and liberalization within the European Community and the Internet seems to have affected the way the non-IT companies acted. There seems to be no need to have a subsidiary in the field. For a long time there has been no need to produce locally, as elimination of trade barriers and falling transportation costs made it profitable to exploit advantages of scale by concentrating production of goods. Today, logistics is typically outsourced, and so is post-sales service; billing is done from home or by a middleman, and marketing and sales are handled by a combination of middlemen and the Internet. The results rather point to elimination of existing subsidiaries (Dahlén & Åkerblom, 2000). Other potential means of increasing commitment, such as adjusting products or services to local tastes etc., were not studied.

These conclusions stand in sharp contrast to behaviour in the e-commerce group of companies: they all, at entry, established an organization of their own, by purposely not relying upon standardization on the

Internet. The perceived need to adjust to local circumstances made the companies go for a local presence. Why is behaviour so homogeneous on this point? Obviously, there are alternatives available, as shown, for example, by Amazon. Perhaps, as the e-commerce companies all market consumer products, these are perceived to be sensitive to local tastes. At this point there is no answer. A guess is that one of the founders of Boxman, the initiator of e-commerce in Sweden, has been influential in promoting his view on how to conduct entry into a foreign market. Possibly, others have imitated him. Another guess is that we will see other e-commerce companies choosing not to establish their own strongholds in foreign markets. This does not necessarily mean that there are no increasing commitments, but they may take other forms such as adjusting production facilities back home, for example (Johanson & Vahlne, 1977).

However, increasing commitment in the e-commerce firms was visible in the form of continued investments in building competence and capacity in the local organizations. The same was true for the Internet consulting agencies. This is consistent with the effort to build a position in the respective markets.

Finally, given the long-term perspective applied in the four older cases, the results of this study should be seen as an account of the first wave of internationalisation of the companies. This can be compared with the first five years of the internationalisation of Sandvik, Volvo and Facit, which was almost as rapid. The role of experiential learning cannot be expected to have an effect until the outcome of those first years has been perceived in the firms. Will they continue on the same path?

Moreover, there is a sampling problem. Evidently, the cases studied are those where the firms were extremely quick in going abroad. There might be others that have been more cautious and which have not attracted as much attention. Ten years from now we might have a situation in which some of those early starters have disappeared for various reasons and, in which some others, slower starters, have appeared on the scene. A study at that time might very well give a different picture.

Furthermore, some studies of the internationalisation of the firm have indicated that the behavioural model of internationalisation is not only behavioural but also rational in the long run (Barkema *et al.*, 1996; Li, 1995). Thus, studies of survival rates have shown that those firms which follow the model have higher survival rates than others. And Luo (1999) also demonstrated that experiential learning had a strong effect on performance in firms engaging in China. This effect is stronger the greater the environmental dynamism, complexity and hostility the firm meets

(Luo & Peng, 1999). This means that we have reason to expect a high failure rate among several of the rapid internationalisers in our sample.

Altogether, we can see some obvious differences between the new companies and the old. We can also see some differences between the three subsamples of new companies. But our impression is that the differences are not so great as to lead us to conclude that the firms of the new economy are of a different nature from those of the old, nor that the new business environment is qualitatively different from the old.

Implications for the Internationalisation Process Model

The central change mechanisms of the model are learning, relationship formation and development, and commitment decisions. Partners learn about each other, build trust and decide to develop the joint business. Learning is considered to be critical as the model assumes that engagement in international business is characterized by uncertainty. There are many unknowns, especially at the beginning. The question is, then, is there less uncertainty today compared with, say, the 1950s and 1960s? As stated earlier, that may be the case due to decreasing psychic distance and improved ability to deal with such distances. Secondly, if the new Internet technology imposes a certain way of doing business, similar forall parties concerned, uncertainty decreases and a joint culture may be formed. So perhaps the uncertainty connected with the international aspect is decreasing. Remaining, or in this period even increasing, is of course the general uncertainty connected with competition, technological development and an unknown future (cf., Regnér, 1999). This uncertainty is more relevant to the second dimension of internationalisation: deepening commitment is about competing and doing a better job for the customer. But this is also a matter of experiential learning, so nothing has changed.

In the model it was assumed that decision makers "keep risk-taking at a satisfactory level". For companies controlled by venture capitalists, this assumption indicates that the development reflects that high risks are indeed taken in the individual company and that losses over several years are tolerated. This is quite consistent with the model, although it allows for a more rapid development than is usually assumed in the references to the model.

Another assumption is that the internationalisation process proceeds with little attention paid to strategy. But in these days "everyone" is trained in strategy-making and implementation, and one gets the impression from the case companies that the level of "strategic thinking" is higher and that strategic intentions are referred to when motivating action. However, we have reason to be cautious in assuming that the strategizing will have an impact on the long-run behaviour of those firms that survive. It is also probable that in companies where the field organization is eliminated and decision-making is re-centralized, the managers at headquarters are more likely to take a "strategic view" rather than to see opportunities evolving in the local market. Vahlne *et al.* (1996) found perceptions being affected by roles: somewhat simplified, field people saw opportunities while headquartered individuals saw risks. This may, on the other hand, be different in venture–capitalist-controlled companies.

New Perspective

When finally revising this paper one year after writing the version above, we decided not to modify it in the light of the dramatic changes that had taken place in the IT world. Some of the new economy firms no longer exist, and several have withdrawn to the domestic market or to just a few foreign markets. On the whole, we think that the development of the firms in response to the dramatic changes has supported the view of our model. In the model, current activities are critical since experiential knowledge is built on them and they strengthen the commitment. The firms performed almost no current activities in the foreign markets. As the chairman of Icon Medialab said when they closed some of the foreign units: "It was so easy to expand. Market activities were only a matter of order receiving". Thus they did not learn anything about the customers and markets. Nor did the customers learn anything about the firms. And there was no commitment leading to the interdependence that is the glue that binds the firms to each other. In the good times, the firms expanded rapidly in order to exploit what they thought was a first mover advantage, which, however, was no advantage at all because they did not invest in relationships with the customers.

References

Åkerblom,V., & Dahlén, H. (1999). *Samband mellan Internetanvändning och Internationell verksamhet för små och medelstora företag. (The Connection Between Internet Use and International Operations of SMEs).* Master's Thesis in Marketing, School of Economics and Commercial Law, Gothenburg University.

Andersson,V., Havås, M., & Marasovic, M. (1999). *Internationalisering i Internetkonsultbranschen — kan uppsalamodellen förklara den? (Internationalization in the Internet-consultancy Industry — Can the Uppsala Model Explain?).* Master Thesis in Marketing, School of Economics and Commercial Law, Gothenburg University.

Barkema, H. G., Bell, J. H. J., & Pennings, J. M. (1996). Foreign entry, cultural barriers, and learning. *Strategic Management Journal, 17,* 151–166.

Dagens Industri, (2000). January 7.

Downes, L., & Mui, C. (1998). *Unleashing the Killer App — Digital Strategies for Market Dominance.* Cambridge, Mass.: Harvard Business School.

Ekström, M., & Persson, C. (1999). *The Internationalization Process of E-commerce Companies — a Case Study on Bokus, Boxman, Dressmart and LetsBuyIt.* Thesis, Integrated Master's Program, School of Economics and Commercial Law, Gothenburg University.

Hörnell, E., Vahlne, J.-E. and Wiedersheim-Paul, F. (1973). *Export och utlandsetebleringar (Export and Foreign Establishments).* Stockholm: Almqvist & Wiksell.

Johanson, J. & Vahlne, J.-E. (1977). The internationalization process of the firm — a model of knowledge development and increasing foreign market commitments. *Journal of International Business Studies,* Spring/Summer, 23–32.

Johanson, J. & Vahlne, J.-E. (1990). The mechanism of internationalization. *International Marketing Review,* 11–24.

Levitt, T. (1983). The globalization of markets. *Harvard Business Review,* May/ June.

Li, J. (1995). Foreign entry and survival: effects of strategic choices on performance in international markets. *Strategic Management Journal, 16,* 333–352.

Luo, Y. (1999). Time-based experience and international expansion: the case of an emerging economy. *Journal of Management Studies, 36(4),* 503–534.

Luo, Y. & Peng, M. (1999) Learning to compete in a transition economy: Experience, environment and performance. *Journal of International Business Studies, 30(2),* 269–296.

Lundqvist, M., Olsson, L. & Kjellman, C. (1999). *Småföretagens Internationalisering — en komparativ studie av konsument och producentvaruföretag. (Internationalization of Small firms —* a Comparative Study of Consumer and Business-to-business Firms). Master's Thesis in Marketing, School of Economics and Commercial Law, Gothenburg University.

Mougayar, W. (1998). *Opening Digital Markets — Battle Plans and Business Strategies for Internet Commerce.* McGraw-Hill.

Nordström, K. A. (1991). *The Internationalization Process of the Firm — Searching for New Patterns and Explanations.* Institute of International Business, Stockholm School of Economics.

Nordström, K. A. & Ridderstråle, J. (1999). *Funky Business.* Book House Publishing.

Penrose, E. T. (1959). *The Theory of the Growth of the Firm.* Basil Blackwell.

Regnér, P. (1999). *Strategy Creation and Change in Complexity — Adaptive and Creative Learning Dynamics in the Firm.*

Vahlne, J.-E., Nordström, K. A. & Torbacke, S. (1996). Swedish multinationals in Central and Eastern Europe — entry and subsequent development. *Journal of East-West Business, 1(4),* 1–16.

Winram, S. & Steib, M. (1999). *The European Internet Report,* June, Morgan Stanley DeanWitter.

Chapter 10

Internationalisation — Real Options, Knowledge Management and the Uppsala Approach

Peter J. Buckley, Mark Casson and Mohammed Azzim Gulamhussen[1]

Introduction

Scandinavian literature on the internationalisation strategy of a firm emphasizes the incremental and sequential nature of both the export process and the foreign direct investment process (see, for example, Johanson & Vahlne, 1977; Johanson & Wiedersheim-Paul, 1975; Strandskov, 1986). Firms acquire experience of one foreign market before entering the next: they do not enter all major markets at the outset. In this way they benefit from the lessons learnt in the early stages of expansion and avoid making too many big mistakes. There are two other theories, however — namely internalisation and globalisation — which seem to imply that, on the contrary, firms will internationalise in a single discrete step involving simultaneous entry into all markets. This conflict between the theories is more apparent than real, however. This paper shows that the theory of organizational learning implicit in the Scandinavian approach in fact complements these other approaches, by highlighting factors which they omit. A formal model is presented which clarifies these

[1]This chapter relies heavily on three earlier pieces of work: Casson (1994), Buckley and Casson (1998) and particularly Casson (1999).

Critical Perspectives on Internationalisation, pp. 229–261.

complementarities and so enriches all three areas of theory. This paper is an attempt to show the relevance of the real option analysis in the internationalisation process.

It turns out that this model includes, as a special case, an international analogue of Penrose's (1959) theory of the growth of the firm. This is because it embodies, in addition to Scandinavian insights, one of Penrose's key ideas, namely that it is prohibitively costly for any team of managers to diversify in several directions at once. It touches on an even more fundamental issue too: the scope of the rational actor model in analysing managerial behaviour. It is widely believed that rational action implies that managers do not make mistakes. It is claimed that, in consequence, behavioural models of learning may provide a better account of managerial behaviour than does the rational action approach.

This argument ignores the possibility that rational managers will take account of information costs, however. The model presented here shows that, when information is costly, rational managers will make mistakes because the optimal frequency of mistakes is greater than zero. Because the model assumes rationality it can actually predict the kind of mistakes that will be made and the frequency with which they will occur. It shows that the entire internationalisation strategy of a firm can be interpreted as a strategy designed to reduce, but not eliminate, the incidence of mistakes in individual market entry strategies. This illustrates one of the main strengths of the rational action approach: it facilitates simple mathematical modelling which not only captures existing insights in parsimonious terms, but deepens these insights and reveals new ones as well.

Real Options

Real options reduce risk by providing the flexibility to respond to new information as it becomes available. The key to the successful exploitation of real options is to foresee the kind of information that is likely to become available and to plan the options in order to exploit this information at an early stage. Its use in internationalisation theory puts the Uppsala approach into a wider context.

Almost everyone has heard about financial options — in particular 'put' and 'call' options based upon stock market prices (for a review see Dempster & Pliska, 1997). These options involve a contract between two parties. This contract creates a right to buy or sell an asset at a future time at a pre-specified price — either a fixed price, or a price specified by some agreed rule. This right can be traded: it can be bought and sold, just like the underlying asset to which it relates. The main object of option theory, as developed in finance, is to price such options correctly.

There is a good deal of confusion about the relation between real options and financial options. There are two opposing views that can be found in the popular literature, and both of them are wrong. The first is that real options and financial options are basically the same thing — that real options relate to real assets, and financial options relate to financial assets, but that the underlying principles are the same. The second view is that real options and financial options are fundamentally different: real options are about the timing of irreversible investment decisions, whilst financial option theory is about the valuation of 'derivative' contractual instruments. Those who take the second view believe that those who take the first view are misled by the use of the same term — option — to describe two different phenomena. In fact, the first view is closer to the truth than the second, in the sense that financial options are simply a special case of real options, and the same principles — as described above — apply to both. The mistake of the first view is to suppose that the difference lies simply in whether the asset is real or monetary. The nature of the asset is important, but the key issue is whether the asset is tradable or not, rather than whether it takes a real or monetary form. In practice, almost all monetary assets are tradable, but the converse does not apply: not all real assets are non-tradable. Because some real assets are tradable, tradability is a separate issue from whether the asset is a real or monetary one.

The nature of the option is also important too. Some options are contractual, and others reflect the physical properties of the asset. For example, some options are exercised by buying and selling an asset, whereas others are exercised by retaining ownership of the asset and reallocating it to an alternative use. The importance of distinguishing between contractual and non-contractual options is reflected in the second view described above. Where this view goes wrong is to suppose that different principles apply to the valuation of contractual options and non-contractual options. In fact they do not. The principles are the same. This is fortunate, because it means that there is, in fact, just one body of option theory, and not two. Financial option theory is just a special case of a more general theory of options which is based on the principles set out above. Real option theory is the body of theory that has applied these general principles to non-contractual options on non-tradable assets, and neglected their applications to financial options. The

Table 10.1: Classification of Options by Type of Option and Type of Asset, with Examples.

	Type of asset		
	Tradable		Non-tradable
	Monetary	**Real**	**Real**
Type of option			
Contractual			
Formal	Bond or currency option	Commodity option Equity option	Option to purchase land or building Option to acquire a non-quoted firm
Informal			'First refusal' option to acquire a firm in which a minority stake is held
Non-contractual	Holding money as a source of liquidity		Option to up-size, down-size or re-locate a factory: see also Table 10.2

applications of real option theory given below clearly demonstrate that the principles commonly ascribed to real option theory apply to financial options as well.

These remarks are elaborated in Table 10.1. The table classifies different types of options using two main dimensions. The first dimension, indicated by the columns, specifies whether the asset is tradable or not. A tradable asset is an asset which can always be bought and sold. When there are no transaction costs or other 'market imperfections', the purchase price of a tradable asset is equal to its selling price. This is a crucial property used in standard option pricing models in the theory of finance. The columns also identify a secondary distinction between real and monetary assets, but as indicated above, this is of no real significance. It is of no significance because, as emphasized above, it is the economic value of the asset that matters in option theory, and the physical form that the asset takes is of no consequence unless it affects some other more relevant aspect of the problem too.

The second dimension, indicated by the rows, specifies whether the option takes a contractual form or not. This distinction is not important for the mathematical structure of the models, but it is important in understanding how an option model is applied. The distinction shows that option theory can be used to value the flexibility provided both by contractual arrangements and by the physical properties of an asset. A minor distinction is between contractual arrangements of a formal and an informal kind. Whilst formal arrangements are the most conspicuous, informal arrangements may be of greater consequence where long-term corporate strategies are concerned — for example, informal options agreed with partner firms to acquire or divest joint venture companies.

The options of greatest relevance to IB theory appear in the bottom right-hand corner of the table. They are real options rather than financial options. They include options to vary the size, location, timing and utilisation of an investment project once the initial phase of it is complete. These are non-contractual options, which are highly relevant to location issues in IB. Another important set of options discussed above are contractual options to acquire or divest assets owned wholly or partly by other firms. These contractual options are highly relevant to ownership issues in IB. Between them, these two issues — ownership and location — dominate the modern economic theory of IB (Buckley & Casson, 1976; 1998). It follows that real options have a key role in generating a dynamic version of IB theory.

Techniques of Analysis

Much of the technical difficulty in contemporary financial option theory stems from the commitment to continuous time models. Continuous time is a reasonable approximation to reality in stock markets and currency markets where trading is virtually instantaneous, but it is a poor approximation to the circumstances under which non-contractual decisions relating to the deployment of real assets are made. Here, discrete time models, based on dividing up time into a finite number of periods, are generally more realistic. Since discrete time models are much simpler to solve than continuous time models, there is much to be gained from studying options from the outset in terms of discrete time. This is the approach adopted in this paper.

The discrete time models used in this chapter involve rational intertemporal decision-making under uncertainty. All the models can be solved by explicit analytical methods, although for certain types of model approximations are useful. The general method of solution is a recursive technique. This technique solves for the rational choices in the final period, conditional on the choices made in the previous periods, and then uses these results to determine the optimal choices in preceding period. This method is repeated until the initial period is reached. Initial decisions are optimised on the assumption that, in the light of these decisions, the most appropriate choices in subsequent periods will then be made. This determines a comprehensive contingent plan of action covering every period.

Most of the models are presented in numerical rather than algebraic form. This is the most convenient way of expounding models like the present ones, which involve choices between discrete strategies over discrete periods of time. It is straightforward to re-formulate the models in algebraic form, and interested readers may like to do this for themselves. The only difficulty is that the derivation of solutions is relatively tedious, and the algebraic inequalities that characterise the optimum strategy are cumbersome to write down. Because the present paper has a mainly expository role, numerical examples are preferable because they are much quicker to present and are more readily understood.

To illustrate the discrete time approach, consider the following numerical example, which places a standard financial option problem in a discrete time framework. Because the example involves a tradable financial asset, it possesses the special feature that the purchase price of the asset is always equal to its selling price. The decision-maker has to decide whether to purchase a contractual option which will allow him to buy the asset in the future at a pre-specified price, if he wishes to.

Example 1. Consider a single indivisible asset whose future value may be either 20 or 10, depending on whether conditions are good ($s = 1$) or bad ($s = 0$). Conditions are good with probability p. The asset can be purchased today ($t = 0$) for 15 units, or purchase can be deferred until tomorrow ($t = 1$), when tomorrow's price will be known. A call option can be purchased today for two units, which gives the right to purchase the asset tomorrow for 15 units — i.e., for the same price as today. The objective of the risk-neutral decision-maker is to maximize the expected profit v. Because of the short period of time elapsing between today and tomorrow, discounting is ignored.

There is an element of irreversibility in today's purchase because a purchaser cannot guarantee to sell the asset tomorrow for the price at which he bought it. Such a guarantee can only be acquired through the separate purchase of a 'put' option, which allows him to sell the asset at a pre-specified price, such as the price at which he bought it. To keep the model simple, the put option is ignored.

The problem is represented using a decision tree in Figure 10.1. Starting from the top of the figure, the decision maker has three initial alternatives:

1) To purchase the asset immediately;
2) To purchase the call option instead;
3) To defer a decision on purchasing until later.

Once conditions have been revealed, the decision-maker faces further decisions. If he has purchased the option then he must decide whether to exercise it or not. The net rewards, derived from the data given above, are indicated by the numbers along the bottom of the figure. If conditions are good then it pays to exercise the option, whereas if conditions are bad then it pays not to exercise it. The optimal choices are indicated by the thicker branches in the figure. If the decision-maker has deferred a

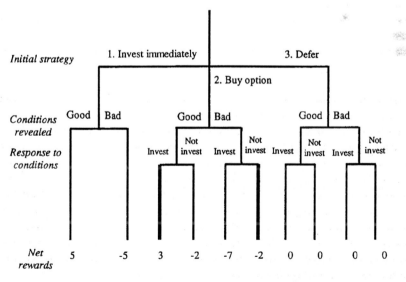

Figure 10.1: Decision Tree for Appraisal of Option Purchase.

decision then he can decide whether to purchase the asset the following day. However, the special conditions assumed in this problem mean that this decision is of no consequence. Since the purchase price is always equal to the value of the asset, the decision-maker is indifferent to purchase, whatever conditions prevail. It is assumed for simplicity that in these circumstances the decision-maker will choose not to make a purchase.

It follows from this discussion that three main strategies need to be considered: Let v_i be the expected value of the ith strategy; then

$$v_1 = (20p + 10(1 - p)) - 15 \qquad\qquad = -5 + 10p \qquad (1.1)$$
$$v_2 = ((20 - 15)p + 0(1 - p)) - 2 \qquad = -2 + 5p \qquad (1.2)$$
$$v_3 = 0 \qquad\qquad\qquad\qquad\qquad\qquad\qquad\qquad (1.3)$$

The first term in equation (1.1) is the expected revenue from an initial investment when it is sold in the following period, whilst the second term is today's purchase price. The first term in equation (1.2) is the value of the option when exercised, weighted by the probability that conditions are good. The second term is its value (zero) when conditions are bad, and the third term is its purchase price.

Selecting the highest value of v for any given value of p gives the solution:

$$
i = \begin{array}{lll}
1 & \text{if} & p > 0.6 \\
2 & \text{if} & 0.4 < p < 0.6 \\
3 & \text{if} & p < 0.4
\end{array} \qquad (2)
$$

Thus as the probability of good conditions increases from zero to one, the decision-maker switches from no purchase to option purchase, to immediate purchase, illustrating his growing confidence that conditions will be good. The inequalities specified here assume that when two strategies are of equal value, the strategy with the lower number is always chosen; this convention is used throughout the chapter.

The solution is illustrated graphically in Figure 10.2. The vertical axis measures the expected profit and the horizontal axis measures the probability of good conditions. The schedule V1V1' indicates the expected value of the initial purchase strategy. The relatively low intercept and steep slope shows that this is the riskiest strategy. The investor is exposed to a serious risk of capital loss if conditions turn out to be bad. The schedule V2V2' indicates the value of the option strategy. Holding an

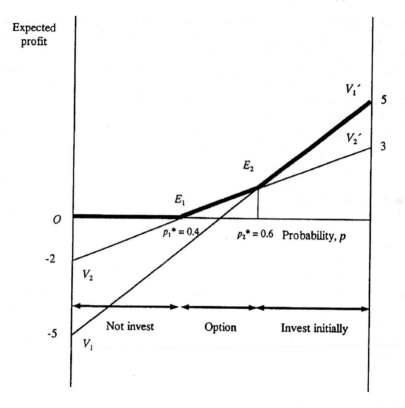

Figure 10.2: Graphical Solution of the Financial Option Problem.

option eliminates the risk of capital loss, whilst offering the prospect of a capital gain by preserving the right to purchase the asset at a pre-specified price equal to the initial price. The option therefore provides a speculative opportunity whilst controlling the risk involved. The horizontal axis represents the null value of the third strategy.

To maximize expected profit it is necessary to identify the upper envelope of the three schedules. This is the schedule OE1E2V1′, which has kinks at the points E1, E2, where some pair of strategies has equal value. For any given value of p, the optimal strategy is the one that forms the portion of the envelope at the relevant point along the horizontal axis. The kinks E1, E2, correspond to the two critical values of probability p1* = 0.4, p2* = 0.6, where switches of strategy take place. At the first switch point, the no purchase strategy and the option strategy are of equal value, whilst at the second switch point the option strategy and the immediate purchase strategy are of equal value.

The same diagrammatic technique can also be used to measure the value of an option. Suppose that the decision-maker does not know that an option can be purchased for two units. A decision rule is required to determine when to purchase an option. Let a be the unknown value of the option. Equation (1.2) then becomes

$$v2 = -a + 5p \tag{3}$$

and the decision rule is to purchase the option if

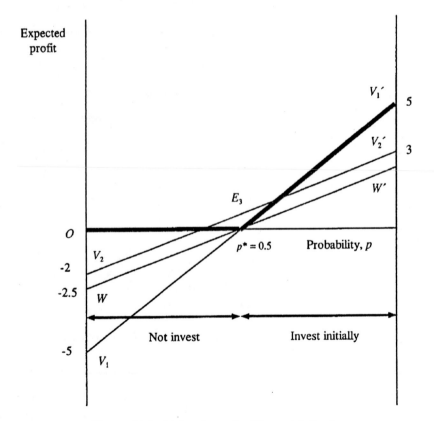

Figure 10.3: Valuation of a Financial Option.

v2 > max[v1, v3]

i.e., if

$$a < \max[-5 + 10p, 0] + 5p \qquad (4)$$

The determination of the value of the option for p = 0.5 is shown in Figure 10.3. This involves a two-stage procedure. In the first stage the maximum expected value obtainable from the two alternative strategies is determined by constructing the envelope OE3V1' from the higher of V1V1' (representing strategy 1) and the horizontal axis (representing strategy 3). In the second stage, a line WW' is drawn parallel to V2V2' through the envelope OE3V1' so that it touches the envelope at the lowest possible point. Given the assumed value for p, this happens to be the point E3 where the line V1V1' intersects the horizontal axis. The vertical distance between V2V2' and WW' is a measure of the value of the option. The decision rule is to purchase the option only if this distance is a positive one. The distance in the figure can be measured by comparing the intercepts V1 and W on the left hand vertical axis. The value of the option is 2.5. Since its purchase price is only 2, the option should be acquired when p = 0.5. This agrees with the result obtained in Figure 10.2, which showed that the option should be purchased whenever p was in the range between 0.4 and 0.6.

The Timing of a Real Investment: A Simple Role for Contractual Options in International Business

Consider a firm contemplating entry into a foreign market. The firm has identified an investment opportunity which it alone can exploit. Exploitation of the opportunity begins in period 2, but the investment expenditure can be incurred in either period 1 or period 2; the problem is to determine which is best. It is convenient to assume that the second period, beginning tomorrow, is very much longer than the first. Because the period is much longer, it is difficult to justify ignoring issues relating to the discount rate. However, to keep the model simple it is convenient to take the rate of discount as fixed and specify the entire problem in terms of discounted values. Discounting is introduced explicitly below.

The opportunity generates a known flow of income with present value 20 units. To appropriate this income stream, the firm needs to acquire a site for the erection of a factory. Conditions in the local market for industrial property are very uncertain, however (as they are in many transitional economies). At the moment, a site is available at a price of 15 units, but in the following period a similar site could be become available for either 10 units or 20 units, depending upon whether supply conditions in the property market are good or bad. Conditions are good (the price is 10 units) with probability p.

Once the site has been bought, the factory must be erected immediately, and once this has occurred, the site has no alternative use, and no resale value. The owner of the site is willing to fix the price for a sale tomorrow at 17 units, provided that a non-refundable deposit of two units is paid. The reservation on the site can be cancelled tomorrow if desired. Cancelling the reservation would allow the firm to make a spot purchase at a price of 10 units if conditions were good.

This example has been chosen to illustrate the close connection between real options and financial options, as described earlier. The situation closely resembles the financial option problem discussed above. The principal change is that the asset in which the firm invests is no longer tradable. The future value of the asset depends not upon what it can be sold for, but only upon what it can be used for. The purchase is technically irreversible, but economically it incurs little risk because the owner is certain that the asset is worth 18 units from the outset. The only risk is that the owner may pay more for the asset than is really necessary.

Because the asset is not tradable, a wedge can be driven between its purchase price and its value to the firm. This is reflected in the fact that, whether it is purchased for 10, 15 or 20 units, it is still worth 20 units to the firm. By contrast, above, the asset was always worth what it was purchased for at the time.

There are three dominant strategies, each of which corresponds to one of the strategies in example 1:

1) invest at the outset;
2) place a deposit (the call option) and exercise it if the spot price is high; cancel the order and purchase spot if the price is low;
3) defer the decision, and invest only if the price is low.

The expected profits generated by these strategies are:

$$v1 = 20 - 15 \qquad\qquad = 5 \qquad\qquad (5.1)$$
$$v2 = 20 - 2 - 10p - 15(1 - p) \qquad = 3 + 5p \qquad (5.2)$$
$$v3 = (20 - 10)p \qquad\qquad = 10p \qquad\qquad (5.3)$$

The first equation shows that initial purchase carries no risk, since both the value of the asset (18 units) and the purchase price (15 units) are known at the outset. The second equation shows that the option will not be exercised if conditions are good — a cost of 10 units is incurred with probability p — but will be exercised if conditions are bad — a cost of 15 units is incurred with probability 1) — p. The third equation shows the profit to be made by deferring the decision when conditions turn out to be good.

Expected profit is maximized by setting

$$i = \begin{array}{ll} 1) & \text{if } p < 0.4 \\ 2) & \text{if } 0.4 < p < 0.6 \\ 3) & \text{if } p > 0.6 \end{array} \tag{6}$$

The solution is illustrated in Figure 10.4. The conventions are the same as for Figure 10.1. The expected values of the three strategies are represented respectively by the schedules V1V1′, V2V2′ and OV3′ The maximum attainable value of profit for an given value of p is indicated by the height of the envelope V1E1E2V3′. The figure shows that when the future purchase price of the asset is expected to be very high (p is low) the investment will be made at the outset (when strategy 1) is chosen), whilst if it is expected to be very low (p is high) the investment will be deferred (when strategy 3) is chosen). A deposit will be placed on the asset (strategy 2)) if the firm believes that a high or low price will occur a probability in the mid-range of values between 0.4 and 0.6. Indeed, it is readily established, using the method described in the previous section, that the option is most valuable when the uncertainty is greatest, i.e., when p = 0.5.

The similarity between this example and the previous one is illustrated by the appearance of the same critical probability values, p1* = 0.4, p2* = 0.6. Indeed, a comparison of Figure 10.4 with Figure 10.2 shows that the two figures are almost identical except for the fact that all the schedules have been pushed upwards by five units. This explains why the critical values are the same. The only substantial difference arises from the fact that the role of the strategy 1) in the previous example has now been taken over by strategy 3), and vice versa. The role of strategy 2) — the option strategy — remains exactly the same. The interchange of the roles of strategies 1) and 3) is explained by the fact that in the previous example risk was eliminated by not purchasing the asset, whilst in the present example it is eliminated by purchasing the asset at the outset.

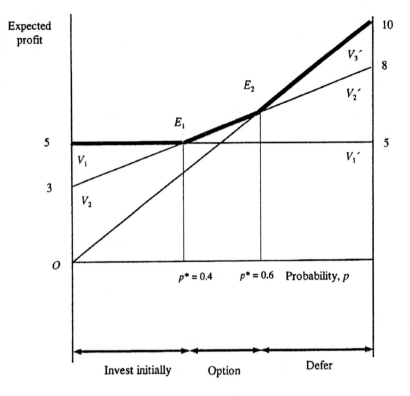

Figure 10.4: Option to Purchase a Real Asset with an Uncertain Future
Price but Known Value in Use

Although the new model relates to a real asset rather than a financial
asset, it is still driven by the same kind of speculative forces as before.

Uncertain Demand Conditions

The previous section discussed a contractual option governing the purchase of a real asset. This is only one of several types of option relating
to real assets, and it is certainly not the most important one so far as IB
is concerned. When real options were introduced (Casson, 1999), the
emphasis was on their role in coping with uncertainty about demand for
the asset's services — and specifically with uncertainty about the foreign

Table 10.2: Classification of Non-tradable Real Options by Source of Uncertainty and Type of Asset, with Examples.

Type of option	Source of uncertainty		
	Cost of supply	Intensity of demand	Either supply or demand, or both
Contractual	Option to purchase land or building		IJV
Non-contractual	Build flexibility into sources of input supply	Build flexibility into range of demands that can be satisfied	Build in potential to up-size, down-size or re-locate plant at low cost

demand for the product from which the demand for these services is derived. The previous example, by contrast, focussed on uncertainty about the supply of the asset instead.

Both demand and supply are potential sources of uncertainty, and the relation between them is illustrated in Table 10.2. The columns of the table distinguish three sources of uncertainty: supply, demand, and a combination of the two. The rows of the table distinguish two types of option: contractual and non-contractual. The most important type of contractual option is the IJV, which is useful in coping with uncertainty in both demand and supply. Non-contractual options involve issues such as the size, timing, location and versatility of investments. Both contractual and non-contractual options can take numerous forms — indeed, there are far too many to do justice to them all in a single paper.

The remaining sections of this paper concentrate on a few important cases, beginning with some simple cases relating to non-contractual options that reduce the risks relating to uncertainty in demand. By switching attention from uncertainty about supply to uncertainty about demand some classic examples of real option models are obtained.

Demand uncertainty is an important factor in foreign market entry decisions. Entry is often deferred, even when it would be profitable to go ahead immediately, because it would be even more profitable to wait until later. The strategy of deferring foreign market entry was discussed by Buckley and Casson (1981), but only under conditions of certainty. Under these conditions, the main motive for deferring entry is to await further growth in the market. Once uncertainty is introduced, another motive for waiting is introduced — namely, to dispel uncertainty about whether the market is likely to grow or not. Entry is postponed until some crucial information relating to the prospective size of the market has become available. This is the gist of the example that follows.

Consider an initial investment in a foreign market. This could be an investment in marketing and distribution facilities, or it could involve investment in production facilities as well. As before, there are two periods, with the second period being very long. Investment today generates a revenue of two units today, and a revenue of 20 units tomorrow if conditions are good and 10 units if they are bad. Demand conditions are good with probability p. If the asset is not purchased until tomorrow then only tomorrow's revenues are obtained. The purchase price of the asset is 15 units in both periods. The advantage of purchasing tomorrow is that the purchase decision can be made when the state of demand is known. An asset purchased today cannot be sold off again tomorrow: the entire purchase price is a sunk cost.

By deferring the entry decision, the firm can guarantee that it will not make a loss. When the decision is deferred, the optimal strategy is to enter if and only if demand conditions are good. This generates an expected profit of 5p. It follows that deferred investment with conditional entry dominates a strategy of not investing at all.

As a result of this, there are only two strategies worth distinguishing:

1) invest at the outset;
2) defer the investment decision, and invest tomorrow only if demand conditions are good.

The expected profits generated by these strategies are:

$$v1 = 10(1-p) + 20p + 2 - 15 \qquad = -3 + 10p \qquad (7.1)$$
$$v2 = (20-15)p \qquad\qquad\qquad = 5p \qquad\qquad (7.2)$$

The first two terms in equation (7.1) express expected revenue in period 2): namely, 10 units when demand conditions are bad, and 20 units when they are good. The third term captures the revenue generated in period 1), while the final term is the outlay on the investment. The derivation of equation (7.2) has already been explained. There is no revenue stream and no outlay when demand conditions are bad, because the firm does not invest in this case. There is no revenue from period 1) either, because investment does not take place until period 2).

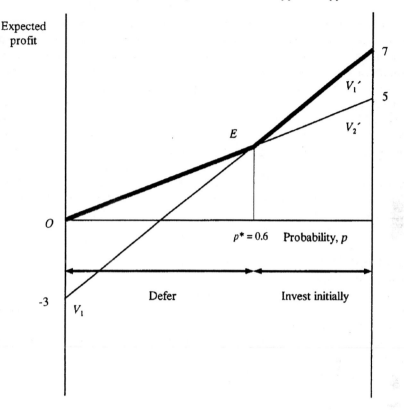

Figure 10.5: Decision to Defer Investment when Future Demand is Uncertain.

Expected profit is maximized by setting:

$$
i = \begin{array}{ll} 1 & \text{if} \quad p > 0.6 \\ 2 & \text{if} \quad p < 0.6 \end{array} \tag{7}
$$

The solution is illustrated in Figure 10.5. The expected profit generated by immediate investment is indicated by the height of the schedule V1V1', while the expected profit generated by deferral is indicated by the height of the schedule OV2'. The maximum attainable profit is indicated by the envelope OEV1', which has a kink at E. The point E identifies the critical probability p* = 0.6 at which the firm switches from deferral to immediate entry. Thus for low values of p, where the firm is pessimistic about demand conditions, entry is deferred, whilst for high values of p, where the firm is optimistic about demand conditions, entry is immediate because the firm is so confident that conditions will be good.

Scale and Reversibility of Investments

In the previous example the only strategy conferring option value was deferment. In practice, however, real option value is often generated by choosing an alternative, more flexible, form of investment. This section examines a variant of this strategy which is particularly relevant to foreign market entry (for a similar application to corporate growth see Kulatilaka & Perotti, 1998).

Suppose that there is an alternative to the irreversible investment described in the previous section, in the form of a smaller investment which is partially reversible. This small investment can be upgraded to a full investment the following period if desired. It involves an initial outlay of 10 units, seven units of which can be recovered if the investment is abandoned the following period. The cost of an upgrade is assumed to be six units. The small investment yields the same revenue as the large investment in the initial period — namely two units. This is because the market is initially small, and can be served just as adequately from a small investment as from a large one. However, the small investment is much less effective in the second period. Because of its small scale it can generate an income of only 5 units whatever the size of the market.

The obvious way to exploit the small investment is to use it for initial entry and then either scale it up, if demand is strong, or liquidate it if demand is weak. The alternative to scaling up is to liquidate the investment in the second period and put the proceeds towards a purchase of the larger asset. This is uneconomic, however, because the cost is 15 – 7 = eight units, as against six units for the upgrade. The alternative to liquidation is to keep the asset in use, but this is uneconomic because the income from use is five units whereas the proceeds from liquidation are seven units.

It follows that there is only one additional strategy which is worth considering:

3) Invest on a small scale with a view to scaling up if demand is buoyant and liquidating if demand is weak.

The expected value of the new strategy is

$$v3 = -10 + 2 + (20 - 6)p + 7(1 - p) \qquad = -1 + 7p \qquad (9)$$

The first term in (9) is the initial outlay, and the second term the revenue from period 1); the third term is the expected profit from an upgrade when demand conditions are good, and the final term is the expected proceeds from liquidation when conditions are bad.

The new solution is:

$$i = \begin{array}{lll} 1 & \text{if} & p > 0.67 \\ 2 & \text{if} & p < 0.5 \\ 3 & \text{if} & 0.5 < p < 0.67 \end{array} \qquad (10)$$

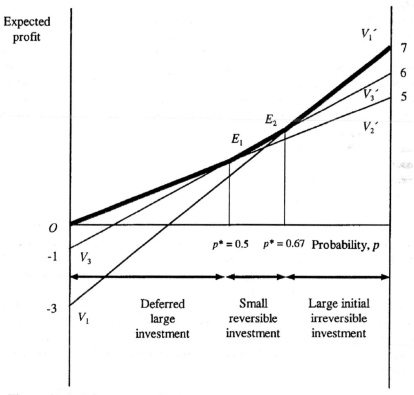

Figure 10.6: Advantages of a Small-scale Reversible Initial Investment when Future Demand is Uncertain.

The solution is illustrated in Figure 10.6. The value of the new strategy 3 is indicated by the height of the schedule V3V3'. This intersects OV2' at E1 and V1V1' at E2, determining the critical probabilities p1* = 0.5, p2* = 0.67 between which the small scale investment is preferred. This is a good example of the way that small flexible investments are preferred when future demand conditions are highly uncertain.

Investment in Information-Gathering as a Real Option

While the previous example clearly demonstrated the advantages of small reversible investments, the value of the option that was generated was not sufficiently large to make the strategy dominant. It was efficient only when there was a high degree of uncertainty. Given the prevalence of such investments in real-world market entry situations, this suggests that something important may have been omitted from the model.

The obvious omission is investment in the collection of information. So far it has been assumed that information about the state of demand is automatically revealed in the second period whether the firm has invested in the first period or not. Under these conditions, deferred investment is very attractive when market prospects are poor because investing at the outset confers no information advantage. On the other hand, the problem with making an irreversible investment at the outset is that it is too late to do anything useful with the information once it has been obtained.

Suppose now that information on demand conditions can only be obtained in the second period if an investment has been made in the first period. While the values of both of the initial entry strategies remain unchanged, the value of the deferred entry strategy is dramatically reduced. Because it now confers no information advantage, the value of the deferred investment strategy falls to

$$v2 = 10(1 - p) + 20p - 15 \qquad\qquad = -5 + 10p \qquad (11)$$

It is now totally dominated by the initial full scale investment strategy, because the only remaining difference between them is that the initial investment generates two units of profit from period 1) whereas the deferred investment does not.

The deferred investment strategy previously dominated the null strategy of no investment in either period, but as deferment is now less profitable, this is no longer the case. It is therefore necessary to re-introduce the null strategy explicitly into the strategy set. It is convenient to intro-duce it as a replacement for the deferred investment strategy. The new strategies that need to be evaluated are therefore:

1) Invest on a large scale at the outset;
2) Do not invest at all;
3) Invest on a small scale at the outset with a view to scaling up if demand is buoyant and liquidating if demand is weak.

The new solution is:

$$i = \begin{array}{ll} 1 & \text{if } p > 0.67 \\ 2 & \text{if } p < 0.14 \\ 3 & \text{if } 0.14 < p < 0.67 \end{array} \qquad (12)$$

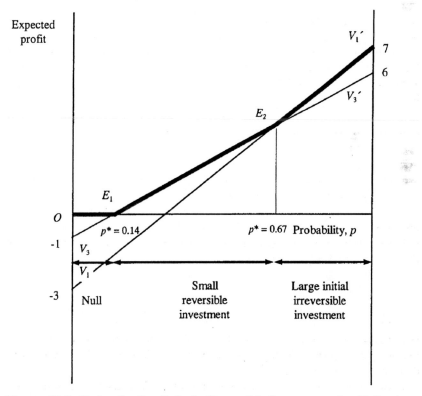

Figure 10.7: Role of a Small Scale Reversible Investment for Collecting Information on Demand Conditions in a Market.

The modified solution is illustrated in Figure 10.7. The schedules V1V1', V3V3' remain in their previous positions (see Figure 10.6). The value of strategy 2), which is now the null strategy, is represented by the horizontal axis. V3V3' intersects the horizontal axis at E1, corresponding to a critical probability $p1^* = 0.14$. It intersects V1V1' at the same point, E2, as before, corresponding to the critical probability $p2^* = 0.67$. The range of probability values for which the small reversible strategy is chosen has therefore more than tripled as compared with the previous case.

This modified example shows very clearly why a small scale reversible investment is so often chosen as an initial entry strategy. It can act as a 'listening post', helping the investor to collect information on the future prospects of the market. Using another metaphor, it can be described as a 'toe in the water': it is an exercise in collecting important information which affords the option of a quick withdrawal if necessary. This metaphor is also consistent with the picture of FDI as a process of increasing commitment to the foreign market, as described in the Uppsala model of the internationalisation of the firm (Johanson & Vahlne, 1977; Johanson & Weidersheim-Paul, 1975).

Quality of Judgement and the Performance of the Firm

When the present model 'rationalizes' marketing errors, however, it does not rationalize errors in the internationalisation strategy itself. While management chooses, within the model, whether or not to improve its own subjective estimates of the state of each market, it does not choose whether to improve its estimates about the type of market in order to make a better choice about investigation or about the sequence of market entry. This is because of the focus of the model on the 'hands on' investigations that are carried out after a commitment to market entry has been made.

It would be possible, in principle, to extend the analysis back in time to a period before the management was required to make the internationalisation decision. At this stage management could consider investing in information which would improve the quality of the subjective probabilities used to determine the internationalisation strategy. Since the cost of additional information would itself be uncertain, however, this would introduce a third variety of uncertainty into the model. Indeed the process could be continued back even further until a time was reached in which the management had just a few simple theories about how information on various subjects might conceivably relate to this issue, and a small amount of initial information with which to prime the learning process. It would then be possible to impute subsequent successes and failures to the reliability of these early beliefs and their relevance to subsequent situations. With the regression of the quest for information further into the past, the cultural heritage of the management each would emerge as the key to its performance.

In the absence of such ambitious analysis, however, the present model does at least provide a simple basis for relating the accuracy of the subjective beliefs as inherited from culture and past experience, to the performance of the internationalisation strategy (Buckley & Chapman, 1997). Generally speaking, the more accurate are the beliefs, the better will be the performance of the firm. The relation between accuracy and performance is not a continuous one, though, because, as noted earlier, errors in probabilities translate into errors in strategy only when critical probability thresholds are exceeded. This amplifies the earlier comparison between two firms in which it was just the relevance of the home country marketing experience which affected subsequent performance. It suggests that it is not just the firm's own experience in its home market that is important, but the culture it acquires from its domestic environment too.

To analyze the impact of beliefs upon performance the modeller must, of course, specify what the true situation — unknown to the management — really is. Suppose, for example, that each market is of a different type, so that correct beliefs are represented by $q_2 = q_3 = 1$, $p_2 = p_3 = 0$. Suppose also that there is no correlation, $k = 0$. Under these circumstances a simultaneous strategy is almost certainly preferable to a sequential strategy because, with both foreign markets being different, the sequential approach offers no economies of scope to information.

A very optimistic management might take the view that all the markets were of the same type, so that both foreign markets were exactly like the domestic market: that is, $q_2 = q_3 = 0$. With expected costs of internationalisation well below their actual level, the firm could decide to internationalise when in fact the null strategy of remaining a domestic firm might be better. Moreover, being so confident in its beliefs, management may not investigate the states of individual markets either, so that costly errors may be perpetrated in marketing strategy too. Thus the firm will expand into the two foreign markets simultaneously without any investigation, and make losses as a result. Misguided subjective beliefs therefore provide a simple rationalization for impetuous globalisation.

At the other extreme, so far as strategy is concerned, is the management that wrongly believes that both foreign markets, though different from the home market, are of the same type, but recognizes that it does not know what state this is. This firm will opt for the cautious strategy of sequential internationalisation when in fact simultaneous internationalisation with investigation at each stage would definitely be better. This kind of firm is typically commended in the internationalisation literature, although, as this example makes clear, its strategy is inefficient in certain circumstances.

Evaluation of the Scandinavian Approach

The preceding analysis has immediate relevance to the evaluation of alternative theories of the firm. To begin with, the analysis highlights the importance of subjective beliefs about the similarity and dissimilarity of different markets. It shows that the advantage of a sequential approach to expansion is greatest when foreign markets are believed to be different from the home one but are likely to be similar to each other. Given that they are indeed similar, the sequential approach maximizes the economies of scope that the first investigation affords. Conversely, the advantage of the simultaneous strategy is greatest when the foreign markets are believed to be similar to the home one, and, if different, to be different in their own particular way. This means that experience gained from any particular market will be of little relevance elsewhere.

The strategic management literature advocating globalisation (Porter, 1980) clearly adopts this latter view. The markets of different industrialized countries are claimed to be basically similar — at least so far as the preferences of young high-income consumers are concerned — and any variation tends to be imputed to local factors peculiar to each market. Globalisation therefore appears in the present model as a specific response to a particular configuration of the international market system.

Internalization theory is often alleged to favour a rather similar strategy. This is because of the theory's emphasis on the public good properties of knowledge developed in the domestic market, and the advantage of exploiting these properties internally through expansion of the firm. In fact, however, most authors in this tradition have been very aware of the 'psychic costs' to the firm of entering foreign markets (Buckley & Casson, 1976). Internalization theorists have tended to assume that all markets are different, so that there is always a cost of entry. Because all markets

Table 10.3: Classification of Theoretical Approaches to Internationalisation.

Foreign Markets	Home and Foreign Markets	
	Same	**Different**
Same	Globalisation	Scandinavian
Different	—	Internalization

Note: Because globalisation assumes that foreign markets are essentially the same as the home market it follows that differences between foreign markets must be small. But in so far as these small differences are idiosyncratic to each market, the logic of simultaneous internationalisation will be more secure.

are different, the scope economies of accrued experience of market entry have not been emphasized in the same way as in the Scandinavian literature. The internalization view has supported the simultaneous approach simply because there is little point in deferring entry if the costs cannot be reduced using experience gained in other markets first. Simultaneous entry is also promoted by the fact that, where technological knowledge is concerned, patents expire and trade secrets leak out, so that early entry into all markets is advisable before the potential monopoly rents are dissipated. Internalization theory, in other words, highlights a particular kind of pre-emptive advantage.

Where internalization theorists have argued for sequential entry is has generally been in terms of the "Penrose' effect — that simultaneous internationalisation of the firm will overstretch its managerial resources. The Penrose argument is, however, quite distinct from the argument for sequential internationalisation based on economies of scope available from the learning process. The two approaches are, in principle, rival explanations of the sequential expansion of the firm, although they can be regarded as complementary and mutually reinforcing within a synthetic view. While this chapter is committed to elaborating the learning approach, it has been useful, from the standpoint of practical application, to have incorporated the Penrose theory within the model as a special case.

The difference between the internalization approach and the globalisation approach lies not, therefore, in the recommended internationalisation strategy but rather in the perceived profitability of internationalisation per se. Because internalization theory recognizes psychic costs that globalisation theory discounts, it more often favours the null strategy of remaining at home and licensing the technology to other firms overseas. Licensing to foreign firms with local knowledge of market conditions is an important element of internalization theory precisely because the psychic costs of foreign market entry are fully recognized.

It can be seen that, by elimination, the Scandinavian approach focuses on those situations where foreign markets are unlike the home market but very similar to each other. The older Scandinavian literature associated with the Uppsala school emphasizes the need to expand in stages in a manner reminiscent of (but not coincident with) the product cycle model (Vernon, 1979). The more recent literature, on the other hand, emphasizes the importance of speeding up the learning process by improving communication between foreign subsidiaries.

Recall that the net advantage of the sequential approach depends on, amongst other things, the excess of the cost of investigation over the cost of communication between subsidiaries. To encourage subsidiaries to learn from each other, it is desirable not only to improve headquarters — subsidiary communication but to encourage subsidiaries to communicate directly with each other. Organizational learning needs to be decentralized, in other words. This is an important aspect of the thinking underlying the 'heterarchy' or the 'network' firm (Chesnais, 1988; Hedlund, 1986). Whilst the discussion of the heterarchies tends to focus on the organizational restructuring of the mature multinational enterprise, the present model emphasizes the more general advantage to the

Table 10.4: Information Gathering Versus Investment Deferral Decisions.

	Do Not Defer Commit Resource Time t	Defer Commitment of Resource 'Real Options'
Do Not Collect Information (Measure things you would otherwise not know).	1 Gung-ho Investor	3 Cautious but Uninformed Investor
Do Collect Information Research Prudentially	2 Uninformed Investor	4 Sophisticated Investor

firm of building up the heterarchy in stepwise fashion from the very start of the internationalisation process.

As indicated earlier, learning by doing is a satisfactory alternative to systematic investigation if the costs of making a mistake are not too great. To control these costs, firms will tend to make small commitments to begin with, and only increase their commitments once experience has been gained. Thus sequential entry into markets is accompanied by incremental expansion in these markets over time. Because systematic investigation reduces the likelihood of mistakes (in the model above it eliminates it altogether — which is clearly a very extreme case) it supports a greater initial commitment. Thus sequential expansion will be associated with different degrees of initial commitment according to the way that knowledge of markets is acquired. This coincides with the general thrust of the Scandinavian approach.

International Joint Ventures as Real Options

International joint ventures are primarily contractual real options. Although an IJV's physical assets may embody a certain degree of flexibility, the distinctive feature of an IJV from an option perspective is the flexibility afforded by the joint ownership arrangement. There are many different types of IJV. This section presents an example which has been chosen to illustrate the option perspective on IJVs in the simplest possible way.

The basic idea is that a partner in an IJV possesses both a 'call option' to buy out the other partner, and a 'put' option to sell out to the other partner, depending upon how the IJV performs in the future (Chi & McGuire, 1996; Kogut & Zander, 1993). The question arises, however, as to why the other partner would be willing to trade on especially favourable terms. One reason is that transaction costs are lower between the partners than they are between ordinary firms because the partners have got to know and trust each other. They share the gains from this trust by trading equity with each other on mutually favourable terms. This means that the partners possess options to trade on these terms instead of on the terms that would prevail if there were no previous connection between them.

Another explanation is that one of the partners is better informed than the other. Their reputation for being better informed gives them an advantage in negotiations over equity purchase. As the IJV evolves, the more sophisticated partner makes offers to the less sophisticated partner which the latter is willing to accept. In this way information rents accrue to the partner that is better at valuing the joint venture — i.e., is better at forecasting the IJV's future stream of profits. This mechanism for appropriating information rents will only work, however, if the other partner receives no rival offers from third parties. One reason why they may not receive such offers is that other firms are not so well informed about the prospects for the IJV because they lack the 'inside knowledge' that is shared by the partner firms. They therefore lack the confidence to make rival offers. The other partner may not possess sufficiently tangible evidence to go out and solicit such offers to test the offers received from the more sophisticated firm. It is this case of asymmetric information which is the basis of the example that follows.

Consider two firms which can go into partnership by sharing ownership of equity on a 50:50 basis. One firm provides finance and the other provides the human capital, such as the ideas. The issue is analyzed from the standpoint of the financial investor, which is the more sophisticated firm. This investor, it is assumed, has identified a small high-technology start-up venture which requires capital in order to fund further R&D. The owner of the start up will sell 50 percent of his equity for five units, or sell out completely for 10 units. These sales must be effected at the outset (period 1)), before the outcome of the R&D is known.

In the future (period 2)) the outcome of the R&D is revealed to the owners of the firm. The financier knows that if the research is successful then the project will be worth 20 units, whereas if it is unsuccessful then it will be worthless. The partner, however, is not so good at valuing projects, and believes that if the outcome is successful then it will be worth only 12 units, whilst if it is unsuccessful, it will still be worth 7 units. These beliefs are reflected in negotiations between the firms, in which the sophisticated firm extracts maximum rents from the unsophisticated one. The unsophisticated partner is willing to sell his 50 percent stake for $12 - 5 = 7$ units if the outcome is good, and to buy the financial investor's stake for $7 - 5 = 2$ units if the outcome is bad. The outcome does not become public knowledge, so these offers will not be affected by rival bids. The partners come to an informal understanding on these terms when they enter the IJV. Because of the trust between them, they both honour these terms in the following period, even though their initial contributions have been 'sunk' by the start of the second period.

The financial investor has three main alternatives:

1) Acquire the firm immediately;
2) Enter a joint venture immediately and review the situation in the next period;
3) Avoid the project altogether.

If he participates in the IJV then it always pays him to exercise the call option if the outcome is good because the unsophisticated partner undervalues the project. Thus instead of earning 50 percent of 20 units, namely 10 units, the investor can pay out an additional seven units to obtain an additional 10 units, i.e., the entire 20 units, for himself. Similarly, it always pays to him exercise the put option when the outcome is bad. This is because the unsophisticated partner overvalues the project, since he is willing to pay two units to buy more of a project that is actually worthless. Thus the sophisticated partner will not continue with the IJV in its initial form, but will either take over the IJV, or divest his share of it, depending on the outcome of the R&D.

Let the probability of a successful outcome perceived at the outset by the sophisticated investor be p. Then the expected profits of the three strategies are:

$$v1 = -10 + 20p \tag{13.1}$$
$$v2 = -5 + (20 - 7)p + 2(1 - p) = -3 + 11p \tag{13.2}$$
$$v3 = 0 \tag{13.3}$$

The first term in equation (13.1) is the purchase price for an outright acquisition, and the second term is the profit from the entire project when its outcome is good. The first term in equation (13.2) is the cost of buying a stake in the IJV. The second term is the expected profit generated by exercising the call option, and the third term is the expected profit generated by exercising the put option.

The solution is:

$$i = \begin{array}{lll} 1 & \text{if} & p > 0.78 \\ 2 & \text{if} & 0.27 < p < 0.78 \\ 3 & \text{if} & p < 0.27 \end{array} \tag{14}$$

The solution is illustrated in Figure 10.8. As before the expected profit associated with the ith strategy (i = 1,2) is indicated by the height of the schedule ViVi', with the horizontal axis indicating the expected profit of the null strategy (strategy 3)). The envelope OE1E2V1' indicates the

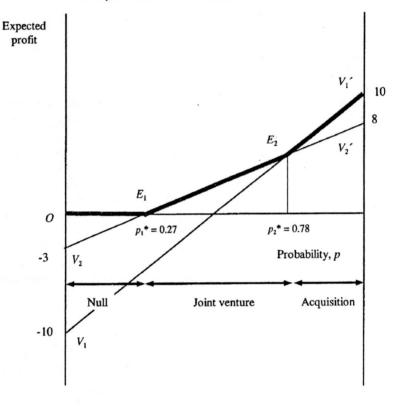

Figure 10.8: An International Joint Venture as a Real Option.

maximum attainable profit. The IJV is the preferred strategy between the critical values p1* = 0.27, p2* = 0.78, which correspond to the switch points E1, E2. The figure reveals the IJV as a classic option strategy — namely one that is pursued when the investor is highly uncertain about the outcome of a project.

It is possible to extend this model by taking the exercise of options as a repeated process but this is beyond the scope of this short paper.

Conclusions

Real options provide a way of rationalizing many practical aspects of business behaviour which until recently defied analysis: the seeming irrationality of procrastination and delay in committing resources to new foreign markets, and the cautious incremental approach to investment that is so often pursued once the market is entered.

The application of real options to IB issues has been discouraged by confusions over the relation between real options and financial options. This paper has sought to clear up some of this confusion by demonstrating that a single set of four key principles underlie both branches of options theory. The principal difference between the two branches of theory lies in the fact that one deals mainly with tradable assets and the other deals mainly with non-tradable ones.

Options reduce risk by providing the flexibility to respond to new information when it becomes available. The key to a successful exploitation of real options is to foresee the kind of information that is likely to become available, and plan the options to exploit this information from an early stage. Flexibility can take many forms: IJVs provide flexibility through contractual options, whereas small reversible investments in versatile assets provide flexibility in a non-contractual form. These forms of flexibility can be combined — for example, by holding a portfolio of IJVs, each of which operates versatile assets, and utilises information by-products from other IJVs, as well as supplying its own information by-products to them.

This paper has introduced and synthesized ideas rather than presented an exhaustive treatise on its subject. Much work remains to be done in producing algebraic versions of the numerical models presented above, and in simulating the algebraic models to determine the sensitivity of various option strategies to the parameters which govern them. This paper has focused on applications to manufacturing, but real options also apply to marketing and R&D (see, for example, Huchzermeier & Loch, 1997). New models can be generated by modifying the assumptions of the models presented above. The new models can be made more realistic than the ones presented here — for example, by introducing oligopolistic rivalry (Lambrecht & Perraudin, 1996) — but they are also likely to be more complicated too.

Insights from these models can be used to construct 'dynamic' versions of existing static theories. The real option perspective can be applied to standard IB theories, including classic theories such as the Product Cycle model and its variants (Vernon, 1966; 1974; 1979). The real option perspective can provide a formal analysis of the leads and lags in the internationalisation process which is missing from many orthodox accounts of the subject.

References

Buckley, P. J. & Casson, M. C. (1981). Optimal timing of a foreign direct investment. *Economic Journal, 91*, 75–87.

Buckley, P. J. & Casson, M. C. (1998). Models of multinational enterprise. *Journal of International Business Studies, 29(1)*, 21–44.

Buckley, P. J. & Chapman, M. (1997). The perception and measurement of transaction cost. *Cambridge Journal of Economics, 21(2)*, 127–145.

Campa, J. M. (1994). Multinational investment under uncertainty in the chemical processing industries. *Journal of International Business Studies, 25(3)*, 557–578.

Capel, J. (1992). How to service a foreign market under uncertainty: a real option approach. *European Journal of Political Economy, 8*, 455–475.

Casson, M. (1996). Internationalisation as a learning process: a model of corporate growth and geographical diversification. In V. N. Balasubramanyan & D. Sapsford (eds), *The Economics of International Investment*. Cheltenham: Edward Elgar.

Chi, T. & McGuire, D. J. (1996). Collaborative ventures and value of learning: integrating the transaction cost and strategic option perspectives on the choice of market entry modes. *Journal of International Business Studies, 27(2)*, 285–307.

DeMeza, D. & van der Ploeg, F. (1987). Production flexibility as a motive for multinationality. *Journal of Industrial Economics 35(3)*, 343–351.

Dempster, M. A. H. & Pliska, S. R. (eds) (1997). *Mathematics of Derivative Securities*. Cambridge: Cambridge University Press.

Dixit, A. & Pindyck, R. S. (1994). *Investments under Uncertainty*. Princeton, NJ: Princeton University Press.

Hirshleifer, J. & Riley, J. G. (1992). *The Analytics of Uncertainty and Information*. Cambridge: Cambridge University Press.

Huchzermeier, A. & Loch, C. H. (1997). *Evaluating R&D Projects as Real Options: Why More Variability is not Always Better*. Fontainebleau: INSEAD, Working Paper 97/105/TM.

Johanson, J. & Vahlne, J.-E. (1977). The internationalization process of the firm — a model of knowledge development and increasing foreign market commitments. *Journal of International Business Studies, 8(1)*, 23–32.

Johanson, J. & Wiedersheim-Paul, F. (1975). The internationalization of the firm: four Swedish cases. *Journal of Management Studies*, October, 305–322.

Jorgenson, D. W. (1963). Capital theory and investment behaviour. *American Economic Review 53*, 247–259.

Jorgenson, D. W. (1967). Investment behaviour and the production function. *Bell Journal of Economics and Management Science, 3*, 220–251.

Kogut, B. & Kulatilaka, N. (1994). Operating flexibility, global manufacturing and the option value of a multinational network. *Management Science, 40(1)*, 123–139.

Kogut, B. & Zander, U. (1993). Knowledge of the firm and the evolutionary theory of the multinational corporation. *Journal of International Business Studies, 24(4),* 625–645.

Kulatilaka, N. & Perotti, E. C. (1998). Strategic growth options. *Management Science, 44(8),* 1021– 1031.

Lambrecht, B. & Perraudin, W. (1996). *Real options and Pre-emption.* Discussion Paper, Department of Economics, Birkbeck College, University of London.

Marschak, J. & Radner, R. (1972). *Economic Theory of Teams.* New Haven, CN: Yale University Press.

Mello, A. S., Parsons, J. E. & Triantis, A. J. (1995). An integrated model of multinational flexibility and hedging policies. *Journal of International Economics, 39,* 27–51.

Rangan, S. (1997). *Do Multinationals Shift Production in Response to Exchange Rate Changes? Do Their Responses Vary by Nationality?* Evidence from 1977– 1993. Fontainbleau: INSEAD, Working Paper 97/84/SM.

Rivoli, P. & Salorio, E. (1996). Foreign direct investment under uncertainty. *Journal of International Business Studies, 27(2),* 335–354.

Schmitzler, A. (1991). *Flexibility and Adjustment to Information in Sequential Decision Problems: A Systematic Approach.* Berlin: Springer-Verlag, Lecture Notes in Economics and Mathematical Systems, 371.

Shackle, G. L. S. (1970). *Expectation, Enterprise and Profit.* Cambridge: Cambridge University Press.

Van Mieghem (1998). Investment strategies for flexible resources. *Management Science, 44(8),* 1071–1077.

Vernon, R. (1966). International investment and international trade in the product cycle. *Quarterly Journal of Economics, 80,* 190–207.

Vernon, R. (1974). The location of economic activity. In J. H. Dunning (ed.), *Economic Analysis and the Multinational Enterprise.* London: Allen & Unwin. 89–114.

Vernon, R. (1979). The product cycle hypothesis in a new international environment. *Oxford Bulletin of Economics and Statistics, 41,* 255–267.

Wiseman, J. (1989). *Cost, Choice and Political Economy.* Aldershot: Edward Elgar.

Chapter 11

Knowledge and Time: A Forgotten Factor in the Internationalisation Process of Firms

Anders Blomstermo, Kent Eriksson and
D. Deo Sharma[1]

Background

Internationalisation is a journey out into unknown territory. On this journey, knowledge based on experience is critical. It takes time to gain such experience. In many studies it is presumed that time is a valid indicator of knowledge though this is not discussed or tested. The role played by time in the internationalisation process of firms has been unclear. Many researchers have even used time to operationalize experiential knowledge.

According to research (Cavusgil, 1980; Johanson & Vahlne, 1977; Luostarinen, 1980), internationalisation is based on experiential learning. It is sometimes also said that the internationalisation process of a firm is a learning process. In reviews of internationalisation research, Andersen (1993) and Leonidas and Katsikeas (1996) find that little attention has been paid to the dimension of time in internationalisation. It has even been called the hidden dimension of internationalisation (Kutschker, Bäurle & Schmid, 1997). A large body of the international business

---

[1] The authors appear in alphabetical order and have contributed equally to this article.

Critical Perspectives on Internationalisation, pp. 263–283.
Copyright © 2002 by Elsevier Science Ltd.
All rights of reproduction in any form reserved.
ISBN: 0-08-044053-5

literature does not consider time (Anderson & Gatignon, 1986; Beamish & Banks, 1987; Buckley & Casson, 1976; Dunning, 1980; 1988; Gatignon & Anderson, 1988; Williamson, 1975). Except for the study by Eriksson, Johanson, Majkgård and Sharma (2001). They investigated with help of LISREL the effect of time on experiential business knowledge, institutional knowledge and internationalisation knowledge.

The objective of this chapter is to further our understanding of the internationalisation process by investigating the effect of time on knowledge and learning. A general assumption in the international business literature is that knowledge is based on experience from domestic operations and when firms go abroad they base their activities on that knowledge. Recently several contradicting evidence has appeared in the literature (Eriksson, Majkgård & Sharma, 2000; Knight & Cavusgil, 1996; Oviatt & McDougall, 1994) identifying an increasing number of firms which were global from their inception. The question posed is: What is the role of time in the internationalisation process? The aspect of time discussed is the length of time spent in foreign operations, which we call duration.

Time is a complex phenomenon with many different faces (Hassard, 1991). All are not treated in this chapter. For example, the timing of foreign market entries is not dealt with. Nor does it consider order or sequence of moves in internationalisation.

In the first section of the chapter, we present a review of the treatment of time in international business literature. More specifically, we identify three distinctive roles of duration in the literature. In some studies, duration is treated as an antecedent to knowledge. In others, it is used as an indicator of experiential knowledge. Still others regard it as a consequence of experiential knowledge. In the second section, we use research on organizational learning theory and internationalisation-, business- and institutional knowledge to discuss duration of foreign operations and learning. Lastly, implications for future research are discussed.

Time and Knowledge

While the duration of foreign operations is an important issue in the literature on the internationalisation process of firms, the main part of international business literature does not, for theoretical reasons, consider duration at all. For example, in the research based on the eclectic approach (Dunning, 1977; 1980; 1988), the transaction cost approach

(Williamson, 1975), and the internalization theory (Buckley, & Casson, 1976) time is not discussed (Anderson & Gatignon, 1986; Beamish & Banks, 1987; Gatignon & Anderson, 1988).

A large body of international business literature, frequently referred to as behavioural studies, is based on implicit or explicit references to time. Instances of implicit references to time are words such as development, evolution, stages and sequence. We meet them in export development studies, implying that this area is concerned with changes over time (Leonidas & Katsikeas, 1996), in the evolutionary theory of multinational firms (Kogut & Zander, 1993), in studies on stages of internationalisation or export behaviour (Bilkey 1978), and in research on sequences of organizational forms (Johanson & Wiedersheim-Paul, 1975).

We review this literature with regard to its assumed relations to knowledge. We do not claim that the review is exhaustive, but it does provide a coherent picture of how the issue of duration has been treated in research on the internationalisation of firms. Given that, in the literature, internationalisation is considered as a history-dependent process, it is logical to start by looking at the research in which duration of foreign operations is an antecedent to experiential knowledge.

Duration as an Antecedent to Knowledge

The general line of thinking is based on the assumption that duration of foreign operations influences knowledge in the internationalisation process of firms. One relatively widespread view is that there is a direct positive correlation between duration and experiential knowledge, (Root, 1994) as depicted in Figure 11.1. According to this view, as firms operate abroad, 'rational decision making displaces or limits the behavioural factors (fears, anxieties, ethnocentric bias, and so on) that dominate earlier decision making' (Root, 1994). The longer firms operate abroad, the more they learn, and the more rational decision-making becomes.

Others do not presume such a direct relation between duration and experiential knowledge. They assume that the need for information changes according to the stages of internationalisation. The problems and opportunities that firms are exposed to at different stages are different. New exporters, for instance, are exposed to problems concerning issues such as international transfer of funds and documentation (Yang *et al.*, 1992), but as the firm operates longer abroad and becomes international, problems in understanding overseas commercial practices and different

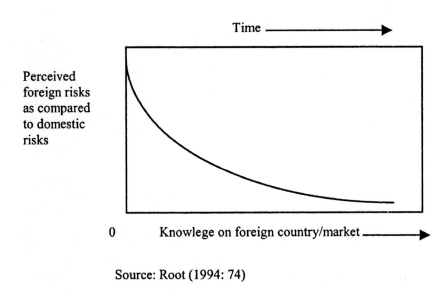

Source: Root (1994: 74)

Figure 11.1: Relationship between Time and Knowledge.

product standards become a greater concern (Bilkey, 1978). According to this view, new fields of knowledge become sequentially relevant and are included in the stock of knowledge of the firm.

In the product life-cycle model proposed by Vernon (1966), Wells (1972) and others, the order of events is important. The model identifies a number of stages in the internationalisation of industries and describes how firms react to changing competitive conditions as their foreign and domestic markets for products expand, mature, and decline. The model claims that many products go through a trade cycle, during which the United States is initially an exporter, then loses its export markets and finally becomes an importer of the product (Wells, 1968). While Vernon's (1966) reference to time is only implicit, Wells (1972) discusses time explicitly. Wells identifies four phases in the international expansion of firms. Phase one is based on a firm's export strength. In phase two, foreign production starts. In phase three, foreign producers become as competitive in export markets. In phase four, import competition in the US market begins. Thus, products are first innovated and produced in the US market. As the market potential abroad grows production moves abroad. And as the product becomes standardized, low-cost production in other countries becomes important. Over time, the technology becomes standardized and the location of production moves overseas. The product life-cycle model claims that time is important in learning and accumulating production knowledge.

Perlmutter (1969) explicitly mentions time in his work on the evolution of the international orientation of firms. He suggests that initially firms are ethnocentric, but as they learn more on international markets, institutions, rules and regulations, they become polycentric and, ultimately, geocentric. The evolution process of firms is thus based on the accumulation of knowledge and experience of international operations and markets. This process, whereby firms move from ethnocentricity to geocentricity, is time-consuming. Building trust between persons of different nationalities is a central obstacle in the process, and can only be overcome through the experience of interaction with each other over time. 'The route to pervasive geocentric thinking is long and tortuous' (Perlmutter, 1969).

In the internationalisation process model of Johanson and Vahlne (1977), time is only implicitly present. Indeed, the words 'time' and 'duration' do not appear in their article. In the formulation of their model, however, they stress that the present state of internationalisation is one important factor in explaining the course of subsequent internationalisation. Thus, history or path dependence is a basic characteristic of the model. Moreover, experiential knowledge must be acquired gradually through operations in the foreign country. In discussing what they call 'change aspects', Johanson and Vahlne conclude that market experience can only be acquired through a long learning process in connection with current activities. This is their explanation for internationalisation often being a slow process. Experiential knowledge is usually associated with particular conditions in a specific market and cannot be transferred to other individuals or other markets, which implies strong history dependence.

A similar reference to duration is made in a study by Buckley and Casson (1988). They discuss international cooperative agreements, including joint ventures and emphasize the importance of trust, reputation and commitment in governing these agreements. They point out that establishing trust and a reputation in international market is a slow process and say that one reason 'why reputation building may be slow is that cheating is often a covert practice — it is more viable if it goes undetected — and so it may be a long time before parties can be certain whether or not an agent has cheated' (Buckley & Casson, 1988). Thus, trust and reputation are by-products of experience gained over time. The importance of time in building cooperation and trust is recognized.

An explicit reference to time is obvious in the strategic options theory proposed by Bowman and Hurry (1993) and Kogut (1983). The basic thinking in this model is that 'firms are sequentially approaching foreign entry with learning gained from past entry experience' (Chang, 1995). It is argued that learning from earlier foreign market entry experience enables firms to build up firm specific capabilities or internationalisation knowledge. These capabilities are then used in subsequent market entries.

Duration as Operationalization of Knowledge

Most frequently time is used explicitly to operationalize knowledge. In those articles, it is assumed that duration of foreign operations is a valid indicator of experience, though this assumption is not tested. The factor of time is operationalized in three ways:

1) number of years in foreign operations;
2) whether or not previous foreign operations have been carried out;
3) number of previous foreign entries.

First, the most frequently used operationalization in the research is the number of years in foreign operations or foreign experience. These studies implicitly assume a direct correlation between duration of export activities and experiential knowledge accumulated in the internationalising firm (cf., Figure 11.1), and that this relation is linear.

A large body of research has followed the pioneering Wisconsin studies in which Bilkey and Tesar (1977) empirically identify six stages in the export expansion of firms. Bilkey and Tesar found that there are differences in foreign experience, indicated by number of years of export experience, between firms in different stages of export expansion. In this research, length of export operations is one of the main criteria used to classify exporting firms with regard to stages of export development. Similar approaches, in which years in export operations is used to distinguish stages in export development, have been applied by Cavusgil (1980; 1984), Czinkota (1982), Ursic and Czinkota (1984), Naidu and Rao (1993) and Naidu and Prasad (1994).

Wiedersheim-Paul *et al.,* (1978) and Crick (1995) used number of years of exporting as a measure of experiential knowledge in the process of export development. Weinstein (1977) also used 'the amount of overseas experience the agency had at the time of the investment' (Weinstein, 1977) to explain foreign market entry and foreign market selection of US-based advertising agencies abroad. Maclayton, Smith & Hair, (1980), explicitly operationalized knowledge in terms of years of operations abroad and found that overseas business experience had no correlation with a firm's evaluation criteria of foreign markets. Also, Wilson (1980) measured previous experience by the number of years a firm had been multinational.

In an interesting study Erramilli (1991) explicitly investigated the effects of length of foreign operations on market entry mode selection and market country selection. The purpose of his research was to examine the effects of experiential knowledge on country market selection and foreign market entry mode selection. He used number of years of foreign operation of the firm as an operationalization of experience. He concluded that the duration of foreign operations had a slightly significant effect on the choice of market country and a strong effect on the choice of entry mode in a country.

Finally, Terpstra and Yu (1988) studied US advertising agencies abroad. They did not operationalize experience in number of years abroad, but conclude that experience in number of years abroad would capture international operations experience better than the measure they used, the ratio of foreign billing to total billing by the firm.

Other researchers have operationalized experience using duration as a dichotomous variable. Davidson (1980; 1983), and Davidson and McFetridge (1985) studied US firms and state that aggregate experience operationalized by pre-presence of a subsidiary in a foreign market increases a firm's propensity to make subsequent investments in that country and a preference to acquire a wholly owned subsidiary. It is argued that the pre-presence of a subsidiary in that country is a source of experiential knowledge to the firm reducing uncertainties associated with foreign operations. Davidson (1980) also argued that firms with no pre-presence in a country lack experience of that country and perceive greater uncertainty and a greater lack of knowledge about foreign markets and foreign institutions. Those firms over-estimate risks and under-estimate benefits. Firms with pre-presence in a country, on the other hand, accumulate knowledge and their risk perception goes down. Managers perceive that they are in a better position to estimate costs and benefits. Franko (1976) and Caves and Mehra (1986) also used pre-presence in a country as a measure of experience. This operationalization of experience has also been used by Kogut and Singh (1988), Madsen (1989), Gripsrud (1990) and Hennart and Park (1994).

A third measure is used by Chang (1995) when he applies sequential options theory in a study of Japanese firms abroad. Chang operationalizes experience by the number of previous foreign entries of the firm at the time of a new entry. He found that accumulated previous foreign entry experience strongly affects the next foreign market entry. The time dimension is indirectly present in this operationalization.

The preceding review shows that a great number of researchers have used duration of international operations to operationalize learning and experiential knowledge in internationalisation. Thus, a direct relation between duration and experience is taken for granted. Several of them, but not all, have also concluded that experience measured in that way has a strong influence on important internationalisation and export development variables.

Duration as a Consequence of Knowledge

In the literature on international ventures, longevity of operations is frequently used as a measure of performance. Pre-mature termination of an international venture is considered a symptom of failure, an acceptance by the firm that the performance of the venture was less than satisfactory. In international joint ventures, for example, a pre-mature termination may show the inability of the joint venture partners to cooperate and resolve conflicts. Thus, Franko (1976) and Contractor (1986) use longevity as a measure of success for international joint ventures. Geringer and Hebert (1991) found a strong correlation between joint venture performance and longevity of the venture measured in number of years. They reported a positive correlation between parent firm perceptions of the extent to which the venture performed well and the original goals and duration of the venture. Harrigan (1988), and Parkhe (1991) also used longevity as an indicator of success in studies of joint ventures.

Longevity is also frequently used as a performance measure indicating success of foreign entry. In a study of entry mode selection and financial performance, Woodcock, Beamish and Makino (1994) found a positive relationship between the duration of a foreign venture and its financial performance. Ventures with a short life performed poorly compared to older ventures. These researchers conclude that there is a stable relation between entry mode, age and performance.

Li and Guisinger (1991) investigate the performance differences of different market entry modes abroad. They define performance as the failure rates of individual foreign market entry modes in the American market. Their results show that the new ventures had the lowest failure rate, followed by joint ventures. Acquisitions had the highest failure rate. Li (1995) also found in a related study that the longevity is affected by learning and experience in foreign operations.

Although all of these studies explicitly use longevity as a consequence their reference to the role of knowledge is only implicit. In studies of foreign entries of Dutch firms, however, Barkema, Bell and Penning (1996), and Barkema, Shenkar, Vermeulen, and Bell (1997) test hypotheses within a framework of organizational learning and use longevity as an outcome of learning. Their research demonstrates that knowledge development has a significant impact on longevity of operations.

Antecedent	Operationalization	Consequence
Vernon (1966)	Bilkey & Tesar (1977)	Franko (1976)
Wells (1968, 1972)	Weinstein (1977)	Contractor (1986)
Perlmutter (1969)	Wiedersheim-Paul et al. (1978)	Harrigan (1988)
Johanson & Vahlne (1977)	Cavusgil (1980, 1984)	Geringer & Hebert (1991)
Kogut (1983)	Davidson (1980, 1983)	Li & Guisinger (1991)
Buckley and Casson	Maclayton et al. (1980)	Parkhe (1991)
(1988)	Wilson (1980)	Woodcock et al. (1994)
Yang et al. (1992)	Czinkota (1982)	Li (1995)
Bowman & Hurry (1993)	Ursic & Czinkota (1984)	Barkema et al. (1996)
Root (1994)	Davidson & McFetridge (1985)	Barkema et al. (1997)
Chang (1995)	Caves & Mehra (1986)	
	Kogut & Singh (1988)	
	Terpstra & Yu (1988)	
	Madsen (1989)	
	Gripsrud (1990)	
	Erramilli (1991)	
	Naidu & Rao (1993)	
	Naidu & Prasad (1994)	
	Hennart & Park (1994)	
	Crick (1995)	

Figure 11.2: Three Features of International Duration and Knowledge in International Business Literature.

The different ways in which time, duration, length or longevity are used in international business studies are summarized in Figure 11.2.

Duration of International Business Operations and Knowledge Development

A common starting point of almost all the studies reviewed is the assumption that firms initially operate locally and that their knowledge (Bilkey, 1978; Johanson & Vahlne, 1977; Perlmutter, 1969; Vernon, 1966) reflects their operations in their local contexts. Knowledge is based on experience from those operations. This experiential knowledge is embedded in the routines and administrative structure developed to manage domestic operations. When they go abroad, firms base their activities on those routines and embedded knowledge, which, however, frequently does not help them to understand situations and conditions in specific foreign markets. Firms must learn both about doing business abroad and about the conditions in particular foreign markets. This requires experience gained over time from doing business in those markets.

Empirical analysis has demonstrated that three different but interrelated components of knowledge are critical in internationalisation: internationalisation knowledge, foreign business knowledge and foreign institutional knowledge (Eriksson *et al.*, 1997). Internationalisation knowledge concerns knowledge of the firm's capability and resources to engage in international operations. This knowledge is embedded in the routines, norms and structure of the firm. A critical consideration in internationalisation is the compatibility of the firm's existing resources and those needed in a particular foreign market (Johanson & Vahlne, 1977; Madhok, 1997). Thus, internationalisation knowledge governs the need and search for business and institutional knowledge about foreign markets. Business knowledge is knowledge on customers, competitors and market conditions in particular foreign markets. Institutional knowledge refers to knowledge of government and institutional framework, rules, norms and values in the particular markets. It has been demonstrated that lack of internationalisation knowledge leads to lack of business knowledge and institutional knowledge about foreign markets (Eriksson *et al.*, 1997). Lack of business knowledge and institutional knowledge, increase the perceived cost of future internationalisation. They inhibit further internationalisation.

Since the internationalisation process is characterized as a process of learning and knowledge development, we base the following discussion on organizational learning literature. According to Duncan and Weiss (1979) in Weick (1991) "Learning is the process by which knowledge about action-outcome relationships and the effect of the environment on these relationships is developed". It seems to be a common view in organizational learning literature, as in internationalisation process theory, that firms learn from their past experience by transforming this experience to useful knowledge. It is also a common notion that learning is a dynamic, albeit mostly incremental, phenomenon unfolding over time and linked to current and previous knowledge (Cohen & Levinthal, 1990; Garvin, 1993).

In Argyris and Schön's (1978) discussion of organizational learning, the organizational theory-in-use is a central concept. It can be specified in terms of Weick's (1991) definition of learning given above, with the addition that an organizational theory-in-use is embedded in the routines, norms and values of an organization. In the present context of experiential knowledge development in the internationalisation process, internationalisation knowledge can be seen as the firm's theory-in-use with regard to international business strategy. Lack of internationalisation knowledge is perceived when the theory-in-use is vague, undifferentiated or irrelevant. Such lack of internationalisation knowledge leads to, as mentioned above, lack of business and institutional knowledge about foreign markets.

According to organization learning literature, a distinction can be made between lower and higher order learning. The former takes place within the existing framework of a firm's theory-in-use and associated routines, systems and norms, while the latter denotes a restructuring of this framework (Argyris & Schön, 1978; Corsini, 1987; Fiol & Lyles, 1985). When the theory-in-use is applied to business problems that evolve, errors are normally detected. The extent to which those errors are compatible with the existing framework, or are peripheral or of otherwise limited significance, corrections are made within the framework. Such lower order learning may result in differentiation, specification and extension of the theory-in-use and in marginal modification of routines and systems. This is also what March (1991) calls a strategy of exploitation, which allows for economies of scale. If experiences concern areas that are fundamental to the firm, or repeated error corrections do not lead to the expected outcomes, a restructuring of the organizational theory-in-use and the corresponding norms, strategies and assumptions may take place. Such higher order learning may also occur as a result of accumulation of a number of errors together questioning assumptions of the received theory-in-use. This is a strategy of exploration (March, 1991).

The relation between the two forms of learning is such that higher order learning is based on lower order learning. In practice, learning contains elements of both lower and higher order. The relative importance of the two can be seen as an economic problem. The theory-in-use together with associated routines and norms determine the organization's capacity to absorb new knowledge (Cohen & Levinthal, 1990). Restructuring of the theory-in-use and the corresponding routines as a consequence of new knowledge is difficult and costly. Organizational learning therefore tends to be a mostly incremental process, in which new knowledge is absorbed primarily within the existing framework and restructuring occurs only occasionally when the received theory-in-use no longer seems workable. Thus, for economic reasons, firms will rely on lower order learning as long as is possible.

In the context of the internationalisation process, lower order learning means that foreign business and institutional knowledge is developed. This is because in the international development of a firm, experience from international business operations, in the form of actual observations or practical acquaintance with facts or events, is gained by the managers and the recording systems of the firm. This experience is interpreted and evaluated based on the firm's theory-in-use, that is, internationalisation knowledge. Much of this experience presumably concerns relatively peripheral areas of the firm, such as particular foreign markets, and is accommodated within the existing framework in the form of differentiations, extensions or just peripheral corrections, with reconsideration of the knowledge about other areas of the firm necessary. Differentiations and extensions of theory-in-use are incremental learning that reduces the lack of knowledge of the firm. When experience is not consistent with received theory-in-use but does not call for reconsideration of the theory, peripheral corrections may be made. They represent incremental learning that increases the lack of knowledge.

Some experience is of the kind that contradicts fundamental assumptions associated with the existing framework and calls for a restructuring of the received theory-in-use and the related routines, strategies and norms. This experience will lead to discontinuous changes in internationalisation knowledge. Similarly, over time, experience of many types is retained in the memory of the firm. The accumulation of such experience may result in the discovery that the outcome of actions over time has not been in accordance with the theory-in-use and a restructuring of this theory is required. Thus, although much of this experience has been accommodated within the existing framework as lower level learning, it may, when accumulated in the books or other parts of the memory of the firm, eventually lead to reconsideration and restructuring of the theory-in-use.

In the literature on duration and experiential knowledge reviewed earlier, it is either argued that duration of foreign operations is an antecedent that reduces the lack of knowledge and, consequently, uncertainty regarding international operations, or it is assumed that duration of foreign operations is a valid indicator of experiential knowledge. This would appear to be an instance of lower order learning. As time passes, a firm differentiates its knowledge about how to do international business and how foreign markets work. No distinction with regard to the three kinds of knowledge is made in the literature. However, internationalisation literature is not univocal in this respect. There are a number of instances in the literature that suggest that firms, when operating abroad, learn that these operations are more difficult than they initially expected. The lack of knowledge increases with experience as suggested by O'Grady and Lane's (1996) study of the psychic distance paradox. Similarly, Johanson and Vahlne (1977) argue that in some situations, characterized by market instability and heterogeneity, operations abroad may lead to a greater lack of knowledge. According to this view there is a gap between knowledge according to the theory-in-use and the felt need for knowledge.

There is, however, one situation which all internationalising firms are exposed to. This is when they, a time after the first step abroad, are reached by signals from foreign markets. An instance of this is the psychic distance paradox formulated by O'Grady and Lane (1996), where they find that after a few years a number of Canadian firms discovered that the US market was not as similar to the Canadian market as they had expected. There is reason to expect that when going abroad many firms are optimistic, in the sense that their ideas are based on past experience from domestic operations, about the development of international operations. After going abroad, it takes some time before an evaluation of the experience from the first steps abroad may be made. There is reason to expect that, in many cases, a discontinuous restructuring of a firm's internationalisation knowledge will occur after a number of years of foreign operations.

Discussion and Concluding Remarks

The chapter demonstrates that time in the form of duration of foreign operation is relevant in explaining development of experiential knowledge in the internationalisation process.

We consider theory-in-use as a set of assumptions held by a firm, about what the firm can do under different circumstances and what kind of knowledge is required for different purposes. Knowledge changes over time to support the theory-in-use and reduce perceived need for additional knowledge. Learning in the field of institutional conditions is, until this point, a matter of learning about the need for more and better information. The theory-in-use is not questioned. Due to its experiences in connection with foreign operations, after a time, a firm may realize that its particular theory-in-use is not valid and that a restructuring is required. Evidently, restructuring of such a theory is not a continuous process. It takes place when the accumulated experience says that the theory no longer corresponds to reality. This may occur through a specific event such as a decision to enter a market in a new way, a particular action by a customer, a competitor, or a cooperating partner, or it may occur as a result of some unexpected outcome. It may also follow from a long period of incremental deviations from expectations. Thus, we have no reason to expect that a restructuring of the theory-in-use should take place at any specific point of time.

Internationalisation is not a single event. It is a process of knowledge development with a history and a future. However, the internationalisation knowledge development process is not straightforward, it is discontinuous (Eriksson *et al.,* 2001).

All firms know that the acquisition of business knowledge will require interaction with actors abroad. Business knowledge development increases over time depending on new and existing foreign ventures. Consequently, most firms are aware that business conditions are complex.

At home the firms have concentrated their learning efforts on direct business matters while institutional matters are taken for granted and when going international they just continue on that ethnocentric track and believe that they can handle the foreign institutional environment until they after some time discover that their institutional learning was an illusion. Obviously, there is strong reason to strengthening the awareness of the specificity of the domestic institutional environment and the wide international variations of such environments. Over time as firms operates abroad, they realize that institutions are more complex than expected

(Eriksson *et al.*, 2000a; O'Grady & Lane 1996). In this respect duration has a important influence on institutional knowledge.

The discussion on theory-in-use can be compared with Kuhn's (1970) concept of scientific revolution, where current scientific activities are performed within a framework of a current scientific paradigm, and where these activities are assumed to add to the validity of the paradigm. Yet, in the course of performing these activities, anomalies may arise, which lead to the construction of competing paradigms which may eventually replace the earlier one. Both business knowledge and institutional knowledge development correspond to current within-paradigmatic scientific development, while internationalisation knowledge change captures a revolution in the theory-in-use.

When firms operate many years in the domestic market and develop routines, structures and mental models, their ability to learn from other firms abroad are limited. These firms find it easier to absorb new knowledge that relates to their existing domestic knowledge base. Consequently, such firms start their internationalisation process in countries that are culturally similar their own. On the other hand, Born Globals, with such limited domestic experience have not yet developed routines and processes for handling international issues, make it easier for them to adapt to international expansion. These new firms lack strong ties and legitimacy in the domestic market. They are exposed to high level of uncertainty that concern potential clients and their precise needs and demands. For the same reasons, Born Globals lack knowledge of foreign business culture that may impact their business transactions. These firms are open minded, i.e., they use double loop learning questioning present practices and cause-effect relationship. They use a search and evaluation process that is based on exploiting existing opportunities. These opportunities are evaluated on their own merits, with the firms' current knowledge base being far less of a constraint for future operations.

New firms with weak ties may receive a different set of knowledge from their environment. They are able to see technological and market opportunities from a different angle and they are more innovative concerning the needs of its clients and markets. Born Globals manage uncertainty by being adaptive and flexible regard to country market selection as well as entry mode selection. Adaptiveness is made possible as Born Globals are not bound by specific successful experience of the past. This may concern both which foreign markets to enter as well as the entry mode selection in specific markets. Adaptiveness is also made possible as the problem of unlearning old knowledge does not arise.

These firms may jump to far distant countries and need not pursue a gradual stepwise process of foreign establishment. In other words, the internationalisation process of Born Globals is characterized by the strategy of exploration.

This chapter has several managerial implications and also implications for future research. Our literature review shows that firms that have already developed an international absorptive capacity have it easier to go abroad. It is important to build international relationships early (Majkgård & Sharma, 1998). It is more difficult for firms with long domestic experience to change their routines and processes to an international strategy. These firms have already a cemented knowledge platform.

The discussion call for more research on the development of the treatment of time in international business literature. We need quantitative research on the effect of time on learning in the internationalisation process of firms. More specific, the effect of time on institutional knowledge, business knowledge and internationalisation knowledge (Eriksson *et al.*, 1997; 2001). More research is also required on learning in the early internationalisation. Intensive case studies of the nature of this development should be fruitful. Is it really a matter of revolutionary changes and if so which are the driving forces in those changes and what are their consequences for instance in terms of the internationalisation capability of the firm? Another interesting issue is to investigate the effect of variation in terms of operations in different countries on the internationalisation process (Eriksson *et al.*, 2001). Finally, research on firms that are 'born international' with regard to the role of time appears to be an interesting field. Does Born Globals mean that no development of internationalisation knowledge is needed?

References

Andersen, O. (1993). On the internationalization process of firms: A critical analysis. *Journal of International Business Studies, 24(2)*, 209–232.

Anderson, E. & Gatignon, H. (1986). Modes of entry: A transactions cost analysis and propositions. *Journal of International Business Studies, 17(3)*, 1–26.

Anderson, J. C. & Gerbing, D. W. (1988). Structural equation modeling in practice: A review and recommended two-step approach. *Psychological Bulletin, 103(3)*, 411–423.

Argyris, C. & Schön, D. A. (1978). *Organizational Learning: A Theory of Action Perspective*. Reading, Mass.: Addison-Wesley.

Armstrong, J. S. & Overton, T. S. (1977). Estimating non-response bias in mail surveys. *Journal of Marketing Research, 14(3)*, 396–402.

Barkema, H. G., Bell, J. H. J. & Penning, J. M. (1996). Foreign entry, cultural barriers, and learning. *Strategic Management Journal, 17(2)*, 151–166.

Barkema, H. G., Shenkar, O., Vermeulen, F. & Bell, J. H. J. (1997). Working abroad, working with others: How firms learn to operate international joint ventures. *Academy of Management Journal, 40(2)*, 426–442.

Beamish, P. W. & Banks, J. C. (1987). Equity joint ventures and the theory of the multinational enterprise. *Journal of International Business Studies, 19(2)*, 1–16.

Beamish, P. W. & Inkpen, A. C. (1995). Keeping international joint ventures stable and profitable. *Long Range Planning, 28(3)*, 26–36.

Bilkey, W. J. (1978). An attempted integration of the literature on the export behavior of firms. *Journal of International Business Studies, 13*, 39–55.

Bilkey, W. J. (1982). Variables associated with export profitability. *Journal of International Business Studies, 12(2)*, 39–55.

Bilkey, W. J. & Tesar, G. (1977). The export behaviour of smaller sized Wisconsin manufacturing firms. *Journal of International Business Studies, 8(1)*, 93–98.

Bollen, K. A. (1989). *Structural Equations with Latent Variables*. New York: John Wiley & Sons.

Bonaccorsi, A. (1992). On the relationship between firms size and export intensity. *Journal of International Business Studies, 23(4)*, 605–635.

Bowman, E. & Hurry, D. (1993). Strategy through the option lens: an integrated view of resource investments and the incremental-choice process. *Academy of Management Review, 18*, 760–782.

Buckley, P. J. & Casson, M. (1976). *The Future of the Multinational Enterprise*. London: Macmillan.

Buckley, P. J. & Casson, M. (1988). A theory of cooperation in international business. In F. J. Contractor & P. Lorange (eds), *Cooperative Strategies in International Business*. Lexington, MA: Lexington Books. 31–55.

Calof, J. L. (1994). The relationship between firm size and export behavior revisited. *Journal of International Business Studies, 2*, 367–387.

Carlson, S. (1974). International transmission of information and the business firm. *The Annals of the American Academy of Political and Social Science, 412*, 55–63.

Caves, R. & Mehra, S. (1986). Entry of foreign multinationals into U.S. manufacturing industries. In M. Porter (ed.), *Competition in Global Industries*. Cambridge, MA: Harvard Business School Press. 449–482.

Cavusgil, S. T. (1980). On the internationalization process of firms. *European Research, 8*, 273–281.

Cavusgil, S. T. (1984). Organizational characteristics associated with export activity. *Journal of Management Studies, 21(1)*, 3–22.

Chang, S. J. (1995). International expansion strategy of Japanese firms: Capability building through sequential entry. *Academy of Management Journal, 38(2)*, 383–407.

Cohen, W. & Levinthal, D. (1990). Absorptive capacity: A new perspective on learning and innovation. *Administration Science Quarterly, 35*, 128–152.

Contractor, F. J. (1986). International business: an alternative view. *International Marketing Review, 3(1)*, 74–85.

Corsini, R. (1987). *Concise Encyclopedia of Psychology*. New York: Wiley.

Crick, D. (1995). An investigation into the targeting of UK export assistance. *European Journal of Marketing, 29(8)*, 76–94.

Czinkota, M. (1982). *Export Development Strategies: US Promotion Policies*. New York: Praeger Publishers.

Davidson, W. H. (1980). The location of foreign direct investment activity: country characteristics and experience effects. *Journal of International Business Studies, 11(2)*, 9–22.

Davidson, W. H. (1983). Market similarity and market selection: Implications of international marketing strategy. *Journal of Business Research, 11*, 439–456.

Davidson, W. H. & McFetridge, D. G. (1985). Key characteristics in the choice of international technology transfer mode. *Journal of International Business Studies, 16(2)*, 5–21.

Duncan, R. & Weiss, A. (1979). Organizational learning: Implications for organizational design. In B. Staw & L. L. Cummings (eds), *Research in Organizational Behavior*, 1. Greenwich, CT: JAI. 75–132.

Dunning, J. H. (1977). Trade, location of economic activity and the MNE: A search for an eclectic approach. In B. Ohlin, P. Hesselborn & M. Wijkman (eds), *The International Allocation of Economic Activity*. New York: Holmes & Meier.

Dunning, J. H. (1980). Towards an eclectic theory of international production: some empirical tests. *Journal of International Business Studies, 11*, 1, 9–31.

Dunning, J. H. (1988). The eclectic paradigm of international production: A restatement and some possible extensions. *Journal of International Business Studies, 19*, 1, 1–31.

Eriksson, K., Johanson, J., Majkgård, A. & Sharma, D. D. (1997). Experiential knowledge and cost in the internationalization process. *Journal of International Business Studies, 28(2)*, 337–360.

Eriksson, K., Johanson, J., Majkgård, A. & Sharma, D. D. (2001). Time and experiential knowledge in the internationalization process. *Zeitschrift Für Betriebswirtschaft, 71(1)*, 21–44.

Eriksson, K., Johanson. J., Majkgård, A. & Sharma, D. D. (2000). Effect of variation on knowledge accumulation in the internationalization process. *International Studies of Management & Organization, 30(1)*, 26–44.

Erramilli, M. K. (1991). The experience factor in foreign market entry behavior of service firms. *Journal of International Business Studies, 22(3)*, 479–501.

Fiol, C. M. and Lyles, M. A. (1985). Organizational learning. *Academy of Management Review, 1(4)*, 803–813.

Franko, L. G. (1976). *The European Multinationals: A Renewed Challenge to American and British Big Business.* Greenwich, CT: Greylock.

Garvin, D. A. (1993). Building a learning organization. *Harvard Business Review, 71(4)*, 78–91.

Gatignon, H. & Anderson, E. (1988). The multinational corporation's degree of control over foreign subsidiaries: An empirical test of a transaction cost explanation. *Journal of Law, Economics, and Organization, 4(2)*, 305–335.

Geringer, J. M. and Hebert, L. (1991). Measuring performance of international joint ventures. *Journal of International Business Studies, 22(2)*, 249–263.

Gripsrud, G. (1990). The determinants of export decisions and attitudes to a distant market: Norwegian fishery exports to Japan. *Journal of International Business Studies, 21(3)*,

Harrigan, K. R. (1988). Joint ventures and competitive strategy. *Strategic Management Journal, 9*, 141–158.

Hassard, J. (1991). Aspects of Time in Organization. *Human Relations, 44(2)*, 105–125.

Hayduk, L. A. (1987). *Structural Equation Modeling with LISREL: Essentials and Advances.* Baltimore: Johns Hopkins University Press.

Hennart, J. F. and Park, Y. (1994). Location, governance, and strategic determinants of Japanese manufacturing investment in the United States. *Strategic Management Journal, 15*, 419–436.

Johanson, J. and Vahlne, J.-E. (1977). The internationalization process of the firm — a model of knowledge development and increasing foreign market commitments. *Journal of International Business Studies, 8(1)*, 23–32.

Johanson, J. and Wiedersheim-Paul, F. (1975). The internationalization of the firm — four Swedish cases. *Journal of Management Studies, 12(3)*, 305–322.

Jöreskog, K.-G. and Sörbom, D. (1993). *LISREL 8: Structural Equation Modelling with the SIMPLIS Command Language.* Chicago: Scientific Software International.

Knight, G. A. and Cavusgil, S. T. (1996). The Born Global Firm: A challenge to traditional internationalization theory. *Advances in International Marketing, 8*, 11–26.

Kogut, B. (1983). Foreign direct investment as a sequential process. In C. P. Kindleberger & D. Audretsch (eds), *The Multinational Corporation in the 1980s.* Cambridge, MA: MIT Press. 36–56.

Kogut, B. & Harbir S. (1988). The effect of national culture on the choice of entry mode. *Journal of International Business Studies, 19(3)*, 411–432.

Kogut, B. & Zander, U. (1993). Knowledge of the firm and the evolutionary theory of the multinational enterprise. *Journal of International Business Studies, 24*, 625–646.

Kuhn, T. S. (1970). *The Structure of Scientific Revolution.* Chicago: University of Chicago Press.

Kutschker, M., Bäurle, I. & Schmid, S. (1997). The "three es" of internationalization. *Management International Review, 37(2)*, 101–124.

Leonidas C. & Katsikeas, C. S. (1996). The export development process: An integrative review of empirical models. *Journal of International Business Studies, 27(3)*, 517–551.

Li, J. T. (1995). Foreign entry and survival: effect of strategic choices on performance in international markets. *Strategic Management Journal, 16*, 333–351.

Li, J. T. and Guisinger, S. (1991). Comparative business failures of foreign-controlled firms in the United States. *Journal of International Business Studies, 22*, 209–224.

Lord, F. C. and Novick, M. R. (1968). *Statistical Theories of Mental Test Scores*. Reading, MA: Addison-Wesley.

Luostarinen, R. (1980). *Internationalization of the Firm*. Helsinki: Helsinki School of Economics.

Maclayton, D., Smith, M. & Hair, J. (1980). Determinants of foreign market entry: a multivariate analysis of corporate behaviour in the US-based health care industry. *Management International Review, 20(3)*, 40–52.

Madhok, A. (1997). Cost, value and foreign market entry mode: The transaction and the firm. *Strategic Management Journal, 18(1)*, 39–61.

Madsen, T. K. (1989). Succesful export marketing management: Some empirical evidence. *International Marketing Review, 6(4)*, 41–57.

March, J. G. (1991). Exploration and exploitation in organizational learning. *Organizational Science, 2(1)*,

Naidu, G. M. & Prasad, V. K. (1994). Predictors of export strategy and performance of small and medium-sized firms. *Journal of Business Research, 31(2–3)*, 107–115.

Naidu, G. M. & Rao, T. R. (1993). Public sector promotion of exports: a needs-based approach. *Journal of Business Research, 27*, 85–101.

O'Grady, S. & Lane, H. W. (1996). The psychic distance paradox. *Journal of International Business Studies, 27(2)*, 309–333.

Oviatt, B. M. & McDougall, P. P. (1994). Toward a theory of international new ventures. *Journal of International Business Studies, 25(1)*, 45–64.

Parkhe, A. (1991). Interfirm diversity, organizational learning, and longevity in global strategic alliances. *Journal of International Business Studies, 22(4)*, 579–601.

Perlmutter, H. V. (1969). The tortuous evolution of the multinational corporation. *Columbia Journal of World Business*, 9–18.

Root, F. J. (1994). *Foreign Market Entry Strategies*. New York: AMACOM.

Terpstra, V. & Yu, C.-M. (1988). Determinants of foreign investment by US advertising agencies. *Journal of International Business Studies, 19(1)*, 33–46.

Ursic, M. L. & Czinkota, M. R. (1984). An experience curve explanation of export Expansion. *Journal of Business Research, 12*, 159–168.

Vernon, R. (1966). International investment and international trade in the product cycle. *Quarterly Journal of Economics, 80(2)*, 190–207.

Weick, K. E. (1991). The traditional quality of organizational learning. *Organization Science, 2(1)*, 116–124.

Weinstein, A. K. (1977). Foreign investment by service firms: The case of multinational advertising agencies. *Journal of International Business Studies, 8(1)*, 83–91.

Wells, L. T. (1968). A product life cycle for international trade? *Journal of Marketing, 32*, July, 1–6.

Wells, L. T. (Ed.) (1972). *The Product Life Cycle and International Trade*. Boston: Harvard Business School, Division of Research.

Wiedersheim-Paul, F., Olson, H. S. and Welch, L. S. (1978). Pre-export activity: The first step in internationalization. *Journal of International Business Studies, 8(1)*, 47–58.

Williamson, O. E. (1975). *Markets and Hierarchies: Analysis and Antitrust Implications*. New York: The Free Press.

Wilson, B. D. (1980). The propensity of multinationals to expand through acquisitions. *Journal of International Business Studies, 11*, 59–65.

Woodcock, C. P., Beamish, P. W. & Makino, S. (1994). Ownership-based entry mode strategies and international performance. *Journal of International Business Studies, 25(2)*, 253–273.

Yang, Y. S., Leione, R. P. & Alden, D. L. (1992). A market expansion ability approach to identify potential exporters. *Journal of Marketing, 56*, January, 84–96.

Zeithaml, V. A., Parasuraman, A. & Berry, L. L. (1985). Problems and strategies in service marketing. *Journal of Marketing, 49(2)*, 33–46.

Zucker, L. G. (1991). The role of institutionalization in cultural persistence. In P. J. DiMaggio & W. W. Powell, (eds), *The New Institutionalism in Organizational Analysis*. Chicago & London: University of Chicago Press. 83–107.

Chapter 12

The Fifth Dimension —
Expectations in the Internationalisation
Process Model

Amjad Hadjikhani and Martin Johanson

Introduction

The internationalisation process model (IP-model) (Johanson & Vahlne, 1977; 1990) is one of the predominant models for understanding how firms internationalise their business. The model has four dimensions: market commitment, market knowledge, current activities, and commitment decisions. These dimensions and the model as a whole have been reviewed and tested in a large number of studies. Over the years, criticism has been directed against the IP-model from various angles. Some describe the model as deterministic (Reid, 1981; Turnbull, 1987); some, like O'Grady and Lane (1996), criticize the model for its inability to define managerial behaviour; and some, like Hedlund and Kverneland (1985), claim that lack of knowledge is no longer a factor limiting the pattern and geographical extent of internationalisation. Critics attack the model for the way it assumes passivity and ignores risk-taking and for the stress given to the influence of past experience on firms' commitment behaviour.

This paper does not aim to verify or test the different studies supporting or criticizing the internationalisation process model (IP-model). It rather espouses the views of the critics and sees them as voices needing particular attention. The study recognizes the urgency of the researchers'

Critical Perspectives on Internationalisation, pp. 285–303.
ISBN: 0-08-044053-5

claim that there is a discrepancy between the actual behaviour of firms, on the one hand, and the behaviour the commitment and knowledge concepts in the IP-model are able to define, on the other. By paying serious attention to the voices of the critics, the authors hope to equip the IP-model with a new conceptual tool. The ultimate aim is to contribute to the development of the IP-model and to increase its ability to analyse different market conditions, even situations like the imbalance between experience and commitment pinpointed by the critics. The paper exposes firm internationalisation as an active market process integrating the future into the past and present. It builds on what was implied by Hayek (1945) and Simon (1957) — that expectations are one of the crucial variables driving business. The concept of expectation is deployed so as to reduce the discrepancy and imbalance between commitment and knowledge.

The IP-model has been criticized for treating firms, if not as passive, at least as defensive (Cavusgil, 1980; Turnbull, 1987). In light of the model, according to this criticism, firms react but never act, and internationalisation is thereby understood as a defence, a way to decrease uncertainty. Another criticism concerns the relationship between experience and market commitment (i.e., the balance and imbalance in the development of these two variables). There are situations characterized by an imbalance between market commitment and market knowledge. Studies have documented the fact that firms sometimes make large market commitments without any experiential knowledge. A firm may jump from the stage of exporting to the stage of large joint-venture commitments. Such a firm is more risk-taking than the IP-model postulates and leaps into the unknown. It is not so much that experiential knowledge is unimportant, as that in some cases other factors are the driving forces.

Another example of imbalance occurs when an international firm's market knowledge erodes or becomes obsolete due to market changes. Both institutional and business knowledge can become obsolete and the changeability and unpredictability of market conditions can force a firm to make new decisions about whether to maintain a commitment or to reduce it. Once again, other factors than experience seem to be driving the process of internationalisation. The opposite can occur; that is, a firm's long-term presence in a market may provide much experience but not require any large investment because of the low priority given to the market.

In sum, the critics implicitly pinpoint the imbalance between commitment and experience. Risk-taking behaviour, or the fact that firms actively search for information and make strategic decisions without experience, is a manifestation of that imbalance. The question, then, is why firms behave in a specific way that the concept of experience is inadequate to explain. Within this theoretical space, this paper introduces the concept of expectation to enrich the IP-model and answer the critics. This study accepts that the four elements in the IP-model are not sufficient to analyse firms' international behaviour in every circumstance. The concept of expectation introduces the future dimension, which can explain why commitment decisions are made despite an imbalance between experiential knowledge and market commitment.

The claim of this paper is that a firm's investment decisions and market activities are based not only on experience but also on what the firm expects from the future in its international market. We propose that by integrating expectations as an intermediary variable between state aspects and change aspects, we can satisfy the critics and enhance the model without rejecting its main ideas or theoretical basis. We start by introducing two types of expectation and give them a role in the model. After that, we discuss expectations in relation first to market knowledge and then to market commitment. The next two sections address the concept of expectation's impact on the model with respect to change aspects, commitment decision, and current activities.

Expectation and the IP-Model

While the IP-model is silent on the topic of expectation, a number of studies have focused their attention, implicitly or explicitly, on expectation (see, for example, Cyert & March, 1963; Lachmann, 1977) According to Lachmann (1977) expectation is not a formalized calculation based on known history. It is anticipations, wishes, and hopes about the unknown future that arise, in turn, from each individual's experience. In accordance with that reasoning, entering a foreign market can be viewed as an interplay between experience and expectation (Lachmann, 1986). The process is similar to that of the man who is waiting for a bus that did not turn up on time. His increasing commitment is based not only on pure experiential knowledge (he has taken the bus before) and objective knowledge (he has the timetable, which says that it should have arrived), but also on the expectation that the bus will appear soon. Knowledge without the anticipation of future value does not supply a ground for decision. Expectation incorporates knowledge and elaborates a map of the future (that the bus will arrive soon) and that affects his decision. In this paper, we will argue that there are two types of expectations: institutional expectations and network expectations.

Institutional or general expectations (Gabarro, 1978; Lindskold, 1978; Sitkin & Roth, 1993) are created when an actor gives common values to market conditions (Sitkin & Roth, 1993). We see an instance in a firm penetrating a new foreign country but lacking experiential knowledge. The only driving force for market entry and commitment are the firm's general beliefs about institutional factors and their future development (Halinen, 1994; Young & Wilkinson, 1989). As business in the foreign market increases, the knowledge gained is used to refine the vague maps and the actor's position becomes progressively more crystallized. In this context network expectations are defined as beliefs about the future actions of counterparts. To explain in terms of incrementality, in its market entry a firm will construct values for specific actors in addition to those for the institutional market. In this phase, expectations are specific and point at several interrelated actors (see also Bies, 1987; Butler & Cantrell, 1984; Hadjikhani, 1996). The evolution of expectations from institutional to network relies on the development of knowledge not only of a specific partner but also of other interrelated actors in the market. This explanation implies that market expectations are composed either of institutional expectations alone or of both institutional and network expectations. The assumption is that network expectations also contain institutional expectations.

To include expectations in the IP-model it is necessary to position the concept in the model. Expectations are proposed as an intermediary element binding market knowledge and market commitment to current activities and commitment decisions. Expectations, as discussed, are presumed to have their ground in what firms have committed and what they know. Thus market commitment makes up the frame for what it is worthwhile to expect and market knowledge for what it is possible to expect. Current activities and commitment decisions, on the other hand, have their basis in market expectations, which are built not only on what firms have experienced and committed, but also on what they expect from institutional and business actors. It follows, as depicted in the Figure 12.1 below, that expectations stand between the state and change aspects.

The model withholds the crucial assertion that expectations connect the state and change aspects to each other. The postulation is as follows: if

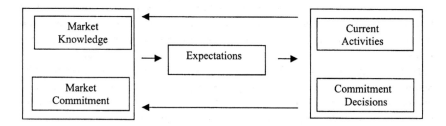

Figure 12.1: Expectations in the Internationalisation Process Model.

the state aspect is given and has resulted in some investment and knowledge, there must be a driving force for the firm's current decisions and actions. The future is not completely a repetition of the past. Without expectations, a firm is assumed to act blindly on the basis of its former experience without observing changes in the path. The postulation is, as well, that without market expectations, there will be no current decisions or activities. This expression implies that any further change in market decisions or activities requires changes in expectation.

Decisions on commitment escalation depend on how a firm assesses the future. This requires that expectations be incremental. While we have a low level of knowledge about business actors and expectations are largely composed of institutional knowledge and beliefs about the future, commitment is expected to be low. As market activities and knowledge increase expectations become more specific. This is because the firm's knowledge about local actors and their relationships has been extended. In the process, local actors' function and identity become ever more transparent, leading to network expectations. Expectations also explain an imbalance between commitment and knowledge. In other words, in cases where experiential knowledge provides general vague information but commitment is high, the reason is because of a positive future evaluation. A high degree of imbalance entails a high risk as commitment is based on low experiential knowledge. In the following, the attempt is to connect expectations to the four dimensions of the IP-model.

Expectations and Market Knowledge

A firm's knowledge reduces uncertainty and is the tool that fosters creativity (Sullivan & Nonaka, 1986) or expected utility (Cyert & March,

1963). This implies a view of action as a temporal process or as a behaviour process, in the sense that firms learn about their environments in
order to undertake actions that will promote their activities in the future.
Expectations are what enterprises will develop in the future through what
they know about their context, but expectations are by no means independent of such things as a firm's hopes or wishes (Simon, 1957). Thus
the knowledge a firm has about a specific market constitutes the plan or
mental map or frame for what the firm will be able to imagine concerning
the market. Expectations and knowledge are tied to each other and
bound to the market.

Knowledge itself can be divided into a) knowledge that comes from
experience and b) knowledge obtained from other sources. In the context
of internationalisation, knowledge comprises information about context,
such as about general market conditions in a foreign country. Studies in
risk calculation (Campa, 1994; Cosset & Roy, 1990; Kobrin, 1980;),
country risk (Feder & Ross, 1982; Feder & Uy, 1985; Makhija, 1993),
and political risk (Miller, 1992) are of measures that aim to generate
general information on what a firm can expect from the market. This
information generates expectations, but at a general level. It does not
pinpoint a specific transaction partner but considers the probability of
political or market changes. Market commitment is attached only to
institutional expectations and comes with a high risk. Institutional
knowledge is connected to vague expectations about market behaviour.

The incremental growth of knowledge explains the development in
expectations from general to more specific. Studies of the use of bridgeheads (Blankenburg Holm & Chetty, 2000; Bridgewater, 1999) have
found that firms achieve foreign market penetration by relying on partners or firms that they have some knowledge about. When an actor has
no knowledge about the foreign market, it relies on what the partner
knows to construct its market expectations and consequently decide its
commitment. The theory of bridgeheads implies that, for example, a
bounded trust relationship can give access to markets in which the actor
has no exchange experience. Expectations arising from the bounded relationship create general expectations about the other market. These can be
reached through the information obtained from the partner about that
other environment. Firms relying only on general market expectations
reduce the risk by trusting other firms that have an exchange relationship
in the foreign market. In a sense, expectations of new opportunities
derive from general knowledge and from the relationship with trusted
partners.

Such a postulation is consistent with the theory of network inter-dependency. A firm that penetrates a new market via a partner that already operates in that market becomes connected to others in the new market, although network interdependency can exist without being realized. Network expectations are crystallized by realization of the connection. The key to the expectations that derive from a bounded relationship is that the actor has no knowledge about the connected firms or about the nature of their interdependencies. Possibly a relationship is being established only for the purpose of, for example, access to the distribution channel of a firm in a foreign market. It follows that the knowledge of the exchange partner about actors in the distribution channel constructs the focal firm's expectations. The critical factor is that when experiential knowledge is not extended beyond the bounded relationship, expectations are composed mainly of beliefs about the behaviour of institutions and a few market actors. Besides these few relationships, all other actors in the environment are seen in a general context constituting a vague expectation. Small firms, for example, that depend on large international companies may lack network expectations because they do not have knowledge about those firms in foreign markets with which they are, nevertheless, interdependent. Such a firm's current commitment is constructed on the basis of market expectations, that is, on the basis of beliefs about the future behaviour of a few specific counterparts and others in the environment about which the firm has no experiential knowledge.

The incremental development of expectations is interwoven with increasing market activities and knowledge that result in progressive uncertainty reduction and increasing trust in the behaviour of the market actors. Expectations depend on how a firm assesses the future. A low level of knowledge generates general, non-specific and vague market expectations. Through increasing market activities, market knowledge and expectations develop progressively and become more specific. In the process, actors' functions and identities become progressively clearer, and trust relationships evolve for market exchange.

Expectations and Market Commitment

Johanson and Vahlne (1977) define market commitment as the amount of resources invested in a specific market and the cost at which these resources can be transferred to other markets. Expectations can be explained as the anticipations of a firm about the value of a specific strategy (Barney, 1986). From an internationalisation perspective, firms, in making commitments, assign values to the future development of foreign markets. Expectations are consequently the plans, hopes, and wishes that the strategy aims to achieve through the resources committed. At each moment, the firm has plans about its operation in the future. The plans — sometimes formalized and sometimes not — consist of means (the knowledge and resources controlled by the firm) and ends (what the firm aims to do with the means in order to exploit a business opportunity). From an internationalisation point of view, the plans contain information about which specific market to target, which product to buy or to sell, which entry mode to use, and also which problems and obstacles will be encountered during entry.

The assumption of stable change in the market has permitted researchers to explain, for example, that a gradual increase in knowledge determines an increase in commitment and vice versa. Conceptually, the internationalisation model treats expectations as an appendage to market commitment and knowledge. Instead of expectations, it seems that terms such as "interdependence" play the role of predicting commitment behaviour. Narrowly understood, interdependence dictates resource commitment, and therefore there is no need for inclusion of the concept of expectation. This could also be the reason that the IP-model has no explicit concern with explaining commitment in terms of the future. Eventually, the theory contains the concept of expectation, but it has a latent function. Insofar as there is a positive and equal correlation between commitment and knowledge, or the bonds between actors develop along a smooth curve, evidence of expectation is suppressed, since other concepts account easily for the internationalisation process. Essentially, expectations manifest themselves when uncertainty in the market is high given the level of market commitment, or, as mentioned, when there is a large imbalance between experience and commitment. Within this frame, the concept of interdependence, for example, has no function if it does not contain a future dimension. The basis for the term is its process nature. Thus, a firm's predictions are interwoven with its commitments and with the reaction of others in its network. Building on this base in the internationalisation model, the concept of expectation entails incrementality (i.e., expectations move from a state of vague expectation to more specific and detailed expectations). The incremental process of expectation is interwoven with increasing market activities and knowledge, which progressively reduce uncertainty and increase trust in the future behaviour of actors in the market. Decisions on escalation of commitment or of market penetration by actors outside the market lie in how those actors assess the ambiguous future. Market knowledge and market commitment make up the frames for the movement from vague perceptual maps to more crystallized understandings of the positions of the actors in the market, understandings which then become the basis for future commitment decisions and business activities.

Expectations and Current Activities

Hunt (1991) and Oliver (1980) explain that expectations are the probabilities firms assign to the occurrence of positive or negative events should they engage or aim to engage in some interaction with others in a market. Expectations are judgements about a firm's future position in the market in relation to other actors. Expectations are a result both of past experience and of information "sailing" around. Thus a firm's expectations and business activities are always a result of its knowledge, and from that it follows that firms tend to search for phenomena similar to those that have generated positive experiences for them in the past or for other actors that they trust. The higher the commitment and experience a foreign firm has in a local market, the higher the probability of occurrence of the expected outcomes.

Johanson and Vahlne (1977; 1990) indicate that the main dimension in current activities is business. Doing business, i.e., buying and selling, is the objective of firms entering a new market, and therefore finding and exploiting business opportunities is the main activity. Business opportunity can be defined as when the firm has either the means, combined in space and time, or the ends, but not both. That is, the firm has identified the customer or the supplier but has not yet been able to identify how to pay, how to transport, or which product to buy or sell, or vice versa. We argue that both finding and exploiting business opportunities cause change and that expectations are instrumental in that change.

During the internationalisation, process *search* is the initial activity, which results in a firm's finding something. Search occurs when a firm has identified the ends and the means but has still not been able to combine them in reality; that is, it has to search for one of them in order to be able to combine them and to transform the opportunity into business. Thus, a precondition for search is that the firm knows either the ends or the means. This knowledge can either be experiential in its nature or objective (the firm has been taught or informed by others). Obviously, the firm knows what it does not know and decides to search for it. Thus search is characterized by what the firm knows that it needs and by what it expects to find, because if the firm does not believe that it will find what it is searching for, search is a meaningless activity. Expectations are the analysis of the past and present to construct values for the market, and on the foundation of the firm's knowledge it evaluates what to do and how to do it and begins to search for it. How and where the firm searches when preparing to participate in a foreign market are a result of the interplay between the firm's experience and its expectations, and with these as a starting point the firm begins its search activities. Searching and finding business opportunities are therefore often a repetition of past behaviour.

Expectations are seldom perceived as sufficient in the search for business opportunities. The uncertainty is too great — more knowledge is needed and the market in question has to be analysed more thoroughly. The firm begins to search for knowledge. One way of doing this is to collect information about the market. In light of the firm's expectations it collects information, searching for the conditions it believes have to prevail if its expectations are to be realized. Thus search activities involve looking actively for something already identified — a problem has occurred and the firm believes that it already knows the solution but has to find it. Analysing the market by collecting data and information, however, while it provides some insight, cannot by itself give the firm unique insight into the market (Barney, 1986). This kind of knowledge can be codified and is, moreover, comparatively easy and cheap to distribute, which usually means that it is accessible to many firms. Consequently, acquiring such knowledge does not give the firm a competitive advantage over other firms. Still, this type of information can reduce the perceived market uncertainty.

The triadic interaction of experience-expectation-search involves behaviour characterized by limited knowledge but still rational and very much in accordance with common sense. The firm consciously realizes that its knowledge is not perfect or that it perceives uncertainty. The familiar is perceived as less uncertain. A firm does business in a market to which it is committed and when a problem occurs, uncertainty increases; that is, someone else is acting in an unpredictable way and this forces the firm to act. According to this model, the firm is active only when it reacts to problems, which is making internationalisation into a quite rational but passive activity. However, sometimes, or rather usually, more or less constantly, things take place that are, to a large extent, beyond the control of the firm. The firm makes discoveries while doing business. Two sources of discovery may be distinguished: discovery as a result of search and discovery as a result of exploitation. These discoveries cannot be viewed as results of a purposeful and intentional search process, in the sense of searching in a specific way to achieve expected results. Instead, the discoveries are a result of something that the firm did not know that it did not know. Discoveries are surprises and findings that beforehand were unknowable. In effect, the process of acting in a foreign market can be viewed partly as a journey of discovery into the unknown, an attempt to discover new ways to do things better than they have been done before (Hayek, 1980); and the acquisition of market knowledge through the experience of foreign market participation and adjustment can be viewed as a revision of expectations in response to newly acquired market experience (Kirzner, 1973).

Barney (1986) argues that the knowledge acquired through market analysis is never critical and does not give a firm any advantage, although he admits that sometimes firms can stumble onto information that gives them a knowledge advantage. The discovery process is a wide-open road where any firm could end up. A number of unexpected coincidences occur and since they are beneficial to the firm they must be viewed as luck (Barney, 1986). This view implies, however, that there are only two types of governance mode: the hierarchy and the market transaction. As has been made clear, discovery also occurs when firms exploit business opportunities. This exploiting of business opportunities, according to Johanson and Vahlne (1990), mainly takes the character of long-term exchanges, usually called business relationships, with other specific firms. While the hierarchy gives the firm unique knowledge about itself, attributing discoveries to market transactions implies that all necessary knowledge is embedded in the price, which is, in turn, accessible to all firms in the market. Knowledge is not a problem. If one accepts, however, that there is a third governance mode, the business relationship, the conditions change. Trust is assumed to be the driving mechanism and the existence of the business relationship is a consequence of the fact that the price does not provide enough information. Critical experience and expectations of positive outcomes, very much synonymous with trust, are to be found not only within the boundaries of the firm, but also in business relationships. Unique discoveries about the foreign market are consequently made during the internationalisation process, as well, and not only within the boundaries of the firm. We do not suggest that discovery is the result of a lack of experiential knowledge. It is rather the other way around: a firm that has gained a good deal of experiential knowledge realizes that it has to expect discoveries in its network.

In the light of the preceding discussion concerning search and discovery, we suggest that what a firm will search for is dependent on which type of expectation is predominant. When a firm has been active in the market for a long period, network expectations are predominant and the firm will search mainly in its existing network. But the firm will also realize from what it has learned that discovery is impossible to avoid. On the other hand, if the firm has mainly institutional expectations it will search for what it knows from other markets, that is, for phenomena with which it is familiar. This seems to be the case when the firm has limited experiential knowledge either because it has been active in the market only for a short time or because its experiential knowledge has eroded due to rapid and extensive market changes. Thus the type of expectation and business activity will also be a result of the knowledge the firm possesses.

Expectations and Commitment Decision

A commitment decision is a desire to invest in and devote to a specific market tangible and intangible resources with varying degrees of transferability, a desire that is transformed into action. Johanson and Vahlne's (1977) focus was on the investment of tangible resources, but recent studies have shown that commitment can be intangible (Hadjikhani, 1996) and have an attitudinal (Gundlach *et al.*, 1995) or affective component (Kumar *et al.*, 1995). This makes commitment an enduring intention that is based not on calculation but rather on shared values, loyalty, and affective attachment (Gundlach *et al.*, 1995). Commitment is a series of ongoing small decisions (Staw, 1987) that can decrease uncertainty and the costs of continuously seeking new buyers or sellers (Gundlach *et al.*, 1995) or markets. However, when a firm invests in a specific market it becomes vulnerable (Morgan & Hunt, 1994), since it thereby excludes alternative markets and its dependence on the specific market increases.

We propose that a firm's expectations of a market will affect the amount, the character, tangible and/or intangible, and the transferability of the resources committed. A decision to commit additional resources seems to consist of two steps. First, there must be a desire to stay in the market and to do business with other actors in that market, and second, this desire must be transformed into *action*. Although in the model a commitment decision is viewed as a change aspect, it results, due to the limited transferability of the resources, in stability. This constitutes, according to Anderson *et al.*, (1994), Gundlach *et al.*, (1995), Kumar *et al.*, (1995), the main dimension of commitment and is reflected in the state aspect market commitment. Firms that control resources with low transferability strive to achieve stability (Anderson & Weitz, 1992), durability and consistency (Dwyer *et al.*, 1987), and continuity (Kumar *et al.*, 1995), since these are the basis for development and growth (Anderson *et al.*, 1994; Kumar *et al.*, 1995; Morgan & Hunt, 1994).

The first step implies that the decision is dependent on the state of internationalisation and that the firm attaches a positive value to the development of the market (Moorman *et al.*, 1992). In the light of this, we begin with the apparently trivial proposition that there is a positive relationship between positive expectations and an additional commitment decision. A firm with positive expectations, either institutional or network, will probably make a decision to commit additional resources to a foreign market. Since experiential knowledge is based on activities and the activities in the foreign market tend to be related to business, we suggest that high experiential knowledge and positive network expectations will result in the firm's committing resources to specific actors in the foreign market. In this case, network expectations mostly play a supporting role. However, the firm also acts in relation to various political actors, and these activities also result in experience that is an important input for institutional expectations that strengthen the reasons for investing in the market.

We can also consider another situation, maybe less trivial, where there is a strong relationship between expectation and commitment decision. It can happen that a firm facing unpredicted changes increases its commitment, despite the fact that its market knowledge is decreasing. In such a case, expectations gain in significance (Kobrin, 1978; Staw, 1981). Firms with low or quickly eroding market knowledge acting in a rapidly changing market may commit resources in the expectation of future prosperity. Their actions in this case resemble those of commitment and decision-making at an individual level. Expectancy theory (Vroom, 1964) explains the escalation of commitment by the fact that decision-makers have the propensity to take risks under conditions of uncertainty (Kahneman & Tversky, 1979). Thus firms can even escalate their commitment to a failing course of actions in response to the uncertainty of a market in turmoil (see Brockner, 1992; Staw & Ross, 1978). According to Brockner (1992) and Staw (1981) the feedback from previous activities, that is what one learns from doing, forms the basis for commitment escalation. Knowledge developed while carrying out activities related to a commitment will reinforce the commitment. Knowledge and commitment are bounded in space and time, which alleviates perceived uncertainty, but also explains commitment escalation to a failing course of action when the experience is of negative character. The firms' behaviour does not follow linear route; rather former experience in a market creates high expectations for the future.

Defining expectation in terms of the IP-model, decisions on commitment escalation depend on how the firm assesses the future. Low knowledge generates general and vague expectations. With increasing market activities, market knowledge and expectations develop progressively and become more specific. In the course of this process, local actors' functions and identities become progressively more transparent and trust relationships evolve for market exchange.

Final Comments

The aim of this paper is not to present a completely new model. Rather, the paper attempts to adapt the IP-model with the goal of amplifying its analytical fields. Studies criticizing the IP-model advance views that need serious consideration. The attempt in this paper is to enrich the model with an analytical tool that enables it to analyse even those behaviours beyond the scope of analyses of progressive internationalisation behaviour. Incorporating the concept of expectation can disarm those critics whose attacks have their origin mainly in the imbalance between experience and commitment. The paper identifies expectation as a concept distinct from the other four concepts in the model and postulates that firms actively envision the future when making commitment decisions.

Generally, the IP-model (Johanson & Vahlne, 1990) implicitly merges expectations with the factors of knowledge and commitment. The concept of expectation does not affect the model insofar as firms and market changes are stable. Yet a smooth and progressive development is possible only where there is an assumed balance between experience and commitment. In light of such an assumption, international firms act on the basis of commitment and knowledge and in consequence, market expectations and strategic visions are unimportant. This paper asserts that there always exists an imbalance between experience and commitment. Expectations are formed on the assumption that the future will not be exactly like the past; firms can have strategies or visions for the future that do not rely entirely on past experience. They may decide on strategic risk-taking or respond to the unforeseen behaviour of others. This study found that the factor of imbalance is the source of many criticisms of the IP-model. In response, it incorporates the concept of expectation to rectify the shortcomings identified by the critics. Instead of rejecting the IP-model, the paper's aim is to expand its generalization ability. In the light of criticisms of the IP-model, this paper raises a very simple question: to what extent does expectation fit into the IP-model and how can the concept of expectation increase our understanding of firm internationalisation? In answer to that question, we suggest that the role of expectations is especially significant when there is a clear imbalance between commitment and knowledge; for instance, when firms take more risks and accept a higher level of uncertainty than experience justifies. It covers cases where a firm's behaviour is more active than reactive. It also covers cases where a firm de-internationalises; that is, decreases its business and resources in a market, sometimes to such an extent as it leaves the market.

First of all, when it comes to a clear imbalance between commitment and knowledge, firms sometimes take more risks than the IP-model suggests. According to the first version of the model, when a firm has low market knowledge and a low market commitment, it should, due to perceived uncertainty, invest few resources and begin limited business operations in a market that is perceived as culturally close to the firm. However, we suggest that if such a firm were responding to institutional changes, such as deregulation, legislative changes, privatisation, and so forth, or to changes in the business environment, such as growth, increased demand, or technological development, for example, its expectations might convince it to take great risks, despite the uncertainty. In this case, it seems that institutional expectations have a stronger impact on the commitment decision than network expectations. Moreover, expectation can help us explain why the process of internationalisation evolves more quickly than the IP-model contemplates. The model assumes that a firm has to learn before it can increase its level of internationalisation. However, positive expectations can partly supplant the need for learning through activities in the market and can thereby increase the pace of the internationalisation.

Second, expectations drive internationalisation. But the concept of expectation also implies that internationalisation is not simply a reactive process. It is also an active process, where firms actively search for business opportunities and make commitment decisions. Including the factor of expectation enriches the model with an understanding of the search for new opportunities and new market entries and of commitments beyond those justified by experiential knowledge. The concept of expectation also offers us an explanation for how experiential knowledge is developed during the active search process. Firms make discoveries when searching for business opportunities. Viewing internationalisation as both an active and reactive process also increases our understanding, above all, of why firms begin to do business internationally.

Thirdly, since market changes can drastically reduce the value of experiential knowledge or market commitment, the rule of incrementality in the IP-model can be preserved by incorporating the concept of expectation. Negative expectations help to explain why firms scale back international operations and exit foreign markets, despite having a high level of market commitment and market knowledge. In the same way, taking account of positive expectations can increase our understanding of why firms whose experiential knowledge has been reduced or committed resources have been lost through political changes might prefer to remain in a market

Finally, the concept of expectations adds knowledge on why managers choose alternatives with varieties of risks. With this factor management and strategic actions do gain an identity in the model. In this way, it becomes easier to analyse why firms suddenly become committed largely in a foreign market with a high risk.

In sum, without expectations there is no real driving force for commitment. The addition of this new concept has some consequences for the IP-model. First of all, expectations together with experience can explain changes in market commitment better than can experiential knowledge alone. Further, expectations can also account for risk-taking behaviour that exceeds the level that our knowledge of a firm's experiential knowledge would lead us to expect. Moreover, despite the fact that managers' strategic behaviour or environmental changes can reduce the value of experiential knowledge, with the factor of expectation, the rule of incrementality in the IP-model can be preserved. The factor of expectation describes why firms maintain commitments when they have little or even no experiential knowledge. Finally, the factor of expectation enriches the model with an understanding of the search for new opportunities and new market entries and of commitments beyond the level dictated by experiential knowledge.

References

Anderson, E., Lodish, L. M. & Weitz, B. A. (1987). Resource allocation behavior in conventional channels. *Journal of Marketing Research, 24*, February, 85–97.

Anderson, J. C., Håkansson, H. & Johanson, J. (1994). Dyadic business relationships within a business network context. *Journal of Marketing 58*, October, 1–15.

Barney, J. B. (1986). Strategic factor markets: expectations, luck and business strategy. *Management Science, 17(1)*, 99–120.

Bies, R. J. (1987). The predicament of injustice: the management of moral outrage. In B. M. Staw & L. L. Cummings (eds), *Research in Organisational Behavior* 9. Greenwich: JAI Press.

Bridgewater, S. (1999). Networks and internationalization: the case of multinational corporations entering Ukraine. *International Business Review, 8*, 99–118.

Brockner J. (1992). The escalation of commitment to a failing course of action: toward theoretical progress. *Academy of Management Review, 17(1)*, 39–51.

Butler, J. K. & Cantrell, R. S. (1984). A behavioral decision theory approach to modelling dyadic trust in superiors and subordinates. *Psychological Reports, 55*, 19–28.

Campa, J. M. (1994). Multinational iInvestment under uncertainty in the chemical processing industries. *Journal of International Business Studies, 25(3)*, 557–578.

Cavusgil, S. T. (1980). On the internationalization process of the firm. *European Research, 8*, November, 273–281.

Chetty, S. & Blankenburg Holm, D. (2000). Internationalization of small to medium-sized manufacturing firms: a network approach. *International Business Review, 9*, 77–93.

Cosset, J.-C. & Roy, J. (1991). The determinants of country risk ratings. *Journal of International Business Studies, 22(1)*, 135–142.

Cyert, R. M. & March, J. G. (1963). The behavioral theory of the firm. (2nd ed.) Cambridge, Massachusetts: Blackwell Publishers.

Dwyer, F. R., Schurr, P. H. & Oh, S. (1987). Developing buyer-seller relationships. *Journal of Marketing*, April, 11–27.

Feder, G. and Ross, K. (1982). Risk assessments and risk premiums in the Eurodollar market. *Journal of Finance*, June.

Feder, G. & Uy, L. (1985). The determinants of international credits creditworthiness and their implications. *Journal of Policy Modelling, 7*, 133–156.

Gabarro, J. J. (1978). The development of trust, influence and expectations. In A.

G. Athos & J. J. Gabarro (eds), *Interpersonal Behavior: Communication and Understanding in Relationships*. Englewood Cliffs, NJ: Prentice Hall. 290–303.

Gundlach, G. T., Achrol, R. S. & Mentzer, J. T. (1995). The structure of commitment in exchange. *Journal of Marketing, 59*, January, 78–92.

Hadjikhani, A. (1996). *International Business and Political Crisis*. Uppsala: Almqvist & Wiksell.

Hadjikhani, A. & Johanson, J. (1996). Facing foreign market turbulence: three Swedish multinationals in Iran. *Journal of International Marketing, 4(4)*, 53–73.

Halinen, A. (1994). *Exchange Relationships in Professional Services: A Study of Relationship Development in the Advertising Sector*. Doctoral dissertation, Turku School of Economics and Business Administration.

Hayek, F. A. (1936). Economics and knowledge. *Economica*, n.s. *4*, 33–56.

Hayek, F. A. (1945). The use of knowledge in society. *American Economic Review, XXXV(4)*, 519–530.

Hunt, S. D. (1991). *Modern Marketing Theory: Critical Issues in the Philosophy of Marketing Science*. Cincinnati, OH: South-Western.

Johanson, J. & Vahlne, J.-E. (1977). The internationalization process of firm a model of knowledge development and increasing foreign market commitments. *Journal of International Business Studies 8*, Spring/Summer, 2332.

Johanson, J. & Vahlne, J.-E. (1990). The mechanism of internationalization. *International Marketing Review, 7(4)*, 11–24.

Kahneman, D. & Tverski, A. (1984). Choice, values and frames. *American Psychologist, 39*, 341–350.

Kirzner, I. M. (1973). *Competition and entrepreneurship*. Chicago & London: The University of Chicago Press.

Kobrin, J. S. (1978). When does political instability result in increased investment risk. *Columbia Journal of World Business 13*, Fall, 113–122.

Kobrin, J. S. (1980). Foreign enterprises and forced disinvestments in LDCs. *International Organizations 34*, Winter, 65–88.

Kumar, N., Scheer, L. K. & Steenkamp, J.-B. E. M. (1995). The effects of perceived interdependence on dealer attitudes. *Journal of Marketing Research 32*, August, 348-356

Lachmann, L. M. (1977). *Capital, Expectations and the Market Process*. Kansas City: Sheed Andrews and McMeel.

Lachmann, L. M. (1986). *The Market as an Economic Process*. Oxford: Basil Blackwell.

Lindskold, S. (1978). Trust development, the GRIT proposal, and the effects of conciliatory acts on conflict and cooperation. *Psychological Bulletin, 5(4)* 772793.

Makhija, M. V. (1993). Government intervention in the Venezuelan petroleum industry: An empirical investigation of political risk. *Journal of International Business Studies, 24(3)*, 531–555.

Miller, K. D. (1992). Industry and country effects on managers' perspective of environmental uncertainties. *Journal of International Business Studies, 24(1),* 693–714.

Moorman, C., Zaltman, G. & Deshpandé, R. (1992). Relationships between providers and users of Market research: the dynamics of trust within and between organizations. *Journal of Marketing Research, 29,* August, 314–328.

Morgan, R. M. & Hunt, S. D. (1994). The commitment-trust theory of relationship marketing. *Journal of Marketing, 58,* July, 20–38.

Nilson, T. (1995). *Chaos Marketing, How to Win in a Turbulent World.* London: McGraw-Hill.

Oliver, R. L. (1980). A cognitive model of the antecedents and consequences of satisfaction decisions. *Journal of Marketing Research, 17,* November, 460–469.

Rotter, J. B. (1980). Interpersonal trust, trustworthiness, and gullibility. *American Psychologist, 35(1),* 17.

Shapiro, S. P. (1987). The social control of interpersonal trust. *American Journal of Sociology, 93(3),* 623658.

Simon, H. (1957). Administrative Behaviour, a Study of Decision Making Processes in Administrative Organization. (2nd ed.). New York: Macmillan.

Sitkin, S. & Roth, N. (1993). Explaining the limited effectiveness of learning remedies for trust/mistrust. *Organization Science, 4(3),* August, 367–392.

Staw, B. (1981). The escalation of commitment to a course of action. *Academy of Management Review, 6(4),* 577–587.

Staw, B. M. & Ross, J. (1978). Commitment to a policy decision: a multi-theoretical perspective. *Administrative Science Quarterly, 23,* 40–64.

Sullivan, J. J. & Nonaka, I. (1986). The application of organizational learning theory to Japanese and American management. *Journal of International Business Studies,* Fall, 127–147.

Vroom, V. (1964). *Work and Motivation.* New York: Wiley.

Young, L. C. & Wilkinson, I. F. (1989). The role of trust and cooperation in marketing channels: a preliminary study. *European Journal of Marketing, 23(7),* 109–121.

Chapter 13

What Determines the Internationalisation of Corporate Technology?

John Cantwell and Elena Kosmopoulou

Introduction

Innovation has been increasingly internationalised during recent decades, and while internationalisation is not itself a new phenomenon the number of large firms involved, and the importance of the technological activity that is carried out abroad has greatly increased (Bartlett & Ghoshal, 1989; Cantwell, 1995; Dunning, 1993). The largest US and especially European companies have made a major contribution to this process. The pursuit of international competitiveness at a country level follows historically defined trajectories, as part of different national and regional systems of innovation (Cantwell, 2000; Lundvall, 1988; Nelson, 1993).

At the firm level, the internationalisation of technological activities encourages the creation and diffusion of innovation by tapping into locally-specific resources and effectively deploying individually localised exchanges with indigenous firm capabilities in various sites (Cantwell & Janne, 1999a; Dunning & Wymbs, 1999; Kuemmerle, 1998; 1999a; 1999b; Pearce, 1989; 1999; Zander, 1998; 1999). The world's largest firms in recent years have moved from employing international R&D as a means of better exploiting established competencies in accordance with the conditions of local markets and production conditions, towards the creation of local centres of excellence with differentiated but complementary sources of expertise. The geographical dispersion of research facilitates the multi-technological development of firms, and becomes positively

Critical Perspectives on Internationalisation, pp. 305–334.
ISBN: 0-08-044053-5

associated with corporate technological diversification (Breschi *et al.*, 1998; Cantwell & Piscitello, 1999; Zander, 1997). Consequently, firms pursue their technological diversification partly through the internationalisation of the process of competence creation, complementing their domestic activity with suitably locally differentiated foreign-located lines of development (Cantwell & Piscitello, 1999; 2000).

Development of an Analytical Framework

In this context, we begin from but then explore how to go beyond two background propositions on the determinants of the internationalisation of corporate technological activity which can be found in the literature (see in particular Patel & Pavitt, 2000). While these propositions may be useful starting points for explaining cross-country and cross-industry variations in the degree of internationalisation they are insufficient. In showing that there are two further factors which also determine differences in the extent of technological internationalisation between countries and industries, we present a more general and comprehensive framework for the analysis of the international location of innovative activity in large firms.

The two background propositions are as follows. First is the supposition that large firms from small countries tend to be more highly internationalised in their technological development strategies, while large country multinational corporations (MNCs) tend to be less internationalised. The reason is that the constraints of small country size compel large firms originating from such economies to become internationalised more rapidly. Taken alone this proposition is an overgeneralisation and may be misleading, since for example British firms have been highly internationalised for a long time while Swedish firms have been little internationalised until relatively recently. More importantly for our argument, the cross-national group pattern in the degree of internationalisation within each industry varies from one industry to another.

To explain the foundation for the second proposition, while firms develop a wide range of technologies to support a narrower range of products (Granstrand *et al.*, 1997; Pavitt *et al.*,1989), the geographical dispersion of production in multinational firms exceeds that of technological activity (Cantwell & Hodson, 1991). We might infer from this that technology is internationalised more in support of the geographical spread of production and markets, than the other way round, and indeed until recently this has been largely true (Cantwell, 1995; Cantwell & Piscitello, 2000). Until around 1980 international direct investments tended to be market-seeking or natural resource-seeking, and not technological asset-seeking. So historically when the internationalisation of technology followed the internationalisation of production, which in turn was motivated by a search for markets or resources, the share of foreign-located research tended to be greatest where it was needed to adapt products to locally differentiated markets (as in food products) or to adapt resource extraction to local conditions (like mining); and not in research-intensive industries, in which a higher proportion of research is directed towards the development of entirely new products and processes rather than simpler adaptation.

Thus, the second background proposition is that less research-intensive industries tend to be relatively more internationalised in their technological activity (in terms of foreign research shares) than are highly research-intensive industries. However, taken alone this is (also) an over-generalisation that may be misleading. Chemicals, pharmaceuticals, petrochemicals and office equipment (computing) are all research-intensive industries that have on average a substantial internationalisation of technological endeavour among large firms. More importantly again for our purposes, the ranking from highly internationalised industries down to the least internationalised is not uniform if we compare the cross-industry distribution for the firms of different nationalities of origin. So rather than explaining why on average food and pharmaceuticals are highly internationalised industries while aircraft is not, we need to be able to explain why the food firms of some home countries of origin are highly internationalised in their technological efforts, but the food companies of other countries are not.

To clarify the nature of the supplementary arguments that are necessary to build upon but qualify and go beyond the received wisdoms that technological development tends to be more internationalised on average in firms from smaller countries and in less research-intensive industries, we develop a new framework that embraces elements of these existing contentions. Yet at the same time our approach provides a more comprehensive explanation of the complex variations across countries and industries in the degree of internationalisation of technological activity that is observed in practice among large firms. Our framework introduces two new components in order to establish more precisely the determinants of the internationalisation of corporate innovative effort.

Home/ Host Country Perspective

Outward   Inward

		Outward	Inward
Level of Analysis	Industry	High Degree of Internationalisation (H)	Local Deterrence in the Primary Industry (L)
	Technology	Exploration for Diversification (M)	Local Attraction for Diversification (M)

Where: H   High internationalisation of technological activity in the industry or technological field in question

M   Medium-intensity internationalisation of technological activity in the industry or technological field in question

L   Low internationalisation of technological activity in the industry or technological field in question

Figure 13.1: The Effect of Leading Locally-owned National Groups on the Degree and Structure of Internationalisation of Innovation.

First, national groups of large industrial firms have unique and distinctive international technological profiles that reflect the path-dependent and historically bounded competencies that were originally developed in their home country (Cantwell, 2000). In industries in which national groups of firms are strongest as technological leaders the extent of internationalisation of technology development will be relatively high (Cantwell, 1989). However, such multinational firms utilise their international networks for innovation in large part to promote their own comparative technological diversification (Cantwell & Piscitello, 2000). The investment that they conduct abroad tends to be more oriented towards general technological systems, relevant to most industries, which are either core to the current technological paradigm (such as information and communication technology or new materials) or carried forward from past paradigms (such as mechanical devices and instruments), while they tend to retain at home a higher proportion of technological development in the primary fields for their respective industries. Conversely, from the perspective of inward investment, in the industries in which the host country is technologically strongest, the vibrant local presence of strong indigenous companies tends to deter foreign-owned firms of the same industry from conducting substantial levels of local development in the primary technologies of the industry in question. At the same time, the strongest firms of other industries might be attracted to locate development of the relevant technologies in such a centre of excellence, which lines of development for them would represent diversification from the primary technologies of their own industries. Since they are in another industry, they are not direct competitors of the local leaders.

In other words, the intensity of technological competition influences cross-sectoral patterns of international expansion. Competitive strengths in an industry on the part of a national group of firms encourage outward investment in foreign-located technological development but discourage the inward investment of foreign-owned companies in the same industry. However, the foreign-owned firms of other industries (which are not major competitors in output markets) may be attracted to source technology from a centre of excellence in the primary field of development in which local firms lead. Likewise, while the leading local companies tend to retain at home much of their development of their own primary technologies (given local expertise), what they locate abroad will be geared towards the foreign development of related or complementary fields.

Thus, in general in the case of an area in which local firms are strong we expect to observe roughly the pattern illustrated in Figure 13.1 in terms of the degree of internationalisation of technological activity at the level of the industry, and at the level of the equivalent technological field. First, we expect outward investment in innovation to exceed inward investment, given the balance of corporate strengths. However, second, while in the case of outward investment the internationalisation of the industry will tend to exceed that in the corresponding technological field (since strong domestically owned firms diversify abroad), within inward investment the pattern tends to be the other way round (since foreign-owned firms in the same industry are those most deterred by the presence of dominant local companies).

However, to bring in now the second new component of our framework, an essentially reverse trend may be observed in industries and

Home/ Host Country Perspective

		Outward	Inward
Level of Analysis	Industry	Dependence On Local User(s) or Supplier(s) (L)	Deterrence due to Established Local Inter-Firms Linkages (L)
	Technology	Exploitation of User(s) or Supplier(s) Capabilities (M)	Local Attraction for Diversification (M)

Where: M   Medium-intensity internationalisation of technological activity in the industry or technological field in question

L   Low internationalisation of technological activity in the industry or technological field in question

Figure 13.2: The Effect of Tight Localised Coupling of Capable Downstream User (or Upstream Supplier) Firms as the Source of Innovation on the Degree of Internationalisation of Technological Activity.

countries in which the basis of strong local technological competitiveness is a tight interrelatedness of companies in the industry with downstream local user firms or upstream supplier firms as the sources of innovation and as a crucial feedback to in-house innovation. This type of relationship places great importance on mutual trust and locally-specific knowledge creation because it demands a commitment of substantial resources and "has a cumulative and continuous property with a time dimension" (Lee, 1998) that induces national industrial groups to remain local in their innovative orientation (Lundvall, 1985; 1988). Hence, the more that the production of a national industrial group is aimed at local intermediate good markets, or depends upon locally-specific suppliers of innovative equipment or other inputs, the less internationalised they will tend to be in their research strategy.

We might expect this argument to apply in an industry such as metals, or machine tools, yet the same inward-looking approach to innovation may also be relevant to other industries with a strong indigenous advantage linked to inter-company and inter-industry interrelatedness. This is particularly likely to apply in the case of Japan, where a closely knit network of firms (such as in the form of Keiretsu) supports a broad dispersion of development across complementary technological fields (Scherer, 1997). For example, we have a variety of industries in Japan such as the chemical, the computer, the electrical equipment, etc. whose technological development relies for support upon, and in turn helps to support competence development in a focus industry, most notably motor vehicles. In this case the chemical, computer, and electrical equipment industries can be regarded as to a greater extent than usual intermediate-good oriented and much of their technological effort is directed to the innovative support of the car industry. Of course, this does not mean that these industries provide only for the local market or that in some later stage of their development they will not become more international in their innovative activity. Instead, the Japanese chemical industry is, for example, among the leading national groups in paints.[1]

However, in general in a case in which the technological strength of local firms depends upon a tight localised inter-industry coupling of user-producer interaction in innovation, we expect to observe roughly the pattern illustrated in Figure 13.2, distinguishing again between the level of the focus industry and the level of the equivalent technological field. First, we expect outward investment in innovation to be low, quite likely to the extent that it is even weaker than inward investment. Yet in this case both outward and inward internationalisation in the industry will tend to be lower than in the corresponding technological field (since the firms of related industries may be better able to diversify into this field abroad or to tap into local excellence, while within the industry local firms would find it difficult to establish similar linkages or to operate more independently elsewhere, and foreign-owned firms find the inter-knit structure of the local industry a barrier to entry).

[1] Kansai Paints and Nippon Paints Co., Ltd. are according to *Chemical Week* magazine among the leading top ten paints and coatings firms (fourth and sixth respectively), ranked by 1994 sales (*Encyclopedia of Global Industries* 1996).

Data and Methodology

Already in the 1960s work conducted by Schmookler (1966) and Scherer (1965) related firm size, and the volume of investment to the determinants of the rate and direction of inventive activity as measured by corporate patenting. Growing recognition since then of the importance of technology and technological change for the competitiveness and growth of both firms and countries led to a continuous effort in the exploration of the causal relationships between patenting activity and measured economic variables. There is almost unanimous agreement about the importance of patent statistics, although there is considerable debate among scholars about the essence of what exactly is being measured. A brief examination follows, to explain how we use corporate patent statistics in what follows.

Patents are an indirect measure of (the composition of) advances in knowledge inputs into the technological learning processes of firms. They provide a good proxy measure of the cross-sectoral distribution of technological activity for large firms (Cantwell, 1993), which tend to have a high propensity to patent (Mansfield, 1986). The database used for the study consists of patents granted in the US to the largest world firms. The data presented here are patents granted to 792 of the world's largest industrial firms, derived from the listings of *Fortune 500* (Dunning & Pearce, 1985). Of these 792 companies 730 had an active patenting presence during the period 1969-1995. Moreover, 54 companies were added to these. They include (mainly for recent years, but occasionally historically) enterprises that occupied a prominent position in the US patent records, some of which are firms that were omitted from *Fortune*'s listing for classification reasons (e.g., RCA and AT&T were classified in the service sector).

Patents granted in the US are a rich, historically consistent and often unique source of information. The patent record includes the name(s) of inventors, details about the time of application and granting of the patent, and the name of the firm to which the patent has been assigned (from which we can infer the name and location of the parent company, following a consolidation process as described below), as well as the location of residence of the first-named inventor, which as a general rule reflects the location of the research facilities that have led to the invention. Moreover, each patent document provides a historically consistent classification of the type of technology associated with each invention provided by the examiners of the US Patent and Trademark Office, who continuously update the US patent class system by reclassifying all earlier patents accordingly. Inventions have to satisfy three criteria in order to be entitled to a patent: novelty, non-obviousness and usefulness. The US system is referred to as the first-to-invent system, in contrast to the EU and the Japanese, which are first-to-file systems.

The year 1984 is used as the base year in the consolidation process. In other words firms were consolidated in their 1984 form with respect to patents granted between 1969 and 1984, but post-1984 acquisitions have been taken into account. To identify the corporate groups, companies have been grouped according to their country of origin (home country of the parent company) and allocated to the industry of their primary output, according to the product distribution of their sales. As stated already, each patent granted to the world's largest firms has been classified into a type of technological activity. This classification scheme collects together appropriate classes and sub-classes from the US patent class system. Usually patents are assigned to several technological fields, but here the primary classification is used in all cases. For the purposes of our study patents have been aggregated into six periods (dividing 1969–1995 into six). An extensive literature discusses the advantages and disadvantages of the use of patent data as a comparable indicator of technological activity (Archibugi, 1992; Griliches, 1990; Pavitt, 1988). These comprehensive accounts aim to raise caution as to the potential problems of interpretation of these data and state the limitations of the method rather than undermining its significance.

Although a detailed analysis is beyond the scope and scale of this paper one point that is significant to what follows is worth reiterating here. Small and medium-sized firms tend to have a relatively low propensity to patent their inventions. However, we only deal with the largest and most technologically advanced firms whose propensity to patent is high. This study focuses on patenting activity by the largest firms originating from the US or from selected European countries arranged by their nationality of ownership and examines the extent of internationalisation of their research facilities, and also looks at the patenting of all the world's largest firms which is sourced from research located in the equivalent set of host countries (the US and certain European countries).

For the purposes of an analysis based upon Figure 13.1 above we need an empirical measure of the nationality of technological leaders among large firms in each industry. The revealed technological advantage (RTA) index provides a proxy measure of the technological specialisation of each national group of firms, either across industries (as used here), or across types of technological activity (not used here, but see Cantwell, 2000 for such a comparison). Therefore, in this context, the RTA is defined as the share of US patents granted to the national group of firms in question in a particular industry, relative to that national group's share of US patents granted to large firms in all industries.

$$RTA_{ij} = (P_{ij}/\Sigma_j P_{ij})(\Sigma_i P_{ij}/\Sigma_i \Sigma_j P_{ij}),$$

where: P is the number of US patents
          i is the primary industry of output
          j is the national group of firms

The index gives values around unity. The greater the value, the more a group of firms has a comparative technological advantage in the industry in question. The index controls for inter-sectoral and inter-country variations in the propensity to patent (Cantwell, 1993; 2000). We use this form of the index to establish the profile of national technological strengths and weaknesses — that is, the industries in which the largest firms originating from a given country are technological leaders.

Revisiting the General Cross-country and Cross-industry Pattern of Internationalisation

In Tables 13.1 and 13.3–13.6 we examine the internationalisation of research through the US patenting activity of the largest industrial firms of the most internationalised countries, by distinguishing between patents that are attributable to research outside the home country and those due to research located in the home country of the parent company. It soon becomes evident that the use of aggregate data at a global level provides only a partial picture of the degree of internationalisation that characterises the firms of particular countries or particular industries.

Table 13.1 sketches the overall picture of the extent of internationalisation of technological activity in the world's largest firms. It examines the share of their US patenting from research in foreign locations organised by the nationality of the parent firm through the period 1969–1995. In the world total a mild upward trend is observed. This tendency becomes much more obvious once Japanese-owned firms are excluded, and moreover a slight acceleration in the internationalisation process can be observed during the more recent periods. However, when including the

Table 13.1: Percentage of US Patents of World's Largest Firms Attributable to Research in Foreign Locations, Organised by Nationality of Parent Firm, During 1969–1995.

Country	1969–72	1973–77	1978–82	1983–86	1987–90	1991–95
France	8.16	7.74	7.17	9.19	18.17	33.17
Germany	12.77	11.05	12.07	14.47	17.05	20.72
Netherlands	50.40	47.37	47.65	53.99	53.96	55.69
Sweden	17.82	19.90	26.20	28.94	30.60	42.42
Switzerland	44.36	43.63	43.78	41.59	42.99	52.47
United Kingdom	43.08	41.24	40.47	47.09	50.42	55.79
Sub-total	28.41	25.27	24.64	27.12	30.38	34.98
United States	4.96	5.89	6.40	7.53	7.91	8.62
Belgium	50.00	54.24	56.27	71.21	56.04	67.25
Canada	41.19	39.30	39.49	35.82	40.12	43.96
Italy	13.39	16.03	13.85	12.59	11.14	16.47
Japan	2.63	1.88	1.22	1.26	0.92	1.08
Other Countries	16.58*	19.92	22.38	20.40	17.39	8.73
Total of all Countries	**10.04**	**10.53**	**10.50**	**10.95**	**11.28**	**11.27**
Total excluding Japan	**10.08**	**11.59**	**12.25**	**13.88**	**15.76**	**16.53**

Source: US patent database compiled by John Cantwell of the University of Reading, with the assistance of the US Patent Trademark Office.
Notes: * Less than 100 patents.

Japanese-owned companies the absolute values of the world total percentages may be misleading, as the rising share in US corporate patenting of the little internationalised Japanese firms held back the increase in the aggregate proportion of patenting attributable to foreign-located research (Cantwell & Harding, 1998). The relatively low degree of internationalisation of the largest US and the Japanese firms drives down the global average, such that the latter provides only weaker recognition of the more highly international orientation of European firms, because of the dominant share of US patenting accounted for by US-owned and Japanese-owned national groups.[2]

---

[2] Half of the US corporate patents granted to the world's largest firms are assigned to US-owned companies, and about one-sixth are due to Japanese-owned large firms.

In sum, the overall picture in Table 13.1 shows that in line with the first background proposition outlined above, the largest firms which originate from small countries such as Switzerland and especially the Netherlands (see Cantwell & Janne, 1999b), as well as Belgium tend to have a much higher level of patenting from international sources than do those of larger countries. At this general level the UK is the major exception to the proposition of an inverse relationship between the size of a domestic technological system and the internationalisation of that country's largest firms. The high degree of internationalisation which British-owned firms have inherited is linked to the role of Britain as an imperial power with strong overseas interests, and a long-standing liberal economic policy with respect to inward and outward capital movements as well as trade. In contrast, Swedish multinationals remained constrained for longer by the needs of the more locally integrated domestic economic and technological system of which they were part, despite the smaller size of their home country — and so they evolved internationally only in a 'tortoise-like' fashion (Zander, 1994).

Table 13.2 traces the comparative advantage in innovation of national industrial groups over the 1969–95 period as a whole, in order to be able to apply the framework suggested by Figure 13.1 and to identify the national origins of the technological leaders in each industry. RTA values above one denote comparative technological advantage in an industry. Smaller countries have a narrower range of industries in which their firms compete successfully as worldwide technological leaders. To take a few highlights, the largest US-owned firms are technological leaders in the pharmaceuticals and office equipment (computing) industries, German-owned companies are leaders in the chemicals and metals industries, UK-owned firms in the food products and coal and petroleum products (oil) industries, French-owned firms in the electrical equipment and aerospace industries, Dutch-owned firms in electrical equipment, Swiss-owned companies in pharmaceuticals, Swedish-owned firms in mechanical engineering, and Japanese-owned firms in the motor vehicle industry.

Table 13.3 provides a view over the 1969–95 period as a whole of inter-industry, and cross-national group comparisons of the extent of internationalisation of technological development in the largest firms. There is not an even distribution of international R&D across national groups and industries, which would reflect in a uniform fashion their average contribution to foreign-located innovative activity. In food, as suggested by Figure 13.1 the leading groups, namely UK-owned (66%) and Swiss-owned firms (69%) as well as French-owned firms (62%), are the

Table 13.2: Revealed Technological Advantage (RTA) of Selected Nationally-owned Groups of Firms, Across Industries, During 1969–1995.

Industry	United States	Germany	United Kingdom	France	Nether-lands	Switzer-land	Sweden	Japan
Food, Drink, and Tobacco	1.16	0.00	4.74	0.48	0.19	1.18	0.03	0.41
Chemicals	0.75	2.58	1.10	0.96	0.89	2.78	0.31	0.76
Pharmaceuticals	1.24	1.05	0.87	0.94	0.00	3.98	0.84	0.22
Metals	0.69	2.19	1.03	1.34	0.45	0.94	2.37	1.00
Mechanical Engineering	1.19	1.01	1.01	0.24	0.00	1.69	6.74	0.32
Electrical Equipment	0.84	0.67	0.51	1.12	3.29	0.36	0.87	1.54
Office Equipment	1.46	0.02	0.11	0.49	0.00	0.00	0.00	0.80
Motor Vehicles	0.64	1.58	1.24	1.07	0.00	0.00	0.87	1.82
Aircraft and Aerospace	1.65	0.22	0.84	1.35	0.00	0.00	0.00	0.00
Coal and Petroleum Products	1.43	0.02	2.79	1.64	0.00	0.00	0.00	0.08
Instruments	0.82	0.28	0.02	0.00	0.00	0.00	0.62	2.46
Other Manufacturing	1.13	0.16	0.94	1.31	0.00	0.46	1.58	1.01

Table 13.3: Percentage of US Patents of World's Largest Firms Attributable to Research in Foreign Locations, Organised by Nationality and Industrial Group of Parent Firms, During 1969–1995.

Industry	United States	Germany	United Kingdom	France	Nether- lands	Switzer- land	Sweden	Japan	Total
Food, Drink and Tobacco	6.53	0.00*	66.42	61.79	0.00*	69.12	0.00*	2.55	22.24
Chemicals	6.36	20.67	33.13	11.81	49.89	41.55	16.52	1.52	14.21
Pharmaceuticals	10.99	17.98	19.25	4.84	N.A.	59.36	15.33	0.83	16.16
Metals	6.16	7.79	46.03	8.83	63.44	41.33	18.89	0.75	10.32
Mechanical Engineering	7.08	7.04	56.47	1.27	N.A.	29.48	32.25	0.80	12.47
Electrical Equipment	6.57	14.09	30.03	24.31	51.93	34.19	36.16	0.92	9.74
Office Equipment	11.41	3.62	11.73	31.97	N.A.	N.A.	N.A.	3.49	10.34
Motor Vehicles	5.60	8.32	24.39	6.28	N.A.	N.A.	11.35	0.81	5.68
Aircraft and Aerospace	2.34	0.82	3.06	3.83	N.A.	N.A.	N.A.	N.A.	2.39
Coal and Petroleum	4.25	0.63	83.90	12.25	N.A.	N.A.	N.A.	0.52	15.08
Instruments	5.80	3.51	74.29*	N.A.	N.A.	N.A.	32.13	0.77	3.37
Otherland	7.92	11.44	28.22	26.67	N.A.	29.03	26.41	2.87	10.39
Total	6.80	14.98	45.76	15.92	51.72	44.66	27.61	1.22	10.81

Source: As for Table 1
Notes: * Less than 100 patents for the group of firms from all research facilities
N.A. Not Applicable

national groups responsible for the high foreign share in the world total (22%), but in this industry internationalisation is not high for the US-owned (7%) or German-owned companies (0%). In chemicals (world average ratio 14%), the high overall share abroad is primarily due to the high internationalisation of German companies, the world leaders in this industry (21%) which is again consistent with the scheme of Figure 13.1. In pharmaceuticals (world total 16%) it is the firms of the US (11%), Switzerland (59%) and to a lesser degree Germany (18%) that sustain an above-average industry foreign share to match their technological prowess (Table 13.2), and in petrochemical products the high overall foreign share is due entirely to the largest British-owned firms (84%), once more the technological leaders in this industry. At the other end of the spectrum, the instruments industry is one of the least inter-nationalised according to the world total (a mere 3%), but not for Swedish-owned firms (32%).

Table 13.4 reorganises the same data instead by the type of technologi-cal activity rather than the industry of corporate ownership, and this differs from Table 13.3 by virtue of the 'multi-technology' character of production in any industry (Granstrand *et al.,* 1997). Partly as a result of this spread of the development of many technologies across industries, the dispersion of internationalisation of technological sectors in Table 13.4 is narrower than for the world total of industries in Table 13.3. Hence, the larger number of sectors is around average. Most of the inter-national innovation within sectors in Table 13.4, as in Table 13.3, is due mainly to only a handful of national groups. More importantly, in con-trast to Table 13.3, there is evidence of international technological diver-sification as proposed in Figure 13.1. Food, for example, is a technological sector on which stronger German-owned firms in industries other than food have placed the greatest emphasis upon diversifying into abroad (27%), while from a leading position in the industry US-owned companies abroad have very low activity (5%).

To elaborate further, Tables 13.3 and 13.4 show how individual national groups expand their research activities in a varied manner that has little to do with the average position of the relevant industry and tech-nology. While in the more highly internationalised food, chemical, phar-maceutical and oil industries not all national groups have above-average foreign research shares, on the other side, instruments is one of the least internationalised industries (in the global average position), but Swedish-owned firms are internationalised, in an area in which they seem to be less constrained by domestically integrated structures than in other industries.

Table 13.4: Percentage of US Patents of the World's Largest Firms Attributable to Research in Foreign Locations, Classified by Type of Technological Activity and Nationality of Parent Firms, During 1969–1995.

Technological Sector	United States	Germany	United Kingdom	France	Nether-lands	Switzer-land	Sweden	Japan	Total
Food, Drink and Tobacco	4.91	26.97	61.72	30.91*	20.59*	47.62	23.94*	0.42	13.62
Chemicals	6.19	16.24	54.15	11.46	40.94	43.41	23.70	1.22	12.49
Pharmaceuticals	11.32	26.96	30.65	13.01	39.87	54.25	20.29	1.43	18.79
Metals	6.34	12.73	50.68	10.29	45.87	42.13	25.83	1.17	10.41
Mechanical Engineering	7.33	10.88	51.41	11.51	58.35	40.30	34.03	1.15	12.14
Electrical Equipment	6.80	13.63	32.55	23.74	52.96	36.61	25.91	1.17	9.36
Office Equipment	7.21	23.53	27.57	37.86	45.17	33.00	18.18	1.17	7.84
Motor Vehicles	7.00	9.24	19.20	9.16	76.60*	16.67*	16.58	0.84	5.57
Aircraft and Aerospace	1.21*	3.06	9.84	0.90	64.29*	25.00*	6.25*	2.94	2.58
Coal and Petroleum	3.43	5.63	68.74	2.44	40.74*	62.96*	20.00*	1.37	8.62
Instruments	7.32	12.65	36.54	11.70	60.79	52.25	27.26	0.95	8.77
Other	6.05	10.64	38.75	16.44	52.58	42.38	19.19	1.49	9.33
Total	6.80	14.98	45.76	15.92	51.72	44.66	27.61	1.22	10.81

Source: As for Table 1
Notes: * Less than 100 patents for the group of firms from all research facilities
N.A. Not Applicable

In the most internationalised sectors of food, pharmaceuticals, chemicals and oil the main contributors are the national groups that are technological leaders in the relevant industries, as suggested from Figure 13.1.

The greatest internationalisation occurs in technological areas that do not always coincide with the core fields of the most internationalised industries, especially when individual national groups are considered separately. Significantly above average in its degree of internationalisation is the pharmaceutical technological field, which is due again largely to German-owned and US-owned firms, and to a lesser extent due to Swiss-owned companies, but the internationalisation of food technologies is in good measure due to the diversification abroad of German-owned firms from other industries. Likewise, unlike the indigenous companies of the comparatively weak computing industry in Germany, German-owned firms in other industries show great interest in developing computing technologies abroad. Further, unlike the high internationalisation of research in the coal and petroleum product industry, research in petrochemical technologies is below average in its degree of internationalisation.

Moreover, foreign-located activity is lowest not only in aircraft but also in the motor vehicles industry and technological area (see the totals in Tables 13.3 and 13.4) in contrast to what might be expected if the siting of research abroad were simply to facilitate adaptation to foreign markets. Internationalisation in the motor vehicle industry, like in the Japanese national system of innovation as a whole and to a lesser extent in the Swedish system, seems to be constrained by the importance of localised vertically integrated linkages for generating and transmitting innovation, as proposed in Figure 13.2.

Turning to the organisation of these data from the perspective of inward rather than outward investment, the focal point in Tables 13.5 and 13.6, we examine the degree of foreign penetration in each of our selection of host countries. In Table 13.5 the foreign shares of local activity are classified by industry and in Table 13.6 by the field of technological activity as derived from the US patent class system.

Considering the world as a whole in Table 13.5 (as in Table 13.3), foreign penetration is highest in the industrial sectors of food, pharmaceuticals, petrochemicals, chemicals, and machinery. Looking more closely, however, host country variations again suggest a more complex picture which reflects the pattern suggested by Figure 13.1. The foreign penetration of the food industry is much below average in the UK (15% as against the national average of 34%) in which local firms

Table 13.5: Percentage of US Corporate Patents of World's Largest Firms Attributable to Research in Host Countries Due to Foreign-owned Firms, Organised by the Industrial Group of Parent Company, During 1969–1995.

Industry	United States	Germany	United Kingdom	France	Netherlands	Switzerland	Sweden	Japan	Total
Food, Drink, and Tobacco	17.50	99.64	15.45	55.25	82.16	29.77	83.33*	4.84	22.24
Chemicals	14.61	6.49	29.55	33.31	11.60	3.78	13.32	5.30	14.21
Pharmaceuticals	9.91	13.91	50.34	19.34	100.00*	4.13	2.87	16.40	16.16
Metals	10.92	9.87	29.62	11.20	48.68	15.00	1.81	2.24	10.32
Mechanical Engineering	5.05	25.84	47.16	52.00	100.00	14.81	1.48	6.67	12.47
Electrical Equipment	6.01	30.01	43.48	27.85	4.11	40.62	22.91	1.33	9.74
Office Equipment	1.41	86.34	76.71	56.76	100.00	100.00	100.00*	16.06	10.34
Motor Vehicles	3.50	8.35	13.18	21.83	100.00	100.00*	3.27	2.15	5.68
Aircraft and Aerospace	0.14*	15.18	10.54	2.85	100.00*	100.00*	100.00*	100.00	2.39
Coal and Petroleum Products	10.22	80.47	19.43	10.31	100.00	100.00	100.00*	18.50	15.08
Instruments	0.87	29.90	97.79	100.00	100.00*	100.00*	2.16	0.43	3.37
Other Manufacturing	4.57	56.64	26.71	30.66	100.00*	14.49	13.21	3.29	10.39
Total	7.11	16.87	33.73	25.86	26.50	15.25	9.93	3.52	10.81

Source: As for Table 1
Notes: * Less than 100 patents for the group of firms from all research facilities

Table 13.6: Percentage of US Corporate Patents Attributable to Research in Host Countries Due to Foreign-owned Firms, Classified by the Type of Technological Activity, During 1969–1995.

Technological Sector	United States	Germany	United Kingdom	France	Netherlands	Switzerland	Sweden	Japan	Total
Food, Drink, and Tobacco	8.28	30.85	20.73	45.71*	80.43	24.66	16.92*	6.68	13.62
Chemicals	9.81	8.09	35.54	21.19	46.45	4.92	10.20	6.05	12.49
Pharmaceuticals	15.78	8.05	41.55	37.61	13.24	2.54	5.23	9.39	18.79
Metals	5.68	28.78	34.86	20.37	30.56	17.47	7.89	2.31	10.41
Mechanical Engineering	6.73	25.73	28.35	26.58	52.32	23.58	7.22	3.82	12.14
Electrical Equipment	5.09	25.13	39.45	28.66	6.76	47.49	7.72	3.10	9.36
Office Equipment	5.32	29.37	50.53	40.46	3.80	63.59	22.34	2.06	7.84
Motor Vehicles	5.38	7.01	20.79	21.62	66.67*	10.00*	1.23	2.17	5.57
Aircraft and Aerospace	0.86	9.09	0.87	4.76	0.00*	14.29*	14.29*	2.94	2.58
Coal and Petroleum Products	4.61	14.14	18.32	9.09	92.83	23.08*	0.00*	3.34	8.62
Instruments	5.13	20.63	37.05	30.58	13.23	36.87	27.19	2.56	8.77
Other Manufacturing	5.49	16.33	19.75	16.06	33.17	19.17	5.58	3.12	9.33
Total	7.11	16.87	33.73	25.86	26.50	15.25	9.93	3.52	10.81

Source: As for Table 1
Notes: * Less than 100 patents for the group of firms from all research facilities

are technologically strong (Table 13.2). In pharmaceuticals Switzerland, Sweden, France and Germany have low levels of foreign research penetration, in line with Figure 13.1 in the case of the Swiss and German leaders, while the UK has attracted considerable foreign attention. The UK pharmaceutical case might be thought of as an exception to Figure 13.1, but it seems that there are only a few cases of such centres of excellence in which inward investment is encouraged and outward investment discouraged in the same industry (comparing Table 13.3 and 13.5), and such centres do seem to be exceptional and are difficult to create. In chemicals Switzerland and Germany (whose firms are the leaders — see Table 13.2) together with the Netherlands have witnessed minimal penetration in comparison with the tendency in the world as a whole. Moreover, the two countries of major comparative strength in coal and petroleum product technology — that is the UK and the Netherlands — have both developed strong research bases in petrochemicals at home that have allowed little scope for foreign penetration.

The world total in Table 13.6 reveals again a quite different view of international activity when considering the type of technological activity (as opposed to the industry) that is sited abroad. As seen already from the identical world total column in Table 13.4, differences with the equivalent industries shown in Tables 13.3 and 13.5 are apparent in petrochemicals and in chemicals that now feature below average, while mechanical engineering is now above average. This suggests that oil companies use their foreign-located development more for mining and the mechanical technologies involved in the extraction of crude oil, rather than to innovate in petrochemicals themselves. A similar pattern, even if to a lesser extent, may apply in other industries. The level of international activity in food is also considerably less as a technological field as opposed to an industry (Cantwell & Santangelo, 1999; 2000). Thus, although in terms of the absolute level of activity firms tend to do most abroad in the same line of innovation as at home (Patel & Vega, 1999), namely in the primary technological field of their own industry — it is after all scarcely surprising that chemical firms develop mainly chemical technology and so on, whether at home or abroad — in relative terms in their foreign-located activity they tend to diversify away from the primary field of their own industry, becoming proportionally more active in the development of complementary and supporting technologies.

Moreover, Tables 13.5 and 13.6 show, from the host country's perspective, in which industries and technologies the world's largest firms tap into local host country research expertise, and the degree of accessibility they enjoy. Countries such as the US, the UK and Germany, while they play host to local technological development in a wide variety of industries and technologies, do not tend to experience penetration in their domestic research to the same extent in those activities in which their indigenous firms are strongest, as indicated in Figure 13.1. Foreign ownership of research facilities is of little significance in the US in computing, for instance, in the UK in food (in both the relevant industry and technological field), in both countries in petrochemicals (at least in the technological field), and in Germany in chemicals and pharmaceuticals (in both the industry and technological area). These are all signs of the deterrence of technological leadership.

However, from a weaker position France is to almost the same extent open to foreign-owned research as its indigenous firms are themselves internationalised in food and computing, but to a rather lesser degree in mechanical engineering technologies (in comparison with the machinery industry). Lastly, from a position in which local strength comes mainly from the firms of other related industries, although the Swedish instrument industry receives little local development by foreign-owned firms in the industry, there is significant penetration in instrument technologies by the foreign-owned firms of other industries, consistently with Figure 13.2.

The Explanation of Variations between National Industrial Groups of Firms

Although national groups of firms have distinctive technological profiles, a comparative analysis of their competitive position, their degree of internationalisation and of foreign-owned inward investment in the equivalent countries reveals some common underlying determinants, which have been illustrated in Figures 13.1 and 13.2 above. The most technologically competitive national industrial groups tend to be also as expected the most internationalised in the cross-country distribution of each country of origin. However, the home countries of these leading national groups tend to receive comparatively lower inward investment in technological development in the equivalent industries, as proposed in Figure 13.1.

UK-owned firms lead in the food industry (Table 13.2), to be followed only at a distance by US-owned and Swiss-owned firms. British-owned firms are also highly internationalised in both the food industry and the food technological field (66% and 62% in Tables 13.3 and 13.4). However, foreign-owned firms when considering technology-based investment in the UK, seem overwhelmed by indigenous competitiveness, and have only a modest innovative presence in the country (15% and 20% in Tables 13.5 and 13.6). Moreover, it is clear that UK-owned food industry firms are more internationalised as a whole than are UK-owned firms in the development of food technology as such (that is, the food firms conduct abroad the development of non-food technologies to a greater extent than at home); while foreign-owned firms are more attracted to the UK to develop food technology than in the food industry itself (it is the firms of other industries that in part source food-related technology from a UK location).

Likewise, Swiss-owned, and in particular German-owned firms are the technological leaders in the chemical industry (Table 13.2). Both national groups have a high degree of internationalisation (42% and 21% in Table 13.3). Swiss-owned firms have become just slightly more internationalised in the primary technological sector (43% in Table 13.4) than in the industry (which may be due to the even greater strength of the Swiss pharmaceutical firms, and their emphasis on the development of related chemical technologies abroad), but the German group remains consistent with Figure 13.1, and is more active internationally in the chemical industry than in chemical technologies (16% in Table 13.4). However, both host countries (Switzerland and Germany) receive minimal attention from foreign-owned research in this industry (4% and 6% in Table 13.5), although the local sourcing of chemical technologies by foreign-owned firms of other industries is indeed slightly higher (5% and 8% in Table 13.6).[3]

Swiss-owned and US-owned firms have the strongest technological base in the pharmaceuticals industry (Table 13.2). Swiss-owned companies are very active internationally in this industry (59% in Table 13.3) and also, although to a lesser extent, in the corresponding technological sector (54% in Table 13.4). At the same time Switzerland has little to fear from foreign penetration in either pharmaceutical technologies (4% in Table 13.6), or the even weaker inward innovation from foreign-owned firms in the industry (3% in Table 13.5). US-owned firms in the pharmaceutical industry are, with respect to the US average, quite internationalised in both the industry (11% in Table 13.3), and very slightly more in the primary technology (11% in Table 13.4). Further, despite the accessibility of the US as a host to foreign-owned innovation, much more

---

[3] For a more detailed analysis of the technological profiles of international research activity within industries, see our earlier discussion paper (Cantwell & Kosmopoulou, 2000).

is accomplished in the technological field than is achieved in the industry itself (10% and 16% in Tables 13.5 and 13.6).

The technological advantage of Swedish-owned firms in machinery is without any serious challenge from other national groups that cluster around average. Swedish-owned firms in this industry are highly internationalised in their organisation of innovation, even if the internationalisation of the technology is just above that of the industry (32% and 34% in Tables 13.3 and 13.4). The relative strength of the development of mechanical technology abroad may be due to the close relationship between the mechanical engineering industry and other industries in Sweden. On the other hand, innovation by foreign-owned firms in Sweden is consistent with Figure 13.1, since although low, innovation in the relevant technology is greater than it is in the industry (1% and 7% in Tables 13.5 and 13.6).

Dutch-owned firms have the strongest position in the electrical equipment industry (Table 13.2). Correspondingly, Dutch-owned firms are highly internationalised in both the industry and primary technology (52% and 53% in Tables 13.3 and 13.4), and the Netherlands has a low degree of penetration by foreign-owned research, but one which is higher for the firms of other industries accessing local innovation in electrical technology (4% and 7% in Tables 13.5 and 13.6).

In the computing industry, US-owned firms are without hesitation the industry leaders, and have a relatively high share of foreign-situated research, which is higher in the industry than in the technological sector (11% and 7% in Tables 13.3 and 13.4). However, Tables 13.5 and 13.6 show once again an indication of entry deterrence in their own home country. Foreign-owned research in the US industry is very low especially when compared to the high interest in computing technologies (5% in Table 13.6), and suggests the interest of foreign investors from other industries in acquiring US computing technologies.

In motor vehicles German corporate strength is quite prominent as Table 13.2 shows. The industry, on the whole, is moderately internationalised in terms of innovation and the German-owned national group is consistent with this picture (8% and 9% in Tables 13.3 and 13.4). However, foreign-owned innovation, although low in Germany, is higher than what one would expect for a leading group (8% and 7% in Tables 13.5 and 13.6), which may be due to the relocation of the technological efforts of the UK component companies in Germany at the time when the indigenous UK vehicle industry declined. UK competitiveness on the other hand is exaggerated (Table 13.2) because the motor-vehicle industry includes both a relatively weak vehicle assembly industry and the much stronger vehicle and transport component firms. This amalgamation of a weak car industry and much stronger component firms helps to account for the average industry but the somewhat higher technology internationalisation (always in respect to the relevant country and industry average figures — 24% and 19% in Tables 13.3 and 13.4).

The leading national groups in aircraft and aerospace, US-owned firms and French-owned firms (Table 13.2) operate in an industry with a relatively low propensity to patent. However, despite the difficulties of small numbers, and taking into consideration the special situation of this industry, both the US and French cases conform to the theoretical framework of Figure 13.1. US-owned firms have high — with respect to the industry — outward internationalisation (2% in Table 13.3) while the US has low inward investment in the technology (1% in Table 13.6, but 0% in the industry in Table 13.5). Comparing the aircraft industry with the national average, France as well has much lower inward investment (3% and 5% in Tables 13.5 and 13.6) than the extent to which its firms engage in outward development abroad (4% and 1% in Tables 13.4 and 13.5). Furthermore, inward research activity by foreign-owned firms in both countries is much higher in the primary technological field than it is in the industry as a whole (see Tables 13.5 and 13.6).

UK-owned firms in coal and petroleum products (oil) lead the industry and technological field (Table 13.2) and have a long-standing international tradition (84% in Table 13.3 and 69% in Table 13.4). In comparison, in line with the contentions of Figure 13.1, foreign-owned innovation in the UK remains at exceedingly low levels in both industry and technological field (19% and 18% in Tables 13.5 and 13.6).

However, the reverse trend is observed in the metals industry, in which localised user-producer interaction with the firms of other industries is often of great importance in innovation. As illustrated in Figure 13.2, we expect to observe considerably lower outward internationalisation in this industry than the strength of the relevant national groups might otherwise indicate, accompanied by a consistently higher internationalisation of the primary technology with respect to the industry. For inward investment, foreign penetration of the industry in centres with strong indigenous firms is also lower as suggested by Figure 13.2, but somewhat higher in the technological field compared to the industry (in which latter respect the scheme of Figure 13.2 is in line with that of Figure 13.1).

Swedish-owned companies are the technological leaders in the metal industry and the metals technological field (Table 13.2). The Swedish-owned industry's internationalisation is relatively low (19% in Table 13.3) while the internationalisation of the technological field is moderate (26% in Table 13.4). Foreign-owned innovation, although at a low degree, is higher in the technological field than in the industry, indicating again that local capabilities are tapped into indirectly more by non-metal industry firms (2% and 8% in Tables 13.5 and 13.6).

Besides the Swedish-owned, German-owned and French-owned firms are leaders in the metals industry too (Table 13.2). Both national groups and their home economies follow patterns that are consistent with Figure 13.2. They have a moderate level of internationalisation that is more prevalent with respect to the primary technological field (13% and 10% in Table 13.3) than in the metals industry (8% and 9% in Table 13.4). Moreover, inward investment in the industry is lower than is the level of outward internationalisation with respect to the relevant national averages, and more to the point, the industry is significantly less affected by foreign penetration (10% and 11% in Table 13.5) than the field of the primary technology (29% and 20% in Table 13.6).

Although the theme of Figure 13.2 is most obvious in the case of metals, the same internationalisation-suppressing effect is relevant to other national industrial groups for which a strong indigenous advantage is inward-looking. The higher the degree to which innovation depends upon localised inter-industry linkages within or between companies, the less will be the imperative and the capacity to internationalise, not because of the inability to compete in markets on a global scale, but instead because the main driving forces behind innovation lie in the form of location-specific relationships with other local industries.

Even if this is true, to some extent, for a number of national industrial groups, it is in Japan that this framework has greatest relevance, due to the particular form of historically developed business organisation as in the keiretsu structure (hub and spike). Japanese-owned firms have a leading position in motor vehicles, instruments, and electrical equipment (Table 13.2). Yet the internationalisation of innovation in these industries is moderate in terms of both industry and even country levels, and in all three cases the internationalisation of Japanese-owned firms is higher in the development of primary technologies than in the corresponding industries (in motor vehicles 0.81% and 0.84%; in instruments 0.77% and 0.95%; in electrical equipment 0.92% and 1.17% in Tables 13.3 and 13.4 respectively). Further, inward penetration from foreign-owned firms is generally very low in Japan, and the local sourcing of the relevant primary technologies is more common among foreign-owned companies from other industries (motor vehicles 2.15% and 2.17%; instruments 0.43% and 2.56%; electrical equipment 1.33% and 3.10% in Tables 13.5 and 13.6 respectively).

Conclusions

Our results support the conclusions that first, the internationalisation of the corporate research and development tends to be higher in an industry in which a national group of firms is especially technologically strong, and the firms in question tend to diversify their technological activity through such international operations. Second, inward penetration in locations of domestic technological excellence tends to be low in the same industry, but attracts to a greater extent the investments of stronger firms from other industries to source the primary technology of the industry of host country excellence, since for them local technological cooperation need not be constrained by market rivalry. However, third, national groups of firms whose technological strength is bound up with inter-industry linkages in innovation in their own home country (or national system of innovation) have greater difficulty in internationalising their technological base, both in an outward and in an inward direction.

To conclude, while we must be careful in our cross-country cross-industry analysis that in looking at the trees we do not lose sight of the forest, we have seen that restricting ourselves to a panoramic or 'average' view may be misleading if it skates over the complexity that is associated with substantial variations in the quality and type of the timber. Our picture is altogether richer when we compare the experiences of different national groups with varying strengths in the degree of their inter-nationalisation of corporate technology at an industry level and at the level of technological fields instead of just examining the totals that represent global average values.

What is especially notable from our findings is the restatement they provide of the significance of technological ownership advantages as a condition for internationalisation (Cantwell, 1989; Dunning, 1995). Some commentators have attempted to present the latest phase of asset-seeking investments of MNCs abroad which promotes their corporate technologi-cal diversification — a facet that we have also emphasised ourselves, both here and elsewhere (Cantwell & Piscitello, 2000; Dunning & Wymbs, 1999) — as somehow in conflict with the notion that MNCs require some initial ownership advantages. Instead, we observe that the augmenting and strengthening of ownership advantages through internationally dispersed innovation is complementary to the initial advantages of firms developed in their home base. It is the technological leaders of each industry with the strongest inherited ownership advantages that are best able to develop an international network of innovation (Cantwell, 1995) and so extend their advantage.

Acknowledgements

The authors wish to gratefully acknowledge financial support from the project on 'Dynamic capabilities, growth and long-term competitiveness of European firms (Dynacom)', funded under the EU's Targeted Socio-Economic Research programme (contract number SOE1-CT97-1078).

References

Archibugi, D. (1992). Patenting as an indicator of technological innovation: a review. *Science and Public Policy, 19(6)*, 357—368.

Bartlett, C. & Ghoshal, S. (1989). *Managing Across Borders: the Transnational Solution.* Boston: Harvard University Press.

Breschi, S., Lissoni, F. & Malerba, F. (1998). Knowledge proximity and firms' technological diversification, *mimeo*, CESPRI, Università L. Bocconi.

Cantwell, J. A. (1987). The reorganisation of European industries after integration: selected evidence on the role of multinational corporations. *Journal of Common Market Studies, 26(2)*, 127–151.

Cantwell, J. A. (1989). *Technological Innovation and Multinational Corporations.* Oxford: Basil Blackwell.

Cantwell, J. A. (1993). Corporate technological specialisation in international industries. In M. C. Casson, & J. Creedy (eds), *Industrial Concentration and Economic Inequality.* Aldershot: Edward Elgar.

Cantwell, J. A. (1995). The globalisation of technology: what remains of the product cycle model?. *Cambridge Journal of Economics, 19(1)*, 155–174.

Cantwell, J. A. (2000). Technological lock-in of large firms since the interwar period. *European Review of Economic History, 4*, 147–174.

Cantwell, J. A. & Harding, R. (1998). The internationalization of German companies' R&D. *National Institute Economic Review, 163*, 99–115.

Cantwell, J. A. & Hodson, C. (1991). Global R&D and UK competitiveness. In M. C. Casson (ed.), *Global Research Strategy and International Competitiveness.* Oxford: Basil Blackwell.

Cantwell, J. A. & Janne, O. E. M. (1999a). Technological globalisation and innovative centres: the Role of corporate technological leadership and locational hierarchy. *Research Policy, 28(2-3)*, 119–144.

Cantwell, J. A. & Janne, O. E. M. (1999b). The internationalization of technological activity: The Dutch case. In R. van Hoesel & R. Narula (eds), *Multinational Enterprises from the Netherlands*. London: Routledge.

Cantwell, J. A. & Kosmopoulou, E. (2000). *What Determines the Internationalization of Corporate Technology?* University of Reading Discussion Papers in International Investment and Management, 284, September.

Cantwell, J. A. & Piscitello, L. (1999). The emergence of corporate international networks for the accumulation of dispersed technological competences. *Management International Review, 39(1)*, (Special Issue), 123–147.

Cantwell, J. A. & Piscitello, L. (2000). Accumulating technological competence — its changing impact on corporate diversification and internationalization. *Industrial and Corporate Change, 9*, 21–51.

Cantwell, J. A. & Santangelo, G. D. (1999). The frontier of international technology networks: Sourcing abroad the most highly tacit capabilities. *Information Economics and Policy, 11*, 101–123.

Cantwell, J. A. & Santangelo, G. D. (2000). Capitalism, profits and innovation in the new techno-economic paradigm. *Journal of Evolutionary Economics, 10*, 131–157.

Dunning, J. H. (1993). *Multinational Enterprises and the Global Economy*. Wokingham: Addison-Wesley.

Dunning, J. H. (1995). Reappraising the eclectic paradigm in an age of alliance capitalism. *Journal of International Business Studies, 26(3)*, 461–491.

Dunning, J. H. & Pearce, R. D. (1985). *The World's Largest Industrial Enterprises 1962–1983*. Farnborough: Gower.

Dunning, J. H. & Wymbs, C. (1999). The geographical sourcing of technology-based assets by multinational enterprises. In D. Archibugi, J. Howells & J. Michie (eds). *Innovation Policy in a Global Economy*. Cambridge and New York: Cambridge University Press.

Granstrand, O., Patel, P. & Pavitt, K. L. R (1997). Multi-technology corporations: why they have 'distributed' rather than 'distinctive core' competencies. *California Management Review, 39*, 8–25.

Griliches, Z. (1990). Patent statistics as economic indicators: a survey. *Journal of Economic Literature, 18(4)*, December, 1661–1707.

Kuemmerle, W. (1998). Strategic interaction, knowledge sourcing and knowledge exploitation in foreign environments: an analysis of foreign direct investment in R&D by multinational companies. In M. A. Hitt *et al.*, (eds), M*anaging Strategically in an Interconnected World*. Chichester: John Wiley.

Kuemmerle, W. (1999a). The drivers of foreign direct investment into research and development: an empirical investigation. *Journal of International Business Studies, 30(1)*, 1–24.

Kuemmerle, W. (1999b). Foreign direct investment in industrial research in the pharmaceutical and electronics industries — results from a survey of multinational firms. *Research Policy, 28(2–3)*, 179–193.

Lee, Kong-Rae (1998). *The Sources of Capital Goods Innovation: The Role of User Firms in Japan and Korea.* Chur: Hardwood Academic Publishers.

Lundvall, B. A. (1985). *Product Innovation and User-Producer Interaction.* Aalborg: Aalborg University Press.

Lundvall, B. A. (1988). Innovation as an interactive process: from user-producer interaction to the national system of innovation. In G. Dosi *et al.*, (eds). *Technical Change and Economic Theory.* London: Frances Pinter.

Mansfield, E. (1986). Patents and innovation: an empirical study. *Mangement Science 32*, 173–181.

Nelson, R. R. (1993). *National Innovation Systems: A Comparative Analysis.* Oxford: OUP.

Patel, P. & Pavitt, K. L. R. (2000). National systems of innovation under strain: the internationalization of corporate R&D. In R. Barrel, G. Mason & M. Mahoney (eds), *Productivity, Innovation and Economic Performance.* Cambridge & New York: Cambridge University Press.

Patel, P. & Vega, M. (1999). Patterns of internationalization of corporate technology: location vs. home country advantages. *Research Policy,28(2–3)* 145–155.

Pavitt, K. L. R. (1988). Uses and abuses of patent statistics. In A. van Raan (ed.), *Handbook of Quantitative Studies of Science Policy.* North Holland, Amsterdam.

Pavitt, K., Robson, M. & Townsend, J. (1989). Technological accumulation, diversification and organisation in UK companies, 1945–1983. *Management Science, 35*, 1.

Pearce, R. D (1989). *The Internationalization of Research and Development by Multinational Enterprises.* London: Macmillan.

Pearce, R. D. (1999). Decentralised R&D and strategic competitiveness: globalised approaches to generation and use of technology in multinational enterprises (MNEs). *Research Policy, 28(2–3)*, 157–178.

Scher, M. J. (1997). *Japanese Interfirm Networks and Their Main Banks.* London: Macmillan.

Scherer, F. M. (1965). Firm size, market structure, opportunity, and the output of patented inventions. *American Economic Review, 55*, 1097–1123.

Schmookler, J. (1966). *Invention and Economic Growth.* Cambridge, Mass.: HUP.

Zander, I. (1994). *The Tortoise Evolution of the Multinational Corporation — Foreign Technological Activity in Swedish Multinational Firms, 1890–1990.* Doctoral dissertation, Stockholm School of Economics.

Zander, I. (1997). Technological diversification in the multinational corporation — historical evolution and future prospects. *Research Policy, 26*, 209–227.

Zander, I. (1998). The evolution of technological capabilities in the multinational corporation — dispersion, duplication and potential advantages from multinationality. *Research Policy, 27*, 17–35.

Zander, I. (1999). How do you mean "Global"? An empirical investigation of innovation networks in the multinational corporation. *Research Policy, 28(2–3)*, 195–213.

Chapter 14

Developing an Internally Driven Growth Strategy in Network Organizations: An Organizational Learning Approach

Peter Lorange

Introduction

In this paper, we will discuss how to develop strategies in network organizations, based on utilizing organizational learning as a main driver.
After introducing a conceptual scheme for growth, to be implemented
largely in flat, project-based, temporary network organizations, we shall
specifically indicate three strategic archetypes where different approaches
to network organization designs might be appropriate. These situations
will be complementing the more traditional, "business-as-usual" strategic
settings in normal firms, typically organized along more conventional,
often functional, divisional, or matrix lines. A case study will then be
introduced to illustrate these issues, based on Nestlé's worldwide pet-food
business. Specifically, we shall illustrate that various network-driven strategic growth initiatives can complement the challenge of inducing growth
in the more classical organizational structures, usually related to business-as-usual strategy settings. We shall then discuss organizational learning as a specific driver of growth in the various strategic modes, including
business-as-usual. In the latter, however, we will not expect organizational learning to be a major force, but rather, that conventional planning and budgeting will be the main drivers for strategy development.
When it comes to the three network-based strategic archetypes, we shall
indeed expect organizational learning to be *the* major driver for the

Critical Perspectives on Internationalisation, pp. 335–354.
Copyright © 2002 by Elsevier Science Ltd.
All rights of reproduction in any form reserved.
ISBN: 0-08-044053-5

development of the growth strategies.

The paper will conclude with some generalizations regarding growth-driven strategies and organizational learning in network organizations.

A Conceptual Scheme for Strategy Development: A Human Resource-based Focus

Our claim (Chakravarthy & Lorange, 1991; Chakravarthy, Lorange & Cho, 2001) is that there are two critical underlying dimensions of the development of growth strategies in business organizations, keeping in mind that *the* essential strategic resource is the firm's *people*, with their organizational competencies, experiences, insights, and facility for making judgments. It will be *this* human resource base that one must build upon to develop growth strategies, based on how the two critical issues stated below are tackled:

- First, what is the organization's ability to *see* interesting business opportunities, ideally based on new ways to serve the customer? How can the organization reposition itself so as to serve the client/customer in novel ways, offering them new benefits, even of which they may yet be totally unaware? How can the organization "lead the customer", as opposed to the classical "adaptation to the customer" market-driven orientation? (Kumar *et al.*, 2000; Lorange, 2002);
- Second, how can the organization *mobilize* its relevant human resources to serve such identified opportunities? This is a matter of identifying the appropriate competencies, typically imbedded in the heads of people, and of mobilizing them by combining them into meaningful competence clusters, in the form of workable teams. This must be based on providing inspiration and incentives for these people to work together in such ways that they commit to the strategic challenge at hand — i.e., flexibility, not silo thinking!

Let us combine these two dimensions — the ability to "see", and the ability to "mobilize" — into a conceptual scheme for strategic growth (see Figure 14.1).

We see from this figure that the typical strategic mode will be "protect and extend". The strategic challenge here will be to nurture the step-by-step evolution of one's business, incrementally adding to the basic strategic directions already laid out. One can say that strategy development is

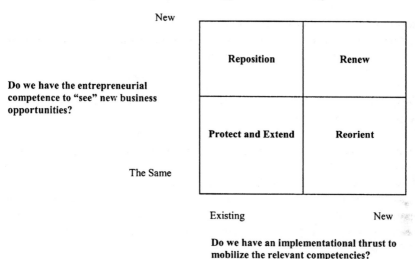

New

Do we have the entrepreneurial
competence to "see" new business
opportunities?

The Same

Existing   New

Do we have an implementational thrust to
mobilize the relevant competencies?

Figure 14.1: Four Strategic Growth Challenges.

emergent, that the past also largely defines the future (Mintzberg, 1994; Quinn, 1995). Utilization of classical planning processes to identify how to proceed incrementally, and how to delineate the tasks to be carried out by the various organizational players, can be applied here (Chakravarthy & Lorange, 1991; Lorange, 1980). One can expect to see a classical organizational design here, along hierarchical lines. The key is mainly to develop an efficient organization, based on a division of labour that can address fairly straightforward incremental strategic challenges, involving relatively well-understood changes as these relate to predictable opportunities (Hrebiniak & Joyce, 1984). These are typically slight changes in patterns of task specifications and resource utilization, to implement incremental strategic thrusts.

When it comes to the other three strategic archetypes in our conceptional scheme — "reposition", "reorient", or "renew" — the situation is different. Here, we usually face much more radically adaptive challenges — calling for less traditional organizational designs (Jarillo, 1988). For instance, we may want to extend into new markets, by "repositioning" our business. This calls for a strong capability to "see" new business opportunities. This may often imply a task force organization, a project team, working in a "flat" mode, perhaps under the leadership of a champion — an internal entrepreneur, to "push" this strategic repositioning by seeing new opportunities. As such a strategy materializes over time, more formality could be gradually introduced in the organizational design. In the initial stages, though, one can expect the radical "seeing" growth task to be more effectively undertaken through a flat, project-based, non-hierarchical organizational form, bringing the eclectic minds together! Typically, these members of such project-based, creative teams will also have another job — another "hat" in the established "protect and extend" based hierarchical organization. It might be normal to spend some time in a "reposition", creative project team, as well as some time attending to functional roles as part of a "protect-and-extend" strategy (Galbraith, 1996; Galbraith *et al.*, 1998).

Similarly, in the "reorient" situation, the challenge is to add new competencies to one's strategy. This may mean putting together, creative, "flat", eclectic project teams, perhaps orchestrated by an internal entrepreneur. While the key is to get the reorient strategy going in the short run, this may eventually lead to more formalization, a convergence towards a more traditional hierarchical organization. In the short term, a project organization to reorient the strategy would probably be based on teams of executives who, once more, wear two hats, one being in the "reorient" world, the other "protect-and-extend".

The even more radical situational context, the "renew" strategy, involves *both* "seeing" a new opportunity *and* the development of a new competency, also calling for a project organization. In this case, it would be more of a full-time task, given the more radical, new challenges, consequently diminishing the "two-hat" set-up for executives in this contextual setting. Key people could migrate from the other "reposition" and/or "reorient" project organizations. However, as this "renew" strategy gradually takes hold, one can expect to see the transformation of the "pure" or full-blown network organization into more of a "two-hat" world, and then eventually a hierarchical one. In the shorter run, however, the "renew" type project organizational mode will be totally "flat", enlisting designated talents that can contribute to do so.

In summary, we see an organizational set-up that approaches the task of internally generated growth and strategic renewal in several complementary ways — a hybrid approach! On the one hand, we have the main thrust of the strategic growth map, "protect and extend". This involves a classical organizational design, backed by an equally classical administrative system for setting and implementing strategic direction — planning and budgeting processes. On the other hand, three complementary strategic archetypes also exist, with different organizational set-ups for "reposition", "reorient", and "renew". The organizational constructs usually consist of temporary project teams, "flat", and often with an internal entrepreneur as the catalyst/leader (Chakravarthy & Lorange, 2001).

The question is now: how is the strategic direction delineated? We know that in the classical case of "protect and extend", and with a conventional, formal organizational structure, classical planning and control will do the job! But what about the other three archetypes? Here, with these temporary network organizational settings, we cannot rely on classical planning and budgeting. Why can we not apply conventional administrative systems to the project-based, temporary organizational settings? The answer rests on the fact that we are now dealing with fluidity in tasks and the lack of specificity in the adaptation challenges, leading to rapidly changing, temporary patterns of organizational roles and resource commitments. This will make it difficult for formal administrative planning and budgeting processes to function effectively. Rather, we feel that organizational learning will be a dominant source for strategic direction-setting in these contexts, based on a sense of "making good even better" to handle the key evolutionary tasks in the heads of the people working on the strategy. This "learning as you go" approach will thus be essential to strategic development in these networked organization contexts. In order to further explore this argument, let us now examine more closely one such organization, Nestlé's worldwide pet-food business. This hybrid business consists simultaneously of both a more formal organizational design and a more networked project-oriented design.

Nestlé Friskies Pet-Food

Nestlé entered the pet food business in 1985, when they acquired the US multinational Carnation corporation, which had also developed the Friskies brand. At the time of the acquisition, Friskies was primarily sold in the US, with minimal sales in Europe, and negligible sales elsewhere in the world, including in Japan. The global pet-food business is organized as a free-standing organizational entity, which is relatively simple, with activities in the US, Western Europe, Japan, Australia, and South Africa. The initial main focus of Carnation was on pet food for *cats*, not for dogs or other animals. Furthermore, it was primarily the so-called *wet* (i.e., canned) food that was produced. Friskies has become one of

Nestlé's nine worldwide strategic brands, along with Nestlé, Maggi, Nescafé, Libby's, Perrier, Nestea, Nestlé Foodservice and Buitoni. Most of Nestlé's food activities are organized as a matrix, with each country — or market — representing the bulk of Nestlé's portfolio, reporting into three geographical zones. Product strategies are pursued through global SBUs, reporting to a worldwide SBU head. The zones and the SBUs work in a matrix. However, a few businesses — notably water (including Perrier), pet-foods (including Friskies), and, to some extent, Nescafé — have different forms of this, forming their own global organizations.

The pet-food business has grown significantly. America is still the major market, again with heavy emphasis on the wet canned product for cats. The European market has also grown significantly, and significant markets have grown in Japan and in Australia as well — all focusing initially on wet cat food. For all of these markets, it is especially critical that the cats are being fed a product with the utmost concern for quality, since cats are known to be fickle in their eating habits — more discriminating, not forgiving, as dogs. Quality is therefore *the* key issue. A main challenge, however, is due to the fact that dry food is growing faster than the wet, and that the dog food segment is outgrowing the cat food. We might see the business in the United States largely as the "protect and extend" business — i.e., how to develop the basic Nestlé pet food further, around "wet-cat", penetrating further established distribution channels. Nestlé has strong, proprietary know-how regarding wet cat food's taste, and the consumer is largely conservative — he buys cat food based on the fact that it must work!

The manager in the US, Mr. Harris, feels that a "protect and extend" strategy is not enough — the business must be based on entrepreneurial spirit. By contrast, one normally *manages* businesses in Nestlé's global matrix world, which involves typical focuses on trade-offs and compromises — i.e., less on pushing entrepreneurship. However, the pet food business can be relatively entrepreneurial, because it is independent, and also relatively clear, easy, and simple, focusing on only a few markets. You know to whom you are selling. In the US, 60 percent is sold through traditional grocery chains — however, entrepreneurism is dampened when selling only to the few large chains — a negotiation business! But 40 percent is sold through other channels which are much more entrepreneurial!

R&D is vital for identifying new business growth. There are two R&D centres, in the US and France. The US-based R&D manager is now responsible for projects and priorities worldwide. This arrangement is one year old, and backed up by semi-annual coordination meetings between

R&D and the key business unit leaders worldwide: Messrs. J. Harris, Mannami (Japan), and T. J. Gallagher (Europe). Doing managed, coordinated R&D is considered increasingly essential. It is felt that this is now much better than before, when each market more or less independently contracted with one of the R&D centres.

With this as a background, let us now move on to the "reposition" strategic challenge. The development of the wet cat-food businesses into new markets such as Europe is an example. Initially, this was started as a project-based network organization. Over time, a more formal European organization was developed. This was eventually headed up by a European manager for the pet food team, Mr. J. Gallagher. He had a strong career history as an "internal entrepreneur", someone who would get things done! As noted, the pet-food business was run on its own, as a European team, autonomous from the "normal" Nestlé business, which is organized country by country, with an SBU matrix overlay. We can see this business development in Europe, therefore, as essentially replanting the already tried US-based "wet cat" business concept, but now in a new business setting: Europe.

Let us now turn to an example illustrating the "reorient" situation: the development of *dry* cat food, both in the US and Europe. This would call for the introduction of new competencies, say, in R&D, manufacturing, packaging, logistics, distribution, and marketing. The task would now be to serve existing customers in new ways. At Nestlé, we saw a team-based approach for tackling this, where, both in the US and in Europe, special-purpose, cross-functional, organizational units were put in place to develop dry cat food. Needless to say, these teams worked closely together; they were perhaps best described as two parts of one team, and, with the main wet cat food business, "borrowing" from this business for critical staffing requirements. The "reorient" flavour of the dry cat teams, both in the US and Europe was clear — namely, to serve the customer with new know-how. Further, the flat, temporary nature of the teams was clearly noticeable.

We now turn our focus to the perhaps most challenging example of business renewal, the "renew". Both the dry and wet cat-food business in Japan illustrates the "renew" business challenge well. We are talking about a geographic expansion into an entirely new market with an entirely new attitude towards the customer, above all with an almost religious emphasis on all aspects of quality. This includes not only product quality, with precise requirements for colour and taste consistency, but also the packaging, appearance of the cans, etc. Similarly, Nestlé pet food

Japan developed a product servicing strategy based on new know-how, and the principal that no production should take place in Japan (Andersson & Holmström, 2000; Forsgren *et al.*, 2000; Lorenzoni & Baden-Fuller, 1995). All sourcing came from Nestlé's global network, notably from the US, but also from Australia, France, Thailand, Indonesia, Liechtenstein, etc. Thus, a new competency in terms of logistics capabilities had to be developed. Figure 14.2 gives a view of the business cum network arrangement for Nestlé Friskies, Japan.

Let us now look at some of the more salient features of this network approach. As noted, all of the products sold by Friskies Japan are imported. In 1999, about 6,000 containers, with some 100,000 tons of products, were shipped from ports in the USA, Australia, France, Thailand, Indonesia, and Liechtenstein. Most of the products were manufactured in Nestlé's Friskies factories in Australia and the USA. Those coming from Thailand and Indonesia were made on production lines owned by outside suppliers, following recipes developed by Friskies Japan and under their supervision. Additional countries of some sourcing in 1999 (in very small amounts) were France and Liechtenstein. Friskies Japan was, in principle, free to source from wherever it wanted. But building relationships with country-based organizations for sourcing takes time! One would thus aim for stability.

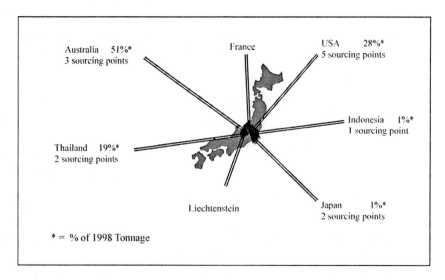

Figure 14.2: Japan — 100 Percent of Goods Sourced from Overseas.

Imports coming into Japan from the USA represented about 40,000 tons in 1999. From the outset, the ordering and transport of finished goods would have been relatively easy if all of the products had been made in the same factory. But they came from five different factories, locations, and states, each specialized in a different product range. Logistics was thus a big challenge, particularly since global sourcing usually takes three to four months. Neither excess inventories nor stock-outs were "permissible".

At least three conditions may have to be fulfilled when importing high volume consumer goods from overseas, if one wants to ensure an efficient management of stocks, to be kept down to a minimum. Each would require the development of unique know-how or competencies:

1) an efficient system of sales estimates;
2) precise coordination between Friskies Japan and the Friskies factories in sourcing countries. Therefore, there is a logistics manager — with three assistants — one for each major country, residing in Japan;
3) deciding on the port of unloading in Japan, with the possibility to change the destination of the ship at the last minute.

Let us examine a few aspects of this example of the know-how challenges of this "renew"-based network organization further. First of all, why should this be a "network" organization? As noted, we see a virtual operation at work, with no factories and no product development centre in the country. It is totally dependent for supplies from other Nestlé factories around the world. Logistics and communications are therefore of primary importance, as is the need to anticipate and estimate precisely how sales will evolve in the different geographical regions of the country. Limiting costs of storage and time for imported products at sea is also vital. It calls for a finely tuned timing regarding the arrival of finished products by containers, often with a last-minute choice of the port of entry, where the containers should be unloaded, so as to ensure the smoothest operation possible.

Thus, the Friskies Japan organization concentrates on sales, marketing, and logistics, with 90 percent of its total staff in those functions. Speed and flexibility are key. It is important for all to act fast — hence, the flat network organization. Flexible sourcing of products is a key factor in the speed of serving the customer, in contrast to the typical mass production approach in more traditional, functionalised hierarchies, where the response to the market would typically be lower.

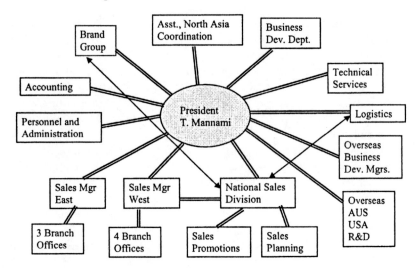

Figure 14.3: Friskies Japan — The Virtual Company.
===== Primary Organizational Links
——— Special Coordination Links

Also, strong competition, especially from the Mars corporation, calls for quick response. Direct, face-to-face contact among key executives in the network is vital. This is quick and action-oriented. There are only a few meetings and few reports. An ad hoc management style prevails, where — again — speed is key! Organizational "space" is abundant in this network! Figure 14.3 shows us that the network centres *around* the boss, the internal entrepreneur, Mr Mannami. Fast communication is vital.

The Japanese market does not have its own Research and Development Centre either. Friskies Japan relies on projects carried out in Nestlé's international Research and Development network with, as noted, two of Nestlé's Research and Development Centres. They work exclusively on pet-foods, one in St. Joseph, Missouri, USA, and the other in Amiens, France. In a typical pyramidal organization, things can easily take too much time. There is a potential conflict between the extreme network organization of Japan and the more conventional organizational forms on the rest of the world.

The role of vision appears to be essential in making the network function. Top management has a clear operational vision — namely, to become a leader in the pet-food business within a relatively short period of time. This vision is widely shared with all employees. In this type of organization, it seems especially vital, thus, that all share the vision, including at the operating level, so that each individual can understand his role(s) in the network based on this. In a more classical hierarchical organization, on the other hand, the extreme attention to vision-sharing may not be so crucial, since the more specialized tasks will be more clear-cut. Perhaps somewhat paradoxically, some stability is also important — the same people in the network need to know each other well, and must know their roles, including exactly how they interface!

In such a "flat" organization, top management must be very close to the operational level (see Figure 14.3). The CEO must have an operational mind! He works face to face with many. Any questions must be handled directly with the person in charge, not up/down a formal hierarchy! There are no management committees. The managers typically have several hats — two to three functions each. Each manager is therefore rather broad-minded. Emphasis is also put on educating people to know other areas, to create a general management point of view, not narrow specialists, but executives who appreciate the whole. It is felt that this leads to more innovation and new ideas, with these breakthroughs being driven from the market-based network, not from the R&D centres!

The most remarkable fact are the people who have made this Nestlé operation work. They seem to have adapted well to new challenges: the importance of information and communication of all kinds, the speed of decision and execution, the globalisation of exchanges, and the abolition of borders and frontiers to trade. It is interesting to contrast this with the much more conventional, hierarchical organization in place for the rest of Nestlé Japan. This seems to perform less well, with much less growth. Interestingly, people appear to prefer coming to work at the networked Nestlé Friskies Japan organization rather than at the conventional part of Nestlé Japan.

The Individuals Learning Dimension and the Link to Strategy

There are some generalizations to be drawn on the importance of organizational learning, particularly as it applies to the three network-based strategic archetypes identified in Figure 14.1. Organizational learning in fact *drives* the development of strategies in such settings (Dromgoole & Gorman, 2000). To establish this point, let us examine more closely the notion of organizational learning.

Corporate learning is an organizational construct that can be seen to provide learning support at three levels — for the individual, for groups within the organization, and for the organization in a broader context. A key question for us is: How, if at all, can these corporate learning activities support the development of effective strategies? First, it provides executive development support for *individual* executives serving their personal development needs. The individual executive typically enrols in programs that build up *his* or *her* individual competencies, thereby also supporting the build-up of organizational capabilities that the firm needs to pursue regarding the running of its business, and the pursuance of its strategies, and/or their implementation. This seems to be more directly linked to the more conventional "protect & extend", rather than to the network-based strategic archetypes.

The individual learner's needs to build his own individual learning network to be more effective in flat, ad hoc organizational settings will therefore be key. To become a better strategist in such settings, the learner might consider issues such as the following:

- How can I learn as an individual? What kinds of co-learners would I be looking for in my learning network? Would there be colleagues from my own firm, from my own function? Or would there be executives from other functions? From different firms? From different national cultures?
- How can my learning network help me to get up to speed to learning right away and faster, so that I can better practice "making good even better?"
- How can I develop in my own mind a clarification of my own value as an active member of a learning network? What can *I* contribute that might be of benefit to the other individual learners? To "give" means to learn!
- Web-based dialogue space can also be key virtual learning Net may become increasingly critical for the individual. How can I link up virtually with fellow colleagues, students, professors, and data bases, interactively addressing key challenges for learning?

A firm's learning goal is not, however, primarily to further strengthen individual specialized know-how development, despite the fact that this can lead to excellent executives for "protect and extend" settings. Rather it is to encourage flexible, eclectic, individual learning, to achieve maximum benefit for the individual from learning from others, from diverse cultures, from a variety of backgrounds and firms. This would help prepare the individual to contribute to strategy development in the network-based settings. This also leads us to our next challenge, how to achieve organizational learning — critically important for network settings.

Organizational Learning — A Key Driver of Strategy in Networks

A second complementary learning task is to develop networks for effective organizational learning — i.e., to create a learning infrastructure around the organizational units — an organizational, even a corporate learning network (Senge, 1990). The intent of this is to stimulate organizational learning by *teams* of executives, complementing individual learning. In part, this may mean developing a shared view on new markets and market extensions — for all in an organizational unit — or even with the entire firm — to better understand how to serve one's customers in new ways — learn how best to interface with them dynamically. It can further imply the repositioning of one's value delivery by learning how to add new knowledge or competencies as the main driver for growth — again, it will be crucial to gain understanding throughout learning within the entire organization! How can several members of an organization learn to develop a shared view on the new know-how needed for redefinition of key characteristics of the value chain? How can the organization learn how to do it differently? Both challenges — serving the customer in new ways and introducing new know-how — imply a reorientation of learning towards *seeing* these types of knowledge build-up as *the* main drivers for growth. This shapes the learning agenda! Therefore, this learning must be shared extensively within the organization, a key purpose of organizational learning! And, both learning challenges imply the redefinition of one's strategy. Figure 14.4 illustrates these learning challenges. We see that they compare directly to the two dimensions in Figure 14.1.

How then can effective learning be built up to enhance organizational learning in network settings? First, one must focus heavily on action-oriented learning programs, where the aim is to create organizational learning networks that enhance strategy development. These will naturally

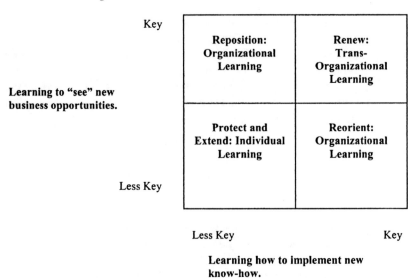

Figure 14.4: Learning, to Support the Strategic Growth Challenges.

tend to be focused primarily on one's own company, on one's own problems and challenges, on one's own strategic setting. Take the introduction of dry cat food in Nestlé Friskies Japan as an example. Trial and error led to the conclusion that it would become practically impossible to import the many varieties of dry cat food packs needed. As the business grew, the organization learned how to handle this — to import larger bags, and to repack these at local packaging lines in Kobe and Tokyo. The organizational team learned a new logistical game, and the requisite know-how needed for this.

Organizational learning means the establishment of an effective organizational learning network. It may even be most effective when it is part of one's day-to-day business practice, perhaps particularly supported by best-practice bench-marking processes. Top management's insistence on organizational learning will be essential, and it will be crucial to break down organizational silos. Jack Welch, formerly of GE, is perhaps the best known proponent of how to create an effective organizational learning network. He always asked a line executive who has come up with a good new approach to a challenge or a problem: "Whom have you shared this with?" It is "forbidden" not to share — problem-solving without sharing is unacceptable! (*The Economist*, 1999)

Trans-organizational Learning — A Strategic Process!

The third, complementary learning mode in network settings that we shall examine is the establishment of trans-organizational learning in networks. This is meant to foster more learning to achieve radically new insights, for instance to renew one's businesses through *both* new customer/market realignment *and* new know-how/technology — i.e., learning how to develop radically new "renew" strategies. Our claim is that learning to achieve this will ideally imply "looking outside" one's own organization for new growth, beyond the borders of one's existing businesses, interacting more widely! Hence, we may, thus need a more widely-focused, trans-organizational learning focus in our network organization. This could also imply that one must learn to *undo* one's established business positions and existing modes of operation as one develops a new one: GE is a classic example! (*The Economist*, 1999)

A good example of looking for new business between existing businesses — in other words, of trans-organizational learning — comes to mind: Nestlé has developed a new line of yoghurts — LC-1 — based on adding so-called probiotic bacteria to conventional yoghurts, thereby creating a product that also strengthens one's immune system (Rogers, 2000). It does not alter the taste of food, and is beneficial to health — a combination of a health-enhancing ingredient *and* a food carrier. Not only has the LC-1 yoghurt become a huge success, but the bacteria ingredient is now introduced in other food carriers — i.e., creating several new ways of serving the customer, "reorient". A special LC-1 bacteria is now also being introduced on the US market allowing the customer to add it to the foods of his choices, such as breakfast cereals and juices. We have a new product for a new market, a "renew"! What about introducing the LC-1 bacteria in pet foods? Which would be the carriers? Dry? Wet? How would the immune systems of the animals react? Cats? Dogs? We can see the rudiments of entirely new performance-based pet-foods — again "renew" cases. But this requires broad networking among many sources at Nestlé, with the pro-biotic bacteria expert from the R&D staff in Lausanne, with several food carrier applications development units, bringing pro-biotic bacteria competencies to the pet-food R&D laboratories in St Louis and/or Amiens, "borrowing" from Nestlé's pro-biotic yoghurt marketing experience, involving outside laboratories for verification of clinical testing, etc.

The executives behind this must be able to mobilize more widespread learning, now also drawing on a trans-corporate learning network, drawing on selling to new customers, focusing on how to make use of the product's properties, and un-learning traditional business applications! The latter corresponds to GE's focus on systematically "destroying" classical outmoded business value creation propositions.

The questions now are: How do we establish trans-organizational learning networks? What is involved? There are several lessons to be had from the development of effective learning and strategies in complex network settings:

- In order to have the organization — with its many networked sub-entities — to directionally go in one direction, a top-down general sense of direction must be provided. The new CEO of Nestlé provided this in several ways, issuing guidelines for real internal growth, providing four "pillars" for strategic direction and giving a blueprint for future success via value-added products;
- An emphasis on more entrepreneurial-driven, risk-taking executives, known for their commitment to and motivation for specific strategic ideas. At Nestlé, Harris, Gallagher, and Mannami would all fit this label;
- Emphasis on smooth, triangular team interaction among the business leaders, key market executives and R&D. The attitude should be open, not "tunnel vision". A sense of proximity must be created — a "meeting place"!
- "The creative Web requires a mindset very different from that of the traditional hierarchical corporation. The issue of trust is crucial. Trust concerns the faith that one's fellow participants will be able to achieve success" (Conklin & Tapp, 2000);
- A clear recognition of new customer trends — i.e., through the possibility of adding value in the pet-food business by combining a traditional pet food "carrier" and an LC-1 bacteria; this works because the consumer wants it!

What About the Firm's Strategic Needs?

As we saw in Figures 14.1 and 14.4, there is one business-as-usual growth challenge, plus three additional key network strategic challenges facing the normal firm, on which the learning might also focus. It turns out that these seem to generally correspond with the three levels of learning that we have discussed in the previous sections.

Referring to Figures 14.1 and 14.4, we see that the marginal extension of the present business — the "protect and extend" — might typically require only relatively non-earthshaking learning, perhaps based primarily on the individual learning networks of the executives. "Reposition" and/or "reorient" would require more widespread organizational learning, largely based on organizational learning networks, for shared understanding of how to serve the customer base in new ways and possibly the same for making use of new know-how. The most involved learning would be in the case of "renew". This *does* require earthshaking learning, most likely through trans-organizational learning networks for thinking "out of the box".

Clearly established learning network concepts should be the backbone of any learning. As seen earlier, we recommend *three* complementary learning network activities comprised in the conceptual lay-out of a balanced learning approach, to support the firm's strategies with the relevant knowledge needed for aggressive business value creation. These networks again must support the development of knowledge for the individual, for the organizational entity, and for the organization based on the more extensive supra-organization network.

This has several implications. The learning must be designed not only to support "what might be good for the individual to learn", but also learning related but *new* information, such as evolutionary ideas concerning service to the customers and the extensions of knowledge bases needed — i.e., to going from supporting the build-up of general knowledge for the individual to supporting the input of knowledge for specific strategic business solutions! Again, this goes beyond the "protect and extend" strategic mode, mostly embedded in the heads of individuals, towards supporting strategic knowledge for pursuing internally generated growth (Gilbert & Lorange, 1997).

The approach must also support learning to envision and to verify more fundamental market shifts and their knowledge implications. Specifically, is this way of seeing the market's more relevant development and the requisite knowledge for this the most appropriate? The development of an organizational learning network, focused on, say, project-based task-force problem-solving can be crucial here. Is this idea the best, seen and judged by the organization as a team!? This is associated with the build-up of relevant strategic knowledge to support the "reposition" and/or "reorient" strategic archetypes!

As noted, teaching reconceptualization and implementation of truly radical ideas will also be vital (Strobel, 2000). This represents a focus on breaking from the past, the key being to find the relevant competencies for this. Here the learning approach will be on intra-organizational learning networks, taking the form of, say, brainstorming around project-based implementation in an industry, and scenario discussions for where the industry might go — to "see", to share, and to communicate. This is mostly applied to the "renew" strategic archetype.

A firm could thus have a clear, all-inclusive, design concept of its own strategic learning, as a way to drive its overall strategic direction, perhaps representing an explicit portfolio of foci, the individual learning supported by individual learning networks, complemented by organizational learning networks, as well as the intra-organizational learning networks. This should represent a deliberate design, to meet the individual's, the group's, and the firm's dynamic and strategic learning needs. This design must be linked to a clear conceptual strategic scheme.

A final implication could therefore be a shift toward more systematic learning as a way to enhance growth strategies in network contexts. The classical planning and control processes — effective as they might be in "protect and extend" settings — need to be complemented by "investments" in organizational learning approaches for the other, complementary network-based strategic settings. This is what seems to take place at GE. We might expect more systematic approaches regarding organizational learning to become in key focus in the future. Or, as Conklin and Tapp observe: "With the shift of responsibility from a hierarchical corporate structure to separate but related work groups, a central issue is the set of systems that can best foster "intrapreneurship" (Conklin & Tapp, 2000). We shall claim that learning processes are likely to become central to answer this plea (Lorange, 2002).

Conclusions

We have argued that internally generated growth strategies may call for the use of temporary network-based organizational focus, driven mainly by internal entrepreneurs. These temporary organizations will be focused on putting together diverse competencies to "see" new business, and to "mobilize" organizational competencies to implement this. We discussed Nestlé's global pet food business as an example.

We have further argued that learning networks must be created — for the individual executives cum strategic learners — for groups of executives gaining a common strategic focus through organizational learning

— and for the organization in its entirety to dynamically strategically reposition itself through intra-organizational foci. The network design must therefore be linked to one's strategic intent — whether this is to support the individual executive cum learner and strategist, whether it is also to go for a complementary organizational strategy and learning dimension, and finally whether one is also meant to stimulate truly radical strategic development and learning for the dynamic repositioning of the firm. Management must not underestimate these strategic repositioning and learning network creation challenges. Too often, strategic change and learning become a routine activity that "peripheralizes" the development and learning strategy challenges, rather than squarely supporting the learning needed to drive the development of the firm's strategies.

References

Andersson, M. & Holmström, C. (2000). The dilemma of developing a centre of excellence — a case study of ABB generation. In U. Holm & T. Pedersen (eds), *The Emergency and Impact of MNC Centres of Excellence*. London: Macmillan.

Chakravarthy, B. & Lorange, P. (1991). *Managing the Strategy Process: A Framework for a Multibusiness Firm*. Englewood Cliffs, N.J.: Prentice Hall.

Chakravarthy, B., Lorange, P. and Cho, H. (2001). The growth imperative for Asian firms, *Nanyang Business Review, 1(1)*.

Conklin, D. & Tapp, L. (2000). The creative web. In S. Chowdhury (ed.), *Management 21C*. London: Prentice Hall.

Dromgoole, T. & Gorman, L. (2000). Developing and implementing strategy through learning networks. In P. Flood, T. *et al.* (eds), *Managing Strategy Implementation: An Organization Behavior Perspective*. Malden, MA: Blackwell.

The Economist, (1999). General Electric: the house that Jack built, Sept. 18, 23–29.

Forsgren, M., Johanson, J. & Sharma, D. (2000). Development of MNC centres of excellence. In U. Holm & T. Pedersen (eds), *The Emergence and Impact of MNC Centres of Excellence*. London: Macmillan.

Galbraith, J. R. (1996). *The Reconfigurable Organization*. San Francisco, CA: Jossey-Bass.

Galbraith, J. R., Lawler III, E. E. & Mohrman, S. A. (1998). *Tomorrow's Organization: Creating Winning Capabilities in a Dynamic World*. San Francisco, CA: Jossey-Bass.

Gibert, X., Lorange, P. (1997) A sstrategy for more effective executive development. In H. Thomas, T. O'Neil & M. Ghertman (eds), *Strategy, Structure and Style*. Chichester: Wiley.

Hrebiniak, L. G. & Joyce, W. F. (1984). *Implementing Strategy*, Macmillan Publishing Company, New York.

Jarillo, C. J. (1988). On Strategic Networks. *Strategic Management Journal 9*, 31–41.

Kumar, Nirmalya, Scheer, Lisa K., Kotler, Philip (2000). From market driven to market driving. *European management journal, 18*, 129–142.

Lorange, P. (1980). *Corporate Planning: An Executive Viewpoint*. Englewood Cliffs, NJ: Prentice Hall.

Lorange, P. (2002). *Developing Strategies in Academic Institutions. The Case of the Business School*. London: Elsevier. Forthcoming.

Lorange, P. (2000). Ultrarapid management processes. In S. Chowdhury (ed.), *Management 21C*. London: Prentice Hall. 151–159.

Lorenzoni, G. & Baden-Fuller, C. (1995). Creating a strategic center to manage a Web of partners. *California Management Review, 37*, 146–158.

Mintzberg, H. (1994). *The Rise and Fall of Strategic Planning*. London: Prentice Hall.

Quinn, J. B. (1989). Strategic Change: logical incrementalism, *Sloan Management Review*. Classic Reprint *20*, 45–60.

Rogers, B. (2000). *The LC-1 Case 20*, No. GM840, IMD, Lausanne.

Senge, P. M. (1990). *The Fifth Discipiline: The Art and Practice of the Learning Organization*. New York, NY: Doubleday.

Strebel, P. (2000). Focusing on breakthrough options. In P. Strebel (ed.), *Focused Energy: Mastering Bottom-up Organizations*, Chichester: Wiley.

Part V

Internationalisation from a Network Perspective

The authors in this section use a network approach to discuss various internationalisation issues. In a network approach, the relationship between the actor and the environment is not viewed as a border but as an interface, full of connections. It is assumed that interaction takes place between the company and specific units within the environment. Thus, it is possible to develop specific interdependencies, or to change existing ones. The interaction includes a systematic combining of resources. This basically challenges the view that there is a distinct border between the resources controlled by the actor/company and the resources that exist in the environment. Instead, the question is how they are combined.

In the first contribution, *Managing Integration of Subsidiary Knowledge in the Multinational Corporation — a Note on the Role of Headquarters*, Ulf Andersson and Ulf Holm describe and analyse how the interplay between the various units within an internationalised company is a result of external business relationships. Each subsidiary can develop as a company in its own right through interaction with its suppliers and customers. This development can then be used in the development of the company's relationships with sister companies. Thus, the development will not be, and does not have to be, channelled through the headquarters. Instead, the international company can work as a network itself, connecting different geographical and technological networks with each other. This provides an opportunity to create an interaction within the company that mirrors but also affects the interaction taking place with external actors in different countries. The way in which the international company is organized can, in this way, more or less capture and exploit as well as help to increase the variety that exists in the entire network.

The second contribution, *Changing Government Strategy of Multinational Corporations in Transition Countries: The Case of Volvo Truck Corporation in India* by Hans Jansson, also focuses on the interaction between the international company and its network in a specific country. Jansson argues that the strategic behaviour of MNCs is changing due to the ongoing liberalization and deregulation in transition countries. Earlier MNCs achieved legitimacy in transition countries directly from government; now, MNCs achieve legitimacy more indirectly by satisfying the social values and norms represented by various interest groups or by the general public in the country.

In the third contribution, *Spatial Determinants on Export Marketing Activity in Marshallian Districts: An Investigation of the Danish Furniture Industry*, Poul Houman Andersen deals with environment from a more spatial perspective. His starting point is that the local environment of a SME (i.e., its location within a district) affects a company's export behaviour. A set of propositions is tested empirically on data from Danish furniture producers, where district versus non-district firms are compared. The results show that companies located within a district cooperate more (compared to firms not located within a district) regarding product adaptation and development. Thus, the conclusion is that "location does matter" in terms of affecting international behaviour.

Henrik Agndal and Björn Axelsson give another illustration of network connections in their contribution, *Internationalisation of the Firm — The Influence of Relationship Sediments*. They begin by noting the importance of individuals and their personal networks, and they consider how these can be used or activated to further the international development of the companies. These networks of personal contacts are the result of the earlier experience of the individuals, which in part also represents the experience of other companies. These experiences — the earlier contacts and knowledge created through them — are combined with some specific capabilities of the new company. This new combination might lead to quite important development steps, as is described in the article.

In the final contribution, *Network Perspective on International Mergers and Acquisitions: What more do we see?*, Virpi Havila and Asta Salmi exemplify the development that can take place in a network due to a merger. Two companies that before the merger had interacted in a certain way develop new ties. This, in turn, may have consequences for all who interact with either of the two companies. We thus get a reaction pattern, "domino effect" of changes in how different actors relate to each other.

Chapter 15

Managing Integration of Subsidiary Knowledge in the Multinational Corporation — A Note on the Role of Headquarters

Ulf Andersson and Ulf Holm

Introduction

At the very end of the 1990s, a Swedish forestry corporation, Aspa, was operating with subsidiaries in nine European countries. One subsidiary, Danke, was a centre of excellence in the sense that it had a history of developing high quality products. Its most prominent products and technical solutions had been developed through intensive co-operation with different customers and suppliers external to the multinational corporation (MNC). Sister subsidiaries that were not as capable as Danke often adapted and used Danke's solutions for their respective markets. Although the prevalent characteristic was that local product markets demanded local adaptations, subsidiary managers felt that exchange of experience had a value. Therefore, they created an informal association through which information from Danke (and other subsidiaries) was mediated. This was managed without instructions from Aspa's headquarters (HQ) although they were informed about its purpose and activities. Involved in meetings, which were held a couple of times every year, were personnel from subsidiary production, development and marketing departments. Aspa's top managers at HQ gave moral support to the group, but they were cautious not to interfere with it and did not partici-

Critical Perspectives on Internationalisation, pp. 359–385.
ISBN: 0-08-044035-5

pate themselves. HQ managers stated that this was a deliberate philosophy since "...everybody turns silent when we attend such meetings".
Thus, the integration of subsidiary knowledge was managed on a basis of
self-interest. As a result, Danke and Aspa's HQ developed a close, informal and intense relationship through which HQ learnt about the development in Danke and its impact on the development of the whole Aspa
corporation.

In this short case illustration, we can observe at least four aspects that
relate to corporate integration of specific subsidiary knowledge. First,
knowledge developed at one location can, through horizontal subsidiary
contacts, be used by subsidiaries in other markets. Second, important
subsidiary knowledge is created through co-operation in business relationships external to the MNC. Third, the HQ did not play the primary
role in the integration of subsidiary knowledge and fourth, in its relation
with Danke, the HQ was the recipient, rather than a sender of knowledge.

Within the theme of adaptive organizations, MNCs are assumed to
achieve global competitive advantage through the accumulation of
knowledge and resources from different parts of the world (Kobrin, 1991;
Kogut, 1985; Porter, 1986; Prahalad & Doz, 1987). This theory — in
which the MNC organization is a "method" of gaining competitive
advantage — builds on the assumption that subsidiaries develop specific
knowledge in their local business settings and that the integration of
certain subsidiaries' knowledge will be beneficial to the MNC as a whole.
This presumes that local environments play a crucial role for the creation
and differentiation of subsidiary knowledge (Birkinshaw & Hood, 1998).
It also assumes that there is a "rational force" from HQ managers, who
will systematically evaluate and tap valuable knowledge for "global
reach" (Bartlett & Ghoshal, 1986).

Research has so far stated that subsidiaries do develop a number of
different activity roles and that some become leading edges for MNC
development (Bartlett & Ghoshal, 1989; Gupta & Govindarajan, 1994).
Although some empirical studies observe the existence of such roles (Forsgren *et al.,* 1992; Holm & Pedersen, 2000), little has been done as yet
dealing with the relation between the driving forces behind subsidiary
knowledge and the integrative mechanisms of that knowledge within the
larger MNC. For instance, does subsidiary engagement in co-operative
relationships external to the MNC, and the gaining of new knowledge
through these, relate to knowledge development among other MNC
units?

Received theory is somewhat ambiguous about the role HQ plays in the corporate integration of subsidiary knowledge. Does HQ play an active, intermediate role, sanctioning knowledge integration, or do subsidiaries integrate their knowledge through autonomous horizontal interaction? Received theory adopts different viewpoints, or mechanisms, for integration of subsidiary knowledge. One is based on HQ control and incitement, which is the predominant perspective adopted amongst researchers on MNC evolution. From such a perspective, we can expect externally generated subsidiary knowledge to be integrated in the MNC on the basis of contact within the HQ-subsidiary relationship, providing HQ with insight that guides them when coordinating exchange between different subsidiaries (Bartlett & Ghoshal, 1989; Gupta & Govindarajan, 1991). We label this "the design path". In a second, externally generated subsidiary knowledge is integrated in the MNC through autonomous horizontal interaction with MNC sister units. Thus, subsidiaries interact more or less on the basis of self-interest and we consequently propose that the integration of subsidiary knowledge relate to the development of interdependent business-like relationships between MNC subsidiaries. We label this "the organic path". In this perspective, the HQ is only one among a number of actors that can influence such a development. MNC competitive advantage, then, will be a matter of an organic growth through lateral contacts, rather than the result of a specific design implemented by HQ. The organic path is closely related to the concept of local rationality and it is driven by the successive interactions and dependencies that some subsidiaries create vis-à-vis other subsidiaries thereby spurring on the exchange of information (Astley & Zajac, 1990; Cook & Emerson, 1984; Pfeffer & Salancik, 1978; Thompson, 1967). In effect, the subsidiary will influence the knowledge development of others (Andersson, *et al.*, 2001; Lane & Lubatkin, 1998).

Although this paper deals with integration of subsidiary knowledge, we have reason to believe that most subsidiaries develop and use most of their knowledge for local purposes. In fact, several obstacles are usually stressed when discussing the integration of subsidiary knowledge in the MNC. One has to do with knowledge being more or less "sticky and tacit" and thus difficult to transfer (Kogut & Zander, 1992; Makhija & Ghanesh, 1997; Nonaka & Takeuchi, 1995). Another speaks of political processes, and stresses that corporate units may not share the same interests, so the diffusion of locally developed knowledge is hindered (Allen, 1977; Bartlett & Ghoshal, 1989). A third aspect concerns the perception gaps between HQ and the subsidiaries that lead to different understandings about the goals and which roles the corporate units play, or should play, and thereby negatively affects the incentive to spread knowledge (Birkinshaw *et al.*, 2000).

It is the assumption of this paper that the obstacles above are apparent. However, it is still the case that some fields of knowledge are more likely to be of global use than other fields and that some subsidiaries more than others will serve as sources of such knowledge. Further, even if most knowledge is bound locally the knowledge that does reach beyond the local subsidiary usage may still be critical for the competitive advantage of the whole MNC.

In the paper, the two "paths" of global integration of subsidiary knowledge are tested by investigating how subsidiary embeddedness in development processes in business relationships external to the MNC relate directly to the importance of a subsidiary for knowledge development within the MNC, and/or indirectly through the formal or informal contact in the HQ–subsidiary relationship. In the following, we discuss subsidiary development and the role of the corporate HQ in the modern MNC. A model is hypothesized and tested using LISREL analysis. Depending on verifications and falsifications of hypotheses, we will determine whether HQ does or does not play a design role in the active integration of subsidiary competence in the MNC. The paper ends with a discussion of the results and concluding remarks.

The Headquarters and Subsidiary Role Development in the International Firm

The internationalisation of the firm can be described as a process of increasing foreign business experiences and resource commitments through activities in foreign markets (Johanson & Vahlne, 1977; 1990). It is argued that lack of international business experience — meaning a high risk of failure when expanding into unknown markets — makes firms start out by taking relatively small steps abroad, often in neighbouring countries with a low psychic distance (Johanson & Wiedersheim-Paul, 1975). In later stages, when the experience is comprehensive and resources are abundant, bigger investments become more common. The internationalisation of the firm, eventually leading to a fully-fledged MNC, will successively contain a variety of geographically spread subsidiaries with a wide range of market experience between them. Thus, the MNC may be considered to be a collection of knowledge and capabilities (Cantwell, 1991; Madhok, 1997).

The process of internationalisation brings about several structural changes. In the early stages when most foreign subsidiaries have a moderate capacity with regard to the level of business activity, the mother-company supplies expert knowledge and vital resources. At this stage, subsidiaries are mainly local and operative, and have a low degree of impact on the strategic development of the MNC as a whole (Forsgren 1989). However, as the internationalisation continues, the management relationship between subsidiaries and the mother company changes. Some subsidiaries will start to adjust the input products received from the mother-company and the home country and adapt them to the specific needs of their local market. Some will also start carrying out their own production and development. Eventually, certain subsidiaries will no longer depend on the mother-company for expertise and the transfer of resources. In this way, the mother-company and the country of origin become less vital for the survival of the subsidiary and, through this, its knowledge development.

We conclude that the internationalisation process of the firm has major consequences for the localization of knowledge creation. First, because it leads subsidiaries to procuring their own resources, which often have an origination external to the MNC. Thus, there will be a more autonomous subsidiary knowledge base.

The External Embeddedness of MNC Subsidiaries

During the internationalisation process of the firm foreign subsidiaries will successively engage in business exchange and develop extensive relationships with local business partners. Thus important business information and certain kinds of operational knowledge will develop on the basis of the subsidiary's local business setting (Amit & Schoemaker, 1993; Grant, 1991; Mahoney & Pandian, 1992; Peteraf, 1993; Teece, *et al.,* 1990). The subsidiary's ability to assimilate this information and to develop its knowledge has much to do with how profound its business relationships are (Holm *et al.,* 1995).

A subsidiary's ability to identify new information from its environment and assimilate it is known as its absorptive capacity (Cohen & Levinthal, 1990; Lane & Lubatkin, 1998). There seem to be two, related, lines of reasoning. First, research on cognition indicates that learning is dependent on existing knowledge. The ability to identify and assimilate is dependent on the richness of the knowledge in existence at that time. Learning is cumulative, and is greatest when the object of learning is related to what is already known (Cohen & Levinthal, 1990; Mowery *et al.*, 1996). The acquisition of new information is not only dependent on the existence of the information as such, but also on the subsidiary's knowledge about areas or problems similar to, or related to, the new information.

Second, implicit in the conceptualisation of absorptive capacity is the assumption that the organization learns from someone else, usually another organization. Thus a subsidiary's absorptive capacity is dependent on its involvement in inter-organizational learning (Hansen, 1999; Kumar & Nti, 1998; Lane & Lubatkin, 1998; Mowery *et al.*, 1996). Consequently, an organization is not equally capable of learning from all organizations. The possibilities of a subsidiary obtaining new information from within another organization, and its ability to assimilate that information, is heavily dependent on the structure of the existing dyadic relationship between the two organisations (Lane & Lubatkin, 1998).

These two lines of reasoning lead to two statements regarding the determinants of a subsidiary's absorptive capacity: First, pre-existing knowledge at the subsidiary level is crucial for the identification and assimilation of new knowledge. Second, the identification and assimilation of this knowledge is mainly carried out within established relationships with other organizations. The structure and nature of these relationships will influence the subsidiary's absorptive capacity.

The discussion of embeddedness in business networks has much in common with the reasoning above (Granovetter, 1985; 1992; Polanyi, 1957; Uzzi, 1997; Zukin & Di Maggio, 1990). The most important facet of embeddedness is the emphasis on the network of inter-organizational relationships for conducting business. The network constitutes an organization's interface with the environment and it is through the inter-organizational relationships that the exchange of information with the environment is handled. Therefore, a subsidiary's relationships can be looked upon as an investment that will influence its future capacity to identify new information and assimilate it. Several scholars have used the concept of embeddedness as it combines the two notions above: the importance of prior knowledge and the importance of relationships (Andersson & Forsgren, 1996; 2000; Grabher, 1993; Uzzi, 1997). Embeddedness in networks is assumed to develop over time, from more arm's-length relationships to relationships based on adaptation and trust (Ford, 1997; Håkansson, 1989; Johanson & Mattsson, 1987; Uzzi, 1997).

This is also in line with Cohen and Levinthal's (1990) notion that absorptive capacity is something that develops over time, is path dependent and therefore builds on prior knowledge of another organizations.

Knowledge about other organizations' capabilities is, therefore, dependent on the level of embeddedness. The higher the level of embeddedness, the greater the pre-existing knowledge of environmental factors of importance for the absorptive capacity. And the higher the level of embeddedness, the greater the similarities between the focal organization and its counterparts in terms of knowledge bases and dominant logic (Lane & Lubatkin, 1998). Thus, embeddedness reflects both pre-existing knowledge and knowledge congruence between partners in the relationships, which in their turn both have a positive impact on an organization's absorptive capacity (Mowery *et al.*, 1996).

This conclusion is highly relevant for subsidiaries belonging to MNCs. The more a subsidiary has deep, extensive relationships with other organizations in its business environment, the greater its ability to identify and assimilate new information from that environment. The depth of the relationship has to do with factors such as mutual adaptation of resources and activities, as well as the existence of trust in the relationship. The scope of the relationship has to do with the number of areas or functions in which the counterparts are related. Focusing on technical development, for example, a high level of embeddedness would mean that the subsidiary and another organization are highly interdependent in terms of technical development activities. For instance, the development of new products in the subsidiary is based on intensive information exchange with the other organization, and development is adapted to meet the requirements of the counterpart. The interface between the subsidiary and the other organization is also broad in terms of the number of technical fields encompassed and the number of people involved.

We conclude that subsidiary external embeddedness reflects its depth in development processes that are conducted in exchange relationships external to the MNC, making the subsidiary maintaining a possible position as bridgehead for linking important knowledge to other MNC units. Next, we will discuss how this knowledge may be integrated in the MNC.

The Global Integration of Subsidiary Knowledge

Ever since strategic management research commenced, the issue of how to design the corporate organization has been of paramount interest.

Although researchers have elaborated on the design problem from different angles, it seems that one common question is how corporate HQ executives should act in order to create a corporate structure that corresponds to their view of the competitive strength of the organization as a whole. Specifically, depending on which problem is being addressed, HQ should decide on matters like: resource distribution, the structure of the information system, the roles of corporate sub-units and the relations between them and the implementation of appropriate values and norms on the basis of what is believed to strengthen the corporate competitive advantage.

A seminal step in this theoretical development — presented some two or three decades ago by Galbraith (1973) and Galbraith and Edström (1976) — addressed the issue of design in terms of the top managers' ability to adapt the organization to meet the requirements of the local environments or to adopt and implement a strategy designed to fit the organization to the environments in which it is active. In this perspective, it is crucial that the top manager is able to obtain appropriate information and process it in the organization. Egelhoff (1988) later adopted this perspective for his study of the MNC. During the late 1980s, several researchers started to address the importance of subsidiary initiatives and of the strength of subsidiary roles for the evolution of the corporation as a whole (Etemad & Dulude, 1986; Ghoshal & Bartlett, 1988; Gupta & Govindarajan, 1991; Hedlund, 1986). Thus it was recognized that some MNC subsidiaries achieved more equal relationships with their HQs and that the corporate system was built by a complex multi-centre structure (Forsgren, 1989) of subsidiaries that no longer only served as implementers of the HQ strategy. This notion addresses the problem of design and questions the efficiency of hierarchy and formal structure as control mechanisms of the corporate organization (Hedlund, 1993).

Still, in most research on MNC development, the issue of the role played by HQ has remained crucial. In fact, the complexity of the corporate structure, the notions of HQ's lack of information about subsidiary activities and the lateral influence among subsidiaries, have all contributed to making examinations of how HQ should manage the corporate evolution more fragmented and more strongly focused. For instance, based on specificity rather than uniformity, Ghoshal and Bartlett (1988) suggest that diffusion of national subsidiary innovations in the MNC can be achieved through the creation of an intensive and co-operative HQ-subsidiary relationship. Martinez and Jarillo (1989) speak of the impact of a number of informal, rather than formal, control mechanisms in the

HQ-subsidiary relationship, while Hedlund (1986), Bartlett and Ghoshal (1989) and others stress the need to create globally shared values among corporate sub units. Accordingly, during the 1990s a "network view" on design issues of the MNC has emerged. In this field, it is basically argued that organizing corporate units with specialized roles within a set of interdependent exchange links creates a competitive advantage for the whole corporation. However, the assumptions about what constitutes a network of relationships differ between researchers in industrial marketing and strategic management (compare for instance the perspectives of Axelsson and Easton, 1992 with Bartlett & Ghoshal, 1989).

In the early 1990s, Ghoshal and Bartlett (1990) expanded their intra-organizational view to an inter-organizational view, meaning that the external network was explicitly addressed. The main conclusion was that the density of external resource links of a subsidiary has a positive impact on the subsidiary's possibility to influence the resource distribution within the MNC. This implies that an increased external resource control of a subsidiary will lead to an intensified contact in the relationship with the HQ. In the diversified MNC, Doz and Prahalad (1993) accordingly stress that important external relationships with customers and suppliers must be incorporated in the task of management, implying that operative subsidiaries will be managed partly on the basis of their linking role to such counterparts. The argument has its relevance as it has been empirically observed that a large portion of the relationships that influence the knowledge development of subsidiaries to a large extent are external to the MNC (Andersson, 1997; Pahlberg, 1996), making external subsidiary embeddedness of particular interest. For this reason the subsidiary may play the role of a crucial bridgehead for linking the MNC to important external network counterparts. However, the more embedded a subsidiary is in the external network of the MNC, the more difficult it will be for HQ to grasp the essence of the subsidiary's development. But as the degree of the subsidiary's external embeddedness reflects investments in important developmental activities that drive the subsidiary knowledge, this will strongly motivate HQ to create a close and intense relationship with it. This leads to the following hypothesis:

H1a: The external embeddedness of a subsidiary is positively related to the intensity in the HQ-subsidiary relationship.

The more intense the relationship between the HQ and the externally embedded subsidiaries, the more insight will the HQ have about the kind of knowledge that the subsidiaries possess. We can therefore speak of the HQ functioning as an intermediate link for knowledge integration within the MNC. In such a scenario, in order to create efficiency and knowledge development in the corporate system, the HQ will create intense relationships with externally embedded subsidiaries and then authorize exchange between those subsidiaries and other MNC units and thus creating flows of important information (Bartlett & Ghoshal, 1986; Porter, 1986). Thus we can formulate the following hypothesis:

H1b: The external embeddedness of a subsidiary is positively related to that subsidiary's importance for MNC knowledge development via the intensity in the HQ-subsidiary relationship.

Together, Hypotheses 1a and 1b reflect the "design path" in which HQ plays an active role in integrating externally generated subsidiary knowledge among MNC units. In the following section we discuss how the external embeddedness of a subsidiary directly relates to subsidiary importance for MNC knowledge development. This represents the "organic path" for MNC integration of externally generated subsidiary knowledge.

The "organic path" of MNC knowledge integration has to do with subsidiaries creating exchange relationships in their external network. But the external network is not isolated from the MNC as relationships often are connected in the sense that changes in one relationship have an impact upon the exchange in another (Blankenburg *et al.*; Cook & Emerson, 1984). Therefore, given that relationships are interdependent, development in the market part of the subsidiary network will have an impact on the activities of the subsidiary's corporate network. For instance, a technical change with regard to a certain market customer will affect the subsidiary's corporate supplier relating to that technology. We posit that the more the subsidiary develops new knowledge outside the MNC part of its network the more it will interact with the MNC counterparts that in some way relate to this network. The "organic path" of MNC integration of subsidiary knowledge is, therefore, a matter of autonomous interaction between subsidiaries. In this process, the counterparts will successively learn about the subsidiary's capabilities, and on the basis of perceived dependence they will adapt their organizational routines in accordance to the requirements developed in the exchange with the subsidiary. The degree of interdependence of a certain subsidiary with the rest of the MNC will reflect the extent to which that subsidiary has a widespread impact on the development of corporate knowledge development. Thus the knowledge attained by the subsidiary will promote corporate learning amongst the sister units, not only because of the others' interest in learning, but also because the knowledge introduces dependence between the corporate units vis-à-vis the subsidiary. We expect that the higher the knowledge development of an MNC subsidiary in its external network, the greater the influence of the subsidiary with regard to the kind of investments and commitments made by the other MNC subsidiaries (Astley & Zajac, 1991).

There is consequently reason to expect that there is a positive relation between subsidiary external embeddedness and the subsidiary importance for the MNC knowledge development. Thus, the following hypothesis can be formulated:

H2: The external embeddedness of a subsidiary is positively related to the importance of that subsidiary for MNC knowledge development.

It should be noticed that the organic path is not a matter of solving how to absorb the "right" knowledge. It is a matter of subsidiaries acting in accordance with their local business interests and their dependencies to other actors in the external and internal business network. While the design path implies strategy formulation and design from a HQ perspective, the organic path stresses the horizontal interactions that successively lead to integration of knowledge between corporate subsidiaries.

The hypothesized model (see Figure 15.1) includes the two primary paths: The "design path" and the "organic path". The first, driven by subsidiary external embeddedness, focuses on a positive relation (H1a) with the intensity in the HQ-subsidiary relationship. If H1b is positive in combination with this, we obtain a picture of the HQ as having an inter-

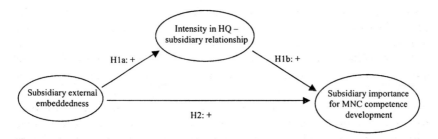

Figure 15.1: The Hypothesized Model.

mediate design role for integrating subsidiary knowledge into the MNC, affecting the knowledge development of other MNC units. In the second path, illustrated by Hypothesis 2, the external embeddedness of a subsidiary affects the importance of the subsidiary for MNC knowledge development. In this path, HQ does not play a role in integrating subsidiary knowledge.

Methods

The Sample

The complexity of the MNC as an organizational form, i.e. its multidimensionality in terms of geographical localization and product lines, makes it particularly difficult to manage and study (Doz & Prahalad, 1993). In terms of management, decentralizing the decisions for global strategic issues down to the management level with responsibility for operational decisions is one way to cope with the increased complexity. The tendency to strengthen the position of the (global) divisions or business areas has been observed in Swedish MNCs by Hedlund and Åman (1984). The reporting from the subsidiaries is directed towards the (global) divisional management to an increasing degree, rather than towards the chief executive office of the MNC. Because of this, our unit of analysis in this paper is the (global) division and its subsidiaries.

With the intention of increasing the likelihood of being able to draw general conclusions from the data gathered, we have selected subsidiaries that can be considered to be representative for the division's activities in conjunction with the division's HQ. We have collected data from 97 subsidiaries holding together 405 important relationships to external customers and suppliers. The subsidiaries belong to 20 divisions within 13 Swedish MNCs. All the divisions have their HQs located in Sweden. Of the 97 subsidiaries involved, 92 are located in Europe and five in North America.

The sample represents a wide spectrum of Swedish industry and includes large and well known companies in industries such as gas applications, hard material tools, industrial equipment, management training, petrochemicals, power distribution, pulp and paper, software and telecommunications equipment. The subsidiaries included are among the largest and most important in their respective divisions. Measured in terms of number of employees, the subsidiaries in the sample account for over 50 percent of the divisions' combined operations on average. In 25 per cent of the divisions the investigated subsidiaries account for more than 80 percent of the divisions' total operations, whilst they account for between 10 and 60 percent in the remaining divisions. The size of the subsidiaries varies between 50 and over 5,000 employees. The average number of employees in the divisions was 5,850 with the variation being from 300 to more than 27,000. Turnover ranged from 0.6 to 23 billion SEK with an average of about 6 billion SEK. All divisions are highly international with, on average, more than 50 percent of their employees being located outside Sweden.

The subsidiaries investigated have their own production and sales so the development of products and of the production process is an important activity in every subsidiary. The subsidiaries studied have a mixture of business relationships with external and corporate suppliers and customers. In this particular study we have excluded the corporate counterparts deliberately to get a clear-cut picture of the subsidiary's external embeddedness and its impact on knowledge development within the corporate system.

Data Gathering

To increase validity and reliability in the assessment of the subsidiaries' relationships with customers, suppliers and HQ, personal interviews have been conducted with three different managers in each subsidiary, the chief executive officer of the subsidiary, the sales manager, and the manager responsible for purchasing. The CEO of the subsidiary was asked to describe the relationship with the HQ and the sales and purchasing managers were asked to describe and assess the three most important relationships with customers and suppliers respectively. The personal interviews were conducted with a standardized questionnaire as a base. During the interview the questionnaire was marked subsequently by one of the two interviewers. Each interview lasted for about two hours. Compared to a mail survey, this method of quantitative data gathering has advantages because it gives the interviewer the possibility to resolve any problems that arise from concepts and interpretation with the respondent.

After interviewing the subsidiary managers in one division, we turned to the HQ and conducted a personal interview with the divisional manager, based on the same type of standardized questionnaire. Through these interviews we gathered information about the HQs' view of each subsidiary's importance for their sister units' development. The HQs' knowledge about the subsidiary's specific business relationships was also checked. This can be seen as a further validation of the questionnaire and of a means of increasing the reliability of the respondents' answers. The study involved personal interviews with more than 300 managers from leading positions in the subsidiaries and the divisional HQs.

An important feature of this research is the choice of suitable respondents concerning measurable variables in relation to the theoretical constructs. Firstly, managers at the HQ of the global division judge variables associated with the importance of each subsidiary for knowledge development in the larger MNC. In turn, the subsidiary managers assess the variables that associate with the theoretical construct external embeddedness of the subsidiary and the intensity in the HQ-subsidiary relationship. This design means that we avoid the potential bias that would arise in the data if the same person estimated all variables. The idea behind separating the assessment is also to get a more reliable measure of the importance of each subsidiary for knowledge development by asking someone outside the subsidiary in question to evaluate this. There is reason to believe that the divisional managers are in a better position to judge the subsidiary's relative importance to the division's knowledge development, than the subsidiaries are themselves.

Construct Analysis

The hypothesized model shown in Figure 15.1 was empirically tested in a LISREL model (Figure 15.2). The validity of the LISREL models is judged by several fit indices. The chi-square test is the most fundamental test of model fit (Bollen, 1989, Satorra & Bentler, 1994). The model chi-square is evaluated in relation to degrees of freedom, and on the bases of these, a probability estimate (p-value) is calculated. This measure is an indication of the distance between the data and the model (Jöreskog & Sörbom, 1993). P-values below 0.05 indicate that the model differs significantly from the data at the five percent level of significance and thus, fails to fit the data (*ibid.*).

Another commonly used fit index is the RMSEA-measure (Root Mean Square Error of Approximation) proposed by Browne and Cudeck (1989). It tests the null hypothesis of close fit between model and data, which could be seen as more meaningful than the null hypothesis of perfect fit. An RMSEA lower than 0.05 indicates "very good" fit, 0.05 to

0.08 a "fair to moderate" fit, 0.08 to 0.10 a "poor" fit, and an RMSEA higher than .10 indicates "very bad" fit (*ibid.*). Other accepted fit indices are the goodness of fit index (GFI), the comparative fit index (CFI), the normed fit index (NFI), and the non-normed fit index (NNFI) (Tanaka & Huba, 1985, Bentler, 1990, Bentler & Bonnet, 1980). Communal to these indices is that values closer to one reflect better fit. However, the normed fit index (NFI) has the disadvantage of not reaching one even when the model is correct and that this phenomenon is exacerbated in smaller samples.

Below, we will first describe the operationalization of the constructs included, then we will evaluate the different forms of validity. Three different forms of validity must be considered: convergent and discriminant validity of constructs and indicators and nomological validity of the entire model (Eriksson, 1998).

External Embeddedness of the Subsidiary

As indicated above, embeddedness is not unidimensional, i.e., a subsidiary can be embedded in one or several dimensions, e.g., in terms of technical development, logistics and/or sales. This makes it difficult to operationalize the concept of embeddedness, since subsidiaries can be embedded in several dimensions. As there are several dimensions of embeddedness and as they do not necessarily have a strong correlation between them, we have to choose one aspect of embeddedness as our measure. In this paper embeddedness is operationalized as technical embeddedness because technical development can be seen to be an extremely important activity for firms' survival.

External technical embeddedness should reflect the value of a business relationship in terms of the subsidiary's capacity to absorb new technology. It is often argued that the development of technology is reflected, above all, in a company's development of new products and/or production processes (see, e.g., Mansfield, 1968). We have therefore chosen the development of products and production processes as our two indicators of external technical embeddedness. As embeddedness also reflects the breadth of the relationship we have used number of different departments involved in each relationship as a third indicator. Together these three indicators mirror both the depth and the breadth of the subsidiary's technical embeddedness. We have fairly reliable data from the subsidiary's own estimation of its degree of adaptation to customers and suppliers and we use this as a proxy for the degree of embeddedness in the subsidiary's relationships. This means that the counterparts' adaptation to the subsidiary is not included in our measurement, which may lead to an underestimation of the subsidiary's degree of embeddedness in its business network. But this problem should not be overstated, since it has been shown elsewhere that adaptation from one side of the relationship is a demonstration of reciprocal commitment and trust (Hallén *et al.,* 1991).

The subsidiary sales and purchasing managers have been asked to assess to what extent the subsidiary has adapted its product and its production technology to a specific relationship with an external customer or supplier. A 5-point Likert-type scale from 1 = 'not at all' to 5 = 'very much' has been used for each indicator. The same managers have also estimated the number of knowledge fields directly involved in each relationship. The answers can vary between 1 and 5 fields of knowledge and correspond to sales, purchasing, production, R & D and subsidiary top management. The higher the number of knowledge fields involved the higher the cognitive capacity in the relationship (Andersson & Dahlqvist, 2000). By simply adding the scores for each of the subsidiary's relationships and then dividing the sum by the number of relationships the subsidiary has, three indicators are created reflecting the average technical embeddedness of the subsidiary's external network. It should also be pointed out that the emphasis has been on the subsidiary's most important product or group of products in the interviews with the subsidiary managers. This means that all questions about business relationships, adaptation, product and production development refer to a specific product or market area rather than to the subsidiary's overall activity. This will certainly increase the relevance of our indicators and should also improve the reliability of the answers given by the subsidiary managers.

Subsidiary Importance for Knowledge Development in the MNC

To receive valid and reliable measures of the subsidiary importance for knowledge development we have used indicators reflecting the subsidiary's importance to its sister units for the development of products and production processes. We have chosen to use the divisional management's recognition of the extent to which each subsidiary is important to its sister units' product and production process development. One benefit of using the divisional management's responses to the questions posed is that it separates them from the responses relating to embeddedness. It also gives the divisional management the opportunity to compare different subsidiaries' contribution to the other units' development. Again, a 5-point Likert type scale has been used (with 1 = very small to 5 = very high).

Intensity in the HQ-subsidiary Relationship

To compose the latent construct intensity in the HQ–subsidiary relationship we have used three indicators, mutual HQ-subsidiary board representation, HQ and subsidiary mutual visiting frequency and time spent by HQ on the specific subsidiary and its activities. To assess the strength of the representation on the board we have asked whether the HQ has any representative on the subsidiary's board and if the subsidiary is represented on the board of the global division. This means that the indicator can take on three different values 0, 1 or 2 depending on whether none, one or the other or both are represented on each other's boards. Visiting frequency is measured as how many times each year representatives from the HQ visits the subsidiary and vice versa. The two scores are added to obtain one measure for visiting frequency. The time HQ spends on each subsidiary is measured by asking how many days during a year the HQ spends on managing the subsidiary and its activities.

To judge convergent and discriminant validity a measurement model where all the constructs and their indicators are included, but in which there are no causal relationships, was estimated. Convergent validity is judged by the R^2-values, measuring the strength of the linear relationships, the t-values, a significance test of each relationship in the model, and the factor loading for each indicator (Jöreskog & Sörbom, 1993).

The constructs in this LISREL model all have good convergent validity, i.e. they are homogenous constructs. As can be seen in Table 15.1, all R^2-values except one are above 0.20, showing strong linear relations between the construct and the indicator (Jöreskog & Sörbom, 1993). However, in the construct intensity of the HQ-subsidiary relationship the indicator mutual representation on boards has a somewhat weaker linear relationship with an R^2-value of 0.18. As this indicator is important from a theoretical point of view, and as it is fairly close to the stipulated 0.20, we decided to let it remain in the construct. The t-values for each indicator are highly significant (lowest t-value 3.65) and the factor loadings are strong. To assess discriminant validity the measurement model tests that only one construct measures a single indicator. Our set of latent constructs exhibited discriminant validity, as the measurement model

Table 15.1: The Constructs and Indicators.

Indicator	Abbre–viation	Factor loading	*t*-value	R^2-value
Subsidiary External Technical Embeddedness				
To what extent has the relationship with this counterpart caused adaptation in the subsidiary's:				
Product development?	PtDev	0.95	8.60	0.89
Production development?	PnDev	0.69	6.47	0.48
Number of fields of knowledge involved in direct contact with people from the counterpart?	KnoFields	0.47	4.46	0.22
Subsidiary Importance for MNC Knowledge Development				
To what extent is this subsidiary important to other divisional units':				
Product development?	ImPtDev	0.82	6.45	0.68
Production development?	ImPnDev	0.68	5.64	0.46
Intensity of the HQ — Subsidiary Relationship				
Mutual representation on Boards	BoRep	0.42	3.65	0.18
Mutual frequency of visits	Visits	0.55	4.53	0.30
Time spent by HQ management on subsidiary activities	Time	0.86	6.13	0.74

demonstrated good fit (Chi^2 was 22.41$_{(df=17)}$ with a *p*-value of 0.12.), while there were no cross-correlation between the constructs.

The next step in the analytical process is to form a structural model by specifying the causal relations in accordance with the four hypotheses. In the following, we test single causal relations with *t*-values and factor loadings between the latent constructs in the model.

Results

By performing repeated iterations, the LISREL analysis advances as the model becomes increasingly fine-tuned and a more coherent representation of the empirical data is reached. Our first step was to test the model with causal relations between the latent construct according to the three hypotheses. This test resulted in a significant model as Chi^2 was $23.80_{(df=17)}$ with a p-value of 0.12. However, whereas both Hypothesis 1b (factor loading $= 0.36$, $t = 2.34$) and Hypothesis 2 (factor loading $= 0.35$, $t = 2.84$) were significant, the relationship hypothesized between the subsidiary external embeddedness and the intensity in the HQ-subsidiary relationship, Hypothesis 1a, was positive although insignificant (factor loading $= 0.19$, $t = 1.45$). The other fit indices, i.e. NFI, NNFI, CFI, GFI and RMSEA, were reasonably good, although the NFI had a somewhat lower value (0.88) compared to the other measures which all were above 0.90. Further, the RMSEA-measure was 0.058 indicating a fair to moderate fit (Browne & Cudeck, 1989).

Thus, the statistical measures indicated that the model-fit could be improved. Therefore, in a second test, we omitted the insignificant relation between external embeddedness and HQ — subsidiary intensity, i.e., Hypothesis 1a. This test resulted in a slightly stronger significance for Hypothesis 1b, i.e. the relation between the intensity of the HQ-subsidiary relationship and the importance of the subsidiary for MNC knowledge development (factor loading $= 0.34$, $t = 2.41$). Hypothesis 2, i.e. the relation between external embeddedness and the importance of the subsidiary for MNC knowledge development was also strengthened (factor loading $= 0.37$, $t = 3.13$). This resulting model, illustrated in Figure 15.2, was significant with a p-value of 0.10 (with $Chi^2 = 25.85_{(df=18)}$).

In conclusion, the results do not support the argument that a subsidiary's external technical embeddedness directly affects the intensity of the HQ-subsidiary relationship and indirectly affects the importance of the subsidiary through the intensity of the HQ-subsidiary relationship. Thus as hypothesis 1a cannot be verified, the design path of external embeddedness is not supported. However, although unrelated to subsidiary external embeddedness, it still seems that the intensity of the HQ-subsidiary relationship affects the importance of the subsidiary for the MNC knowledge development (H1b).

Together, the results imply that the subsidiary's external embeddedness and the intensity in the relationship with the HQ equally explain subsidiary importance for MNC knowledge development. But it seems that the impact of HQ, the design path, stands aloof from the extent to which the subsidiary engages in development processes with actors external to the MNC. Rather, the analysis supports the organic path (hypothesis 2), meaning that subsidiary knowledge development external

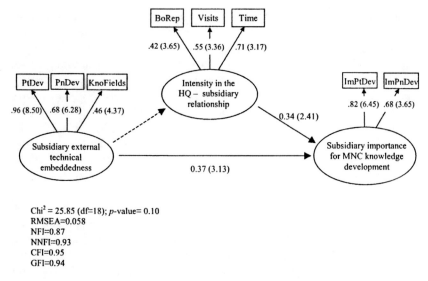

Chi^2 = 25.85 (df=18); *p*-value= 0.10
RMSEA=0.058
NFI=0.87
NNFI=0.93
CFI=0.95
GFI=0.94

Figure 15.2: The Resulting Model.

to the MNC is distributed into the corporate system through autonomous horizontal relationships with sister units.

However, it should be noticed that the RMSEA measure (0.058) of the
received model indicates that further changes in causality could result in
an even better fit between the model and the data (Browne & Cudeck,
1989). Therefore we conducted an explorative procedure and reversed the
causal direction of hypothesis 1b, i.e. the relation between intensity in the
HQ-subsidiary relationship and the subsidiary importance for MNC
knowledge development. This would mean that the subsidiary importance
for MNC knowledge development spurs the intensity in the HQ–subsidiary relationship, rather than vice versa, in combination with subsidiary external embeddedness affecting the subsidiary importance for
MNC knowledge development. In other words, this model proposes that
HQ managers react by intensifying the relationship with the subsidiary
due to the fact that the externally embedded subsidiary has an important
role for knowledge integration in the MNC. The result of this test reveals
an increased *p*-value for the overall model from 0.10 to 0.17. Both relations are significant, with a factor loading of 0.42 and a *t*-value of 3.33
for the relation between subsidiary external embeddedness and subsidiary
importance for MNC knowledge development (H2), and an effect of the

latter on the intensity in the HQ-subsidiary relationship with a factor loading of 0.44 and a t-value of 2.23. The RMSEA is 0.050, which can be considered to be a very good fit (Browne and Cudeck 1989).

This explorative procedure implies that the impact of the organic path plays an important role for MNC knowledge development, not only because of the horizontal integration of the external embeddedness of subsidiaries but also because of HQs' hierarchical integration *vis-à-vis* such subsidiaries. Thus, it seems that the HQ is particularly engaged in creating close relationships with influential subsidiaries.

Concluding Remarks

This paper focuses on the management of the integration of externally embedded subsidiary knowledge in the MNC. Two paths for integration have been analysed: the design path and the organic path. The design path relates to the dominant (traditional) theory in strategic management, which assumes normative integration through hierarchy in the sense that the corporate HQ plays an active role in the integration of knowledge between corporate units. The organic path is, on the other hand, driven by the dependencies that some subsidiaries create vis-à-vis other subsidiaries thereby spurring on the exchange of information and affecting corporate investments in knowledge development in line with these dependencies.

The main conclusion is that subsidiary external embeddedness has a direct impact on the MNC division's knowledge development, supporting hypothesis 2. This is in line with Pfeffer and Salancik (1978) who argue that the subsidiary's ability to control access to external resources produces a dependence situation upon other corporate units. Thus the results support hypotheses 2, the organic path, rather than hypotheses 1a and 1b, i.e., the design path.

The importance of the organic path is strengthened by the result of a further explorative analysis, which implied that the intensity in the HQ-subsidiary relationship is driven by the subsidiary importance for the MNC knowledge development, rather than vice versa. This supports Bartlett and Ghoshal (1989) and Gupta and Govindarajan's (1991) argument that certain subsidiaries will create a more equal and reciprocal relationship with the HQ managers. It seems that a reason for such a development at least partly has to do with the subsidiary's ability to integrate its externally generated knowledge in the MNC. Thus in order to grasp the MNC development it becomes crucial for the HQ to develop intense relationships with those subsidiaries that the HQ managers perceive as being most influential over the corporate knowledge development.

These arguments are consistent with Sune Carlson's seminal study on executive behavior within large corporations (1951). He found that, in meeting with subordinates, the HQ's intention was to get information rather than to take decisions or to give orders or advice. An observation was also that HQ managers tended to spend more time and effort on certain central subordinates to generate information of importance, indicating that HQ managers act by intensifying the contacts with important subsidiaries that already are integrated and somewhat dominant in the corporate system. Therefore, the results in the present study demonstrate that the HQ will develop specific subsidiary relationships beyond the UN-model assumption, i.e. all subsidiaries are treated equally, and the HQ-hierarchical syndrome (Bartlett and Ghoshal 1989), implying that all subsidiaries are not treated as equals. However, it must be stressed that the non-support for hypotheses 1a implies that HQ's lack of knowledge about subsidiary technical development in the external network activities does not trigger an increase in the HQ-subsidiary intensity. It seems that HQ lacks the ability or interest in creating close relationships on the basis of just being externally embedded, although this may be of importance for the technical development of the specific subsidiary. From a geographical and organizational distance, it may be too immense and complicated a task to evaluate each subsidiary's future impact on the MNC long-term development on that basis. Besides, time and resources impose limits on the possibilities HQ has to create intense relationships with more than a limited number of subsidiaries.

The findings are consistent with recent studies on interdependencies in the MNC, which suggest that the superior HQ may stand aloof from the norms, values and interests that develop in the subordinate corporate system (O'Donnell 2000). Rather, it appears that the lateral interdependencies among subordinate units relate to lateral integration of values and norms. Thus, the HQ's attempts to influence the subsidiaries to absorb valuable knowledge across borders seem unlikely or at least problematic. This is particularly the case when the knowledge is highly tacit (Kogut & Zander, 1992) or when the HQ has a vague idea of the subsidiaries' operative roles (Birkinshaw *et al.*, 2000). The complexity of the direct and indirect interdependencies between actors means that the HQ control over the knowledge integration between subsidiaries is limited and HQ is to be considered to be a unit that participates and learns in a similar way as the other corporate units. The role of HQ as a central unit is, in this reasoning, a matter of getting involved in the corporate system of interdependent knowledge flows.

As our analysis disputes the design path it is reason to inquire the role of HQ. It seems that the HQ role is more a matter of keeping up to date with the subsidiaries perceived to be important for the corporate knowledge processes rather than managing the knowledge integration of externally embedded subsidiaries. Perhaps its role is more related to external contacts of importance for the MNC strategic development, inducing acquisitions, joint ventures and dealing with governmental relations etc, than to designing the internal knowledge integration. However, the learning achieved in HQ relevant to the characteristics of the corporation, brought about by creating intense relationships with the most important subsidiaries, is probably crucial for it to be possible to carry out such external strategic development.

References

Allen, T. J. (1977). *Managing the Flow of Technology*. Cambridge, Mass.: MIT Press.

Amit, R. & Schoemaker, P. J. H. (1993). Strategic assets and organizational rent. *Strategic Management Journal, 14*, 33–46.

Andersson, U. (1997). *Subsidiary Network Embeddedness: Integration, Control and Influence in the Multinational Corporation*. Published doctoral dissertation, Department of Business Studies, Uppsala University.

Andersson, U. & Dahlqvist, J. (2000). Business governed product development: knowledge utilization in business relationships. In H. Håkansson & J. Johanson (eds), *Learning in a Business Network Setting*. London: Elsevier.

Andersson, U. & Forsgren, M. (1996). Subsidiary embeddedness and control in the multinational corporation. *International Business Review, 5(5)*, 487–508.

Andersson, U. & Forsgren, M. (2000). In search of centre of excellence: Network embeddedness and subsidiary roles in multinational corporations. *Management International Review, 40(4)*, 329–350.

Andersson, U., Forsgren, M. & Holm, U. (2001). Subsidiary embeddedness, expected performance and competence development in MNCs — a multilevel analysis. *Organization Studies*, forthcoming.

Astley, G. & Zajac, E. (1990). Beyond dyadic exchange: functional interdependence and sub-unit power. *Organization Studies, 11(4)*, 481–501.

Astley, G. & Zajac, E. (1991). Intraorganizational power and organizational design: reconciling rational and coalitional models of organization. *Organization Science, 2(4)*, 399–411.

Axelsson, B. & Easton, G. (1991). *Industrial Networks: A New View of Reality*, London: Routledge.

Bartlett, C. A. & Ghoshal, S. (1986). Tap your subsidiaries for global reach, *Harvard Business Review*, Nov.–Dec., 87–94.

Bartlett, C. A. & Ghoshal, S. (1989). *Managing Across Borders. The Transnational Solution*. Boston: Harvard Business School Press.

Bentler, P. M., (1990). Comparative fit indices in structural models. *Psychological Bulletin*, 107, 238–246.

Bentler, P. M. & Bonett, D. G. (1980). Significance tests and goodness-of-fit in the analysis of covariance structures. *Psychological Bulletin*, 88, 588–606.

Birkinshaw, J., Holm, U., Thilenius, P. *et al.* (2000). Consequences of perception gaps in the headquarters — subsidiary relationship. *International Business Review*, 9(3), 321–344.

Birkinshaw, J. M. & Hood, N. (eds) (1998). *Multinational Corporate Evolution and Subsidiary Development*. London: Macmillan.

Blankenburg Holm, D. & Johanson, J. (1992). Managing network connections in international business, *Scandinavian International Business Review*, 1(1), 5–19.

Bollen, K. A. (1989). *Structural Equations with Latent Variables*. New York: Wiley.

Browne, M. W. & Cudeck, R. (1989). Single sample cross-validation rules for covariance structures. *Multivariate Behavioral Research*, 24, 445–455.

Cantwell, J. (1991). The theory of technological competence and its application to international production. In D. McFetridge (ed.), *Foreign Investment, Technology and Economic Growth*. Calgary: University of Calgary Press.

Carlson, S. (1951). *Executive Behaviour: A Study of the Workload and Working Methods of Managing Directors*, Stockholm: Strömbergs.

Cohen, W. & Levinthal, D. A. (1990). Absorptive capacity: A new perspective on learning and innovation. *Administrative Science Quarterly*, 35, 128–152.

Cook, K. and Emerson, R. M. (1984). Exchange networks and the analysis of complex organizations. *Sociology of Organizations*, 3, 1–30.

Doz, Y. & Prahalad, C. K. (1993). Managing DMNCs: a search for a new paradigm. In S. Ghoshal & D. E. Westney (eds), *Organization Theory and Multinational Corporation*, New York: St. Martins Press.

Egelhoff, W. G. (1988). *Organizing the Multinational Enterprise — An Information-processing Perspective*. Cambridge, Mass.: Ballinger.

Eriksson, K. (1998). *LISREL for Business Analysis*. Department of Business Studies, Uppsala University.

Etemad, H. & Dulude, L. S. (eds) (1986). *Managing the Multinational Subsidiary. Response to Environmental Changes and Host Nations R&D Policies*. London: Croom Helm.

Ford, D. (1997). *Understanding business markets*. London: The Dryden Press.

Forsgren, M. (1989). *Managing the Internationalization Process: The Swedish Case*. London: Routledge.

Forsgren, M., Holm, U. & Johanson, J. (1992). Internationalization of the second degree — the emergence of European-based centres in Swedish international firms. In S. Young (ed.), *Europe and the Multinationals: Issues and Responses for the 1990s*. London: Elgar.

Galbraith, J. (1973). *Designing Complex Organizations*. Reading, Mass.: Addison Wesley.

Galbraith, J. & Edström, A. (1976). International transfer of managers: some important policy implications. *Columbia Journal of World Business*, Summer, 100–112.

Ghoshal, S. & Bartlett, C. A. (1988). Creation, adoption, and diffusion of innovations by subsidiaries of multinational corporations. *Journal of International Business Studies* (Fall), 365–388.

Ghoshal, S. & Bartlett, C. A. (1990). The multinational corporation as an interorganizational network. *Academy of Management Review, 15(4)*, 603–25.

Grabher, G. (1993). Rediscovering the social in the economics of interfirm relations. In G. Grabher (ed.), *The Embedded Firm*. London: Routledge.

Granovetter, M. (1985). Economic action and social structure: The problem of embeddedness. *American Journal of Sociology, 91(3)*, 481–510.

Granovetter, M. (1992). Problems of explanation in economic sociology. In N. Nohria & R. Eccles (eds), *Networks and Organizations: Structure, Form and Action*. Boston: Harvard Business School Press.

Grant, R. (1991). *Contemporary Strategy Analyses: Concepts, Techniques, Application*. Cambridge: Basil Blackwell.

Gupta, A. & Govindarajan, V. (1991). Knowledge flows and the structure of control within multinational corporations. *Academy of Management Review, 16(4)*, 768–792.

Gupta, A. K. & Govindarajan, V. (1994). Organizing for knowledge flows within MNCs. *International Business Review, 4*, 443–457.

Hallén, L., Johanson J. & Nazeem S.-M. (1991). Interfirm adaptations in business relationships. *Journal of Marketing, 55*, 29–37.

Hansen, M. T. (1999). The search-transfer problem: The role of weak ties in sharing knowledge across organization subunits. *Administrative Science Quarterly, 44*, 82–111.

Hedlund, G. (1986). The hypermodern MNC: a heterarchy?. *Human Resource Management, 25(1)*, 9–35.

Hedlund, G. (1993). Assumptions of hierarchy and heterarchy: an application to multinational corporations. In S. Ghoshal & E. Westney (eds), *Organization Theory and the Multinational Corporation*. London: Macmillan.

Hedlund, G. & Åman, P. (1984). *Managing Relationships with Foreign Subsidiaries — Organization and Control in Swedish MNCs*. Stockholm: Sveriges Mekanförbund.

Holm, U., Johanson, J. & Thilenius, P. (1995). HQ knowledge of subsidiary network contexts in the MNC. *International Studies of Management and Organization, 25, 1(2)*, 97–120.

Holm, U. & Pedersen, T. (eds) (2000). *The Emergence and Impact of MNC Centres of Excellence: A Subsidiary Perspective*. London: Macmillan.

Håkansson, H. (1989). *Corporate Technological Behaviour. Cooperation and Networks*. London: Routledge.

Johanson, J. & Mattsson, L.-G. (1987). Internationalization in industry system: A network approach. In N. Hood & J.-E. Vahlne (eds), *Strategies in Global Competition*. London, UK: Routledge.

Johanson, J. & Vahlne, J.-E. (1977). The internationalization process of the firm: a model of knowledge development and increasing market commitments. *Journal of International Business Studies, 8(1)*, 23–32.

Johanson, J. & Vahlne, J.-E. (1990). The mechanisms of internationalization. *International Marketing Review, 7(4)*, 11–24.

Johanson, J. & Wiedersheim-Paul, F. (1975). The internationalization of the firm — four Swedish cases. *Journal of Management Studies, 12(3)*, 305–322.

Jöreskog, K. G. & Sörbom, D. (1993). *LISREL 8: Structural Equation Modelling with the SIMPLIS Command Language*. Hillsdale, N.J.: Lawrence Erlbaum.

Kobrin, S. J. (1991). Is there a relationship between a geocentric mind-set and multinational strategy?. *Journal of International Business Studies, 25*, 493–511.

Kogut, B. (1985). Designing global strategies: profiting from operational flexibility. *Sloan Management Review, 27*, 27–38.

Kogut, B. & Zander, U. (1992). Knowledge of the firm, combinative capabilities and the replication of technology. *Organization Studies, 3*, 383–397.

Kumar, R. & Nti, K. O. (1998). Differential learning and interaction in alliance dynamics: A process and outcome discrepancy model. *Organization Science, 9(3)*, 356–367.

Lane, P. J. & Lubatkin, M. (1998). Relative absorptive capacity and inter-organizational learning. *Strategic Management Journal, 19*, 461–478.

Madhok, A. (1997). Cost, value and foreign market entry mode: The transaction and the firm. *Strategic Management Journal, 18(1)*, 39–61.

Mahoney, J. T. & Pandian, R. J. (1992). The resource-based view within the conversation of strategic marketing. *Strategic Management Journal 13*, June, 363–378.

Makhija, M. V. & Ghanesh, U. (1997). The relationship between control and partner learning in learning-related joint ventures. *Organization Science, 8(5)*, 508–527.

Mansfield, E. (1968). *Industrial research and technological innovation*. NY: W.W. Norton & Company.

Martinez, J. & Jarillo, C. (1989). The evolution of research on coordination mechanisms, in multinational corporations. *Journal of International Business Studies*, Fall, 489–514.

Mowery, D. C., Oxley, J. E. & Silverman, B. S. (1996). Strategic alliances and interfirm knowledge transfer. *Strategic Management Journal, 17*, 77–91.

Nonaka, I. & Takeuchi, H. (1995). *The Knowledge-Creating Company*. New York: Oxford University Press.

O'Donnell, S.W. (2000). Managing foreign subsidiaries: Agents of headquarters, or an interdependent network? *Strategic Management Journal, 21*, 525–548.

Pahlberg, C. (1996). *Subsidiary-Headquarters Relationships in International Business*

Networks. Published doctoral dissertation, Department of Business Studies, Uppsala University.

Peteraf, M. A. (1993). The cornerstones of competitive advantage: a resource-based view. *Strategic Management Journal, 14*, 179–191.

Pfeffer, J. & Salancik, G. R. (1978). *The External Control of Organizations. A Resource Dependence Perspective*. New York: Harper & Row.

Polanyi, K. (1957). *The Great Transformation*. Boston: Beacon Press.

Porter, M. E. (1986). Competition in global industries: a conceptual framework. In M. E. Porter (ed.), *Competition in Global Industries*. Boston: Harvard Business School Press. 15-60.

Prahalad, C. K. & Doz, Y. L. (1987). *The Multinational Mission: Balancing Local Demands and Global Vision*. New York: Free Press.

Satorra, A. & Bentler, P.M. (1994). Corrections to test statistic and standard errors in covariance structure analysis. In A. von Eye & C. C. Clogg, *Analysis of Latent Variables in Developmental Research*. Newbury Park, CA: Sage.

Tanaka, J. S. & Huba, G. J. (1985). A fit index for covariance structural models under arbitrary GLS estimation. *British Journal of Mathematical and Statistical Psychology, 42*, 233–239.

Teece, D. J., Pisano, G. & Shuen (1990). *Firm Capabilities, Resources and the Concept of Strategy. Consortium on Competitiveness & Cooperation*. Working paper no. 90–8, University of California.

Thompson, J. D. (1967). *Organizations in Action*. New York: McGraw-Hill.

Uzzi, B. (1997). Social structure and competition in interfirm networks. The paradox of embeddedness. *Administrative Science Quarterly, 42*, 35–67.

Zukin, S. & Di Maggio, P. J. (eds) (1990). *Structure of Capital*. Cambridge: Cambridge University Press.

Chapter 16

Changing Government Strategy of Multinational Corporations in Transition Countries: The Case of Volvo Truck Corporation in India

Hans Jansson

Introduction

A theoretical framework for analysing MNC strategy towards government in transition countries is proposed. It is based on an institutional approach to strategy and consists of three major parts. In accordance with this approach, the first part deals with the company environment as an external institutional framework and takes up major institutions of importance to this type of MNC strategy. The second part discusses legitimacy as the main rationale behind strategy towards government and identifies three major types of legitimacy relevant for this organizational field. The third part develops MNC strategy towards government by defining and discussing major strategies and heuristics for matching institutional factors. This theoretical framework is applied on Volvo Truck Corporation's strategy towards government in India as an illustration.

Due to the ongoing liberalization and deregulation in transition countries the strategy of multinational corporations (MNC) towards government is changing. This type of strategy is here defined as "government strategy". The increased privatization, deregulation and liberalization of recent years have given companies more space to pursue goals of their own instead of goals being imposed from outside by government, for

Critical Perspectives on Internationalisation, pp. 387–413.

example. This also goes for other groups in society, e.g. other market actors such as customers and suppliers or non-market actors such as political parties and non-governmental organizations. Demands previously canalized through government are more and more replaced by demands from such groups. However, this increasing number of demands on MNCs from various constituents in transition country markets is mainly related to government in one way or another. The wider ramifications of this development revitalize MNC issues that have been dormant for decades, for example the social impact of this increased freedom on host countries, a resurrection of an issue that was much studied and debated in the 1960s and 1970s (see e.g., Dunning, 1993; Jansson, 1982). Since this development changes the role of governments, it also influences MNC strategy towards government. Inter alia, it seems to imply that legitimacy of MNCs in transition countries is changing from being achieved directly from government by following regulations to being more indirect by satisfying the social values and norms represented by various interest groups or by the general public. The foundation for legitimacy is changing. In any case, it becomes more and more clear that MNCs in these countries have responsibilities that go beyond what individual governments require directly. This increased freedom of the MNC makes corporate social responsibility issues vital as well as creating a fear of a backlash against globalisation in many countries from unresolved social issues (World Investment Report, 1999).

Thus, through liberalization MNC environments undergo radical changes, particularly in the emerging markets of transition countries, which makes it interesting to study the strategic behaviour of MNCs in deregulating economies, for example India (Das, 1996; Jansson *et al.,* 1995).

The evaluation of MNCs by other interest groups or stakeholders in these markets increasingly matters for how to gain legitimacy with governments. This is also valid for general types of societal demands not represented by any group, e.g., regarding ethical issues. The common denominator of government demands and these social demands is that they mostly deal with non-business matters, enlarging the scope of MNC strategy by focusing on its wider social environment. An interesting issue, from an international strategic management point of view, is whether the MNC faces another strategic situation regarding these social issues than concerning the more direct business matters. What does MNC strategy look like in an environment of social requirements and expectations?

Government Strategy

The company environment becomes an important strategic issue for government strategy. If the MNC should be able to relate to its complex multilayered and multi-country context in order to achieve legitimacy, the strategy theory needs to be grounded in the environment of the MNC. A larger view of the entire company environment is necessary, since ordinary market-based models are too limited or inadequate. What is especially lacking is how MNC strategy relates to non-economic aspects of its environment. In this article, the MNC environment is defined from an institutional theoretical perspective to consist of institutions or rule-systems, whereas government strategy becomes a matter about how to act towards various groups and in societies characterized by certain values and norms. The strategic perspective is based on the assumption that strategy should match the specific logics prevailing in specific environments. This means that government strategy, which mainly regards the non-business aspects of the environment, cannot be handled according to the business logic prevailing in markets. A social approach to strategy is required, involving a different view on strategy, other ways to analyse the strategic situation and describe strategy. This is accomplished by developing a government strategy framework based on institutional theory. The result is a high-context strategic thinking about MNC government strategy in emerging markets, and where strategy very much becomes a matter of matching the demands of government and related societal groups. This means that the local aspect of international strategy is stressed in this article and not coordination of strategy between different countries (Chou & Cavusgil, 1996; Rugman & Verbeke, 1998; Westney, 1993).

The theoretical framework proposed in this article has been developed within ongoing research about strategy and organization of MNCs in the emerging markets of transition countries, where one main purpose is to find institutionally-based theories for MNCs operating in these markets. The research methodology focuses on case studies of mainly Swedish MNCs operating in East and South Asia as well as in East Europe (Jansson, 2001). The proposed theoretical framework is illustrated with the experience of one of the companies studied, Volvo Truck Corporation's (VTC) production investment in India, which is presented briefly in the appendix. The proposed theoretical framework for MNC strategy towards governments in transition countries is motivated by the fact that this is an under-researched area. There are numerous studies on the impact of MNCs on host countries as well as studies related to corporate social responsibility. But less research has been done about these issues from the point of view of the MNC, particularly regarding the firm's behaviour when being faced by such demands from governments and other groups in transition countries.

The theoretical framework for government strategy consisting of three parts is presented initially. The first part deals with the external company environment and takes up major conditions of importance to government strategy. The second part discusses legitimacy as the main instrumental factor behind government strategy and identifies three major types of legitimacy relevant for government. The third part develops government strategy by defining and discussing major types of matching strategy. Finally, government strategy is illustrated by analysing Volvo Truck Corporation's strategy in India applying the theoretical framework. Finally, conclusions are drawn from this analysis about the usefulness of the theoretical framework for MNC government strategy in the emerging market of a transition country such as India.

The Government Strategic Theoretical Framework

An institutional approach to government strategy is used, which is based on viewing the MNC as an institution (Dunning, 1993; Jansson, 1994b; Whitley, 1992a; Williamson, 1975; 1985; 1991). Strategy is focused on various main heuristics of the organization, implying that strategy is perceived in a broad way, not only being limited to business strategy in markets but also including strategy in other organizational fields, for example towards government. This is a systemic perspective in the way that strategy relates to the particular rules of the social systems in which it is effected (Whittington, 1993). The agency problem is critical in the institutional approach to strategy (Oliver, 1988; 1991; 1997; Tsai & Child 1997; Westney, 1993). Behaviour runs the risk of becoming too deterministic, leaving very little room to organizational discretion. Tsai and Child (1997) introduce a strategic choice perspective into institutional theory and Oliver (1991) somewhat looses the deterministic role of the environment. This is developed further in this article by broadening international strategy beyond the market and by focusing on a wider assortment of strategies based on Oliver (1991) and Mintzberg and Waters (1985). It is also developed how MNCs relate to their external environment, both the interfirm context and the wider context. Institutionalized activities are not only the result of interrelated processes at the individual, organizational and interorganizational levels as in Oliver (1997), but also of processes in organizational fields and societal sectors. This is, e.g., a broader institutional approach to government strategy than found in Murtha and Lenway (1994) or Dunning (1998), and which requires a further specification of the MNC's institutional environment.

Thus, the institutional perspective to strategy implies socially embedded government strategy, which in this article is expressed as a matching strategy. It concerns how the MNC relates to its external environment, dealing directly with the institutions: How to match the values, norms and thought styles of the environment, mainly government, but also systems of property rights and other legal rules such as judicial and penal systems. The state holds a special position, since it participates both as a collective actor, being in direct contact with the MNC, as well as being seen as an external institutional structure, influencing strategy. Other examples of institutions containing values, norms, and thought styles of their own, which might influence MNC strategy towards government, are the educational system, family, clan, religion, country culture system, political system, trade unions, business associations, and business mores.

Institutions

Since institutional frameworks differ between countries, especially between the transition market environment exemplified in this article and developed market economies, the institutional approach takes account of the specific characteristics of the institutional frameworks influencing MNCs. Most MNCs originate within the context of the economic institutions of Western-style capitalism. The effectiveness of carrying over the institutions such a firm represents to quite a different institutional setting depends on the possibilities to match them to those of the domestic institutions of the host country. Institutions are viewed in this article as the rules, procedures, and routines typical of a legitimized social grouping. This rule-like organizational behaviour and the rules behind are defined as institutions and the process regarding how they form, change, and disappear are defined as institutionalization/deinstitutionalization (Jepperson, 1991). Through such basic organizational processes, regular behaviour patterns become ingrained in society leading to a self-activated individual behaviour. These regular activity patterns differ throughout society and therefore society is divided into different social groupings characterized by different regularities or rules. Institutions influence each other. How one part of society is organized affects how other parts are organized.

Scott's (1995) definition of institutions, which integrates different strands of institutional theory, is used to describe three dimensions of institutional content: cognitive, normative and regulative. Ways of thinking and other cognitive patterns within organizations, for example, are not entirely imposed by external institutional factors but are open to multiple interpretations by individual parties (March & Olsen, 1989). Adequate institutional logic or pattern is determined through competition between different individuals, groups, and organizations (Rottenburg, 1996).

The External Institutional Context

To be able to match government demands and other demands in the wider external institutional framework influencing government strategy, it is necessary to make an environmental analysis of these various institutions. The MNC needs to consider the rules prevailing in the market in order to adapt to the behaviour controlled by these rules.

The nature and the grouping of this external institutional context of the MNC is based on Jansson (1994a; 2001), Whitley (1992a; 1992b; 1996), North (1990). MNC strategy is influenced by the rules of the outside institutional world, which is divided into three levels of description or jurisdictions: micro institutions (for example, the MNC), meso institutions (organizational fields), and macro institutions (societal sectors). MNC participates directly in organizational fields, and is influenced by societal sectors. Each institution is characterized by rules of its own. Product/service markets, for example, consist of various organizations such as customers, competitors and suppliers, which share common thought styles, norms and rules. Government consists of ministries and authorities, which share common frames of reference and ways of acting. Government as an organizational field is separated from the political system, which is defined as a societal sector influencing the MNC directly as well as indirectly through the organizational fields. Other essential macro institutions, which are broad ways to organize society, are the legal system, professional and interest associations, business mores (this is the business morale valid when doing business in the country), family/ clan, religion, and country culture. In a country, these meso and macro institutions link to each other in a certain way, creating a specific MNC country environment, organized as an institutional framework.

Major Types of Legitimacy Towards Government

Government strategy is guided and shaped by a quest for legitimacy. Such an acceptance is based on a test or assessment of the actions of the MNC, where ideologies, valuations, and norms are the criteria. From above it is a claim of validity for what one knows is justifiable. From below this claim is justified according to the rules of a certain group expresses as valuations, norms and thought styles. (Cipriani, 1987) To gain legitimacy is a two-way process: the MNC and the actors in its environment are involved in a two-way communication process, claiming and giving legitimacy (Jansson & Sharma, 1993; Jansson *et al.*, 1995; Karlsson, 1991; Kostova & Zaheer, 1999). MNC activities need to be approved by society, e.g., generating income and employment, not polluting the environment or making a contribution in the long run to the development of the country. An organization must prove to the environment its right to exist and therefore it must prove itself beneficial to the society, i.e., it must gain legitimacy. Legitimacy in this sense is externally supplied and externally controlled.

One type of legitimacy is pragmatic (Suchman, 1995) and based on the calculative self-interest of the justifying group. The MNC is supported by government, for example, if it receives some kind of benefits from the existence of the MNC. These benefits can be of an economical, political or ideological nature. Another type of legitimacy is moral (Suchman, 1995) and concerns the impact on society and its welfare at large, where the MNC and its activities are perceived as righteous according to some socially constructed general value and belief system. Legitimacy may be achieved both directly from institutional agents in the organizational field, and indirectly from general values in societal sectors, for example by demonstrating to the stakeholder and/or to the general public that the activities of the MNC in the country take place according to the norms of the stakeholder and/or according to general societal values.

Thus, MNCs may achieve legitimacy directly from different government units or indirectly from other parts of society of importance for gaining legitimacy from government, for example, specific interest groups in the market such as labour unions. Indirect legitimacy might also be claimed through the economic system by being efficient, thereby living up to the values and norms as well as the cognitive structures relevant for the institutional rule complex found in a specific market system. The reason is that in many countries this latter type of legitimacy cannot be taken for granted and is not automatically given, since 'efficiency', due to different values and norms, is interpreted in another way.

Corporate social responsibility is closely related to legitimacy. By demonstrating social responsibility regarding a critical issue for a stakeholder, the MNC could raise its level of legitimacy with this group as well as with government. According to Alkhafaji (1995: 294), there are five key elements among most definitions of corporate social responsibility, e.g., corporations have responsibilities that go beyond the production of goods and services at a profit, they have a broader constituency than just stakeholders, and they serve a wider range of human values than can be captured by sole focus on economics. Corporations can be socially responsible in various types of markets, assist in the building of a social and educational infrastructure, set and raise standards in ethics and quality regarding environmental care, health and safety, and make social investments regarding education, culture, community development and capacity building (Pava & Krausz, 1997; The Prince of Wales Business Leaders Forum, 1998).

By these activities the MNC might raise legitimacy by building reputation and gaining acceptance by governments, communities, and interest groups as well as potentially critical observers. Legitimacy may be achieved by winning the support and commitment of employees, enabling them to contribute to wider civil society, as well as by improving the understanding of local issues, attitudes, culture, and business partners. The MNC strives to achieve legitimacy in various organisational fields and societal sectors, whereas corporate social responsibility is one major way to achieve legitimacy by contributing to the development of society, e.g. in health, infrastructure, education.

In a parliamentary system such as in India, governments are expected to reflect the dominant values and norms that prevail in society. Besides government, legitimacy might also be extended to other stakeholders of relevance to the MNC, legitimacy being defined from the perspective of different stakeholders, interest groups or coalition members of the company. Society is large and complex consisting of several groups and sub-groups with varying norms, values and concepts of what constitutes legitimacy. In this article, these various sources of legitimacy are looked upon from the major stakeholder in society: government. Legitimacy as viewed from government is divided into three main types of legitimacy:

Claim   Justification

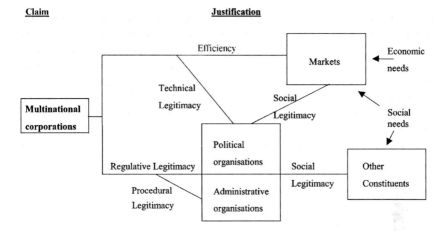

Figure 16.1: Types of MNC Legitimacy Towards Government.

technical legitimacy, regulative legitimacy (including procedural legitimacy), and social legitimacy (see Figure 16.1).

Regulative and Procedural Legitimacy
Host country governments often evaluate MNCs on three main grounds.
The first type of legitimacy is direct and concerns the wider effects of the
market behaviour, e.g. adherence to and respect for host country government laws, rules and regulations, designed to guide, direct, and regulate
the MNC and its operations. This regulative role is mainly the responsibility of the government. This type of more pragmatic legitimacy is
defined as regulative legitimacy. MNCs act politically and learn the rules
of the game and how to gain legitimacy. The priorities of industrial
policy documents, for example, are often public and their content known,
which makes it possible for the MNC to include them in the proposals
submitted to government. Arguments dear to the industrial policy are
highlighted to conform to the letters of the policy. Such conformity to
publicly declared policies increases the chances for getting approvals.
MNCs gain procedural legitimacy from the administrative units by learning the rules and procedures of the bureaucracy and sticking to them.

Technical Legitimacy
The second legitimacy ground is market-based and focuses on the behaviour of companies in markets. This situation, where the company is

evaluated on commercial or technical basis, is defined as technical legitimacy, for example whether MNCs contribute to host country industrial and technological development by improving market efficiency. The efficiency concept is defined as market efficiency, i.e. how efficient companies are operating in markets. This is a value-oriented concept, which is viewed differently by various interest groups in society. Viewed from government, this legitimacy is indirect. It is confined to the economic performance or the efficiency of the firm, which is related to its output and input. This is defined as technical legitimacy, which then connects efficiency and legitimacy. Efficiency is viewed from an outside party, e.g., the government, being the main difference between technical legitimacy and efficiency.

Social Legitimacy
Moreover, in an even wider and more ideological way, efficiency is a societal norm through which such a behaviour is legitimised by society. This is the third ground for legitimacy, which is more moral in kind than the former ones based on administrative rationality or market efficiency. It takes up such aspects as the technological and scientific or rational orientation of the modern welfare state, and concerns the question of the MNC's adaptation to fundamental values and attitudes in society. This third ground concerns how the MNC contributes to the social needs of society. It is a type of moral legitimacy, which is defined as social legitimacy, and which could be expressed through corporate social responsibility.

Matching Strategy

Matching strategy is seen as a main mechanism for relating and joining together in competition internal resources to external environments. It concerns how the MNC responds to changes in the rules of the external framework. Either the MNC is pro-active in relation to the external framework and actively impacts the various rules or acts under their influence, or the strategic response is reactive or passive in relation to the external environment. Matching takes place at three institutional levels: at the micro institutions level, at the meso institutions level, and at the macro institutions level. The basic purpose for matching strategy in markets is efficiency, while the corresponding basic principle in a non-business environment is legitimacy. For government, the matching principle of legitimacy means that the MNC needs to adhere to a number of rules, regulations, values and norms in order to gain, or maintain environmental support. These broad matching principles are generally valid for strategies in these two main types of environments. Since the MNC is active in various countries, it needs to acquire political acceptance by showing respect for national laws and be a good citizen, contributing to national development and economic welfare. In a market environment, however, MNCs gain legitimacy, by being efficient and competitive with regards to production, distribution, and marketing. A majority of the MNC organizations interact with both types of environments, although one type usually predominates. These two major strategic orientations are a further specification of the major organizational fields of technical and institutional environments (Scott, 1983; 1995).

Major Matching Strategies
There are a number of strategies and tactics open to MNCs in matching internal and external institutional frameworks. These are listed in Table 16.1. A strategy is defined as a matching rule, while tactics are defined as decision patterns or heuristics relevant for a specific matching strategy. The pro-active strategies are presented at the top of the table, with the activity of the strategic agent decreasing more and more further down the table, and with the passive strategies and tactics found at the bottom.

According to this table, which is mainly based on Oliver (1991), MNCs could match their external framework in various ways. At one extreme, the MNC is pro-active and is leading the environment, for example through setting quality or environmental standards, which might be imitated by the competitors. By innovating, the MNC through its own actions create the ability to generate change in the external institutional framework, for example when instituting a new industry standard or a new standard for protection of the environment. The rapidly changing world of today puts specific demands on the MNC resources, mainly of flexibility and of being able to quickly concentrate activities to certain projects and areas.

In another more active strategic response, the MNC tries to manipulate constituents of the external framework by coopting, influencing and controlling them, for example, when the MNC wants to replicate its existing rules and routines to the new external environment. These are strategic behaviours that organizations enact in response to pressures towards conformity with the institutional environment (Oliver, 1991).

Table 16.1: Matching Strategies and Heuristics.

Strategies	Heuristics	Examples
Innovate	Generate change	Developing a new product development routine
	Move fast	Creating flexible capabilities and organizational controls
Manipulate	Co-opt	Importing influential constituents
	Influence	Shaping values and criteria
	Control	Dominating institutional constituents and processes
Defy	Dismiss	Ignoring explicit norms and values
	Challenge	Contesting rules and requirements
	Attack	Assaulting the sources of institutional pressure
Avoid	Conceal	Disguising nonconformity
	Buffer	Loosening institutional attachments
	Escape	Changing goals, activities, or domains
Compromise	Balance	Balancing the expectations of multiple constituents
	Pacify	Placating and accommodating institutional elements
	Bargain	Negotiating with institutional stakeholders
	Habit	Compromise
	Pacify	Placating and accommodating institutional elements
Habit	Habit	Following invisible, taken-for-granted norms
	Compromise	
	Pacify	Placating and accommodating institutional elements
Acquiesce	Imitate	Mimicking institutional models
	Comply	Obeying rules and accepting norms

Source: Oliver (1991)

However, a MNC may also replicate a strategy developed elsewhere without even thinking about the necessity to manipulate the environment. This passive strategy of acquiescence is discussed below. The matching strategies of defy, avoid and compromise have ingredients of both an active and passive choice behaviour. A way to neutralize an institutional demand is to co-opt the source of pressure, for example employing officials from government units that is critical to the survival of the MNC. Another option is to try to influence the source, e.g., a government unit, or control it by dominating the institutional constituents and processes. How this will succeed depends upon the bargaining power of the parties. The use of bargaining power may, however, deteriorate the quality of the relationship and even put an end to the relationship. Defying is the other possible matching strategy in such a conflict prone situation. A strong MNC is not susceptible to external pressure and may dismiss government demands by ignoring explicit norms and values. It could also challenge government by contesting rules and requirements or even attack by assaulting the sources of institutional pressure. This could happen, when government tries to force a MNC to relocalize its activities to an area, which would make the company to lose in competitiveness. If the MNC's bargaining position is low, 'avoid' might be a conceivable strategy, for example by disguising nonconformity ('conceal') or 'escape' by changing goals, activities, domains or even country. One heuristic relevant for "avoid" is buffering, where the MNC decouples a part of its organization from the rest of the organization with the purpose to protect it from certain environmental pressures, for example the manufacturing unit in order to stabilize it and increase productivity. In escaping, the MNC could change domain by leaving one country for another, for example depending upon pollution control rules that are too costly to match. When a MNC is confronted with conflicting institutional demands, for example between customer demand for low-priced products and expensive demands for environmentally-safe products, the MNC could compromise between these demands, for example by an heuristic characterized by balancing the expectations of multiple constituents. Another tactic would be to pacify, that is to partially conform to or accommodate one of these institutional elements. A third heuristic is to negotiate or bargain with these institutional stakeholders.

The strategic response of a passive MNC accepting the prevailing rules of the external institutional framework without protest is called "acquiesce", and for which three heuristics are possible. According to the "habit" heuristic, the MNC is not aware of that it matches any pressures from outside, but blindly internalizes taken-for-granted rules and values. Imitation could also take place unconsciously, but not necessarily so, for example of other MNC's successful strategies. When complying, however, the MNC knows what it is doing, for example when incorporating external values, norms, and institutional requirements in its strategy.

Government Strategy Illustrated: The Case of Volvo Truck Corporation in India

Regulative Legitimacy

Regulative legitimacy is achieved by following the rules and regulations of Union and State governments, as well as by following the procedures of the administrative bodies, for example when applying for approvals and when getting products through customs. However, due to the fact that more and more of these regulations have been taken away due to liberalization, the importance of this type of legitimacy has been reduced. This is especially true at the Union government level, while most regulations are kept at the State government level. One remaining problem for VTC at the central level concerns the rules for how money is transferred in and out of India, especially when VTC India wants to remit profits to the Group as pay-back for the initial investment. Since the government monitors these transfers, VTC has to negotiate the terms for how this will be done.

Technical and Social Legitimacy

Technical and social legitimacy are mainly achieved indirectly through organizational fields. The study indicates that their importance increases, while the importance of regulative legitimacy decreases. It is therefore interesting to look closer at how this indirect legitimacy is achieved through the organizational fields.

Product/Service Markets
Before Volvo Truck Corporation's entry, the Indian truck-market was dominated by two major domestic producers. Competition was low with slow or passive research and development efforts, which made product quality and standards not very technologically advanced. VTC's establishment on the Indian market exposes the customers to modern truck technology and standards. One indirect effect of this might be an increase in technical legitimacy. New values and norms are brought into the truck-industry, and where VTC acts as one of the engines in the government's wish to change routines and increase competition in the market. Social legitimacy might also be influenced. As VTC's trucks are more environmentally friendly than competitors' trucks, VTC's customers are

educated, e.g. about how emission levels can be reduced. This might in the future result in a demand for higher environmental standards by the Indian truck manufacturers. However, at present, it is not possible to sell trucks on environmental friendliness, since customers are not yet willing to pay for this feature. However, attitudes are slowly changing and with more VTC trucks on the roads, the environmental issues will increase in importance among customers.

To meet local regulations and get legitimacy, it is important to buy locally manufactured products. Before 1991, MNCs had to follow import restrictions imposed by the central government in Delhi (Jansson, 1982). With most of these rules now abolished, and high tariffs still kept, market efficiency in the Indian market and in world markets has become more important. Because of the low technology and quality levels of the Indian truck industry, local suppliers have to be upgraded to international product standards, i.e., these standards being matched to VTC's. Key suppliers are assisted in developing quality awareness, cost orientation, and logistics to increase delivery security. These efforts are part of a current drive towards reaching international levels of quality with ISO awards, etc. Being a global player, the MNC has the same quality and technology requirements for suppliers in India as on other markets. Through this development initiative, VTC raises the technical legitimacy with the Union and State governments by being able to source parts locally, which is a pre-requisite for operating in the Indian market due to the high imports tariffs.

Labour Markets
Legitimacy was improved by employing mostly locals, whereas VTC gained both technical and social legitimacy from the government through the labour market. VTC intends to further "Indianize" the company by gradually replacing expatriates with Indians. The job opportunities created and the local economic improvements generated by VTC's establishment in Bangalore are other factors, which increase VTC's legitimacy with the state government.

VTC has also created a base for achieving regulative legitimacy in the labour market by adjusting to the general rules and regulations prevailing there, but do not participate in the formulation of new routines to the same extent as in the product/service market. The government's control of the labour market is more strict and regulated. Even if VTC mainly complies with institutional elements, labour groups and other groups in society are also influenced by the values and standards promoted by the

MNC, which could influence social legitimacy. Thus, labour is not only an economic input but also involves various social needs. Corporate social responsibility, in this field, is therefore related to how the company takes care of its employees, e.g. providing appropriate facilities. Interviews with VTC staff at the factory in Hosakote indicated that they were satisfied and proud of their facilities at the plant. VTC has emphasised the importance of having a stimulating working environment, e.g. with modern and well-kept premises with many green areas, a well-run canteen, and a factory with low noise levels and modern equipment with high safety standards. Moreover, by contributing with more money than mandatory to the employees pension funds, VTC assists in improving the employees' social security. The wage rate for many workers is also above the industry average.

The Local Community
VTC is promoting local community development by supporting some voluntary welfare projects, e.g., the building of a new road in a local village; the vaccination of locals; the set up of a small local clinic; the provision of eye-check facilities; and the managing director participating in charity for a hospital. These initiatives are contributing in creating a positive image of VTC, thus enhancing its social legitimacy.

When VTC established the plant in Hosakote, this small community outside Bangalore was obviously affected. The local people had no major previous experience from having a MNC operating there. VTC needed land to build the plant and this resulted in some farmers having to sell their land. According to the law, landowners cannot refuse to sell the land but can refuse a price offer. However, they have to come to an agreement after negotiations with a local government authority and the MNC. In the negotiations, VTC agreed to pay a good price and to hire some locals for the plant, preference was given to locals with the right skills. These actions were taken in order to pacify the "disturbance" created by VTC to the locals.

There is a risk of conflict when a MNC brings Western thought styles to a developing country such as India. If the MNC does not consider local customs, history, culture, tribe structures, religion and caste, the MNC might unconsciously irritate and offend the locals, creating a negative attitude towards the MNC in the local community. VTC was aware of most of these potential areas of conflict and therefore adopted a very open-minded and respectful approach towards the local community in Hosakote in order to balance the different demands. For instance, at some occasions, the local tribe leaders were consulted regarding employment of tribe-members in order to avoid conflicts due to caste. Although respecting the local culture, VTC keep international values at the plant, e.g., no employee is hindered to become a manager due to low caste. There is a balance in the mix of the local traditions and values and the MNC's core values and norms of behaviour. The study demonstrates that VTC seems to have achieved this balance, thus far.

The General Public
As it is still difficult to sell trucks on environmental issues, VTC mostly communicate their environmental friendliness to the Indian media. By proving itself as influencing Indian societal norms, values, and thought styles, legitimacy is improved with the general public and indirectly with government.

Social legitimacy is achieved by influencing social standards. An example of this is the introduction of VTC's core values of quality, safety and environment, which are relatively new to the Indian market. For instance, VTC is introducing its "environmental" technologies, e.g., with the aim to reduce pollution and noise levels. When VTC brings these new values to the market, new standards will be set for the whole truck industry, hence creating benefits for society in general, e.g. less emissions, lower noise levels and decreasing congestion. Moreover, safety, another of VTC's core values, has become increasingly important in the automotive industry, e.g., drivers' safety. Moreover, the gradual improvements in quality and other standards in the Indian truck industry will in the long run provide new opportunities for domestic producers to export their products to , e.g., other Asian markets.

Professional and Interest Organizations
In order to influence government policies and decisions at State and Federal levels, it has become increasingly important to be a member of at least one strong and influential industry association. There are many industry and professional organizations as well as major industry families fighting for government's attention. Volvo Truck became a member of the Confederation of Indian Industry (CII) early in the establishment stage and has nurtured this relationship since then. VTC India's managing director is currently the vice-chairman of CII in Bangalore, which makes it possible to influence its activities and agenda.

Through these associations governments are influenced according to VTC interests in order to increase legitimacy. This has become more important with the changing attitudes of politicians, who now seek assistance from leading industry associations and leaders. This is creating more of a cooperative situation between the associations and governments, which also makes it easier for VTC to approach the government officials by itself and have a constructive dialogue rather than one characterized by suspicion and mistrust.

Technical Legitimacy Summarized

VTC gained a high level of technical legitimacy in India as they transferred state-of-the art technology and introduced many new concepts to the products/service market in India. Moreover, VTC's trucks were of a much higher quality than the Indian manufacturers' trucks. The gap between VTC and domestic producers was huge. Many state governments realized the benefits of having VTC in their state and therefore approached them in the early phases of VTC's project. VTC finally chose Karnataka State, which is promoting the automotive industry, trying to attract many automotive manufacturers. As VTC introduced top of the range trucks they might also contribute to raise the quality level and the efficiency of the whole truck industry as Indian customers now begin to demand the same quality levels from the domestic producers. This effect was expected by Karnataka State, and hence it increased VTC's technical legitimacy with this state government.

Technical legitimacy also seems to be achieved in the labour market by a contribution to its efficiency. This is mainly accomplished by complying with institutional elements at the same time as labour groups and other groups in society are also influenced by the values and standards promoted by the MNC. On financial markets technical legitimacy is obtained by conforming to prevailing rules.

Social Legitimacy Summarized

For VTC, social legitimacy was increased by improving corporate social responsibility, which in the labour field was related to how the company takes care of its employees, e.g. providing appropriate facilities. VTC is also demonstrating social responsibility and thereby winning social legitimacy by promoting local community development by supporting welfare projects. There seems to be a new development of Indian society putting demands on MNCs to assume more responsibility for certain parts of the society such as health issues, infrastructure and the general welfare of people. By fulfilling such demands the MNC justifies its operations to the society. This implies that corporate social responsibility is becoming increasingly important for MNCs operating in India, since this raises the level of legitimacy from many sectors of society. Demonstrating such a responsibility becomes a major way to achieve legitimacy, whereas it becomes a strategic objective for the MNC both from a legitimacy and efficiency perspective. Such a social responsibility based objective mainly becomes a specification of moral legitimacy. It specifies that a MNC contributes to the development of society, not solely creating job opportunities but other contributions too, e.g., in health, infrastructure, education etc.

VTC's Matching Strategy Towards Governments in India

At any time period, interaction between MNCs and various governments can be characterized to be high or low along two main dimensions: the extent of cooperation and competition (Jansson *et al.,* 1995). When analysing the matching strategy of VTC, the relation with the Karnataka State government today is characterized by high cooperation and low competition. Previously, the competitive content of European companies' relationship was higher than presently. A consensus strategy was used, which is characterized by high cooperation and high competition. This changing environmental situation of increased deregulation is also changing matching strategy: from more competitive-orientated strategies of defiance and avoidance to a less competitive one such as compromising. VTC still has to adjust and follow government rules and regulations, but there is more room for negotiations. This is one effect of the liberalization, where both the attitudes of the Union and State governments towards MNCs have changed. This changing situation makes the domination relationship of low cooperation and high competition less relevant for India, while the peripheral relationship could be more relevant in the future, if the liberalization process continues. This peripheral situation of low cooperation and low competition is typical when MNCs do not have to deal with governments very much and therefore can concentrate on the business or efficiency aspects. VTC was the first foreign MNC in the automotive sector that was allowed a 100 percent foreign equity owned subsidiary in India. This illustrates how attractive VTC's investment was to the Indian government and the change of government attitude. VTC as a global truck manufacturer has a legitimate position in the eyes of the State and Central government, and which was used in various ways during the establishment process in India. For example, VTC received incentives from Karnataka State in the form of sales tax exemption and immunity from any new taxes imposed on them in the future. Moreover, the state built a new substation for power supply and laid a completely new fibre-optic cable to Bangalore (40 km from the plant). These are examples of how important Karnataka State believed the establishment of VTC's plant was for the region, the industry and the local community.

Thus, VTC cooperates by compromising. The MNC is very much adjusting and working according to the codes of conduct existing in India. As analysed above, VTC gained legitimacy with government in a number of ways. VTC has been transparent in their operations in India, inter alia to reduce the suspiciousness regarding VTC's plans and intentions, and to create a trustful relationship. This is necessary in a cooperative matching strategy. An example of the good relationship is the fact that VTC has immediate access to government officials and one official is appointed special 'personal' contact. If the MNC has any problems with low-level bureaucrats, who are demanding 'favours', e.g., VTC can approach a higher level official to have the matter resolved. The degree of cooperation is high as both parties are to gain from the relationship. From a government point of view, VTC brings high technology, creates new jobs, raises quality standards etc. Moreover, VTC share their knowledge on environmental issues, creating a debate, which the government advocates. From VTC's perspective, a good relation with the government means they can more easily cope with the Indian bureaucracy and focusing on operating efficiently.

VTC also proved their commitment to the Indian market by introducing their latest models and technology. This manipulation of organizational fields by raising standards contributed to attainment of legitimacy from the government, which makes it easier to promote the own interest in the compromising strategy when balancing the expectations of multiple constituents, mainly by accommodating institutional elements and negotiating with stakeholders. A high legitimacy also improves VTC's efficiency, since the State government, for example, looks upon VTC as an asset and will assist in providing the right conditions for the company. VTC, on the other hand will be able to concentrate on its core activities. Still conflicts between efficiency and legitimacy occur as exemplified by the inspections made at the local factory. VTC's daily work in India is sometimes interrupted by state government officials' visits, the so-called "Inspector Raj", to the plant in Hosakote. The officials come to monitor that VTC operations comply with existing rules and regulations, e.g., labour protection laws. At these visits, VTC must present all the relevant information to the official and with several VTC managers attending the meetings. These types of government activities result in VTC managers "wasting" time on these issues instead of concentrating on the crucial issues of, e.g., operating the plant efficiently. Thus, VTC's efficiency is somewhat distorted due to these government interventions. Previously, these visits were not always announced in advance and were often frequent, but today most visits are scheduled and the number of visits has decreased.

Conclusions

Legitimacy with governments is gained indirectly in various organizational fields by matching the norms, values, and thought styles of these fields. New norms and values are brought into the Indian truck industry by VTC, which seems to be influencing prevailing standards both on the customer and supplier side, for example regarding product quality and pollution. Since these new standards create benefits for the society at large, e.g., less emissions, lower noise levels, and decreasing congestion, they are also relevant for groups outside the product/service market, that is the general public, whereas they become general social standards. Therefore, VTC communicates their environmental friendliness to the Indian media, in that way influencing different stakeholders, and also achieving legitimacy for the activities in India. Professional and interest groups are part of this government strategy. To be able to manipulate stakeholders, the MNC needs to have developed standards of its own. In VTC's case, government strategy is based on its core values regarding quality, safety and environmental concern. This strategy gives VTC legitimacy within these organizational fields, with the general public, and finally with government. VTC is even seen by the government as a role model for other manufacturers within the truck industry. Setting yourself up as a role model can be interpreted as being part of the manipulation strategy. This also demonstrates the close relationship between government strategy and strategy in markets. It highlights the importance for coordinating these strategies in order for them to support each other in the best possible way.

In the other major organizational fields are found more passive matching strategies. VTC can sometimes choose between various rule systems as illustrated with the varying investment incentives from different states. It is also not always clear what the rules are. In the labour market and the local community, VTC compromises by partly conforming to external pressures and by partly promoting its own interest, for example through negotiating with institutional stakeholders. The possibilities to manipulate internal rules for the employees are greater than the external rules. In the former case, this is seen as a control heuristic, while it is, in the latter case, a matter of a mix of placating and accommodating institutional elements. Even if VTC mainly complies with these external rules, labour unions and other groups in society are also influenced by the standards promoted internally, for example, competence and objectivity in selection processes; working conditions at the factory; and wage rates. These strategies demonstrate various ways to achieve legitimacy within an organisational field and indirectly with government. It also shows the importance of corporate social responsibility as part of the government strategy to achieve legitimacy. VTC has also demonstrated social responsibility by participating in local community development activities by investing in infrastructure, for example, a new road in a local village, and social investments, for example in a clinic. This is done to placate local constituents. But the foreign direct investment of VTC also affects certain other constituents of the local community negatively, for example in buying land for the plant, and its Western thought styles conflicting with local village culture, for example institutionalized in the caste system. This is a typical compromise strategy, where the MNC tries to balance the expectations of multiple constituents.

The matching strategy of compromise is also applied by VTC towards the Federal and States governments in India in order to achieve regulative legitimacy. The MNC adjusts and works according to the rules and codes of conduct that exist in India at the same time as the company promotes its own core values. All the three heuristics relevant for this strategy are followed in the balancing of expectations of multiple constituents, mainly by accommodating institutional elements and negotiating with stakeholders. This matching strategy takes place within a relationship structure characterized by high cooperation and low competition between MNCs and government. This means that the previous situation of high cooperation and high competition is changing. European companies were earlier using a consensus strategy, as the competitive content of the relationship was higher than presently (Jansson *et al.,*

1995). This changing environmental situation is also changing matching strategy: from more competitive-oriented strategies of defiance and avoidance to a less competitive one such as 'compromise'. VTC still has to adjust to and follow government rules and regulations, but there is more room for negotiations. This is one effect of liberalization, which has changed the attitudes of both the Union and State governments towards MNCs. This changing situation makes the domination relationship type of low cooperation and high competition less relevant for India, while the peripheral type of low cooperation and low competition might be relevant in the future, if the liberalization process continues and really frees the markets.

There is a close relationship between matching strategy and legitimacy. A main objective of the matching strategy is to improve legitimacy at the same time as a high legitimacy makes it easier to achieve the intended results of the matching strategy. Legitimacy improves the position of the own interest and makes it easier to promote it. VTC gained technical legitimacy in India by improving market efficiency, for example through the transfer of state-of-the-art technology and the introduction of new concepts on the product/service market. It was also achieved on the labour market by a contribution to its efficiency. Regulative and procedural legitimacy is achieved by following the rules and regulations of Union and State governments, as well as by following the procedures of the administrative bodies, for example when applying for approvals and when getting products through customs. As clearly demonstrated by this study, liberalization has rather much changed how to achieve legitimacy compared to the pre-liberalization period before 1991. Social legitimacy is closely related to social responsibility and was mainly gained according to the activities in the labour market and community development activities.

Appendix

Volvo Truck Corporation — A Brief Presentation[1]
Volvo Truck Corporation (VTC) is one of the leading manufacturers of heavy-duty trucks in the world. Today, VTC is a global player with 23,000 employees and production units in ten countries spread all over the world, and with sales on more than 120 markets. In the last couple of years, VTC generated an increase in sales and in 1998 they sold 83,300

---

[1] This summary of VTC builds on Björckebaum and Säle (2000).

trucks. The MNC has long experience within the industry, as their truck operations began already in 1928. Volvo's core values of quality, safety and environmental concern are cornerstones in all operations the company undertakes.

VTC is trying to strengthen the international position even further by investing in big emerging markets such as Eastern Europe, India and China. In June 1998, VTC established a production unit in Bangalore, India. The MNC set up a 100 percent foreign equity owned subsidiary, since the local manufacturers were not perceived suitable for a joint venture. This was the first wholly owned subsidiary set up by a foreign MNC in the Indian automotive sector. Afterwards, other foreign MNCs, e.g. Hyundai, were allowed to do the same. The Volvo factory in Hosakote (outside Bangalore) was built in 13 months, which was seen as a record even by Volvo standards. The initial investment was US$ 80 million. The factory has a capacity of producing 4000 vehicles per annum, while 250 vehicles were manufactured in 1999. Volvo Truck India has 200 blue-collar workers and 100 white-collar workers. Among these, approximately ten are Europeans, while the rest are native Indians.

Volvo Truck India is developing a vendor programme for global sourcing, which aims at exporting parts from India to other manufacturing units in Asia, since costs for production are lower in India. Quality certification is increasing in the truck industry and Volvo follows this development in accordance with their quality commitment.

The most successful trucks produced in India are tractor-trailers and multi-axle heavy trucks. VTC mainly focuses on long-haul trucks (2000–2500 km) but also plans to move into light vehicle segments. Volvo Truck India emphasises their focus on the service and after market. This is also done in order to "avoid breakdowns and reduce operating costs". The Volvo truck is three times as expensive as an Indian truck. Volvo Truck India tries to win market shares by providing the customers with state-of-the-art-technology and giving their customers the ability to make goods transportation more economical and efficient. The major competitors in the Indian market are TATA, Ashok Leyland and some European manufacturers who formed joint ventures with local manufacturers.

Volvo Truck India has focused its presence on the Western parts of India and does not have as many service shops as their competitors, as the reliability of their trucks is much higher, and the high technical skills required repairing and maintaining their trucks. In order to ensure maintenance availability and to expose the Volvo brand, service shops were established even before the first truck had been sold.

References

Alkhafaji, A. F. (1995). *Competitive Global Management: Principles and Strategies.* Lucie Press.

Björckebaum, P. & Säle, P. (2000). *A Swedish MNC's Government Strategy in India. A Case Study of Volvo Truck Corporation.* Masters Thesis in International Business, Graduate Business School, School of Economics and Commercial Law, Göteborg University.

Cipriani, R. (1987). The Sociology of legitimation: an introduction. *Current Sociology, 35(2)* 1–20.

Das, R. (1996). Deregulation and liberalization in India: The managerial response. *Journal of General Management, 21(3),* 48–58.

Dunning, J. H. (1993). *Multinational Enterprises and the Global Economy.* Reading Mass.: Addison-Wesley.

Dunning, J. H. (1998). *The Changing Nature of Firms and Governments in a Knowledge-based Globalizing Economy.* Working Paper No. 98.007, Rutgers University, Graduate School of Management.

Iyer, G. R. (1997). Comparative marketing: An interdisciplinary framework for institutional analysis. *Journal of International Business Studies, 28(3),* 531–561.

Jansson, H. (1982). *Interfirm Linkages in a Developing Economy. The Case of Swedish Firms in India.* Acta Universitatis Upsaliensis, Studia Oeconomiae Negotiorum 14, Uppsala.

Jansson, H. (1994a). *Industrial Products. A Guide to the International Marketing Economics Model.* New York: International Business Press (Haworth Press).

Jansson, H. (1994b). *Transnational corporations in Southeast Asia. An institutional approach to industrial organization.* Aldershot: Edward Elgar.

Jansson, H. (2001). *International Strategic Management in Emerging Markets. Global Institutions and Networks.* Book Manuscript, Department of Business Administration, School of Economics and Commercial Law, Göteborg University.

Jansson, H., Saqib, M. & Sharma, D. D. (1995). *The State and Transnational Corporations. A Network Approach to Industrial Policy in India.* Aldershot: Edward Elgar.

Jansson, H. & Sharma, D. D. (1993). Industrial policy liberalization and TNCs: The Indian experience. *Scandinavian Journal of Management, 9,* 129–143.

Jepperson, R. L. (1991). Institutions, institutional effects, and institutionalism. In W. W. Powell & P. J. DiMaggio (eds), *The New Institutionalism in Organizational Analysis.* Chicago: The University of Chicago Press.

Karlsson, A. (1991). *Om Strategi och Legitimitet — en Studie av Legitimitets Problematiken i Förbindelse med Strategisk Förändring i Organisationer.* Lund: Lund University Press.

Kostova, T. & Zaheer, S. (1999). Organizational legitimacy under conditions of complexity: The case of the multinational enterprise. *Academy of Management Review, 24(1),* 64–81.

March, J. G. & Olsen J. P. (1989). *Rediscovering Institutions.* New York: The Free Press.

Mintzberg, H. & Waters, J. A. (1985). Of strategies, deliberate and emergent. *Strategic Management Journal, 6,* 257–272.

Murtha, T. P. & Lenway, S. A. (1994). Country capabilities and the strategic state: How national political institutions affect multinational corporations' strategies. *Strategic Management Journal, 15,* 113–129.

North, D. C. (1990). *Institutions, Institutional Change and Economic Performance.* Cambridge: Cambridge University Press.

Oliver, C. (1988). The collective strategy framework: an application to competing predictions of isomorphism. *Administrative Science Quarterly, 33,* 543–561.

Oliver, C. (1991). Strategic responses to institutional processes. *Academy of Management Review, 16(1),* 145–179.

Oliver, C. (1997). Sustainable competitive advantage: Combining institutional and resource-based views. *Strategic Management Journal, 18(9),* 697–713.

Pava, M. L. & Krausz, J. (1997). Criteria for evaluating the legitimacy of corporate social responsibility. *Journal of Business Ethics, 16,* 337–347.

The Prince of Wales business leaders forum, responsible business in the global economy. (1998). *Financial Times Guide Number One.*

Rottenburg, R. (1996). When organization travels: On intercultural translation. In B. Czarniawska & G. Sevón (eds), *Translating Organizational Change.* Berlin: Walter de Gruyter.

Rugman, A. M. & Verbeke, A. (1998). Corporate strategy and international environmental policy. *Journal of International Business Studies, 29(4),* 819–834.

Scott, W. R. (1983). The organization of environments: network, cultural, and historical elements. In J. W. Meyer & W. R. Scott, (eds), *Organizational Environments. Ritual and Rationality.* Beverly Hills: Sage.

Scott, W. R. (1995). *Institutions and Organizations.* Thousand Oaks, Cal.: Sage.

Suchman, M. C. (1995). Managing legitimacy: Strategic and institutional approaches. *Academy of Management Review, 20(3),* 571–610.

Tsai, S-H. T. & Child, J. (1997). Strategic responses of multinational corporations to environmental demands. *Journal of General Management, 23(1),* 1–22.

Westney, E. (1993). Institutionalization theory and the multinational enterprise. In S. Ghoshal & D. E. Westney (eds), *Organization Theory and the Multinational Corporation.* New York: St. Martin's Press.

Whitley, R. (ed.) (1992a). *Business Systems in East Asia: Firms, Markets and Societies.* London: Sage.

Whitley, R. (ed) (1992b). *European Business Systems. Firms and Markets in their National Contexts.* London: Sage.

Whitley, R. (1996). The social construction of economic actors. Institutions and types of firm in Europe and other market economies. In R. Whitley & P. Hull

Kristensen (eds), *The Changing European Firm. Limits to Convergence.* London: Routledge.

Williamson, O. E. (1975). *Markets and Hierarchies.* New York: The Free Press.

Williamson, O. E. (1985). *The Economic Institutions of Capitalism.* New York: The Free Press.

Williamson, O. E. (1991). Comparative economic organization: The analysis of structural alternatives. *Administrative Science Quarterly, 36(2),* 69–96.

World Investment Report (1999). *Foreign Direct Investment and the Challenge of Development.* Geneva:

United Nations, UNCTAD.

Chapter 17

Spatial Determinants on Export Marketing Activity in Marshallian Districts: An Investigation of the Danish Furniture Industry

Poul Houman Andersen

Introduction

To what extent do local industrial environments influence the export marketing activities of firms? This issue have gained increasing momentum in political as well as in academic circles. Diverse strands of economic and managerial thought have noted the importance of availability of supplementary resources in local environments for international activities. Regional economics has reflected on the specific economic characteristics of local environments as a distinctive international competitive advantage of associated firms (Christensen & Lindmark, 1993; Maskell, 1996; Porter & Sölvell, 1998; Storper, 1997). Entrepreneurship researchers see the local socio-economic texture as important for understanding the international market expansion of newly established manager-owned firms (Christensen, 1991; Johannison, 1988). Also, students of comparative advantage and of competitive theory regard locally embedded resources as important for international expansion (Porter, 1990).

Even in an increasingly globalising world, local economies remain important. According to some observers, economic forces of globalisation ascribe more significance to unique "locational" attributes as an element for deriving differentiated competitive advantage in the global

Critical Perspectives on Internationalisation, pp. 415–436.
Copyright © 2002 by Elsevier Science Ltd.
All rights of reproduction in any form reserved.
ISBN: 0-08-044035-5

marketplace (Amin & Thrift, 1994). However, despite an ongoing interest in this subject only few attempts have been made to investigate empirically the impact of regional conditions on the export activity of firms. Empirical research has repeatedly been called for (Christensen & Lindmark, 1993; Ried, 1983).

From the view of contemporary internationalisation theory, the role of local contexts presents an interesting challenge. Internationalisation theory has hitherto considered mainly the role of resources internal to the firm as important drivers for understanding the international expansion patterns of firms. However, in recent years, several approaches, which focus on the role of external resource access has come to the fore (Bell, 1995; Chetty & Holm, 2000; Coviello & Munro, 1997; Johnsen & Johnsen, 1999; Snell & Lau, 1994).

The purpose of the present contribution is to add to the body of knowledge concerning the important issue of local milieu. Socio-economic mechanisms of various kinds are expected to exist on the local level due to the socially embedded character of economic relationships in such areas. More precisely we will investigate whether and, if confirmed, why and how economic facets of the local environment may affect the organization of export marketing activities in Danish firms belonging to industrial districts. The paper is structured as follows. First, the proposed significance of the local environment is identified through a literature survey. Then, the export collaboration among SMEs as a special case of committing external resources to internationalisation of the single firm is outlined. What are the economic mechanisms associated with local business environments and how are they believed to support export activities? Based on this overview, a set of propositions and a research strategy are developed. Next, the propositions are tested, using data from the Danish furniture industry. In the concluding chapter, academic as well as political implications and implications for business are debated.

Industrial and Technological Districts and International Business: An Overview

For some time now, international business researchers have noticed the territorial clustering of firms within the same or within functionally related industries as important feature of internationally competitive industries. Local industrial districts or clusters are described in dimensions of economic space such as industrial activities, actors and territory

(Amin & Thrift, 1994; Dalum, 1995; Storper, 1995). Industrial districts are seen as thresholds of international competitive advantage, created through agglomeration of knowledge, skills, learning and experience (Dunning, 1998, Porter, 1998).

The virtues of geographical proximity have been discussed under various headlines. The concept of industrial districts has been (mis?)used to describe an eclectic smattering of industrial networks, including Silicon Valley (Saxenian, 1991), producers of apparel goods in northern Italy (Brusco, 1982; Lazerson, 1993) and Japanese producers of electronics and cars (Fujita & Ishi, 1998). These examples of "districts" include networks of technically interdependent firms, both small and large, which may or may not be agglomerated in physical space. Hence, the concept of industrial districts is in need of some clarification and further conceptual development. Storper & Harrison, (1991) provide a seminal contribution in this respect. In order to define and classify various forms of production systems they develop a vocabulary, including the concept of input-output systems, production units and governance structures.

An input-output system is a collection of activity bundles, which lead up to the production of a specific marketable output. The input-output system may be decomposed into production units, which denote a physically integrated set of activities occurring at a single location. Normally, input-output system will consist of more than one production unit, the propensity depending on whether such activities are subjected to internal and external economies of scale and scope. Hence in cases of external economies of scale and scope, network-like input-output systems prevail, whereas strong internal economies of scale and scope favour the emergence of integrated producers.

As a proceeding step in the development of a classification scheme for various production systems, the authors include the territorial dimension of production. Principally, network-like input-output systems may be dispersed over wide territories without any geographical core or they may be agglomerated. Hence, on the basis of these dimensions a classification of network-based input-output systems can be developed. Applying the dimensions of territoriality and internal and external economies of scale and scope, a scheme of input-output systems can be obtained (Figure 17.1).

In the present context, the most interesting part of Figure 17.1 is found in the bottom half of the figure. Here, we find a scheme for classifying the different types of industrial networks, all characterized by the presence of external economies of scale and scope.

Internal economies of scale and scope

		Weak	Strong
External economies of scale and scope	**Weak**	I. Isolated Workshops (Dina's Beauty Parlour)	II. Process Producers (British Petrol)
	Strong — *Territorial Dispersion*	III. Dispersed Network Production Mostly small units (Lamp producers)	IV. Dispersed Network Production Some large units (Wind Turbine producers)
	Territorial Agglomeration	V. Agglomerated Network Production Mostly small units (Italian Fashion wear)	VI. Agglomerated Network Production Some large units (Toyota City)

"Marshallian" District

Figure 17.1: Types of Input-output Systems — Developed from Storper
and Harrison (1991).

The type of industrial networks described by type three may be found among small and medium-sized producers, where physical space is less problematic in relation to for instance external economies of scale and scope, for instance where product technology interfaces may be relatively standardized. This is the case among lamp producers, which collaborate internationally on the development of new designs. The network identified in cell four, is one where both internal and external economies may be present. For instance, in the case of Danish wind turbine producers, historically present external economies of scale and scope are largely being supplemented and in some cases even replaced by internal economies of scale and scope, as the production technology matures. Moreover, although the wind turbine industry primarily is located in Jutland, Denmark, a number of critical suppliers are located in other regions of Scandinavia (Karnøe, 1995).

Industrial districts, characterized by both internal and external economies of scale and scope, combined with territorial agglomeration are present in the Japanese production system. For instance, Toyota City is an example of first and second-tier suppliers closely located to the "parent" company, Toyota Motors (Dicken, 1992).

The following discussion will focus on type five, which is the closest equivalent to the "Marshallian" industrial district type. It may serve as a convenient denominator as it (despite some other definitions) includes both geographical and functional vectors in its dimensioning of economic space (Brusco, 1982; Pedersen, 1994; Storper & Harrison, 1991). Compared to other types of input-output systems in the Storper-Harrison scheme, Marshallian districts mainly consist of spatially close firms in the same broad industrial sector with both competing and complementary interests and limited internal economies of scale and scope on the firm level. This also means the absence of large producers which may act as configuring the export activities of the industrial district, as in the case of the stainless steel district in the Kolding area in Denmark (Christensen & Phillipsen, 1997).

Different accounts can be found, but industrial district economists broadly agree that both technical and spatial proximity contributes to the locational effects in economic space, although they may not be fully characterised by a technical or geographical boundary. Locational effects to international competitive advantage are considered as powerful and as somewhat neglected in dominating theories of international competitiveness (Krugman, 1991; Lundvall, 1985; Porter, 1990). Broadly, three classes of external economic effects of scale and scope connected to spatial clustering can be identified:

1) Agglomeration effects;
2) Transaction cost minimization effects;
3) Flexibility, learning and innovation effects.

First, concentration of local rivals in Marshallian districts gives rise to external economies of scale, including specialized suppliers, services, labour markets and other types of factor endowments, created by agglomeration of industrial activity (Best, 1990; Krugman, 1991; Piore & Sabel, 1984; Porter, 1994; 1996). This means that SMEs may be able to reap advantages of scale and scope, which previously were restricted to the vertically integrated mass producer (Vatne, 1995). Local organizations, which provide specialized services may arise in favour of the local firms, export activities. The notion of the importance of the specialized labour market as pool of external economies of scale and scope is central in the concept of industrial districts.

Second, local surroundings promote economic cooperation and trust by embedding economic relations in a wider web of spatial relations, which clearly define and sanction acceptable and unacceptable forms of economic behaviour (Curran & Blackburn, 1994; Dei Ottati, 1994). These mechanisms lower transaction costs, and support the availability of venture capital (Christensen & Lindmark, 1993; Kristensen, 1996). Third, locally vested interaction of firms greatly favours the development of a shared grammar or technical language, which may support configurational flexibility as well as innovation and learning among participating firms (Lundvall, 1988; Maskell, 1996). Habitual patterns for inter-firm coordination and configuration of various activities arise from repeated interaction and mutual learning. These features may provide distinct competitive advantage to localized firm networks as compared to other forms of industrial organization. In the place of the large, vertically integrated business, reaping advantages of scale, but which is slow to respond to rapidly changing world market conditions, industrial districts emerge. Such districts are composed of networking firms, which collectively reap the economies of speed and variety needed to cope effectively with volatile market conditions (Best, 1990; Pyke, 1992). The general assumption is that globalisation has led to deepened inter-firm specialization and division of labour. Hence, firm export skills may not necessarily be present within the single firm as export from industrial districts to a growing extent depends on critical capabilities and contacts held by local but external specialists.

Collaborative International Marketing in Industrial Districts: the Case of SMEs

The role of industrial districts to SMEs[1] has been advanced as a particularly interesting avenue to explore, as districts may provide complementary assistance especially to firms with lack of internal resources or capabilities for going international. A distinctive feature of SMEs, which has been identified repeatedly in the business literature, is their limited resource base. Especially in relation to international business the lack of resources has been characterized as a central problem of SMEs. A survey of the literature in this field concluded *"The most common hypothesis is that large companies have size-related advantages that enable them more efficiently in export"* (Aaby & Slater, 1989) Industrial economists of dif-

---

[1] How to demarcate SMEs from larger firms is an often-debated issue and definitions vary from country to country, depending on statistical conventions. In Denmark, SMEs are typically defined as below 100 employees, which is the definition employed here.

ferent sorts have seen market imperfections as impediments of SME internationalisation. Universal consumer norms, removal of trade barriers and shortening product life cycles are among the numerous factors contributing to economies of scale and scope in large-scale operations, tossing the competitive balance unfavourably for SMEs (Douglas & Craig, 1989; Levitt, 1983; Ohmae, 1982).

A second, but related argument against SME internationalisation has been the lack of managerial resources and the perceived greater risks of international operations among SME managers. As the perception of risk is associated with lack of information, the lack of resources for market investigation is expected to expose particularly SME managers to high-risk perceptions associated with international marketing activities. Moreover, the share of total resources invested in the international operations is greater in SMEs as compared to large enterprises, making larger firms less risk averse (Nooteboom, 1989). Thus, research in export behaviour and the internationalisation of firms have seen both the propensity of being an exporting firm and the intensity of exports as positively correlated to size by a number of researchers, although with contradicting empirical findings (see Madsen, 1989 for an excellent overview of empirical findings).

However, an increasing bulk of empirical research in the internationalisation of SMEs has countered the dense relationship between size and export intensity (Bonaccorsi, 1992; Czinkota & Johnston, 1983). This has lead to a questioning of whether SMEs follow the similar rationale as large firms in their international operations (Andersen & Christensen, 1999; Andersen & Kristensen, 1999; Bell, 1995). Whereas the establishment of large companies suggest an increasing internalisation along with growing exports, it has been suggested, that SMEs to a large extent depend on their collaboration with co-specialised and external resources in the conduct of their export activities (Andersen, 1995). Hence, SMEs collaborate with foreign intermediaries; sharing operation costs or developing product programmes on specific export markets (Andersen, 1995; Petersen, 1996). Also, exporting SMEs have a higher propensity for working together with subcontractors than other firms do (Bonaccorsi, 1992). Moreover, SMEs may collaborate with competitors in order to achieve economics of speed and variety (Best, 1990; Storper & Saias, 1997).

Although the co-alignment of external resources with internal skills holds some prosperous possibilities for the SME it also raises a number of questions. Valuable resources are rare and sharing them with business partners comes at a risk. What are the mechanisms allowing SMEs to coordinate and configure export activities together with other firms? The socio-economic mechanisms suggested to be a central feature of locally agglomerated economies might hold a part of this answer. In the following we will discuss the advantages but also the mechanisms allowing for SMEs embedded in industrial districts to access and direct external local resources in favour of their export activities.

The Influences of Industrial Districts on SME Export Activities: Some Propositions

So far, we have focussed on Marshallian districts as a form of industrial organization, which may hold merits in terms of international competitive advantage. From the perspective of the individual SME, belonging to an industrial district provides a number of strategic benefits. SMEs within a district have larger operational latitude as they can mix and match internal and external resources to a greater extent that outsiders. However, supply side conditions, how favourable they may be, are not automatically activated in support of the firm. The utilization of local economic resource endowments depends on the ability of management to configure and coordinate relevant actors in favour of export activities. In the following a number of ways for utilizing local resources in favour of export activities are outlined.

Contributions to studies of export marketing behaviour traditionally have focused on the internal determinants affecting export propensity and intensity. A crucial discussion has concerned the link between export behaviour and the availability of firm resources. Firm size has been seen as a convenient approximation of internal resources (Bonaccorsi, 1992). However, the ability to detect a positive correlation between the export propensity (do firms have export yes/no?) And the export intensity (usually measured as the degree of export turnover to total turnover) has been weak (see Madsen, 1989 for a useful overview of these contributions). Although these findings have not discouraged all, an increasing number of scholars have realized that the international market expansion of the firm should not be seen only in the light of its horizontal position in a chain of value added. It must also be related to its vertical position and the interface between internal and external resources and capabilities (Christensen, 1991; Vatne, 1995). A large, cross-sectional study of the Italian manufacturing sector revealed a partial support for the hypothesis, that small firms (measured in number of employees) are less likely to initiate exports than their larger counterparts. However, the study also revealed that significant differences only occurred when firm sizes were particularly small. Size effects seemed to level off, when the size class exceeds 20 persons full-time employed, suggesting that critical mass is reached already at the micro-level (Bonaccorsi, 1992). Bonaccorsi also suggests the integration of external resources as an important contribution to the current export research, while Ried (1983) scolds traditional models of export behaviour for the lack of context specificity.

Hence, researchers have started to include external resources, such as the firms' access to external economies as part of their functional or territorial position (Christensen, 1991). Recent contributions describe processes of international expansion involving external resources through metaphors such as linking (Fletcher, 1995) and networking (Coviello & Munro, 1997) seeing these perspectives as challenges to more established views (Bell, 1995).Recent developments in the international business conditions have increased attention on the coupling between internal and external resources as determinant of export activities. First, economic volatility created by interdependent forces of cyclical crises in the accumulation of capital and the accelerating pace of technological change demands flexible responses from international as well as domestic oriented firms. Second, improvements in production and information technology have improved the economies of product customerization, thus decreasing the critical mass of scale economies in a number of industries. Last but not least, the globalisation of markets have led to new market expansion opportunities, but also to increased competitive pressure, and the pursuit for marshalling complementary, external resources in favour of export activities.

In these new economic realities, the paradigm of industrial mass-production and the economic rationale associated with it are challenged by economic rationales pertaining to speed and variety (Storper & Saias, 1997). These business conditions are expected to favour especially SMEs vested in local networks for a number of reasons.

Higher risks follow from the instability of economic conditions, and with this transaction costs are expected to increase. Variations in demand and customerized configuration of goods counteracts economies of scale and increases the vertical division of labour in industry as well as the demand for semi-specific assets (Vatne, 1995; Piore & Sabel, 1984).

Several suggestions have been made concerning how territorial proximity supports the development of firms' export activities. The factors promoting trust and exchange of information in the local area may provide easier access to complementary resources for the local firm, which can be mobilized in international market expansion (Christensen & Lindmark, 1993). Moreover, findings have shown that firms may draw upon the collective experience of other firms during their initial export experiences (Bonaccorsi, 1992). Thus it can be proposed, that:

Proposition$_{1a}$:   SMEs in industrial districts are more likely to initiate exports than SMEs in general

Proposition$_{1b}$:   SMEs in industrial districts are likely to have a higher export intensity than SMEs in general

More specifically, a number of areas can be suggested where local SMEs likely may cooperate with each other. One area may concern the organization of export activities. Export activities are often resource demanding in terms of initial investments and transaction costs. Even non-investments form of export organization may call for high monitoring costs (Anderson & Gatignon, 1986). The single firm may not have the necessary critical mass in terms of export turnover. Developing an export sales organization with complementary and even rival firms may therefore be an option for achieving scale economies, which would not be reached individually. Also, firms may entertain various forms of piggybacking arrangements in order to divide various forms of fixed costs in export marketing (Terpstra & Wu, 1990). These could include financing, travel expenses, and other forms of costs. Hence, it can be proposed that

Proposition$_2$:   SMEs in industrial districts are more likely to engage in collaboration regarding other forms of export activity with other firms than SMEs in general

Collaboration may also include international marketing activities, where complementary and even rival firms may co-invest in export market promotion activities. Some anecdotal evidence can be found in support of this proposition. For instance locally recruited supplier associations may jointly promote a certain region in order to attract potential customers (Andersen & Christensen, 1998). In a number of cases, local clusters of firms choose to collaborate on developing an export marketing campaign. For instance, Scottish Whiskey producers join efforts in order to promote the qualities of Scottish Whiskey abroad (Enright, 1998). Other examples include sharing of expenses relating to trade fair participation, distribution of promotion material, etc.

Proposition₃: SMEs in industrial districts are likely to collaborate on export promotion activities than SMEs in general

Also, because of inter-firm collaboration and the existing of highly efficient organizing grammars supporting complex patterns of coordination, industrial districts are expected to support flexible specialization. The patterns of flexible specialization allow the SME to compete on delivery times and entertain product ranges and product adaptation abilities beyond the internal capabilities of the individual firm. Thus by engaging in a flexible and fine-grained division of labour, the district adds systemic value to each participant which is able to draw on a collaborative and flexible production capacity. This also means, that markets can be entered and left without incurring specific investments, allowing the small firm the ability to react on limited export and/or risky market possibilities (Bonaccorsi, 1992). Studies have shown, that accessibility to local advanced users has a positive impact on export market potential (Maskell, 1996).

Proposition₄: SMEs in industrial districts collaborate on export product adaptation and development more frequently than SMEs in general

An essential barrier to internationalisation is the lack of information on international market prospects. Incomplete or lack of information on foreign business opportunities hinders risk-aversive decision makers in considering these market alternatives in sufficient detail. Several investigations have shown, that lack of export information constitutes a major barrier for international expansion (Cavusgil, 1984). Local districts are referred to as information-rich and tapping into the local information sources in order to reach valuable information on export markets may be an important virtue of industrial districts. Thus, it can be proposed:

Proposition₅: SMEs in industrial districts are more likely to exchange market information with other firms than SMEs in general

Data and Methodology

In order to test the propositions, survey data was gathered on Danish furniture producers. The Danish furniture industry is highly export-oriented, yielding an export specialization figure between three and five for the past three decades. The industrial branch is a significant part of the Danish industry, employing approximately eight percent of the workforce in ten percent of the Danish industrial firms. More than 2900 firms are registered as furniture producers, and most of these firms are SMEs. According to the Danish Statistical bureau, less than two percent of the furniture producers have more than 100 employed.[2] Danish furniture is well known for high quality standards and innovative design, and a substantial part of the industrial output is handcrafted. In this sense, the industry has many similarities with the Italian fashion wear industry, which is also known for artisan traditions and significantly high export rates.

Using a commercial database as sampling frame, 617 furniture producers with five employees or more were identified. This criterion was chosen to improve response rates and to weed out those addresses, which did not represent business activities. The larger firms (more than 20 employees) were contacted telephonically prior to sending out the questionnaire, in order to identify a contact person, which could be addressed directly. Participating firms were promised anonymity (although their identity was known to the researcher) and a report of the research results. Two waves (one initial wave and a follow-up wave three weeks later) yielded a formal response rate of 43.7 percent. However, several of the respondents turned out not to be furniture producers, returned a blank questionnaire or stated that they were not interested in participating in the investigation. Hence, the effective response rate was 34.5 percent, or 207 respondents, which is above average for industry questionnaires. Comparing responses to industry data on size and turnover distribution show a fairly good representation of the underlying population in the sample.

The methodology applied here is one of comparing means and standard deviations for district versus non-district firms. Thus, a central task in developing this research strategy is identifying a district and delimiting it from the rest of the population. The furniture district of the Salling area was used in the present study. More than one sixth of all Danish

---

[2] This figure is a bit higher in reality, as the Danish Statistical Bureau uses the number of firm registrations as their nominal base. The same firm makes some firm registrations or entrepreneurs who are planning to establish a business of for reasons such as tax deduction benefits find it feasible to maintain a registration. If weeded out, the actual number of furniture producers would drop and the average size of producers (in terms of person employed) would increase.

furniture producers are found within this relatively small area of western Jutland. Its existence has been fairly well documented in several investigations (Kristensen, 1996; Lorenzen, 1999; Maskell & Malmberg, 1995) and is confirmed by the Danish Association of Furniture Producers, which organizes more than 90 percent of all active Danish furniture producers. These rather anecdotal accounts of the prevalence of this district were followed up by an agglomeration analysis on the postal code area level. This analysis shows that the postal code areas central and nearby the Salling Peninsula are specialized in furniture production both relatively (as compared to their share of total Danish industry) and absolutely (as compared to their total share of Danish furniture producers). The area was delimited using travel-to-work distances as a criterion for spatial demarcation of the district, using the Salling Peninsula as the centre of the circle. Thus, postal codes that are found either within this area or, where more than half of the area is included under the auspices of the circle have been assigned to the district. The propositions have been operationalised, as shown in Appendix A.

Proposition 1a concerned the relationship between localization of firms and the propensity to export. Here, it was proposed, that because of the generally supportive texture of local districts, small and medium-sized firms would have a higher propensity to export as compared to SMEs outside these areas. This proposition is rejected by the results of the statistical analysis (Chi-square: 0.13). The results show (as expected), that a large number of SMEs in the sample holds export activities, both in- and outside the district (84.2 percent inside and 67.5 percent outside).

Although proposition 1a is rejected by the present sample, the role of districts in supporting especially small enterprises still is to be tested. In an Italian context, much similar to the present, Bonaccorsi (1992) suggests that size effects to export propensity levels off at a relatively modest level of employees (the size of 20 persons employed). However, in the present sample, the sub-group of firms from the Salling area with employees below 20 is too small to test statistically.

In a similar line of reasoning than the relating to proposition 1a, the following proposition 1b suggests Marshallian effects on the export intensity of all firms. One-way ANOVA test was used for investigating this proposition. The results are displayed below in Table 17.1 (left side).

Testing proposition 1b show, that the average export intensity of SME exporters within the Salling area is higher than the mean of exporters outside the area. The ANOVA procedure is fluctuating around the 0.05 rejection level of the H0-hypothesis, offering some support to proposition

Table 17.1: Marshallian Effects to Export Intensity.

		SMEs			All firms, irrespective of size		
		Mean Square	F	Sig.	Mean Square	F	Sig.
1998 Export in %	Between groups	3679,3	3,63	.056	8882,4	9,6	***.002
	Within groups		984,5			929,7	
1997 Export in %	Between groups	3675,3	3,71	*.054	8698,5	9,4	***.003
	Within groups	987,8			922,5		
1996 Export in %	Between groups	3679,4	3,74	.059	9116,7	3,7	***.002
	Within groups	984,5			938,0		

* Significant at the .05-level   *** Significant at the .005-level

1b. Hence is a fairly strong association between industrial district affiliation and export intensity. This confirms the assumed Marshallian effects to SMEs export performance. However, the association is much stronger when the test includes all furniture producers, irrespective of size. Here, the H0 hypothesis is rejected. Hence, it can be said that Marshallian effects to export intensity affects all firms, irrespective of size, as shown in the right side of Table 17.1.

Overall, the results are mixed with respect to the proposed hypotheses two to five, as shown in Table 17.2. Albeit SMEs located in the industrial district are more orientated toward collaboration on export marketing than those outside the industrial district, they mainly choose their collaboration partners from outside this area. Hence, only 10 percent of the firms collaborating in the district choose to collaborate with other firms from their district, whereas 75 percent of the partners are found in other areas of Denmark and 15 percent are international partners.

The collaborative orientation on sales activities, i.e., to develop shared product lines or otherwise is clearly stronger within the Salling district, confirming proposition four (significant at the 0.01-level). As this form of cooperative activity is the most resource demanding and most complex in

Table 17.2: Export Collaboration and District Affiliation among SMEs.

Degree of Collaboration on:	Location in Salling	N	Mean Rank	Z	Asymp. Sig. (2-tailed)
Other activities	Yes	16	76,19	−2.024	*.043
	No	108	60,47		
	Total	124			
Promotion	Yes	16	76,56	−1.868	.062
	No	108	60,42		
	Total	124			
Export sales	Yes	16	81,59	−2.690	**.007
	No	108	59,67		
	Total	124			
Information exchange	Yes	16	68,81	−.816	0.415
	No	108	61,56		
	Total	124			

* Significance at the .05-level;   ** Significance at the .01-level

terms of inter-firm coordination, this is perhaps the strongest evidence for the role of Marshallian effects in export collaboration. Information exchange, on the other hand may be characterized as least demanding activity type in the bundle of export collaboration activities discussed here. Even though the mean rank is somewhat higher within the district than outside, the null-hypothesis is not rejected. Therefore, proposition five cannot be confirmed by the present data. Proposition three suggest that collaboration on export promotion are more frequently found among firms in industrial districts. Although the test value is close to rejecting the null-hypothesis (0.062), significant differences between the two populations are not found. However, for the last question on export collaboration activities: Other activities, there is significant differences between firms inside the district as compared to outside firms. Therefore, proposition two is confirmed by the data.

This pattern poses an interesting issue for debate: How come that there are persistent behavioural differences among those firms belonging to the district as compared to firms outside the district? Some tentative explanations may be outlined. One may be that firms in districts collaborate on a host of other dimensions that export, which may lead them to look for partners for collaboration outside the district in order to avoid too strong patterns of similarity. Hence, one would look for complementarity rather than similarity in collaboration in order to avoid rivalry in export market activities. Another and corresponding reason for seeking collaborative partners outside the district may be the "Nashville effect", suggesting that reputation accrues more valuable outside the district than inside as potential partners associates certain virtues with the affiliation of particular locales (Scott, 1999).[3] For the single firm, affiliation with a district is comparable to a brand, associated with a specific reputational capital. Because of this, firms in the Salling area are presumably able to attract and maintain more attractive collaborative partners outside the district than inside.

Concluding Remarks and Directions for Future Work

The role of industrial districts in the export activities of firms is an important topic in the political debate. Export is an important contribution to the creation and sustainment of wealth in the industrialized part of the world. SMEs have contributed to job creation. They are an essential part of the resource support structure utilized by larger firms. They form the hotbed from which the large enterprises of the future are developed. The internationalisation of SMEs ranks high on the agenda world wide of industrial policy makers, and great resources have been issued in support programs, favouring the initiation, development and sustainment of SMEs. At the same time, the theoretical perspective that sees industrial districts as a socio-economic texture of resources locally available is part of a novel approach to the analysis of SMEs international activities.

In general, the notion of Marshallian effects on export collaboration is supported. Both SMEs and larger firms are benefiting from their local affiliation in terms of export intensity. Moreover, small and medium-sized furniture producers in industrial districts holds specific behavioural patterns in terms of export collaboration activities compared to small- and medium-sized furniture producers in general. The study showed, that in the furniture industry, SMEs in industrial districts more frequently join forces with other firms concerning export sales and other firms of export

---

[3] I am indebted to Dr Timothy Clark for pointing out this idea.

activities. In addition, they tend to collaborate more frequently on export promotion activities, albeit this is not statistically significant at the .05-level. However, the study also showed that the underlying logic of collaboration is not as straightforward as suggested in the theory of inter-firm collaboration in industrial districts, the socio-economic links often hailed as a distinguishing mark of industrial districts may not be as obviously linked to inter-firm collaboration as suggested.

Seen from the perspective of academia these results are both encouraging and challenging to the ongoing increasing interest in economic geography among international business scholars. Location *does* matter, and further research on the role of geography to patterns of trade, internationalisation and foreign direct investments seems promising. Also, from the perspective of internationalisation theory, the results provide support to the notion of local resources as important for collaboration.

Also, from a political perspective, the geographical dimension of business may lead to a stronger and better-differentiated industrial policy. Especially in programmes channelling support to SMEs, the role of districts may help in formulating new programmes better fitted to the realities of small business. Hence, studies attempting to investigate the role of industrial districts in marshalling export collaboration in other industrial branches are called for.

Finally, from the perspective of business managers, co-location means co-operation as well as competition. The results presented here points at the importance of a supporting texture of other firms. However, much is still to be taken into consideration, such as to what extent this texture is accessible for the outside firm. These are all questions still waiting to an answer through future research efforts. Moreover, the results produced here needs to be further validated through the study of export collaboration in other industrial districts and in other industrial branches.

Appendix

An Overview of Propositions, Operationalization Measures and Measurement Scale Used[4]

Proposition	Operationalization	Scale
1a: SMEs in industrial districts are more likely to initiate exports than SMEs in general	Do you export? yes/no	Nominal
1b: SMEs in industrial districts are likely to have a higher export ratio than SMEs in general	How did your export develop over the past three accounting years (in percent of total turnover)	Ratio
2: SMEs in industrial districts are more likely to engage in collaboration regarding other forms of export activity with other firms than SMEs in general	Do your firm collaborate (or did it collaborate within the past three years) with other local firms concerning other forms of export marketing activities not mentioned here?	Ordinal
3: SMEs in industrial districts are more likely to collaborate on export promotion activities than firms in general	Do your firm collaborate (or did it collaborate within the past three years)with other local firms concerning export marketing (shared material, shared trade fair participation, shared distribution of promotional material, other)	Ordinal
4: SMEs in industrial districts collaborate on export product adaptation and development more frequently than SMEs in general	Do your firm collaborate (or did it collaborate within the past three years) with other local firms concerning the development of shared package deals to foreign customers or export intermediaries	Ordinal
5: SMEs in industrial districts are more likely to exchange market information with other firms than SMEs in general	Do your firm exchange (or did it exchange within the past three years) export information with other local firms?	Ordinal

[4] As can be seen from Table 17.1, both ordinal-scaled and ratio-scaled data are found, calling for a mixture of analytical techniques, in order to employ the most powerful techniques in each case. Chi-square analysis is utilised testing prop 1a, whereas one-way Anova is used for prop 1b. Props two to five are tested using the Mann-Whitney rank testing procedure for statistical analysis.

References

Aaby, N. E. & Slater, C. (1989). Management influences on export performance: a review of the empirical literature, 1978-88. *International Marketing Review, 6(4)*, 7–26.

Amin, A. & Thrift, N. (1994). Living in the global. In A. Amin & N. Thrift (eds), *Globalization, Institutions and Regional Development in Europe*. Oxford University Press.

Andersen, P. H. (1995). *Collaborative Internationalisation of SMEs — Their Participation in the International Division of Labour*. Copenhagen: DJØF Publishing.

Andersen, P. H. & Christensen, P. R. (1998). *Den Globale Udfordring: Danske Underleverandørers Internationalisering (The Global Challenge: The Internationalization of Danish Subcontractors)*. Copenhagen: Erhvervsfremme Styrelsens Notatserie, Erhvervsministeriets Forlag.

Andersen, P. H. & Christensen, P. R. (1999). Internationalization in loosely coupled business systems: the Danish case. In P. Karnøe, P. H. Kristensen & P. H. Andersen, (eds), *Mobilizing Resources and Generating Competencies*. Copenhagen: Copenhagen Business School Press

Andersen, P. H. & Kristensen, P. H. (1999). The systemic qualities of Danish industrialism. In P. Karnøe, P. H. Kristensen & P. H. Andersen, *Mobilizing Resources and Generating Competencies*. Copenhagen: Copenhagen Business School Press.

Anderson, E & Gatignon, H. (1986). Modes of foreign entry: a transaction cost analysis and propositions. *Journal of International Business Studies, 17(3)*, 1–26.

Bell, J. (1995). The internationalization of small computer software firms — a further challenge to the "stage" theories. *European Journal of Marketing, 29(8)*, 60–75.

Best, M. H. (1990). *The New Competition: Institutions of Industrial Restructuring*. Polity Press.

Bonaccorsi, A. (1992). On the relationship between firm size and export intensity. *Journal of International Business Studies, 23(4)*, 605–635.

Brusco, S. (1982). The Emillian model: productive decentralization and social integration. *Cambridge Journal of Economics, 6*, 167–184.

Chetty, S. & Holm, D. B. (2000). Internationalization of small to medium-sized manufacturing firms: a network approach. *International Business Review, 9*, 77–93.

Christensen, P. R. (1991). The small and medium-sized exporters' squeeze: empirical evidence and model reflections. *Entrepreneurship and Regional Development, 3*, 49–65.

Christensen, P. R. & Lindmark, L. (1993). Location and internationalization of small firms. In L. Lundquist & L. O. Persson (eds), *Visions and Strategies in European Integration: A North European perspective*. Berlin: Springer Verlag.

Christensen, P. R., Phillipsen, K. & Toftild, L. (1997). *Localized or Global Config-uration of International Supply Chains? The Evolution of a Stainless Steel District in Denmark*. Working paper presented at the DRUID theme B workshop, Kolding.

Conover, W. J. (1980). *Practical Nonparametric Statistics*, (2nd ed.). New York: John Wiley & Sons.

Coviello, N. & Munro, H. (1997). Network relationships and the internationalization process of small software firms. *International Business Review, 6(4)*, 361–386.

Curran, J. & Blackburn, R. (1994). *Small Firms and Local Economic Networks: The Death of the Local Economy?* London: Paul Chapman Publishing.

Czinkota, M. R, & Johnston, W. J. (1983). Exporting: Does sales volume make a difference?. *Journal of International Business Studies, 14*, (Spring/Summer), 147–153.

Dalum, B. (1995). Local and global linkages — the radiocommunications cluster in northern Denmark. *Journal of Industry Studies, 2(2)*, 89–109.

Dei Otatti, G. (1994). Trust, interlinking transactions and credit in the industrial district. *Cambridge Journal of Economics, 18*, 529–546.

Dicken, P. (1992). *Global Shift — The Internationalization of Economic Activity*, (2nd ed.). London: Paul Chapman Publications.

Douglas, S. P. & Craig, C. S. (1989). Evolution of global marketing strategy: scale, scope and synergy. *Columbia Journal of World Business*, Fall, 47–595.

Dunning, J. H. (1998). Globalization, technological change and the spatial organization of economic activity. In A. D. Chandler, P. Hagström & Ö. Sölvell (eds), *The Dynamic Firm: The role of Technology, Strategy, Organization & Regions*. Oxford: Oxford University Press.

Enright, M. E. (1998). Regional clusters and firms strategy. In A. D. Chandler, P. Hagström & Ö. Sölvell (eds). *The Dynamic Firm: The role of Technology, Strategy, Organization & Regions*. Oxford: Oxford University Press.

Fletcher, D. (1995). *Australian Countertrade in a Global Context*. Working paper series, Sydney: Faculty of Business, University of Technology.

Fujita, M. & Ishi, R. (1998). Global location behaviour and organizational dynamics of Japanese electronics firms and their impact on regional economies. In A. D. Chandler, P. Hagström & Ö. Sölvell (eds). *The Dynamic Firm: The Role of Technology, Strategy, Organization & Regions*. Oxford: Oxford University Press.

Johannison, B. (1988). Business formation: a network approach. *Scandinavian Journal of Management, 4(3/4)*, 83–99.

Johnsen, R. E. & Johnsen, T. E. (1999). International market development through networks: The case of the Ayrshire knitwear sector. *International Journal of Entrepreneurial Behaviour & Research, 5(6)*, 297–312.

Kristensen, P. H. (1996). *Denmark an Experimental Laboratory of Industrial Organization, vol I–II*. Copenhagen: Copenhagen Business School.

Krugman, P. (1991). *Geography and Trade*. Cambridge, Mass.: MIT Press.

Lazerson, M. (1993). Factory or putting out? Knitting networks in Mondea. In G. Grabher (ed.), *The Embedded Firm*. Routledge.

Levitt, T. (1983). The globalization of markets. *Harvard Business Review*, May–June, 92–102.

Lundvall, B.-Å. (1985). *Product Innovation and User-Producer Interaction*, Aalborg: Aalborg University Press.

Lundvall, B.-Å. (1988). Innovation as an interactive process — from user-producer interaction to national systems of innovation. In G. Dosi *et al.*, (eds), *Technology and Economic Theory*. London: Pinter Publishers.

Madsen, T. K. (1989). Successful export marketing management — some empirical evidence. *International Marketing Review, 6(4)*, 41–57.

Maskell, P. (1996). *Local Embeddedness and Patterns of International Specialization*. Paper presented at the 22nd EIBA conference, Stockholm.

Nooteboom, B. (1989). Diffusion, uncertainty and firm size. *International Journal of Research in Marketing, 6*, 109–128.

Ohmae, K. (1982). *Triad Power*. Free Press.

Pedersen, P. O. (1994). *Clusters of Enterprises within systems of production and Distribution*. CDR Working Paper 94.14, Centre for Development Research.

Petersen, B. (1996). *Explaining Cost- effective Export Market Penetration via Foreign Intermediaries*. Ph.D. Dissertation 4.96, Copehagen Business School.

Piore, M. & Sabel, C. (1984). *The Second Industrial Divide — Possibilities for Prosperity*. New York: Basic Books.

Porter, M. E. (1990). *The Competitive Advantage of Nations*. New York: Macmillan Press.

Porter, M. E. (1994). The Role of location in competition. *Journal of the Economics of Business, 1(1)*, 35–39.

Porter, M. E. (1996). Competitive advantage, agglomeration economics and regional policy. *International Regional Science Review, 19(1 & 2)*, 85–93.

Porter, M. E. (1998). Clusters and the new economics of competition. *Harvard Business Review*, November-December, 77–90.

Porter, M. E. & Sölvell, Ö. (1998). The role of geography in the process of innovation and the sustainable competitive advantage of firms. In A. D. Chandler, P. Hagström, P & Ö. Sölvell (eds), *The Dynamic Firm: The Role of Technology, Strategy, Organization & Regions*. Oxford: Oxford University Press.

Pyke, F. (1992). *Industrial Development Through Small-Firm Cooperation*. Geneva: ILO.

Saxenian, A. (1991). The origins and dynamics of production networks in Silicon Valley. *Research Policy, 20*, 423–437.

Scott, A. J. (1999). The cultural economy: geography and the creative field. *Media, Culture & Society 21*, 807–817.

Snell, R. & Lau, A. (1994). Exploring local competencies salient for expanding small business. *Journal of Management Development, 13(4)*, 4–15.

Storper, M. and Harrison, B. (1991). Flexibility, hierarchy and regional development: The changing structure of industrial production systems and their forms of governance in the 1990s. *Research Policy, 20*, 407–422.

Storper, M. & Saias, M. (1997). *Worlds of Production*. Boston: Harvard University Press.

Terpstra, V. & Wu, C. (1990). Piggybacking: a quick road to internationalization. *International Marketing Review, 7(4)*, 52–63.

Vatne, E. (1995). Local Resource mobilization and internationalization strategies in small and medium-sized enterprises. *Environment and Planning, A 27*, 63–80.

Chapter 18

Internationalisation of the Firm — The Influence of Relationship Sediments

Henrik Agndal and Björn Axelsson

Introduction

Research into the internationalisation of firms has traditionally largely focused on motives, processes, success factors and the organisation of international operations. Even though empirical evidence is scarce, the assumption has generally been that internationalisation is a part of deliberate strategy formation, ignoring the role of serendipity.

This article addresses the influence of specific individuals and their networks on the internationalisation of firms, an issue which has until now been more or less ignored in research. It is thus the aim of this article to contribute to and perhaps further the research into individual networks and their influence on internationalisation.

Initially, some literature is reviewed to identify relevant points of departure related both to the internationalisation of firms and to the role of individuals' contact networks in business. Second, some illustrations showing how individuals and their networks impact internationalisation in practice are provided. These form the basis of a discussion concerning the role of individual networks in internationalisation and a framework of different dimensions of personal relationships is created. Finally, some general implications these findings might have on managerial practice and academic research are discussed.

Critical Perspectives on Internationalisation, pp. 437–456.
ISBN: 0-08-044035-5

Points of Departure

The ways in which firms internationalise have been at the focus of much research. For two decades, the Uppsala internationalisation process model (Johanson & Vahlne, 1977) has exerted considerable influence on the way this research has been conducted (Andersen, 1993). The model portrays internationalisation as a step-wise process in which firms begin their international operations engaging in low-commitment entry modes in nearby markets while, over time, targeting geographically and mentally more distant markets through higher commitment entry modes. Critics have noted, however, that often firms begin their international operations in far off markets or leapfrog, not going through the steps identified in the stage models. Similarly, there appears to be no single model explaining the choice of market entry mode (cf., Andersen, 1993; Melin, 1992).

Motives for internationalisation are generally divided into reactive and proactive motives (Hollensen, 1999). Proactive motives include, for example, the exploitation of economies of scale in research and development, production, management or image, while reactive motives may be a result of market pressure forcing a firm to go international in order to maintain competitiveness. Some literature also attempts to explain internationalisation as a way of exploiting critical resources, developing critical knowledge or identifying market gaps to fill (Engwall & Johanson, 1990). In practice, firms — or more specifically managers in firms — appear to make other judgements, based less on rational decision-making models. Not always do firms exploit those markets that objectively appear to make the most sense. Seemingly rational decisions to exploit favourable local conditions are trumped by other factors like corporate relationships, prior market experience, chance and luck. Rather than talking about strategically sound business plans, a process of orientation, positioning and timing is a more appropriate explanatory model (Axelsson & Johanson, 1992). That is, with less reliance on traditional decision-making models created by earlier business research, descriptions and analyses provided by the network approach are in many cases more appropriate (Blankenburg, 1995).

In addition to the importance placed on inter-firm relationships, seemingly random internationalisation behavior falling outside of traditional explanatory models can also be explained by another factor, the infrastructure of the individual's network or web of contacts. It thus becomes meaningful to distinguish between two network actor levels, the firm and the individual. While firm networks have received considerable attention in later years, individual networks have largely been left unexplored in business research, especially when the international dimension is added (see e.g., Holmlund & Kock, 1998). Within sociology (see, e.g., Burt, 1992) some attention has been devoted to studying individual networks, for example, regarding the possibilities of acting to achieve specific goals depending on the role in the network and network position. These studies, however, rarely relate to firms even if there are some exceptions (see, e.g., Uzzi, 1997).

The Individual in Business Studies

Among business practitioners, the importance of individual networks has long been recognised. In a recent study of the business practices of 13th century merchants in Venice, Dahl (1998) described and analysed the influence of individual networks. Hasselberg (1998) undertook a similar study, charting networking activities among ironworks owners in 19th century Dalarna (Sweden). In research on small and medium-sized firms, a number of scholars also point to the importance of networks as the most crucial factor for entrepreneurs in developing their business ventures (see, e.g., Aldrich *et al.,* 1987; Aldrich & Zimmer, 1990; Birley, 1985; Cromie & Birley, 1992; Dubini & Aldrich, 1991; Johannisson, 1994; Shepherd, 1991).

Dubini and Aldrich (1991) note that networking can be seen as both the actions of an individual [entrepreneur], but also as a part of a firm's activity and structure. Thus, two structures or processes exist at the same time, personal networks or networking connected to the individual and the extended networks or networking associated with organisations. It is argued, "Taken together, these two processes affect the fate of entrepreneurs and their companies" (Dubini & Aldrich, 1991). Johannisson and Monsted, (1998) also argue that "social as well as business aspects must be considered when looking into entrepreneurial networks. They are personal indeed." (Johannisson & Monsted, 1998). Thus, even if the two processes or structures only together explain networks and their roles, in academic research attention has been directed almost exclusively at the former. Johannisson (1994) argues along the same lines, contending that studies of dyadic relations between individuals say little about the network structure as a whole, while macro studies generate little understanding about individual ties.

Within the so-called IMP research tradition several scholars have noted

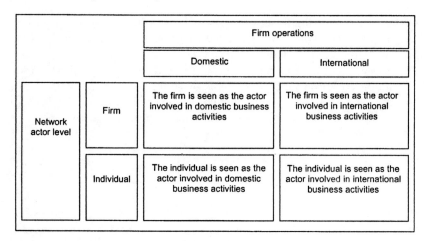

Figure 18.1: Individuals and Firms in Domestic and International
Operations.

the importance of the individual in the interaction between firms. For example, Cunningham and Turnbull (1982) argue that contacts between people are at the heart of organisational interaction, while Hamfelt and Lindberg (1987) note that ties between individuals make up the smallest threads in a network and that it is people who create contacts and trust between organisations.

Based on these arguments, a simple two by two matrix can be constructed to categorise network internationalisation studies (see Figure 18.1). On one axis appears the network actor level, which can be firm or individual. On the other axis one finds firm operations, which can be domestic or international.

To people with experience from the business world, the importance of personal networks is more or less self-evident. Nonetheless, in business research this has largely been left unexplored. A brief review of network literature will reveal a significant number of studies on the firm level, but individual contacts have been more or less ignored. Especially the lower right hand box in the figure (see Figure 18.1), where the individual actor level meets internationalisation studies, is more or less empty. Consequently, a number of important questions remain be addressed by scholars. For example, who makes the decision to internationalise and why? What tipped the scales in favour of one market over another? Is the individual's freedom to manoeuvre greater or smaller if individual networks are considered rather than strategic decision-making models? What implications does such knowledge have for our understanding of business in general and internationalisation processes in particular?

A number of studies of the roles of individuals in on-going domestic business relationships can be found. For example, Turnbull (1979) identified several different roles, including legitimating, informing, negotiating and providing crisis insurance. Similar issues were addressed in Hallén's (1992) study of top executives' ways of creating, cultivating and using personal networks. One similarity between these studies was the role of the network or personal contacts as providing insurance against crises, indicating that perhaps networks were not always utilised on a regular basis. This, however, does not provide a picture of the ways in which personal networks function and certainly does not deal with internationalisation.

A large number of studies dealing with intercultural business communication and business negotiations have been undertaken in the last two decades (see, e.g., Ghauri & Usunier, 1996; Hofstede, 1980). This research focuses on meetings between individuals and how culture influences the outcomes of these meetings. Still other studies look at the importance attached to family networks, for example, in Asia (see Jansson, 1987). Even if they are international in nature, studies of this kind do not look at the roles of specific individuals and how they influence business activities of specific firms. Rather, their aim is to create cultural stereotypes identifying the importance attached locally to specific characteristics or behavior.

Another example of a study of the roles of individuals in internationalisation is the research undertaken by Axelsson, Johansson and Sundberg (1992), who studied 250 international business travellers. More than a quarter of the respondents made their trips primarily to maintain relationships with internal units, customers, and other actors. One-third of the businessmen interviewed travelled mainly to take part of or provide information, while remaining respondents were out to solve specific business problems. Creating and cultivating personal networks was thus an important reason for travelling.

There are also examples of how firms cultivate the networks of individuals as a strategic asset. In a study of career paths (Borg, 1988) it was found that firms consciously tried to create cosmopolitan managers who worked a few years in one country after which they were relocated to another country. This gave the managers the opportunity to build broad personal networks benefiting their firms. Hamfeldt and Lindberg (1987) studied how metallurgic engineers moved internally within firms and externally between firms and were able to show different patterns in how individuals stayed and moved between functions, firms and industries. Quite obviously, the personal networks that evolved had implications for the firms in which the individuals worked. Huber (1991) studied the grafting-in of competence in firms and concluded that this was especially important in times when companies moved into new ventures and needed to transform rapidly. Such situations share some characteristics with foreign market entry, even if Huber's (1991) study did not take an explicit international perspective on the issue.

A great many studies also point out the importance of previous international experience on the decision to initiate internationalisation or to internationalise further (see, e.g., Ali & Swiercs, 1991; Almeida & Bloodgood, 1996; Morgan, 1997; Reuber & Fischer, 1997; Westhead *et al.*, 1998). In the work on which much of current theory of internationalisation rests, Johanson and Vahlne (1977; 1990) argue that attitudes towards the benefits and risks of internationalisation as well as experiential knowledge among managers strongly affect the propensity to internationalise. Somewhat surprisingly perhaps, these studies do not make the seemingly obvious connection between prior international experience and individual networks.

The studies cited above more or less explicitly indicate that individuals and their networks of contacts have great influence on the process of internationalisation. It can thus be argued that individuals — not only in top management positions — may change how a firm directs its efforts at internationalising. The infrastructure of contact networks affects which markets are chosen, the nature of business relations that evolve and which market opportunities that are identified. In the following section of the paper, some illustrative examples of this are provided.

The Influence of Individuals in Internationalisation – Some Illustrations

It can be more or less assumed that individuals and their networks have been crucial for business success as long as there has been a business world. If networks influence domestic business activities, there is every reason to assume that they have at least as great influence on international business activities. It would thus be of interest to study in detail the ways in which individuals direct the internationalisation processes of the firms in which they work or with which they interact. Estimating the overall importance of this phenomenon as well as identifying the patterns in which it moves would be of great importance, both to the academic world and to practitioners. Below follow some examples, case vignettes, of how individuals' contacts led firms to internationalise in specific directions.

Ericsson Entering the Canadian Market

"In an extensive geopolitical analysis of potential markets, among other countries Canada turned up not being suitable for Ericsson's systems of mobile communications, mainly due to strong local competition. In spite of this fact, Ericsson was approached by actors on the Canadian market, and soon started supplying a local firm with equipment. The key factor in Ericsson's expansion into Canada was a technical director in what later emerged as the leading local telecom operator. This individual, a native Hungarian, had been working with telecommunications in Venezuela. In doing so had had frequent contacts with Ericsson. His attitudes towards the company and his personal network led him to suggest Ericsson as a supplier to the Canadian operator, within which he was one of the key individuals. In fact, Canada turned out to be one of the very first markets that Ericsson entered after having carried out the geopolitical analysis." (Blankenburg, 1995)

The case of Ericsson entering Canada shows how the internationalisation process was influenced by an individual's professional relationship with a firm at a time when the relationship was no longer actively maintained. The case also gives an example of how internationalisation can be a response to external stimuli as opposed to proactive strategy. While the process was complicated and the situation uncertain, it is quite clear that had the individual not been around at the time when the decision concerning choice of supplier was made, the story of Ericsson's internationalisation would have developed in a different direction.

Telia Entering Three Asian Markets

"Within a limited period of time, Telia entered three Asian markets as part of three different mobile telecommunications consortia. In each

separate case, Telia had been specially invited to join the winning con-
sortium. Later on, one of the managers at Telia decided to take a closer
look at these market entries. His study showed that all three cases dis-
played some important similarities. They all took place in markets that
had recently been deregulated and the leading actor in all three markets
was an investor from a fourth country who had little experience from tel-
ecommunications operations. The conclusion of the study was that Telia
had been invited to provide the consortia with a measure of legitimacy as
telecom operators.

That was not the end of the story, however. Due to its extensive train-
ing programmes, the Telia Academy had trained hundreds of telecom
officials in these three Asian markets and was known as a capable actor.
This was not the whole truth, though. A deeper study of the individuals
involved in the consortia revealed that they had some expertise of their
own. The main investor involved in the tree consortia had employed an
expert advisor who had been very influential in setting up the consortia.
In fact, the expert advisor had more or less managed the whole process.
The Telia manager's study of the market entries showed that in his youth
some 15 years previously, the advisor to the consortia had worked as a
trainee at Telia in Kalmar in Sweden. Obviously, the expert advisor's
experience with Telia was one of the reasons behind Telia's being invited
to take part in the consortia." (Malmgren & Olausson, 1997)

Much like Ericsson's entry into Canada, the entry of Telia into East Asia
was a result of the influence of a single individual who had established a
relationship in the past that could be reactivated when needed. Again, the
Telia case also shows how a single relationship is critical in the internationalisation process.

Swedish Software Entering the Middle East Market

"Swedish Software entered the Kuwait market over ten years ago having
been invited by a Swedish customer with which they had been working for
a long time on the domestic market. The Swedish customer had opera-
tions in Kuwait and wanted support for a two-year project undertaken for
the public administration. While Swedish Software was working in
Kuwait with its sole customer, they started searching for opportunities to
remain on the market after the project had gone to term. During this
search, they learned about the importance of personal contact networks,

one of the reasons for which is the large number of Arab businessmen who at some point in their career work for the government. Top civil servants normally hold their posts for the duration of their careers, but very often combine this with running private businesses. Only when Swedish Software learned to take into account the private business networks of these key officials were they able to make headway in their search for local business opportunities and be invited to present business proposals. At this stage, Swedish Software also discovered the importance of the middleman. The right middleman would be able to provide access to the right people and market information, thereby helping Swedish Software frame their offerings in the appropriate way. There were thus two main problems. Firstly, how to identify relevant parties and find out who was best suited to help them gain access to broader networks and, secondly, how to frame the offering taking into consideration the interests of the key officials' networks." (Axelsson & Johanson, 1992)

Again, the case shows how internationalisation was initiated by an actor outside the firm. The case of Swedish software differs from the previous cases, however, in that individuals inside the firm then went on to actively establish relationships and use them proactively in achieving internationalisation goals. The firm thus found middlemen and customers due to an understanding of the ways in which the actors, here primarily individuals, were embedded in the business network.

Ericsson Entering the Japanese Market

"The entry of Ericsson into the Japanese mobile telecommunications market has attracted much attention from researchers, and numerous accounts are available. One of the key actors was Morgan Bengtsson, who early on was appointed CEO of Ericsson in Japan. He had previous experience from the Swedish Technical Attaches and joined Ericsson when the Japanese telecommunications market was in its early state of deregulation with openings also for foreign investors. Bengtsson started to systematically map hundreds of individuals belonging to the Japanese network in the telecommunications industry as he believed that such a map would be helpful in understanding and influencing Ericsson's entry into the market. In addition to the map of contacts, Bengtsson had other sources of knowledge about Japan and the telecommunication market. His wife was Japanese and he spoke the language.

The knowledge of the key players on the market together with an under-standing of some of the key characteristics of the Japanese business com-munity is often claimed to have been the reason behind Ericsson's success, which came with the third mobile licence release. In Japan at the time there were three telecom operators and three licenses open for bidding. The first two licenses were given to high-bidders that had spent considerable effort building competence. The third operator had little real interest in tele-communications, but Bengtsson convinced them that with Ericsson's help they could become a major player on the market. The Japanese firm bid for the licence and won, much to the surprise of the market, and Ericsson became the operator's main supplier. The influence of Morgan Bengtsson on the process of Ericsson's entry into the Japanese telecommunications market can hardly be overemphasised.” (Axelsson et al., 1994)

Ericsson entry into Japan differs from the entry into Canada described previously in that in Japan, Ericsson took the initiative. The case thus demonstrates how the individual in charge of the market entry undertook significant efforts in mapping hundreds of key actors in the industry, which put him in a position to objectively assess the market. Just like in the case of Swedish software entering the Middle East, existing contacts were insufficient in explaining internationalisation. Rather, business opportunities were identified when networks were regarded as a strategic resource, which could be actively developed and evaluated.

Scania Entering the Czech Republic

“After the opening of the Eastern Bloc and the transformation of econo-mies like, for example, the Czech Republic, structures in the business community had to adapt to an entirely new situation. An example of a company taking advantage of this is Swedish lorry manufacturer Scania. The company saw an opportunity to expand its business on the Czech market, and found a representative suitable to undertake such a mission. This individual was a former Czech national living in Sweden, who had been working at Scania for a number of years. He now saw an opportu-nity to move back to his old home country, while making use of his experiences in Sweden.” (On-site interview, 1995)

Another category of processes where individuals greatly influence inter-nationalisation processes can also be identified, namely the importance of life history as indicated in the case above. This case also shows how an individual facilitated a market entry, even if he cannot be assumed to have been critical to the long-term success of the venture.

An Australian Wine Merchant Entering the Latvian Market

> *"Since the opening of the Baltic States a lot of new business ventures have been created. There is great demand for many products, and Western firms and individuals are constantly scanning for new business opportunities. A typical example is the expatriated Latvian living in Australia, where he was a wine merchant. When visiting his old home country, he concluded that it would be possible to successfully open a Wine store in Riga. Today, that wine store is known as one of the best in the city."* (On-site interview, 1999)

The cases of Scania entering the Czech Republic and the Australian wine merchant entering Latvia are again different from the previous vignettes. In the case of Scania the firm wanted to set up operations on a new market and found an individual with a personal background in that country. Thanks to his background he was well acquainted both with the new market and the company. The same applies to the Latvian case in which a single individual draws on his experiences from a country and an industry in order to establish a new firm.

Discussion

The cases presented above give rise to a number of questions that have not been explored in any greater detail in the past. They indicate how business processes are influenced by single individuals and their personal networks, in some cases by relationships established a long time ago, in other cases by relationships created for specific purposes. The case vignettes also show how sometimes personal relationships are crucial for certain business deals, and how at other times relationships serve to ensure the smooth implementation of business activities.

Relationship Sediments

In all the cases presented in the previous section the influence of personal relationships between individuals on the internationalisation of firms is apparent. Individuals interpret the context, identify opportunities and enact their environment. While doing so they rely on their previous experience and their networks of personal contact. Often relationships established in the past, *relationship sediments*, appear to play crucial roles as driving forces and enablers of internationalisation.

The cases also hint at how networks can be used as a strategic resource to facilitate action. This should, however, not be seen as an argument in favour of the traditional rationalistic picture presented in classical management literature. In none of the cases is there a question of a top-to-bottom process where the CEO makes a decision to be carried out by other members of the organisation. This might very well be the case in many instances as there are, for example, firms with positions enabling them to shape the structure of the market, and within firms there might be dominating groups of managers. Frequently, however, processes are more random and less controllable, as hinted at in the case vignettes. No single actor controls business activities, regardless of what other actors do or want (Axelsson & Johanson, 1992), of which Ericsson's entry into the Canadian market might be seen as an example. During such non-controllable processes other actors create opportunities, some of which are enacted and others which are not. In identifying, interpreting and taking advantage of such opportunities, the individual and the individual's network of personal contacts — relationship sediments — appears to be crucial.

Of course, no general conclusions concerning the importance of relationship sediments or the frequency with which these influence internationalisation can be drawn from the brief cases presented above. It is, however, possible to point at how potentially important research into these issues is, for purposes of which a model of how the individual relationship sediment fits into the business network can be created.

Modelling the Individual in the Business Network

Considering the reasoning above, it could thus be of interest to create a framework of the different dimensions of relationship sediments that can be identified. Such a framework could, for example, be a tool for the systematic mapping of individuals' contact networks, thereby providing the means of understanding the ways in which specific individuals influence business processes in firms.

The cases presented here hint at some important dimensions, as do several past studies of personal networks. Among others, Burt (1992) distinguishes between contacts that are duplicates and contacts that are complementary. Duplicate contacts give access to more or less similar networks, while complementary contacts add new networks. As far as the number of contacts is concerned, Burt (1992) argues that the higher the number of contacts, the better for the firm as this means access to more networks providing individuals with greater freedom to act and greater access to opportunities.

The creation of such networks can be seen as the creation of an infrastructure, with the individual as a nexus. The individual's network of contacts, be they professional, social, family etc., constitute that infrastructure. In a study of top managers, Hallén (1992) attempts to depict personal networks along two dimensions. Firstly, the individual is seen as part of a network of organisations and institutions, and secondly as part of networks of individuals. This typology covers most of the possible actor groups that could be relevant to study.

In a study of business in Russia, Salmi and Bäckman (1999) discuss the influence of outer and inner circles, also frequently studied in sociological network theory. Inner or "first" circles are referred to as a narrow circle of people that are known and trusted. These individuals form the core of the business network. Outer or "second" circles comprise other individuals with whom business relations are established or maintained, but who do not belong to the first circle. One of the interviewees in Salmi's and Bäckman's (1999) study illustrated this as "*Here, without exception, you must have someone you know everywhere ... This is like a different level: usually the relation is more formal and he is like an acquaintance* (instead of being a friend). *But you definitely need him; to call if you have some problem.*"

These studies all indicate that there are different *dimensions* that must be taken into consideration in a framework of relationship sediments, at least if any real understanding of personal networks is to be attained. For example, it is necessary to consider with whom the relationship exists, its potential uses, and the frequency and ease with which the relationship can be activated. Here it is argued that these dimensions can be summarized into five main categories, which include the type of contact or relationship sediment origin, its importance or role, its structure, availability, and reach (see Figure 18.2). Below each of these categories is discussed.

The category or origin of the relationship sediment can be summarized in present and previous work, profession-related contacts arising from, for example, membership in clubs, family, extended family, and life

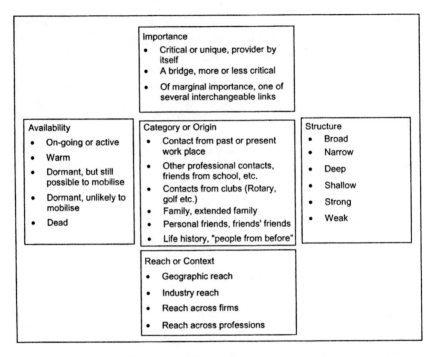

Figure 18.2: Dimensions of Relationship Sediments.

history. Examples of these categories can be found in the case vignettes presented previously. For example, the cases of Ericsson's entry into Canada and Telia's entry into the three East Asian markets show the importance of relationships created at former places of employment, while the cases of the Australian wine merchant in Latvia and Scania entering the Czech Republic indicate the influence of life history.

The structure of the relationship sediment refers to its content, which can be broad, narrow, deep, shallow or any combination of these. It also refers to the commitment of the actors to the relationship, i.e. the strength of the relationship sediment. Examples of this can also be found in the cases. For example, in spite of the long time that had passed since the East Asian consultant spent his traineeship at Telia, this relationship sediment played a crucial role. This might be seen as an indication of a strong and deep relationship sediment, which could also be characterized as narrow because it was useful for that particular business deal only.

The availability of the relationship sediment refers to the extent to which the relationship can be mobilized or activated by the actor. It can be characterized as on-going or active, warm, dormant but with distinct possibilities to mobilize it, dormant with little possibilities of mobilization, or dead. In the cases of Scania in the Czech republic and the Australian wine Merchant in Latvia, the individuals have relationships with their home countries that were probably dormant considering the amount of time that had passed since they emigrated. In both cases, though, it was possible to mobilise the relationships, which can also be said to have been the case in Ericsson's entry into Canada and Telia's entry into East Asia.

The reach of the relationship sediment refers to the context in which it is embedded and the contexts to which it gives access. Dimensions may include countries, industries, firms and professions, but also networks, which can vary in size and number. In all the case illustrations relationship sediments gave access to specific countries and industries, while reach across firms varied with work experience.

The importance of the relationship sediment can be characterized as being a critical provider in itself, a more or less critical bridge to other relationships or network contacts, or of marginal value where it represents one of several ways of achieving the same end. For example, in the case of Ericsson entering Canada the relationship sediment appears to have been critical, while in Ericsson's entry into Japan there appears to have been a conscious creation of multiple, interchangeable relationships.

It should also be noted that the availability and reach (and to some extent the structure and importance) of the relationship sediment are largely related to the individual's role and position as a representative of his or her firm. Some actors are easier to mobilize if the individual represents a potentially important customer — as in the case of Ericsson in Canada — than if he or she is just an individual with whom the company, or any specific individual in the firm, has a relationship. In order to identify who can mobilize whom and for what purpose, it becomes necessary to take into account the context in which the individual operates. Whether this will succeed thus largely depends on the individual's role as representative of a firm. Outside this context the possibilities of mobilizing relationships change. This could easily be related to basic principles of exchange (Bagozzi, 1986), not least to the idea that each party should have something of value to the other party, but also to the notion that each party should be capable of making the offering available. An individual in a certain position is likely to control specific resources and thereby have something of varying interest to different parties.

Naturally, complementary or alternative dimensions to those presented in the framework above (see Figure 18.2) can also be identified. Availability can be complemented by indicators like frequency, regularity, density etc. Generally, however, it is argued that the framework provides a means of charting an individual's network of relationship sediments for purposes of use in business.

Conclusions and Directions for Future Research

This article addresses the issue of individuals' networks as enablers and driving forces in internationalisation. This is a phenomenon well known to practitioners, but which has received very little attention among scholars. Even if the arguments put forward in this article are not entirely new, they might help in formulating some questions for researchers to look more deeply into.

The basic question of the impact of individuals' relations and relationship sediments on internationalisation can be broken down into a number of more tangible questions for future research. Firstly, it is of great interest to try to estimate the relative importance of this phenomenon, i.e. how many of all foreign market entries can basically be explained by the factors discussed in this paper? Further, how many major directional changes of the intended internationalisation of firms do relationships and relationship sediments influence?

Also for managers a high degree of strategic importance should be attached to these issues. If individuals' networks are of vital importance for business activities obviously they deserve attention. Two strategic approaches can be identified. Firms can choose not to track networks and instead hire individuals that have broad networks or ensure that their employees are able to develop international networks, for example, through work rotation programmes. Such an infrastructure would then only be enacted when appropriate — and it would fulfil its function without extensive tracking efforts. A second strategic approach would entail systematic charting efforts of a different nature, based on the presumption that it is indeed possible and meaningful to map networks. One of the first aspects in such an approach is to create awareness of which types of networks that the individuals in the firm can access. In practice, relationship sediments can thus be seen as a bundle of opportunities to enact or a kind of *opportunity networks* for the firm. That is, relationship sediments represent opportunities in the sense that they can be used to envisage and enable business activities for the firm, not least in internationalisation.

Relationship sediments thus represent important assets, and examples of firms systematically addressing this issue can be found. For example, based on the experience gained when entering certain East Asian markets, Telia decided to implement a rudimentary system for tracking and maintaining important contacts and relationships established by employees. In this "relationship bank" descriptions of international projects and names of key actors are recorded for the use in future ventures (interview with Telia manager, Bertil Olausson).

Having discussed the role of relationships and sediments in some detail, it might again be pointed out that by themselves they seldom explain internationalisation. Generally, they offer substantial explanatory power, but are normally complemented by other firm or market-specific factors. In the case illustrations a number of factors acted together with relationship sediments in creating successful foreign market entries. Examples of such factors include, for example, favourable local conditions like in the case of the Australian wine merchant in Latvia, a good product like in the case of Ericsson in Canada, or a solid reputation like Telia in Asia. In many internationalisation processes, however, relationship sediments play the roles of triggers, enablers and directors!

References

Aldrich, H., Rosen, B. & Woodward, W. (1987). The impact of social networks on business founding and profit: a longitudinal study. In N. Churchil *et al.* (eds), *Frontiers of Entrepreneurship Research*. Centre for Entrepreneurial Studies, Babson College. 154–168.

Aldrich, H. and Zimmer, C. (1990). Entrepreneurship through social networks. *California Management Review, 33(1),* 3–23.

Ali, A. & Swiercs, P. (1991). Firm size and export behaviour: lessons from the Midwest. *Journal of Small Business Management*, April, 71–78.

Almeida, J. & Bloodgood, J. (1996). Internationalisation of new ventures: implications of the value chain. In P. Reynolds *et al.* (eds), *Frontiers of Entrepreneurship Research*. Centre for Entrepreneurial Studies, Babson College. 211–225.

Andersen, O. (1993). On the internationalisation process of firms: a critical analysis. *Journal of International Business Studies*, 2nd quarter, 209–231.

Axelsson, B. & Johanson, J. (1992). Foreign market entry — the textbook view vs the network view. In B. Axelsson & G. Easton (eds), *Industrial Networks — A New View of Reality*. London: Routledge.

Axelsson, B., Johanson, J. & Sundberg, J. (1992). Managing by international travelling. In M. Forsgren & J. Johanson (eds), *Managing Networks in International Business*. Philadelphia: Gordon & Breach.

Axelsson, B., Laage-Hellman, J. & Cedergren, A.-C. (1994). *Ericssons Entry into the Japanese Market for Mobile Telephony*. Unpublished case-material: Department of Business Studies, Uppsala University.

Bagozzi, R. (1986). *Principles of Marketing Management*. Chicago: Science Research Associates.

Birley, S. (1985). The role of networks in the entrepreneurial process. *Journal of Business Venturing, 1*, 107–117.

Blankenburg, D. (1995). A network approach to foreign market entry. In K. Möller & D. Wilson (eds), *Business Marketing: An Interaction and Network Perspective*. Boston, MA: Kluver. 375–405.

Borg, M. (1988). *International Transfers of Managers in Multinational Corporations-Transfer Patterns and Organisational Control*. Acta Universitatis Upsaliensis. Studia Oeconomiae Negotiorum 27. Stockholm: Almqvist & Wiksell.

Burt, R. (1992). The social structure of competition. In N. Nohria & R. G. Eccles (eds), *Networks and Organizations: Structure, Form and Action*. Boston, Mass.: Harvard Business School Press.

Cromie, S. & Birley, S. (1992). Networking by female business owners in Northern Ireland. *Journal of Business Venturing, 7*, 237–251.

Cunningham, M. & Turnbull, P. (1982). Interorganiztional personal contact patterns. In H. Håkansson (ed.), *International Marketing and Purchasing of Industrial Goods*. Chichester: John Wiley & Sons.

Dahl, G. (1998). *Trade, Trust and Networks. Commercial Cultures in Late Medieval Italy*. Nordic Academic Press.

Dubini, P. & Aldrich, H. (1991). Personal and extended networks are central to the entrepreneurial process. *Journal of Business Venturing, 6*, 305–313.

Engwall, L. & Johanson, J. (1990). Banks in industrial networks. *Scandinavian Journal of Management 6(3)*, 231–244.

Ghauri, P. & Usunier, J.-C. (1996). *International Business Negotiations*. Oxford: Pergamon.

Hallén, L. (1992). Infrastructural networks in international business. In M. Forsgren & J. Johanson (eds), *Managing Networks in International Business*. Philadelphia: Gordon & Breach.

Hamfelt, C. & Lindberg, A-C. (1987). Technological development and the individual's contact network. In H. Håkansson (ed.), *Industrial Technological Development — A Network Approach*. London: Croom Helm.

Hasselberg, Y. (1998). *Den Sociala Ekonomin: Familjen Clason och Furudals Bruk*

1804–1856. Acta Universitatis Upsaliensis, Doctoral dissertation, Uppsala University.

Hofstede, G. (1980). *Culture's Consequences.* Beverly Hills: Sage.

Hollensen, S. (1999). *Global Marketing — A Market-responsive Approach.* London: Prentice Hall.

Holmlund, M. & Kock, S. (1998). Relationships and the internationalisation of Finnish small and medium-sized companies. *International Small Business Journal, 16(4)*, 46–63.

Huber, G. (1991). Organisational learning: the contributing processes and the literature. *Organizational Science, 2(1)*, 88–115.

Jansson, H. (1987). *Affärskulturer Och relationer. En Studie av Svenska Iindustriföretag i Sydöstasien.* MTC, No. 29.

Johannisson, B. (1994). *Entrepreneurial Networks — Some Conceptual and Methodological Notes.* Institute of Economic Research, Working Paper Series. 1994/8, Lund University.

Johannisson, B. & Monsted, M. (1998). Contextualizing entrepreneurial networking. *International Studies of Management & Organisation, 27(3)*, 109–136.

Johanson, J. & Mattsson, L.-G. (1992). Network position and strategic action. In B. Axelsson & G. Easton (eds), *Industrial Networks — A New View of Reality.* London: Routledge.

Johanson, J. & Vahlne, J.-E. (1977). The Internationalisation process of the firm — a model of knowledge development and increasing foreign markets comittment. *Journal of International Business Studies*, Spring-Summer, 23–32.

Johanson, J & Vahlne, J.-E. (1990). The mechanism of internationalization. *International Marketing Review, 7(4)*, 11–24.

Malmgren, H. & Olausson B. (1997). *A Bird in the Hand Is Worth Two in the Bush or How to Use the Telia Group's International relationships as a Driving Force in Foreign Market Entries.* Uppsala MBA Studies 1997/7. Department of Business Studies, Uppsala University.

Melin, L. (1992). Internationalization as a strategy process. *Strategic Management Journal, 13*, 99–118.

Morgan, R. (1997). Decision making for export strategy. *Small Business and Enterprise Development 4*, 73–85.

Reuber, R. & Fischer, E. (1997). The influence of the management team's international experience on the internationalization behaviors of SMEs. *Journal of International Business Studies*, 4th Quarter, 807–825.

Salmi, A. & Bäckman, J. (1999). Personal relations in Russian business: two circles. Institutions and post- socialist transition. In R. Kosonen & A. Salmi (eds), *Institutions and Post-socialist Transition.* Helsinki: Helsinki School of Economics and Business Administration.

Shepherd, J. (1991). Entrepreneurial growth through constellations. *Journal of Business Venturing, 6*, 363–373.

Turnbull, P. W. (1979). Roles of personal contacts in industrial export marketing. *Scandinavian Journal of Management, 16(5)*, 325–337.

Uzzi, B. (1997). Social structure and competition in interfirm networks: the paradox of embeddedness. *Administrative Science Quarterly, 42*, 35–67.

Westhead, P., Wright, M. & Ucbasaran, D. (1998). The internationalization of new and small firms. In P. Reynolds *et al.* (eds), *Frontiers of Entrepreneurship Research*. Center for Entrepreneurial Studies, Babson College. 464–477.

Chapter 19

Network Perspective on International Mergers and Acquisitions: What More Do We See?

Virpi Havila and Asta Salmi

Introduction

In contemporary business life, mergers and acquisitions form one of the most popular strategies for company growth and diversification. Cross-border deals accounted for a quarter of mergers in 1998, and more are expected as firms go global (*Economist*, 1999). Merger waves thus increasingly involve international operations, and explanations for and analysis of effects of these international waves are in demand (Mattsson, 2000). By and large, the literature on mergers and acquisitions has com-pared the acquiring and the target firms, e.g., the strategic and organisa-tional fit, and the synergy between the two companies (Chatterjee, 1992; Datta, 1991), and has analysed processes relating to, for example, pre-merger negotiations, acquisition behaviour, and post-merger integration (Hunt, 1990; Lindvall, 1991; Nupponen, 1996). Only a few studies look at the (network) context in which acquisitions occur (Forsgren, 1989a;1989b). Motives for mergers and acquisitions have also been listed, including such issues as increase of market share, reduction of competi-tion, quick and economical entry into a business, impulse purchase of a bargain-priced business, acquisition of new technology, and rapid growth (Shrivastava, 1986). International mergers and acquisitions have been analysed and carried out mainly on the premises of the traditional approach to international business, i.e., focusing on top management decision making and based on an understanding of firms as separate units with clearly defined boundaries. It is usually assumed that managerial actions have a major influence on the success of the acquisition or merger (Paine & Power, 1984).

Earlier findings have shown that expected gains from take-overs seldom materialise and that most mergers and acquisitions fail (Chatterjee, 1992; Hunt, 1990; Lubatkin, 1983): the acquisition or merger does not improve the performance or does not measure up to managers' evaluations. Several studies (Jemison & Sitkin, 1986; Shrivastava, 1986; Walsh, 1989) suggest that problems in the integration process are important reasons for merger or acquisition failure. A more recent explanation has pointed to the lack of attention paid to the context of the merging companies: too much effort is concentrated on the mutual fit of the merging companies and too little is spent on analysing their connections to other parties (Anderson *et al.*, 2001). Effects of mergers and acquisitions may spread through the business relationships that are connected, directly and indirectly, to the merging parties; thus the more contextual network perspective becomes relevant. Consequently, the question that arises is: what more do we see, or what do we see that is different, when we study mergers and acquisitions and their effects from the network perspective?

This article aims at investigating network effects of (international) mergers and acquisitions. It thus elaborates on forces of change that are related to mergers and acquisitions, and it shifts attention from pre-merger decision making to the post-merger/post-acquisition network changes. The article is organised as follows. First, we discuss a network view of international business, thus grounding the argument that the mainstream analysis of cross-border mergers is too narrow. Then, we take the network view of mergers and acquisitions, which leads us to discuss change in business networks, including on the one hand, dyad and network change, and on the other, incremental and radical change. We then offer an empirical illustration of one merger and one acquisition and discuss the network effects of these. Finally, we focus on the issue of connectedness and offer implications for future studies of cross-border mergers and acquisitions.

Network Perspective on International Business

The dominant approach in international business literature is to examine the single firm operating internationally or globally. The unit of analysis is a firm, separated from its environment by a distinct boundary, and analysis emphasises a top management perspective and strategic decisions (Forsgren & Johanson, 1992). Like several other Nordic researchers, we view markets and international business from a network perspective, which is based on a different approach to business analysis (Axelsson & Johanson, 1992; Johanson & Mattsson, 1988). This view assumes that international business takes place in a network setting, where business actors are linked to each other through business relationships. Rather than taking the top management view, analysis focuses on the tasks of middle management in handling relationships with other actors, and on everyday interaction through which business relationships are developed and maintained. According to this view, a business enterprise becomes international through connecting actors in different countries (Andersson & Johanson, 1997) and internationalisation means that the firm establishes and develops network positions in foreign markets (Johanson & Mattsson, 1988). In business networks, the actors have positions in the sense that they are directly and indirectly related to specific other actors. A newcomer tries to establish a position of some sort, which is difficult in the short run by reason of the long-term, stable relationships in the existing network, thus the investment nature of current activities in international business becomes emphasised. Our analysis rests on business relationships, and we see that there are several potential actors acting in relation to the focal firm.

It follows that foreign market entry is a process which takes place over time and which is not controlled by any single actor. Axelsson and Johanson (1992) provide three critical issues for entry:

a) orientating process (since, in order to understand relationships and dependencies between actors and connections, the company must enter the network);
b) positioning (i.e., resource commitments and investment processes in order to develop the company's position in the network);
c) timing (i.e., the notion that timing is a matter of seeing opportunities and being able to act promptly).

Empirical studies following these lines have demonstrated complications in the processes. For instance, in entering a turbulent market (Estonian computer markets in the early 1990s) one case company was successful in terms of the timing of its entry, but as it was no longer able to use the earlier investments in these networks, the processes of orientating and positioning were very different from and more difficult than what the company had expected (Salmi, 2000). Several case studies adopting the network perspective to market entry into the changing Eastern European markets have pointed to the need for learning and attention to both old and emerging network relations (Törnroos & Nieminen, 1999).

According to the network view, foreign direct investments are interpreted as investments in positions in foreign networks (Forsgren & Johanson, 1992). They construct a link between a domestic and a foreign network (Chen & Chen, 1998) and they entail investments in specific exchange relationships. It has been typical in the Nordic research tradition to analyse how investment processes abroad are actually carried out by the firm instead of addressing the issue of why foreign direct investments take place (Björkman & Forsgren, 1997). In line with this, we see analysis of processes as fundamental to an understanding of international business. Taking the network approach, we do not look at internationalisation as a separate process but rather as one that is dependent on the network context in which it takes place. Managing the internationalisation process is more a matter of understanding the forces driving and hindering the process than of making specific strategic decisions about the internationalisation. Consequently, in order to understand cross-border mergers and acquisitions, we find it important to analyse the context of the merging companies (networks) and long-term processes involved.

Network Perspective on Mergers and Acquisitions

In general, an implicit assumption in literature dealing with acquisitions seems to be that, through acquisition, the market position of the target firm can be taken over. However, when the network perspective is applied, it is not as clear that this will always be the case:

> *"An important issue ... is whether the buying firm can get control of the other firm's exchange relationships. In other words can the focal firm take over the position as well as the resources. ... the major aim of the acquisition may be to get*

control of the exchange relationships, to change their char-
acter, or to change the connections between exchange rela-
tionships. Control of exchange relationships through
acquisitions is, however, never certain, since there are always
two actors involved." (Johanson & Mattsson, 1992)

Therefore, it is relevant to ask whether business relationships, i.e., relationships to customers and suppliers, can be taken over, i.e., controlled, when buying a company (Anderson *et al.*, 2001). The ensuing question is whether the target company is still as valuable (or the same, even) as estimated if its key connections change as a result of the deal. This is why we see too much attention concentrated on the dyad between the merging parties instead of on the more extensive network.

Mergers and acquisitions do not form any clearly visible line of research within network literature, but some studies can be found that deal with international acquisitions and explicitly use the network perspective. Customarily, these studies focus on the *pre-acquisition phase*. For example, in discussing the motives for an acquisition Forsgren (1989a) refers to the type of relationship that exists between the acquiring and target companies before the acquisition takes place. A study of the entry of a Swedish firm (Atlas-Copco) into US compressor markets (Seyed-Mohamed & Bolte, 1992) reveals that even a firm with ample resources faced difficulties in establishing a position in a moderately structured network. The company thus decided to "buy its way in" through acquisition of an actor already on the inside, and it learned that the network was characterised by person-oriented rather than activity-oriented relationships and that further investments in relationships were therefore required. Also, Forsgren (1989b) discusses foreign acquisitions from a network-oriented approach and concludes that the industrial network structure to which a firm belongs is of crucial importance for its investment behaviour (Forsgren, 1989b). In his study he found that the more involved a firm is in networks abroad, the more likely it is that acquisition will be used as the mode of foreign entry.

If business relations and networks have been seen to affect the propensity to carry out cross-border acquisitions, what, then, can be learned from analysing acquisitions and mergers over longer periods, i.e., what would the network perspective tell us about developments in the *post-merger/post-acquisition phase*? Change, dynamics and long-term processes form the core interest area of network analysis, but focus has rested on change through gradual and incremental steps as network actors interact and adapt to each other. However, there is empirical evidence suggesting that revolutionary change and discontinuities also occur — in fact, some mergers and acquisitions are examples of these (Havila & Salmi, 2000). Andersson, Johanson and Vahlne (1998) also discuss the possibility of revolutionary consequences in situations where there exist no (direct or indirect) relationships between the acquiring and target companies.

We suggest that the evolution of business networks involves both incremental and radical change (Halinen *et al.*, 1999) and that acquisitions form a fruitful context for their analysis. Sometimes mergers and acquisitions are neither reasons for nor results of radical changes, but rather represent incremental changes also in relation to connected parties. But in other cases the acquisition or merger functions as a critical event causing radical change in the network. This may happen, for instance, when one actor, and its connections to other actors, disappears from the network, or when a new actor entering the network initiates new relationships. Mergers and acquisitions can cause radical network changes for primarily two main reasons (Havila & Salmi, 2000). Firstly, the new entity as a whole, or a specific person in the new entity, may be perceived by the connected network actors in such a way that old relationships are disrupted or new ones started. In these cases the surrounding network actors initiate the radical network change even though the inherent reason is the merger or the acquisition. Secondly, the radical network change may be the intended and expected outcome of the merger or acquisition in that managers intend to disrupt old business relationships or start new ones. In these cases the radical change is initiated by the merging entity. However, attention should be given to the fact that network change is an outcome of several interconnected actors; while it may be possible to terminate a relationship through a one-sided decision, it is much less certain that new relationships can be established in accordance with intentional strategies.

To illustrate our argument, the following case description takes a con- textual — network — approach to mergers and acquisitions, and it also analyses the post-merger situations. This empirical study of one inter- national acquisition and one preceding national merger within the Nordic graphics industry shows that the surrounding networks were affected. It also shows how several dynamic processes occur simultaneously, making analysis of single events (mergers and acquisitions) and their effects difficult.

A Nordic Acquisition in the Graphics Industry[1]

Pre-merger Phase

Alpha, one of the companies in focus here, represents the Swedish graphics industry; it has operated for several decades under a name that is well-known in Sweden. Over the years it has had different owners and has thus been involved in several acquisitions. Especially during the 1990s it faced the turbulence of contemporary business life. In the late 1980s Alpha had lost some of its market share due to an increasing competition from foreign firms. Also, the recession in the beginning of the 1990s heightened Alpha's financial crisis. One result was that the number of employees, which in 1992 was over 400, was reduced to approximately 140 in 1993. Alpha produced several different products, whereof one product group accounted for a third of the turnover. About 95 percent of this product group was being bought by a key customer, Theta, with which a long-term relationship had been maintained. In 1995 Alpha was sold to a holding company, the owners of which had the intention of further developing their business within the graphic industry. Accordingly, in 1997 the holding company decided to acquire a competitor for Alpha, namely, Beta, which is located about 200 kilometres from Alpha. So Alpha and Beta became members of a group from 1 January, 1998 (see Figure 19.1).

Post-merger Phase

Alpha and Beta have different local markets and are therefore not competitors with regard to local customers. Alpha also expected to acquire new customers through Beta since Alpha's production process was more complete. Earlier, Beta had been buying the last step of the production process from specialised companies, but after the acquisition it was going to use Alpha for this function. While they did not compete for local customers, Alpha and Beta had earlier competed for some non-local customers, meaning that some of their salesmen had visited the same

---

[1] The empirical data presented in this article has been collected within a larger research project that analyses dynamics within business networks (see Anderson, Havila & Salmi, 2001; Havila & Salmi, 2000; Salmi *et al.*, 1998). The empirical data includes interviews with managers and experts within the field of the Nordic graphics industry during the period May 1997 to March 2000.

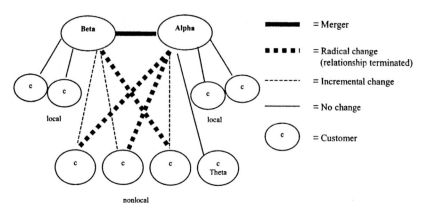

Figure 19.1: The Merger between Alpha and Beta.

customers. Since the two companies offered a similar product, the main way to compete had been to offer a lower price. After the merger, the two companies made plans to coordinate their sales forces so that only one seller would visit each non-local customer, meaning that some of the relationships would disappear. However, in practice, salesmen from both sides were keen on maintaining contact with their existing customers for some time. Moreover, some customers were not totally satisfied with the new unit, but would rather have continued business as before. Thus, perceptions towards the merger were partly negative and different from expectations of the merging company managers. Figure 19.1 illustrates some of the radical and incremental network changes caused by this merger.

During the planning of the division of the work between Alpha and Beta, Alpha was informed that one of its main customers, Theta, had been sold to a Finnish company, Gamma. Thus the period of integration and reformulation of strategies became also a pre-acquisition period in relation to a foreign actor.

The Finnish graphics company, Gamma (acquirer), and the Swedish Theta (target) were former competitors. They had been producing similar products, although mainly for local (domestic) markets. The two companies differed in one crucial respect: Gamma had its own modern production facilities, whereas Theta marketed a product that was produced by Alpha. The top management of Gamma noted that they were quite familiar with all of their competing companies in the Nordic countries;

the companies had followed each other's activities for several years, the market positions were stable and the relationships long-term. Each company also had a dominant position in their national markets due to historical reasons. People knew each other personally very well, as they had met at different industry meetings, associations and trade fairs. Therefore, Gamma expected to be well informed about the target company, Theta. Alpha, in turn, did not foresee that a foreign acquirer would dramatically affect its operations.

The Post-acquisition Phase

The CEO of Gamma expected that Alpha, which had sustained losses during the 1990s, would go bankrupt soon. Gamma decided to stop using Alpha as a supplier for Theta, and instead increased its own in-house production. Since Gamma had free production capacity, clear synergy advantages were expected to be gained as a result of moving production from Alpha in Sweden to Gamma in Finland. An additional reason for the acquisition was that in this way Gamma expected to get somewhat better prices from its suppliers worldwide. This soon proved to be right with regard to some suppliers, which is shown as incremental change in Figure 19.2. This figure shows the radical change and consequent incremental and radical changes in connected relationships.

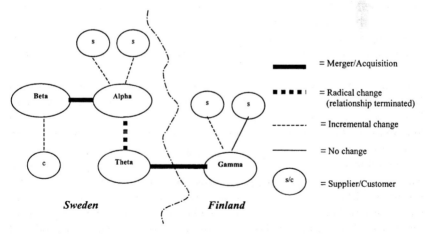

Figure 19.2: Two Parallel Change Processes: The Merger and the Acquisition.

The CEO of Gamma had been involved in several acquisitions in Finland over the years, as a representative of both a buying company and a target company. His experience led him to stress, for example, motivational factors of the involved companies, open information flows and joint decision making. It was decided that the two companies, Gamma and Theta, would in the future act as a genuine group rather than as two individual units, although the headquarters were situated in Finland. Moreover, the acquisition was expected to be appreciated among the personnel of Theta as the new owner operated in the same field and was thus expected to be better informed of the specific features of this business. The former owner of Theta was a conglomerate, and the type of business that Theta was involved in comprised only a minor part of it. A successful acquisition was therefore expected, and optimism prevailed in both the acquiring and target companies.

Two years after the acquisition it seems that the market development has not been favourable and that the new group has experienced unexpected losses. Competitors have been very active; some small aggressive competitors had already appeared on the market before the acquisition. Thus, in practice, the joint operations have not been as easily and smoothly established as expected. Moreover, the traditional approach — being well informed about the target company, together with emphasis on the business cultures and effective integration processes — did not guarantee that all troubles were foreseen or settled. Gamma's active involvement earlier meant that orientation in the Nordic network was easy and the timing relatively successful. Positioning, in turn, involved various processes and influenced several actors — it was a more complicated process than seemed to be expected in the acquiring company.

Network Effects

Gamma's acquisition of Theta has changed radically some parts of the surrounding network after the relationship to the main supplier of Theta was disrupted. For Alpha the loss of its important customer resulted in a need to concentrate on other types of products than had been the case earlier. It also meant disinvestments and dismissal of personnel. In September 1999, Alpha had 80 employees left. Also, Alpha's suppliers were influenced since Alpha's production was cut down and less material was needed; for example, the business relationship with the most important Swedish supplier was, in January 1999, close to termination. One reason for Alpha's survival, despite a loss of a major share of its turnover practically overnight, was that Beta had started to use Alpha for the last step in the production process. In this way, Beta could better serve its existing customers, who, to some extent, could compensate for the one Alpha had lost.

The graphics case shows, among other things, that decisions and results relating to the merger between Swedish Alpha and Beta were influenced by the cross-border acquisition that was conducted by Finnish Gamma at the same time, and that Swedish suppliers to Alpha were quickly affected by the strategic acquisition decision by Gamma, although the companies were located at some distance from one another and were not directly or closely connected. These kinds of changes are all bound to influence how the merger or acquisition processes unfold, and what their outcome — success or failure — will be like.

The Contribution of the Network Perspective: Connectedness

An acquisition always affects the relationship (dyad) between the merging companies. Depending on the pre-merger/pre-acquisition situation, we can talk about radical or incremental change within the dyad. If the two (or several) parties have not been in contact with each other, i.e., have not done business with each other or co-operated in some way, the type of change in the dyad between the merging parties can be classified as radical change. In our empirical illustration this was the case in both the merger between Alpha and Beta and in the acquisition by Gamma. The relationship between the merging parties changed radically as the former competitors had had no (in the Alpha-Beta case) or only little (in the Gamma-Theta case) contacts during the pre-merger/pre-acquisition phase. For example, instead of competing, Alpha and Beta started to collaborate regarding production and sales force with the intention of better serving their existing customers. In the second case, Theta moved its entire production to Gamma and started intensive cooperation in this way.

When we look at the effects on the connected parties after the merger/acquisition in our study we find both incremental and radical types of change in these relations. Incremental network change can be found in the companies' relations with their customers and suppliers; for instance, in some cases the suppliers got more orders. Radical network change is also shown; for example, the merger between Alpha and Beta led to termination of some customer relationships (see Figure 19.1). This was also the situation when Gamma acquired Theta: the relationship between Theta and Alpha was terminated (see Figure 19.2). We do not want to take a stance on whether these changes were 'good' or 'bad', or on how they affect the success or failure of the initial merger/acquisition. Our intention here has been to show that there were network effects and to analyse them on the incremental/radical dimension.

Network effects of the merger or acquisition are caused by connectedness prevailing in business networks. Because of various network interdependencies, indirect relationships that are relatively distant from a focal relationship may be affected (see Håkansson & Snehota, 1995). As we see it, the connectedness has two important dimensions: a structural one and a more processual, or vision-related, one. The former relates to the idea of chains of business relationships and "domino effects" of change in these (Hertz, 1999). This dimension in particular has been illustrated here. For instance, the cross-border acquisition affected relations, which in turn affected others to which the acquirer itself was not directly related. This kind of connectedness is relatively easy to grasp and therefore these chain reactions are more easily mapped out.

The latter dimension of connectedness relates to the perceptions of actors and their network horizons (Anderson *et al.*, 1994). If a merger or acquisition takes place within this horizon and is perceived to require action, the initial merging act creates (incremental or radical) changes in the network, although it may be impossible to follow the route of the structural connections. This dimension is also closely related to timing of activities — when windows of opportunity or sudden threats are perceived, companies tend to react quickly and sometimes strongly. To some extent reactions relate to a specific merger/acquisition, but they may also represent more general "bandwagon" reactions related to the international merger waves.

In general, discussion on acquisitions so far seems to be dominated by the strategic plan, strategic decision, and by one event: the acquisition deal. Some studies have shown that the character of the pre-acquisition phase (regarding network structure) is of crucial importance for the behaviour of the acquiring company (Forsgren, 1989a; 1989b). This means that a sufficiently long-term perspective is needed when studying effects of mergers and acquisitions. The acquisition may well be an outcome of earlier (incremental) processes — thus there are usually more historic reasons and random behaviour behind the merger process than we may infer from contemporary strategic discussions and press releases.

Another notable point of today is that a lot of attention is paid to shareholders (owners and investors); acquisitions are seen as a way to grow rapidly and earn quick returns. However, problems often emerge in the longer run. We argue that network effects take a long time to develop, but they may be crucial for the success of the merger or acquisition; outcomes can only be seen in the longer term, and the contemporary focus on short-term results may therefore be detrimental.

Conclusions

The received way of understanding mergers and acquisitions has focused on the change taking place between the two (or several) involved parties; a lot of attention is directed towards the target company and the integration between the parties. But in addition, the (incremental or radical) change taking place within this dyad may well influence other connected relationships. Thus, the merger or acquisition may be an event that is received and acted upon by other actors, and thus change spreads in the networks. This spread was illustrated in our empirical case, together with the fact that several (international) acquisitions may take place in a parallel fashion, with interfering influence on the network.

This paper argues for a new approach — a network approach — for investigators of mergers and acquisitions. This approach brings to the fore the issue of connectedness, which can be analysed from the perspective of structural features in the network (e.g., mapping out domino effects in the network) or by attending to the visions and perceptions of company personnel, thus bringing in issues that are less concrete but more "in the air". As markets are becoming more global, an increasing number of activities and research on mergers and acquisitions concern cross-border deals. Taking the network perspective, foreign market entry is a process in which orientating, positioning, and timing in the network context provide a basis for analysis of mergers and acquisitions as well. Thus, we would conclude that the traditional focus provides only a partial picture. Orientation and involvement are needed in order to gain information about the network and connections therein. Positioning is a result of the actions of many actors in the network, and it is only partially controlled by the focal actors in the merger or acquisition. Above all, the network view brings to the fore the reasons for changes and the dynamics that business actors encounter. With respect to timing, literature of acquisitions largely focuses on discrete events: take-overs. We should like to stress, however, that these visible deals and acts may be a result of longer-term activities and may also lead to longer-term change processes in the network later on. It seems that presence in the network increases the probability of good timing for mergers and acquisitions.

A major part of our conclusions and their implications are relevant to any merger or acquisition. Basically, it is not of interest whether a merger or acquisition crosses over a national border; firms' boundaries are blurred and networks extend into other countries without visible borders. Actors in several countries are linked via direct and indirect actors and relationships. However, what makes international (foreign) markets different is their relative distance from the company: psychic, geographical and cultural distance and language differences make it more difficult to gain information and understanding about foreign markets. Therefore, mergers and acquisitions in foreign markets are even more risky than domestic ones. Moreover, as our case also shows, change can spread from one country to another, thus creating unexpected network effects to distant "domestic" actors. And considering the large number of acquisitions today, it is more than probable that there are several parallel acquisitions taking place, thus creating interference in network dynamics. Analysis of these dynamics is, in our view, crucial for understanding how merger and acquisition processes unfold.

References

Anderson, H., Havila, V. & Salmi, A. (2001) Can you buy a business relationship? — On the importance of customer and supplier relationships in acquisitions. *Industrial Marketing Management, 30*, 575–586.

Anderson, J. C., Håkansson, H. & Johanson, J. (1994). Dyadic business relationships within a business network context. *Journal of Marketing, 58*, 1–15.

Andersson, U. & Johanson, J. (1997). International business enterprise. In I. Björkman & M. Forsgren (eds), *The Nature of the International Firm.* Copenhagen: Copenhagen Business School Press. 33–49.

Andersson, U., Johanson, J. & Vahlne, J.-E. (1998). Organic acquisition in the internationalization process of the business firm. *Mir (Management International Review), 37*, 67–84.

Axelsson, B. & Johanson J. (1992). Foreign market entry — the textbook vs. the network view. In B. Axelsson & G. Easton (eds), *Industrial Networks. A New View of Reality.* London: Routledge. 218–234.

Björkman, I. & Forsgren, M. (1997). Nordic contributions to international business research. In I. Björkman & M. Forsgren (eds), *The Nature of the International Firm*. Copenhagen: Copenhagen Business School Press. 11–29.

Chatterjee, S. (1992). Sources of value in takeovers: synergy or restructuring — implications for target and bidder firms. *Strategic Management Journal, 13*, 267–286.

Chen, H. & Chen, T.-J. (1998). Network linkages and location choice in foreign direct investment. *Journal of International Business Studies, 29*, 445–468.

Datta, D. K. (1991). Organizational fit and acquisition performance: effects of post-acquisition integration. *Strategic Management Journal, 12*, 281–297.

Economist (1999). How to merge. After the deal. January 9, 19–21.

Forsgren, M. (1989a). Foreign acquisitions: internationalization or network interdependency? *Advances in International Marketing, 3*, 141–159.

Forsgren, M. (1989b) *Managing the Internationalization Process — The Swedish Case*. London: Routledge.

Forsgren, M. & Johanson, J. (1992). Managing internationalization in business networks. In M. Forsgren & J. Johanson (eds), *Managing Networks in International Business*. Philadelphia: Gordon & Breach. 1–16.

Halinen, A., Salmi, A. & Havila, V. (1999). From dyadic change to changing business networks. An analytical framework. *Journal of Management Studies, 36*, 779–794.

Havila, V. & Salmi, A. (2000). Spread of change in business networks: an empirical study of mergers and acquisitions in the graphic industry. *Journal of Strategic Marketing, 8*, 105–119.

Hertz, S. (1999). Domino effects in international networks. *Journal of Business-to-Business Marketing, 5*, 3–31.

Hunt, J. W. (1990). Changing pattern of acquisition behaviour in takeovers and the consequences for acquisition processes. *Strategic Management Journal, 11*, 69–77.

Håkansson, H. & Snehota, I. (eds) (1995). D*eveloping Relationships in Business Networks*. London: Routledge.

Jemison, D. B. & Sitkin, S. B. (1986). Corporate acquisitions: a process perspective: *Academy of Management Review, 11*, 145–163.

Johanson J. & Mattsson, L.-G. (1988). Internationalization in industrial systems — a network approach. In N. Hood & J.-E. Vahlne (eds), *Strategies in Global Competition*. New York: Croom Helm. 287–314.

Johanson, J. & Mattsson, L.-G. (1992). Network positions and strategic action — an analytical framework. In B. Axelsson & G. Easton (eds), *Industrial Networks — A New View of Reality*. London: Routledge. 205–217.

Lindvall, J. (1991). *Svenska Industriföretags Internationella Förvärv — Inriktning och Utfall (Swedish Industrial Companies' International Acquisitions. Direction and Outcome)*. Doctoral dissertation, Department of Business Studies, Uppsala University.

Lubatkin, M.(1983). Mergers and the performance of the acquiring firm. *Academy of Management Review, 8*, 218–225.

Mattsson, L.-G. (2000). *Merger Waves and Contemporary Internationalization of Firms and Markets.* Paper presented at the 16th IMP conference, Bath, UK, September 7-9.

Nupponen, P. (1996). *Post-Acquisition Performance. Combination, Management, and Performance Measurement in Horizontal Integration.* Doctoral dissertation, Helsinki School of Economics and Business Administration, A-109.

Paine, F. T. & Power, D. J. (1984). Merger strategy: An examination of Drucker's five rules for successful acquisitions. *Strategic Management Journal, 5,* 99–110.

Salmi, A. (2000). Entry into turbulent business networks: the case of a western company on the Estonian market. *European Journal of Marketing, 34,* 1374–1390.

Salmi, A. et al., (1998). *Studying Dynamics in Business Networks: The Case of Printing on Paper in Denmark, Finland, and Sweden,* Publications of the Helsinki School of Economics and Business Administration, Series: W-208, June, Helsinki.

Seyed-Mohamed, N. & Bolte, M. (1992). Taking a position in a structured business network. In M. Forsgren & J. Johanson (eds). *Managing Networks in International Business.* Philadelphia: Gordon & Breach. 215–231.

Shrivastava, P. (1986). Postmerger integration. *The Journal of Business Strategy, 7,* 65–76.

Törnroos, J.-Å. & Nieminen, J. (eds) (1999). *Business Entry in Eastern Europe. A Network and Learning Approach with Case Studies.* Helsinki: Kikimora Publications B: 4.

Walsh, J. P. (1989). Doing a deal: merger and acquisition negotiations and their impact upon target company top management turnover. *Strategic Management Journal, 10,* 307–322.

Author Index

Subject Index